Publishing in the Digital Age

Publishing in the Digital Age

The First International Conference on the Publishing Industry and Publishing Education in the Digital Age

Sponsored by

Wuhan University, China
Pace University, USA

November 1–4, 2006

PACE UNIVERSITY PRESS · NEW YORK

Pace University Press
41 Park Row, Rm. 1510
New York, NY 10038

Printed in the United States of America

ISBN 0-944473-89-X (pbk: alk.ppr.)

Contents

Preface *xi*

The First International Conference on the Publishing Industry and Publishing Education in The Digital Age
Sherman Raskin *1*

Educational Publishing in the Digital Era
Robert E. Evanson *3*

Curriculum of Editing and Publishing in the Digital Age
Luo Zichu & Dai Yang *9*

Electronic Publishing in Germany: An Overview of Developments in Industry and Education
Ursula Rautenberg *15*

Publishing, Education and the Digital Age
Henan Sun *23*

Copyright Infringement in Digital Publishing
Shay Humphrey *29*

New Frontier of Digital Publishing in the Domain of Creative Education
Chen Wuwei *37*

Power Law, Long Tail and Book Publishing
Lian Xiaochuan *43*

Digital Surviving and Developing for the Publishing Industry
Zhang Zengshun *55*

Friend or Enemy: The Developing Trend of Popular Magazines in the Digital Era
Li Jianwei *59*

Comparative Analysis of Chinese and American Publishers' Websites
Zhang Zhiqiang & Xing Peng *65*

Publishing Education Within the Environment of Digital Publishing
Zhang Wenhong 77

Education in the Editing and Publishing Specialty Based on Solid Humanity, Market and Technology
Li Xinxiang 83

On Publishing Graduate Education in the Digital Era in China
Huang Xianrong 91

Four Mechanisms that Should Be Introduced into Chinese Publishing Education in the Digital Age
Yao Lei 99

The Actuality, Problems, and Countermeasures of Editing and Publishing Education in China
Liu Canjiao 105

The Cultivation of Publishing Talents in the Context of Digital Publishing
Liang Chunfang 113

On Editorial and Publishing Talent Development
Wu Ping 123

The Multi-Facet Mode of Publishing Human Resource Development in the Digital Age
Sun Fan 129

Comparison and Contrasts in Sino-American Talent Development for Publication
Lin Yuyin 135

Application of a Task-Based Model in the Teaching of Digital Publishing Technology
Wang Qiuju & Wang Hongmei 143

Digital Era Expedites the Naissance of "Reading Studies"—A Basic Course in Editing and Publishing
Gao Hong 149

Digital Technology Promotes China's Publishing Industry
Huang Kaiqing & Zhou Guobiao 157

Tendencies of the Book Industry Under Media Industry Convergence
Wang Songmao 163

Digital Supply Chain: A New Platform for the Chinese Publishing Industry
Zhang Meijuan 171

On Fostering Magazines' Core Competency in the Digital Age
Zhu Jingwen & Sun Jue 177

Research on Tourism Magazines in the Digital Environment
He Yun 181

Application of Digital Technology to Newspaper Publishing and Distribution
Jiang Ling 187

Which Plays the Dominant Role: Content Resources or Technical Resources?
Xiao Lei 191

Open Access Publishing: The Game Playing among Researchers, Libraries and Publishers
Fang Qing & Tao Li 195

Open Access: From the Publishers' Perspective
Xu Lifang & Xu Qi 205

An Expert-Assessment Model for Internet STM Publications
Liu Jinhong 215

The Development of Open Access Repositories
Niu Xiaohong 227

Multimedia Electronic Magazines: Revolution of Magazines in terms of Content and Format in the Age of New Media
Jiang Chengsong & Li Ziwei 235

A Study of Advertising and Marketing of Digital Magazines in China
Wang Bo 245

Self-Publishing on the Internet
He Ziyue 253

Blog Publishing and Its Copyright Protection
Li Yan 261

Research On the Application of OAI—PMH and Its Static Repository
Lu Xiaohua & Tong Wen 269

Analysis of the Marketing Model of POD Publishing
Liu Yongjian & Zou Rui 275

Application of Mobile Payment Based on SIM Cards in Electronic Commerce of the Book Industry
Zhao Dan 281

Terminal Consumption Analysis of the Online Publishing Industry Chain
Wu Mei 289

Investigation on the Networking of China's Copyright Trade
Wang Xiaoyan & Yang Xianghui 295

Transformation and Innovation in the International Book Trade Based on New Technology
Yao Yongchun 307

Comparison and Drawing of Copyright Collective Management in China and Abroad in an Internet Environment
Hu Bo 315

An Exploration of Product Development Tactics of College Textbooks in China
Liu Yindi 325

The Negative Effects of Editorial Planning on Academic Researches
Zhao Jianguo & Chang Chunqiao 333

A Comparative Study of Magazine Advertising of China and Western Countries
Wu Yun 339

The Viability of Copyright Protection Systems
Liu Chunnian 347

Overview of China's Copyright Permissions from 1996 to 2005
Cai Yun 357

Contributors 367

Preface

Fundamental and unprecedented changes have taken place in the publishing industry environment with the coming of the Digital Age. From digitized publishing flow to digitizing of distribution systems and reading style, new technology has swiftly promoted the interactivity and integration of multimedia industry. The traditional publishing industry is facing unparalleled opportunities and challenges, demanding better professional talents. For the healthy development of the publishing industry, successful reform of higher education publishing, and communication and cooperation between international publishing industry and education institutions, The 1st International Conference on the Publishing Industry and Publishing Education in the Digital Age was held on 1st–4th, Nov. 2006 at Wuhan University. It was hosted by Wuhan University China, Pace University USA, China GAPP-WU Advanced Publishing Training Center with the assistance of Hubei News and Press Bureau, Hubei Chang Jiang Publishing Group, Redactor Society of Hubei Province, and Wuhan University Press. Development trends and strategies of the publishing industry in the digital age, publishers' training models, mechanisms and methods were fully discussed at the conference with the following specific aspects:

1. Development of e-publishing technology and its influence on the traditional publishing industry;
2. Influential factors of digital publication (industrial policies, readers, copyright protection, profiting models, etc.);
3. New publishing models in the digital era (open access, publish on demand);
4. Industrial chain and structure of e-publishing;
5. Comparative studies on the publishing industry and its personnel education between China and other countries;

6. Publishers' education objectives, mechanisms, models and methods in the digital age;
7. Structure and quality of publishers in the digital era;
8. Discipline building and curriculum system of editing and publishing specialties in the digital era;
9. Status quo and problems of, and solutions to, China's publishing education.

Specially invited experts and colleagues in publishing and educational circles at home and abroad enthusiastically responded to the calls and contributed a large number of articles. Ninety-seven of them were selected to compile a preprint paper collection for the conference, selections from which have been published after the conference by Pace University Press USA.

Translations from the Chinese are the responsibility of the individual authors. Due to the limited time, mistakes are unavoidable. All criticism will be sincerely appreciated.

Compiler
3-30-2007

The First International Conference on the Publishing Industry and Publishing Education in The Digital Age

Sherman Raskin

November 1 2006 is a special day for Pace University, Wuhan University, GAPP, the United States and China. Today, with the support of Prof. Liu Binjie, deputy administrator of GAPP, Dr. Chen Chuanfu, Dean of School of Information Management of Wuhan University, and Dr. David Caputo, President of Pace University, we have initiated a major International Conference on Digital Publishing inviting professionals worldwide to participate.

The mission is urgent and important as technology changes the face of publishing and the way we publish books, magazines and newspapers. It is also scholarly in spirit and allows publishers and academicians to study the future of the industry worldwide. Most importantly it brings two great nations, China and the United States, together to plan events that will foster publishing education and the publishing profession.

We began this process in September 2004, when Dr. Xu Lifang arrived at Pace University from Wuhan University to serve as a research scholar. Dr. Xu, a young professor, was eager to study the rudiments of publishing with our Pace University professors. In January 2005, Dr. Fang Qing, then chairperson of the Publishing Department at Wuhan University, presently Associate Dean of the School of Information Management, joined his colleague Dr. Xu. Pace was honored to have two esteemed professors from Wuhan University join our faculty that year.

Both scholars audited classes in Marketing Principles and Practices, School Publishing, and Legal Aspects of Publishing. They gave talks on publishing in China today, and had opportunity to personally meet publishing executives in the United States who led major publishing houses and were effecting changes in the industry daily.

They also explored publishing education in the United States, and interviewed the former director of Gayle Research, and, presently, Director of the Denver Publishing Institute, Elizabeth Geiser. They met with Robert Baensch at NYU, Holly Brady of Stanford Publishing Institute, and, of course, Professor Raskin of Pace University. They learned that publishing education in the United States is practical and experiential in nature. Students enrolled in the Pace University Program obtain jobs in the industry upon graduation. An excellent example is Kelly Allen who is presenting a paper this week. She is a graduate of the Pace University Master of Science in Publishing, and presently serves as Director of New Media, Random House. She is also an Advisory Board member of the Pace University Publishing Program. The professors in the Pace Program are executives in the industry who teach what they have practiced for twenty to thirty years. You will have the opportunity to meet Robert Evanson, professor at Pace University and former president of McGraw Hill Education. You will also meet Professor Lian Xiaochaun who worked at Springer Verlag for 14 years, and is now presently a Staff Associate and professor at the Pace Publishing Program, as well as graduate of the program.

Dr. Xu and Dr Fang were able to utilize Pace to further their understanding of the publishing industry and publishing business in the United States. Pace had the opportunity to learn about publishing and publishing education in China from them. The year and their visit were memorable; it was an opportunity to acquire new colleagues and share ideas with them.

One year later, Pace was graced with another prominent Wuhan scholar, Dr. Huang Xianrong, presently chair of the Publishing Science Department at Wuhan University. She too was in pursuit of knowledge and wanted to research the ways in which American publishers pursue their vocation. Dr. Huang was unique in fulfilling goals as well as assisting in signing a Memorandum of Understanding, Cooperation/Exchange between Pace University and Wuhan University.

The goals of the agreement permit Wuhan faculty and Pace faculty to explore the development of cooperative programs. This agreement includes exchange of faculty and establishment of international conferences; for example the digital conference taking place this week. The agreement also supports the exchange of students and the continuation of the research scholar program.

Pace University faculty are very proud of their relationship with Wuhan University and our strong ties with China. Pace University is deeply grateful to our colleagues at Wuhan University for their dedication and hard work in initiating the conference this week. We are proud to be a co-sponsor and a participant today. We want to take this opportunity to thank the leadership and guidance of the GAPP officials.

As Director of the Pace University Publishing Program, I extend President David A. Caputo's deep appreciation for their hard work. President Caputo's global agenda and vision to strengthen greater cooperation between China and the United States has assisted us in moving ahead to make the Memorandum of Understanding a reality. President Caputo is thrilled that the proceedings of this conference will be published both in China and in the United States by the Pace University Press.

Today is a momentous occasion and the beginning of a wonderful relationship between our two universities. Pace looks forward to strengthening these ties and building programs that will support the publishing industry and publishing education both in the United States and China. I personally thank you for the honor of being here today.

Educational Publishing in the Digital Era

Robert E. Evanson

Good morning. Today I would like to present some of the major impacts that the digital age has had, and will continue to have, on education and educational publishers. These are two wonderful professions: publishing and education. Both impact the lives of people in many ways, most we never know about. In the United States, education is our most important issue after homeland security. First I will cover the business and technology trends that impact both professions. Second, I will review the educational/political trends that affect publishers. Third, I will analyze the changes and effects that the trends are having on publishing products, services, and organization. Two demonstrations of products that capitalize on the promise of technology to make a difference in increasing the productivity of teaching and learning will be shown. One product is in the elementary school market; the other is for high school and higher education markets. Fourth, some of the issues that technology has created for educational publishers will be discussed. Lastly, we will draw some conclusions for the future of educational publishers

1. Business/ Technology Trends

Continued technology improvement (lower cost, greater capacity, smaller size) is driving new products and ways of doing business for educational publishers, schools and universities. Moore's and Metcalf's laws are the driving forces, with no let up in sight. For businesses/publishers it means everything from doing business via emails and instant messaging to implementing corporate wide ERP systems. We will discuss and demonstrate some of the newer products that have been enabled by technology. These impacts are, of course, not unique to publishing. They affect all businesses and even warfare (laser guided missiles, instant communication on the battlefield, etc.).

The last several decades have experienced an accelerating rate of discoveries in the sciences. We now have cloning of animals (humans?), genetic engineering, molecular and cell biology and altered foods. It has been said that the half-life of a scientific degree is five years. In other words, half of what one learns in science while in college today is obsolete in five years. There is a story told about Albert Einstein while he taught at Princeton. It seems he wrote up the major question for the end of term final exam. His assistant pointed out that this was the same question as last year! Einstein replied: "That's true, but the answer is different this year." What these trends indicate is the need for continuous lifetime learning, regardless of profession. It has spawned the entire for-profit post secondary industry.

The confluence of these businesses, technologies, and scientific trends has created what is referred to as the Global Knowledge Economy (GKE). This economy, as you probably know, is borderless. Information travels instantly around the globe. As a result, individuals and companies seek the most cost effective ways to do business. This includes everything from outsourced customer service centers to x-ray examinations by physicians to editing of scientific journals. The GKE provides for mobility of individuals and companies who can achieve success by capitalizing on these characteristics, assuming they have the necessary education and skills. It also means that nobody can corner the market, horde information, or achieve a monopoly. Therefore the GKE will be highly competitive for organizations and individuals. All of us must be competitive on a global basis.

Whether it's Peter Drucker or Lester Thurow, you need skills to participate in the GKE. It has been said the currency of the GKE is skills. You need them to enjoy the "good life."

Major publishers continue to gain share, both through organic growth, and also by acquisition. In the US, there are now four major elementary-high school (Elhi) publishers. These are McGraw-Hill, Pearson, Reed Elsevier, and Houghton-Mifflin. There are only three major college publishers (Pearson, Thomson, and McGraw-Hill). In the medical publishing segment, there are two (Reed Elsevier with Saunders/ Mosley and Wolters Kluwer with Lippincott). These companies can make the necessary investments in technology products and systems to stay highly competitive. There are still many smaller niche opportunities, but the risks are higher and/ or the margins may be lower. The larger players feel somewhat threatened by the potential use of technology by the more agile and skilled who may undercut some of their market. This is a fact of life in the educational publishing industry as well as in many other industries.

2. Educational Trends

While the business and technology trends discussed have generated considerable change in the educational publishing business, their customers, the school systems, have also been buffeted by change and, to many, underperformance. In the United States, reading scores have remained relatively flat over the last fifteen years while expenditures have risen over 300% to over $18 billion. See Chart 1. This chart actually masks a bigger problem. As Chart 2 shows, there is a large gap between ethnic groups. Asian-Americans consistently score the highest on reading/math tests administered by the federal government. Hispanic-Americans consistently score the lowest. The gap has not narrowed over the last fifteen years despite many special programs. In New York City alone, the largest school district in the country, over 60% of students

Chart 1: NAEP Reading Scores and ESEA Funding

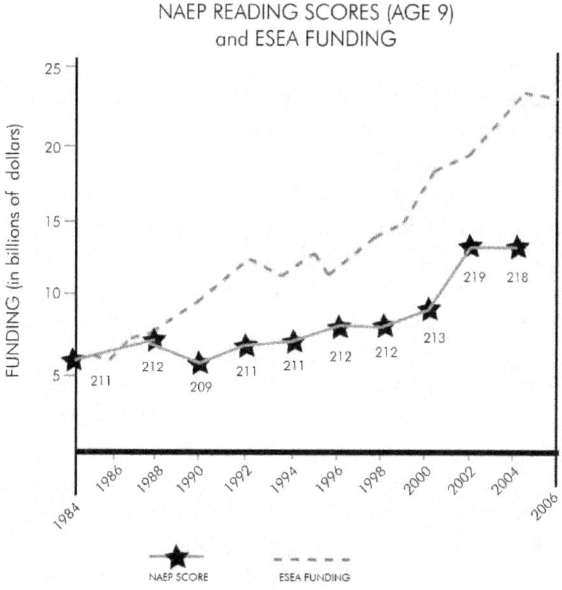

Chart 2: NAEP Reading Scores

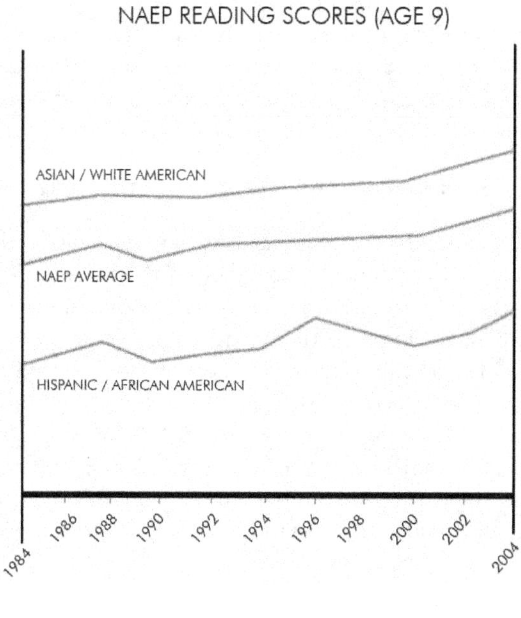

are below grade level in reading and math. This type of data has driven considerable demand for change and improvement by the business community, parents, and politicians.

This performance and lack of progress has resulted in the implementation of standards, assessments and accountability programs in many states. Unlike most other countries, the USA leaves curriculum and other educational decisions to the fifty states. There is not a national standard. Basically, this new system attempts to create accountability by establishing a set of curriculum standards as to what each child should learn for each year and then assessing each child in selected grades to determine progress and hold teachers, administrators, principals, etc. accountable for the results. Governor George W. Bush of Texas was one of the early adopters of this system.

This program was implemented on a federal level when George Bush became president. The No Child Left Behind Act required accountability on the part of schools but also provided significant funding for new reading programs, technology, testing professional development, etc. Every child must be assessed in grades three through eight.

The results must be disaggregated by ethnic and economic categories. Superintendents, teachers, and principals are now accountable for what students learn as opposed to what is taught. Schools now have Profits and Loses. As you might expect this shift has caused much change as well as discomfort in the education community. These changes have created both opportunities and challenges for the publishers who supply curriculum materials and services to the schools.

Internet access in schools is ubiquitous. Almost all schools have personal computers in the back of the classroom (PCBR). Computers are now required at almost all colleges and universities. They are being increasingly integrated into the course material. Universities are spending considerable sums on upgrading classrooms and dorms to support computer use and access. Most universities have a standard course management system.

3. Technology and Educational Publishing

Educational publishers have responded to this trend by developing products aimed at improving efficiency in the schools/colleges and at improving the teaching and learning process. The former would include school administrative reporting, attendance, summarizing and reporting grades, school bus schedules, etc. The latter products are aimed at improving the teacher's effectiveness and/or the student's learning, retention, practice, etc.

There has been a tremendous investment by the US federal government, state and local governments, and individual school districts in computer hardware and infrastructure. This has led publishers to evolve in the development of technology products from a new media group independent of the publishing unit to imbedding technology within the publishing unit, and to creating separate technology profit centers. This shift reflects the increasing importance of these products to the publishers.

Another shift in the industry is one from products to products and service. The educator and the publisher are linked by the results achieved. We will be demonstrating one of these products shortly.

The types of products that exemplify this shift involve more use of PCBR for practice and instruction. This software will allow formative assessments of students on a periodic basis such as weekly, monthly, etc. Most importantly, it will provide the teacher with information about the individual student's performance and instructional needs. This facilitates more customized instruction. These diagnostic reports also help evaluate teacher performance.

We will now run a short demo of a McGraw-Hill product, called Acuity, which has these characteristics.

Let's move to the Higher Education area. Higher Ed has always been more advanced in the use of technology than the ELHI industry. About 75% of all college students receive grades and assignments online and submit assignments via email, and about 50% email or instant message their professors for help. These students are the cyberspace generation. Products that leverage technology to truly improve student learning are few in number. We will now demonstrate one such internet based interactive product.

The product is called ALEKS, which stands for Assessment and Learning in Knowledge Space. It is an online service that is self-paced, provides adaptive assessments, and can be customized for specific courses. Each student will proceed through ALEKS at a different pace and with different assessments and soon, than other students. Now the demo:

There are not many products like ALEKS in the marketplace. However, there are many web based textbooks and, of course, supplemental materials. Recently, Pearson won the California social studies adoption, worth about $80 million, with an electronic text. This is the first such state adoption and could be the start of a new era in digital publishing in the ELHI area. The development cost was apparently about one-half of a basal social studies text.

Another interesting development is the Globaltext project. The project seeks to create internet based textbooks that will be freely available, primarily for developing countries. It was started at the University of Georgia in 2004. So far two books have been published, one in Information Systems and one in Business Fundamentals. The goal is to have about 1,000 electronic textbooks, mainly covering topics taught in the first two years of college.

Many universities have leveraged the internet to create and grow their business. Apollo has over 300,000 students and continues to grow. Dr Robert W. Mendenhall, president of Western Governors University, has observed that "increasingly the world of work is online...most of our business interactions today are with people around the country and around the globe, so in many ways an online education better reflects the workplace than the classroom." Wikiversity is a space for the creation and use of free learning materials and activities, which is a concept similar to the Globaltext project. With this growing use of online texts by universities and with students born in the cyber age, it is absolutely necessary for educational publishers to adapt to this environment.

4. Issues for Educators and Publishers

There remain significant issues that impede the use of technology in educational publishing. In the public elementary and high schools, it is necessary that all children have equal access to computers before instruction, homework, and research assignments can be made. Until each child has a laptop/pc, only assignments that can be worked in the classroom (PCBR) and the computer lab can be made. Some of us think that the federal government should "leave no child unconnected". MIT is working on the $100 computer. As prices continue to decline we may see the day when the schools issue the computer to the child and most textbooks will be electronic.

Today's students are born into the world of cyberspace. Unfortunately, most of their teachers were not. As a result, the acceptance cycle for new and innovative methods is slow. Another impediment to rapid implementation is that each state has its own curriculum standards. To be most effective in the classroom, products must be correlated to those standards. To do so requires considerable flexibility on the part of the publishers as well as significant investment. This is one of the drivers of consolidation in the industry.

Lastly, problems of pricing and copyright persist. In many cases the electronic product is a "by-product" of the development of a basal textbook series. This raises questions on the proper pricing of each component. Additionally, publishers are rightfully concerned about unauthorized use of their electronic products. Movements such as Globaltext and Wikiversity do not provide comfort.

5. Conclusion

In conclusion, there are many forces of change that are affecting the educational community, as we have discussed. This has resulted in many changes in the nature and type of products and services offered by the educational publishing industry. However, when there are many profound changes occurring that are significant for society, many opportunities are created. It is our job to capitalize on these changes, leverage technology, and provide products and services that improve teaching and learning. For companies that do, it is a land of opportunity.

Curriculum of Editing and Publishing in the Digital Age

Luo Zichu & Dai Yang

With the development of the publishing industry in the digital age, the demand for publishing professionals increases constantly. As the training base for publishing professionals, the colleges and universities must strengthen the editing and publishing curriculum according to these new demands for publishing professionals in order to train qualified people. This article discusses course construction for the editing and publishing profession in the digital age from three different aspects.

1. Courses in Editing and Publishing in the Digital Age

Compared with the traditional publishing industry, the publishing industry in the digital age has some main characteristics as follows.

1.1 The Interaction of Multimedia Is More And More Prevalent

We have accomplished the digitization of processing and diffusing information on the web in the digital age, which makes the multimedia characteristic of publications prominent. When an excellent knowledge product comes out, no matter whether it sold well or not at first, it is always followed quickly by other kinds of media. Then there is the thrilling sight of multimedia interaction. In recent years booksellers have become closely related to multimedia interaction. There are "video-leading" publications, whose videos sold well at first and are followed by paper publications, such as *Qiao's Compound*, *Jewel in the Palace*, *Moment in Peking*, and *Show Your Sword*. There are "book-leading" publications, whose paper publications sold well at first and are followed by video and electronic publications, such as *The Hanzheng Street*, *Shen Cong Nao Zai*, *The Totem of Wolf*, and *Children's Encyclopedia in China*. There are "web-leading" publications, which sold well in the form of web composition at first and are followed by paper publications, such as "Losing Love When We Are Graduating," "The First Close Contact," and "Xu's Blog." Multimedia interaction not only makes good use of publishing resources, but also promotes selling and increases the whole efficiency of publishing operations. So it is applied by more and more publishing enterprises.

The wide implementation of multimedia interaction challenges the curriculum of traditional publishing education. The core of traditional publishing education is liberal arts, but managers should master not only the knowledge of liberal arts but also something about science and engineering in the publishing mode of multimedia interchange. The course system for the editing and publishing profession should develop from the core curriculum system of liberal arts to the comprehensive course system of liberal arts and science. So it is necessary to reconstruct the curriculum of the editing and publishing profession.

1.2 Every Publishing Chain Has More and More Technical Content

The main characteristic of the digital age is the development of digital technology. Besides having a decisive influence on the development of publications' productive process, the development of digital technology also has an important effect on other publishing chains, such as the supply of publishing materials, the exploitation of resources, the organization of publications' circulation, and the product's distribution and transportation. From the point of view of technical content, the operation of every publishing chain has much more demand in the digital age than in the traditional age. Take the organization of book circulation for example. In the digital age, the organization of circulation and information flow is achieved mostly on the web. The access to a large amount of digital information improves the velocity and efficiency of circulation and demands more technology be in operation.

With the increase of technical content in publishing chains, publishers are required not only to master some related technical expertise, but also to be very capable of operations. In order to adapt to the new requirements, the editing and publishing profession in colleges and universities should increase the proportion of practical teaching in the curriculum. Besides offering special practical courses, it is advisable to add a period of practice in basic courses. This can intensify the training of students' practice abilities, so we should make students master basic operation skills of every publishing chain by renewing the curriculum. Then students can be rapidly adapted to publishing demands that have more and more technical content.

1.3 The Publishing Process Is More and More Sophisticated

The change in the publishing process is the inevitable outcome of the change of the technical environment. Compared with traditional publishing, the technical environment has had an earthshaking change in the digital age. With the wide application of digital information processing and transmitting technology, many new technologies have appeared in the field of publishing, such as the pre-printing digital processing technique, the net-appending digital technique, the matrix digital technique, the digital technique of direct plate-making and required printing, the proofing digital technique, the network transferring digital technique, etc. The emergence of the new techniques makes the operation of the publishing process flexible. For example, the appearance of the required printing technique enables publications to be sold first and manufactured second. For another example, the appearance of the network transferring technique makes the mode of producing publications varied. We can produce publications locally or in other places, in batches or individually and can choose circulation channels flexibly. Many kinds of patterns can be chosen in the operation of each link.

The flexibility and complexity of the publishing process make the interaction of the various chains of the publishing industry more and more complicated to control. The situation challenges the publishers' decision making and management abilities. So the editing and publishing curriculum in universities should benefit the cultivation of students' comprehensive capabilities.

In a word, the new situation of the publishing industry in the digital age requires more of publishing professionals.

2. Constructing the Editing and Publishing Curriculum in the Digital Age

The rapid development of digital technology is indicative of the digital age. Social productivity improves quickly and social life is altered in all fields. The new social circumstance extensively affects the development of the publishing industry. The effect appears not only in the production technology but also in the management system and operation mechanism of publishing. It is even apparent in the ideological sense and management consciousness of publishers. The effect brings about great change in the demands of publishing professionals. Manifested in at least three aspects. First, it calls for more knowledge. Publishing professionals should have knowledge of liberal arts, society, science and engineering. They should master not only some basic cultural knowledge but also some vocational and management knowledge of the field of publishing. Second, it needs more technology. We need computers and the web to exploit the title resources, to modify and process information, to slot data and make plates, to sell publications on the web, to manage clients, and so on. The work needs higher technology. Third, it requires more integrated management capacities. In the situation of incorporating multimedia, industrial chains networks and the publishing industry running at high speed, if publishers want to operate publishing machines well, they need to not only know how to manage and operate publishing, but also have a group of integrated coordination capability and systematic administration capability.

The above characteristics of publishing professionals in the digital age determine that their specialized knowledge should be composed of three kinds of aspects: basic culture of knowledge, publishing vocational knowledge, the editing and publishing curriculum in colleges and universities should be constructed around this knowledge frame. In concrete design, professional courses in the editing and publishing profession should consist of three kinds of courses as follows, except for the common basic courses that the Education Department sets for all specialties in all colleges and universities.

First, there are some courses about basic culture and history, which can cultivate publishers' cultural qualities. These courses should include foreign language, mathematics, Chinese writing, comprehensive history of China, the history of literature, the development history of science and technology, basic management science, basic economics, an introduction to the culture of science and an introduction to mass communication.

Second, there are some courses about publishing vocational knowledge that can cultivate publishers' vocational qualities. These courses should include basic publishing science, editing theory, editing practice, marketing, management science of publishing enterprises, the logistical organization of publication, basic printing, cover design and layout, publishing history in China, publishing history in foreign countries, publishing law, research on publications, reader science, operation and management of periodicals, operation and management of audio-video and electronic publications, an introduction to the book industry in the world, the foreign publishing trade, and the publishing industry's construction.

Third, there are some courses about operating technology, which can develop students' practical capabilities. These courses should be comprised of basic computer operations, pre-printing digital technique and its application, web design and website construction, database construction, editing software, modern sales technology of electronic commerce technology web publishing information searching, market investigating, planning and decision-making technology, and e-book design and production.

Of course, colleges and universities can offer those courses according to their actual situations. They should form their own distinguishing features and needn't copy the whole.

3. A Variety of Perspectives of Curriculum Construction

Higher publishing education has developed rapidly in our country in recent years. In April 1983, Book Sales Management Profession, which was renamed the Publishing Sales Management Profession, was authorized by the State Education Commission and was established in Wuhan University. Since then, many kinds of publishing degrees have been established one after another at some famous colleges and universities. In 1999, all kinds of publishing professions were merged into the editing and publishing degree, which was then developed. The editing and publishing professional degree has been set up in more than seventy colleges and universities as of today.

By synthesizing the professional courses that are offered in those colleges and universities, we can find that there are many serious problems with the present construction of the curriculum. First, the courses are in a jumble and inconsistent with the training aims. Second, since teachers and contents of courses are arranged with local materials, the curriculum lacks professional content. Third, because we are laying too much stress on theory and making light of practice, it is not beneficial for training students' practiced capabilities. Fourth, colleges and universities are offering courses freely, so the curricula are short of unified basic requirements and the colleges and universities lack essential communication with each other.

In view of the existing problems, the author has several opinions about how to strengthen the editing and publishing professional curriculum.

3.1 Establish Courses for Training Editing and Publishing Professionals

At present, the editing and publishing degree in colleges and universities is formed by merging editing book sales management printing, etc. It is an applied degree which aims at training publishing professionals. The editing and publishing degree has cultivated most of the publishing professionals who are needed by the industry, including in editing, marketing, publishing management, science research education and printing management. Most job assignments for the editing and publishing major graduates are in various kinds of publishing houses. We think that the training aim of the editing and publishing majors should be: training applied publishing professionals who are needed by the publishing industry. We should design curriculums closely around the training aim. The professional courses should consist of all kinds of professional knowledge that is actually needed in the development of the editing and publishing industry which are the core of the curriculum.

Some courses have little or indirect relationships with publishing. For example, some colleges and universities offer the Introduction to Literature as the professional course for editing and publishing. We do not think this is reasonable.

3.2 Ascertain Professional Core Courses with a Preliminary Standard

The professional core course can represent the fundamental distinguishing features of a specialty. It takes responsibility for passing on the most important core knowledge of the specialty. Ascertaining the professional core courses is helpful to standardize the editing and publishing curriculum in colleges and universities and to encourage them to communicate.

There are some basics to ascertaining professional core courses. First, the main content of the courses must be core knowledge necessary to publishers. Second, the professional core courses must have the distinguishing features of the editing and publishing profession; that is to say, the courses have not been offered by other specialties. Third, the knowledge level of course content must be up to the standards of undergraduate education. Fourth, the professional core courses must be universally professional courses that are needed by every branch of the editing and publishing profession.

According to those basics, we should choose eight to ten courses as the professional core courses (there are eight professional core courses in the law degree). Once the professional core courses are ascertained, every school that wants to establish an editing and publishing major must be capable of offering those courses. This is also the prerequisite for forming the distinguishing features of running colleges and universities that offer those professional core courses. Then, we can effectively improve the disorderly and irregular conditions in editing and publishing curriculum.

3.3 Increase the Proportion of Practical Courses

The editing and publishing profession is an applied science, so practical courses are very important. Since the practical teaching of the editing and publishing profession in colleges and universities is in a commonly weak condition at present, we should take measures to accentuate the practical.

Let's take the editing and publishing major at Wuhan University as an example. It has offered many of the three kinds of courses mentioned in the second part of this article, and has made considerable progress in improving the quality of teaching, but apparently only a small portion of students put theory into practice.

Most of the courses rely mainly on classroom instruction and the students' practical courses do not take up a large proportion of course work. There not opportunities for special, comprehensive practice, except in graduate practical courses. Graduate practice is only about forty days, so it is difficult to achieve the aim of training students' practical capabilities. The case of Wuhan University is common in colleges and universities. So it is necessary to accentuate the practical component of course construction.

There are several concrete measures we can take. First, we should increase the proportion of practical courses. Except for a few of the courses (such as publishing history), we should arrange the content of practical teaching in other courses. It is really better to teach less and practice more. Second, we should arrange a comprehensive practice of about a month at the intermediate stage in an undergraduate's four-year study and give students more systematic exposure to fieldwork. Third, it is better to prolong the period of graduate practice for a term or three to five months. Fourth, we should organize and carry out many kinds of extra-curricular practice activities which are beneficial to students' practical capabilities. Students can take active part in summer social practice, teachers' scientific research, professional knowledge contests, and so on. They can heighten their practical capabilities by participating in those extra-curricular practical activities.

REFERENCES

Luo, Zichu. "Constructing undergraduate course system of the editing and publishing profession." *A Vast View on Publishing.* 2004 (1).

——. "Several Opinions about course setting of editing and publishing profession." *Publishing Research.* 2006 (6).

Electronic Publishing in Germany: An Overview of Developments in Industry and Education

Ursula Rautenberg

1. Electronic Publishing in Germany: An Overview of Developments

1.1 A Historical Retrospect

Until the 1980's, the concept of electronic publishing or of computer-assisted publishing was limited exclusively to electronic steps in the production process. New technological developments in the production process, which made it possible to compose books entirely on the publisher's desktop computer until just prior to printing, reduced the number of production phases. Customers and readers took no notice of this at all, as the printed book was—and continues to be—the end result of the production process. In the next step, word processing and layout software provided publishers' production departments with powerful tools for manipulating text. Since the end of the 1980's, at the very latest since 1995, authors have been drawn into the process as well; submitting manuscripts electronically became mandatory in nearly all cases. Around the same time, the user started to become a link in the "electronic chain." The number of PCs in homes and offices climbed quickly, so that electronic consumer goods, at first in the form of CD-ROMs, could complete the chain. From there it was only a short step to electronic books, that is, text files that can be read on a PC or on mobile output devices. The new possibilities of knowledge organization through "hypertexts," the combination of image, text and audio and the transmission of documents and images on the World Wide Web entailed far more momentous consequences; "multimedia" was the buzzword of the 1990's. Thus the technical potential was created for innumerable forms of electronic publishing up to and including E-commerce. By "E-commerce" I mean the execution of commercial transactions in the book trade via electronic means both between particular economic entities (business to business) and also to the end customer (business to consumer). Already in 1993, the motto of the Frankfurt Book Fair was "Frankfurt goes Electronic," and between 1991 and 2000 most publishers had undertaken initial steps towards electronic publishing as a commercial enterprise; after 2000, the rate of publishers entering the electronic publishing market declined markedly. The initial euphoria was soon joined by voices of cultural critique, prophesying the demise of the book and a mass extinction in the book trade.

1.2 The Book Trade's Current Assessment of Electronic Publishing

This historical excursus will be followed with an overview of the current state of affairs and the book trade's own view of the possibilities and limits of electronic publishing. The "Börsenverein des deutschen Buchhandels e.V.," the "German Publishers and Booksellers Association," is the umbrella organization representing the production and publishing segments of the book industry. It attends to the interests of its sector of the industry in economic affairs and cultural politics and follows market developments through its working groups and committees. In 1992 the Association reacted to the apparent triumph of electronic publishing with the establishment of the "Arbeitskreis Elektronisches Publizieren" (AKEP), the "working group on electronic publishing." AKEP has since then regularly surveyed the members of the book trade association in order to investigate developments in all areas of electronic publishing. I'll refer here to the most recent survey, entitled "AKEP Branchenbarometer Elektronisches Publizieren 2006," "A barometer of electronic publishing in the book trade."

The most important trends are:

- More than three quarters of publishers identify the share of electronic products in their total sales in 2006 as no more than 5%. However, more than 50% of the publishers believe that these products will account for more than 15% of their total sales in 10 years.
- The relationship between expenses and receipts is remaining stable. Almost half of the publishers describe it as in balance. In other words, only a quarter of all publishers earned money with electronic publishing. Only 5% of the publishers are expecting significant profits in the next 5 years. It is especially the textbook publishers who are looking optimistically into the future—note the key word "e-Learning"—as well as the large publishing houses with over 100 employees, among which the major players are particularly found in the so-called STM segment (scientific, technical, and medical publishing) or the most important publishers targeting specific professions.
- Revenue from paid content: Paid content as a direct source of revenue for electronic products is considered insignificant by almost 70% of publishers. This form of revenue only plays an important role for around 18%.
- Indirect revenue from advertisement or e-commerce: These play an insignificant role for almost all publishers. Publishers of children's books and self-help books, however, assume that their indirect revenues will increase in the future.

- No revenue: Electronic publishing is used primarily for marketing purposes by large publishers. Especially noteworthy are the dictionary and lexicon publishers, who clearly have great hopes for electronic advertising and marketing tools.

What are the problem areas?

- The decisive factor in determining success is a capable content management system. Over 60% of the publishers complain that industry-wide standards for the use of media-neutral data storage are lacking.
- Business models and payment systems for electronic content are unsatisfactory for three quarters of the publishers.
- The era of offering free content on the Internet is nowhere close to its end for the majority of publishers; the competitive situation continues to exist and will probably become more acute through high-quality content that is made available at no cost by universities and scholars among others.
- Consequently, the debate over a reformulation of copyright becomes an issue. One of the hot topics continues to be the protection of copyrights against piracy. More support from politicians is desired. Digital Rights Management systems are still considered important measures, although a third of the publishers support their replacement by electronic watermarks.
- The digitalization of complete libraries and the "search inside the book" projects of companies such as Amazon and Google, which make content electronically searchable and accessible. The Association of the German Book Trade has developed a counter-model for German publishers and presented it at the Frankfurt Book Fair 2006.

1.3 The AKEP Prize for Innovation

I would like to add some color to this very generalized assessment. Since 2005, AKEP has awarded a prize for innovation in electronic publishing, known as the AKEP Award. The thirty to forty submissions the jury receives each year present a very mixed picture. Particularly the publishers that specialize in products for lawyers or tax consultants are well represented. This is unsurprising, as law texts and legal commentaries belonged to the first text types that were published electronically in Germany; there are many years of experience here. Hans Dieter Beck, the owner of the Beck publishing house in Munich, evaluates the current situation as follows: "We are in a period of strong growth in online publishing, which goes along with a certain decrease in print media." None of the tax or law products have placed in the top three up to now, however. The AKEP Award is a prize for innovation, and particularly publishers for the professions rely on tried and tested solutions for their conservative audiences.

The spectrum among the innovative prize winners reaches from the small press all the way to world-famous dictionary publishers. The winner of the first prize for 2005 is a very small company that operates "soforthoeren.de," a download portal for audio books as sound files in MP3 format. This keeps the experience entirely digital by doing away with the CD-ROM as a physical medium, but it also eliminates the customer's trip to the bookstore. The portal concept involves other ideas as well: For one, communal sales and distribution, which bundles the offerings of many small audio book producers and assumes responsibility for various services. Also, the files are given an electronic watermark through a technology that was developed by the Fraunhofer IPSI-Institute. Thus, violations of copyright can be proven immediately.

The 2006 prize winner is the publisher F.A. Brockhaus. They offer the "Digital Brockhaus Encyclopedia" on a USB flash drive, the only encyclopedia that is immediately usable independent of location and with any Windows PC or laptop. The digital Brockhaus offers a natural language search functionality. One can search for unfamiliar concepts with simple "who - what - where" questions. Brockhaus is in this way innovative and has a decisive market advantage. The representation of connections between related articles in a three-dimensional knowledge space is also innovative. This product required considerable initial investment, as it implemented the current state of research in communications science and computer linguistics. Only a large publishing house that is a leader in a particular field of business can afford such an investment.

2. Education in the Area of Electronic Publishing

2.1 New Occupational Fields and New Career Contours

I need to range somewhat further afield, because the educational and university landscape in Germany is very complex. There is also a certain amount of uncertainty because there are not yet any completely articulated career or educational paths for the electronic segments of the publishing industry. AKEP has compiled some career designations and the necessary qualifications (see figure 1).

The yellow labels indicate areas for which an IT-degree is unconditionally recommended. For the careers with red labels, a university degree is as a rule not required. The educational path to these careers involves an apprenticeship and accompanying vocational school, or another possibility is the study of media design at a technical college. For the career segments labeled in blue, the preconditions are either an apprenticeship in the publishing industry, for example in publishing sales and marketing, or a university degree. Possibilities include a degree in business administration or in book studies at a technical college or a university. This summary represents the ideal, while in reality, specialists for electronic media are still barely employed in the publishing industry except in purely IT-specific activities. Instead, experienced employees in the publishing industry have trained themselves on the job to meet the new demands. In addition, the need for very specialized personnel is not as great as one might believe in the publishing industry. The entry-level employees with the best chances are those who have acquired a core of general knowledge, who can be utilized in many different roles, and who prepare themselves for new responsibilities. It is precisely here that university graduates in book studies, who meet these exact requirements, have an advantage. In addition, they will have studied one or two additional fields in addition to book studies, perhaps learned a foreign language or studied another field of knowledge that, for example, qualifies them for scientific and technical publishers or mass-market publishers. In addition it has to be mentioned that the field of book studies concentrates only on the book in all its forms, while the fields of journalism or communications are responsible for print media such as magazines and newspapers. The distribution networks of current periodical publications run separately from those of the book market, and the training of editors for newspaper and magazine publishers has its own career paths.

Figure 1: AKEP Job-Profiles E-Media, 2002

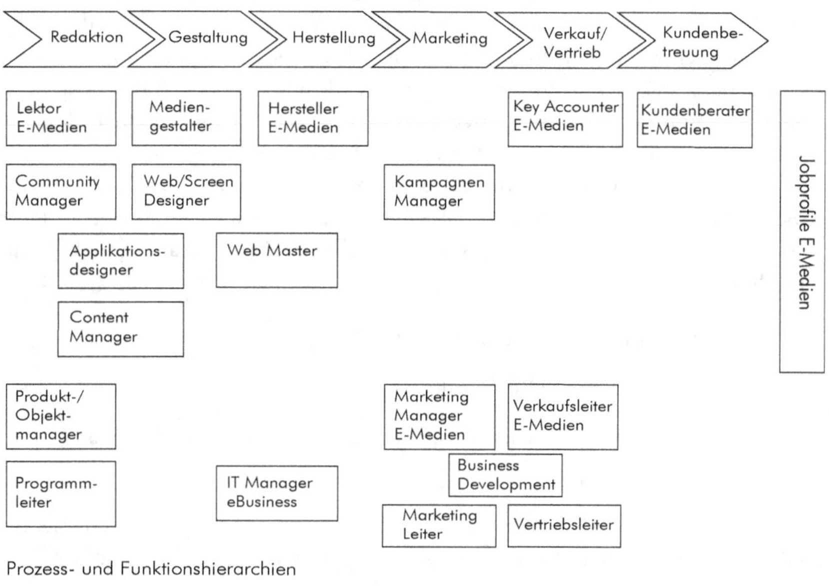

2.2 Book Studies at the University of Erlangen-Nuremberg

The University of Erlangen has the broadest spectrum of disciplines in Germany. Students in book studies can choose their additional subjects from among all other subjects in cultural studies and the humanities. Combinations with business and economics, media studies, or foreign languages are especially popular.

Currently, around 250 students have declared book studies as their major field, with over three quarters of them listing book studies as their primary major. As students can enroll in book studies at only five German universities (Erlangen, Leipzig, Mainz, Munich, and Münster), our students come from all parts of Germany and also from foreign countries. We have eight students from the People's Republic of China of whom four are already in the final phase (master's degree).

The German system of higher education differentiates between universities, which have the exclusive right to grant doctoral degrees, and colleges, which educate students with a focus on practical application rather than on theory and scholarship. Because the book studies program in Erlangen is housed at a university, the course of study must ensure scholarly training at a high level. On the other hand, the field has a strong link to practical application. The curriculum takes into account not only media theory and book history but also the economics and market structures of the modern publishing industry. Focusing on particular career fields as early as possible is mandatory. This focus is obtained through required internships to complement students' coursework and through special course sections with a practical orientation that are offered by editors, distribution specialists, book sellers, or employees of consulting firms. In addition to this, the permanent faculty oversees practice-oriented projects that as a side effect promote knowledge transfer from the classroom to society.

The book studies program in Erlangen has taken note of ongoing developments from the beginning. What is the practical effect in terms of student curriculum? In the winter semester 2007-2008, the "magister artium" will be replaced by new bachelor's and master's degrees that are the final results of a modular, multi-stage, highly structured degree roadmap. The modules must be completed in six semesters leading to the bachelor's degree. Three of these modules have direct relevance for electronic publishing:

- Introduction to Electronic Publishing
- E-commerce in the Book Industry
- Book Typography with an Introduction to Desktop Publishing Software

Other modules also address electronic publishing, of course. For example, the media theory of the book also takes into account book contents in electronic form, and the module on legal matters also addresses new electronic media. It is nonetheless clear that electronic publishing has only a small part in the curriculum. The focus on the history of the book lends the discipline its "depth of field," which media-theoretical disciplines often lack, and the historical focus most directly introduces students to scholarly modes of thought, as such a mindset is required to overcome students' distance from the objects of study. Book theory is important as well, as it is ignored in both technical colleges and in vocational training. It provides an interface to media studies and to research in comparative media. It is precisely the new technologies that show a rapid development towards media convergence and for taking every advantage of the entire chain of creative exploitation in its various output forms. In addition we place great emphasis on economic fundamentals as they relate to the book trade.

It has been already mentioned that the publishing industry has a particular need for generalists who can react to various and constantly changing demands. Our program is tailored for this need rather than for narrowly specialized careers. That segment is adequately addressed by vocational training and technical colleges. The industry is so varied that the graduates are not forced to compete with each other, but rather each one finds the place that corresponds to his training and his disposition. As the survey discussed in the first part of my presentation shows, electronic publishing in Germany is a segment that is growing slowly and continuously but is not a dominant segment of the book trade. It would be premature to train young people very narrowly for it. The inclinations of our students confirm this. Many of them have good technical skills in electronic media and are capable users of desktop publishing programs. It has almost become part of their general everyday skills. Surprisingly often, however, they are most enthusiastic for historical topics, book design, and all aspects of media. The topics of the master's theses upon which one spends six or eight months of one's life reflect this: the "electronic" topics are less in demand.

REFERENCES

"AKEP Job-Profile E-Medien." Arbeitskreis Elektronisches Publizieren / Börsenverein des Deutschen Buchhandels. <http://www.akep.de.>

Arbeitskreis Elektronisches Publizieren / Börsenverein des Deutschen Buchhandels. <http://www.akep.de.>

Buchreport. Special Feb. 2006. pp. 14f.

Kuhn, Axel and Volker Titel. E-Commerce. Auswirkungen auf den Bucheinzelhandel. Erlangen 2004. S. 15-31.

Titel, Volker. Electronic Publishing und E-Commerce im Buchhandel. Ein Forschungsbericht für den Publikationszeitraum 1995 bis 2004. In: Archiv für Geschichte des Buchwesens 59 (2005). S. 201-235.

Publishing, Education and the Digital Age

Henan Sun

1. The Fantasy of a Bestseller

In all the years I have worked in Stirling, I am always being asked the same question, mostly by Chinese publishers: how to make a bestseller.

It seems that everybody wants a bestseller. But what is a bestseller?

1. Everybody Wants a Bestseller

If we define a bestseller as the book that has sold the most copies, possibly the Bible would be a bestseller over many centuries. If it means a book that generated the most revenue, some textbooks and reference books might be listed. But textbooks are not always obvious bestsellers. Major profits often come slowly. Some dictionaries take more than twenty years to develop and will only break even after a number of reprints or new editions. There are long term bestsellers and, over the years, they can become the most profitable publishing products.

We normally identify bestsellers with trade books, fiction and non-fiction. Think of the *Da Vinci Code.* Seven million copies in print, 56 printings in the year after it was first published. But even its publisher asks: how long can it last? So is it fame or reputation that turns a book into a bestseller? And for how long do they produce big money?

Bestsellers are the fantasy of many publishers. But the discounts of trade books nowadays are so enormous that publishers can hardly make any money from them. The profit of a book is not always linked to the number of copies sold or printed. Even with a book printed and sold in large quantities, if the publishers get the calculation wrong, they can still lose money.

It is impossible to guarantee a bestseller. Should we be so obsessed with pursuing something for which we cannot define or set a clear target? Who could have predicted the instant success of the grammar book *Eats, Shoots, and Leaves* in 2003?

We, publishers, will never be able to guarantee a bestseller, however much we spend promoting it. We can hope and dream, but we can never be sure that these hopes will become a reality. Is chasing bestsellers only a matter of carefully managing risk, usually making some money and sometimes huge amounts of money, or is it just a matter of the way the dice fall?

1.1 *Nobody Can Make a Bestseller*

Instead of an obsession with bestsellers, the profitable book is a better objective. Even if it does not sound as attractive, it is more solid for future development. The fact is simple: if all of our books are profitable, we can succeed without ever having a bestseller.

If most of our books are loss makers, we cannot survive even if we have a bestseller. Publishers should be after the profit rather than the fame of producing bestsellers.

The publishing process is a process that demands continuous management input from the publishers. The natural business cycle of the publishing industry has shown us that it calls for long term planning instead of short term bestsellers.

It can be very dangerous for publishers to fantasize too much about a bestseller. Now it is not uncommon for publishers to be too optimistic about the likely sales of a given book. It is not so long ago since a British publisher had a nasty accident in this particular minefield.

In 2000, Dorling Kindersley found itself in severe financial trouble because in the previous year it had overestimated the likely demand for its series of publications related to *Star Wars*. DK was left with some 10 million unsold books. In the six-month period prior to 31 December 1999, the firm ran up a loss of £25m. The outcome was that DK had to be sold to Penguin. Job losses: 350. Also affected were 14,000 people in the UK, and 40,000 worldwide, who were employed as part-time agents for DK products. The chairman later complained that no one had told him about this large print order. If it was true, the management process of the company caused the disaster.

Publishing is of course an industry based on calculating many risks and nobody can guarantee earning money. But the objective of process control is to earn as much as you can and lose as little as possible. What often happens is that publishers do not maximize their earnings when they have a successful book because the publishing process is not well managed.

1.2 What is the Most Valuable?

Productive, long term intellectual property rights are the most valuable assets of a publishing company.

The publisher can make money from publishing the book and explore other subsidiary rights from the copyright. As the copyright holder, the publisher will be able to license different rights to different parties. It is a unique form of property: you can sell it again and again. Successful publishers resell it many times for over a hundred years in some cases. The ownership of copyright is much longer than other kinds of intellectual property.

Over years, the value of the copyrights owned by the publisher represents the brand value of the company in the market. To set up a strategy of improving the value of intellectual properties is the key to secure the future.

2. Publishing Education Serving the Industry

2.1 The Focus of Publishing Education

As publishing becomes more complex and larger in scale, we have created a professional publishing education system. We need two different types of personnel in the industry. We need people who can copyedit the book, proofread the book, design the book, market the book and produce the book. Their jobs fulfill the different functions in the publishing chain. Most courses are focused on basic skills. Only a few are also publishing management focused. But in the future management will be just as important.

Increasingly, we need people who can skillfully manage resources, manage the risks, manage the intellectual properties, manage the finance, make decisions, and take responsibilities. They also need to communicate efficiently with all team members, as well as to think about long term strategies for the company.

The two qualities of skills often exist in the same person but at different stage of his or her career. As publishing education providers, we shall need to provide both the basic and the higher level skills that modern publishers require.

2.2 Integrated Publishing Education

In Stirling, we aim at providing integrated publishing education. We offer two master's degree courses. The M.Litt. in Publishing Studies trains recent graduates with skills required by different functional departments in a publishing house including book editing, book design, marketing, production and electronic publishing. It is for people to enter the business at the junior level.

The M.Sc. in International Publishing Management trains the future managers for the publishing industry at the point when they start to rise to higher management levels. The course uses case study methods to cover risk management, finance management, HR management, production management, strategic planning and project management in the publishing business.

In addition to the degree programmes, we also provide a range of continuous professional development programmes. The Visiting Scholars programmes allow publishers or publishing researchers to spend from one month to one year with us developing an academic or commercial project. They will have staff privileges, comprehensive mentoring and support from the Centre staff.

The intensive publishing training courses will focus on special topics within the business, including copyright trade, editorial, marketing and digital publishing. The effective writing courses will help people develop business writing, textbook writing, technical writing, and professional and academic writing skills.

We put a lot of effort into designing these programmes as an integrated system. We keep close contact with the industry through continuous professional development programmes and keep our degree programmes always up to date. For example, the report from one of our visiting scholars from CIPG has been developed into a core case study for the M.Sc. course.

3. What the Digital Age Has Brought to Chinese Publishers

As the CEO of HarperCollins, Victoria Barnsley has said, "While publishing was once a business of mass production, where one sold ever-increasing print runs of ever-fewer titles to more and more people, the digital age will reverse this. It offers a world in which individual consumers will increasingly be heard, where publishers and authors can, for the first time, have direct contact and relationships with consumers."

The digital age has given publishers an opportunity to make a fresh start. On one hand, it increases the competition. The technology helps lower the entrance barrier of the business; everybody can now become a publisher online.

On the other hand, it gives publishers opportunities to exploit their existing intellectual properties, to market and distribute their books in a different way, and to produce books in low print runs, as a just in time business, transforming the supply chain.

In the digital age, most publishers will experience the opportunities and challenges from the global market. In the digital age, publishers need to re-identify what added value they actually make to content.

3.1 Strengths and Weakness

As Chinese publishers, we have strengths in our market and I am sure that those strengths will help us secure the dominant position in our internal market from international competitors. We have better knowledge about the local market and professional teams with local experience. The cash flows of many publishing houses in China are positive. Businesses and facilities are well developed for our market conditions. The big internal market gives Chinese publishers space for future development and will support Chinese publishers to expand into the international market.

I am very proud that at this year's Frankfurt Book Fair, Chinese publishers, for the first time, had a trade surplus in IP instead of a trade deficit, and licensed out more than eight hundred titles. But if we aim high, there are some weaknesses that we must recognize.

Eight hundred titles compared to the total number of titles we publish every year is still lower than 0.1 percent. Most of the books we licensed are about Chinese culture and Chinese literature. But how many books about China can the international market absorb? If we only concentrate on books about China or related to China, we will never be able to call ourselves international publishers. We have bought a lot of books from Western publishers. How many of them are about the UK or the U.S.?

As publishers, we are the managers of the publishing process. It is the same as managing the process of making clothes, cars and other products. I quite like one car advertisement I saw in Britain. The TV advertisement said, "French car, British Design." We need to increase the international licensing value in our copyrights.

We need to have access to international distribution channels, and know more about local readers either by ourselves or through local agents. We need to set up long term plans as the Japanese car makers have done so well. When they tried to enter the European market, they discovered the secret was to make the car look more European and less Japanese, but still keeping the legendary Japanese reliability and value for money.

We are very good at what we have done, which is about China, because nobody else knows better than us. But to get a bigger share in the international market, knowing China is not enough, we need to learn to use local resources including designers, editors, marketing people and distributors. Only by using them, can we enter a bigger market.

Most important of all, we need to overcome the language barriers. As required by any publishing industry, making things almost right is not enough. Readers have zero tolerance towards any mistakes in books. Being a foreign publisher is no excuse.

3.2 Opportunities and Threats

We have all realized the opportunities and threats the digital age has brought us. It helps break the barriers in traditional book distribution. It gives publishers an opportunity to re-define their future roles.

As Victoria Barnsley said, "for me there are two big questions facing publishers in the 21st century. How we bring added value to the author/consumer relationship in the online world, which still isn't yet clear, and how we'll make money out of it, which is even less clear."

After the failures of many online or digitalization projects, we started to see publishers like CUP and Routledge making money from their well planned digitization projects. It gives publishers new ways to explore existing intellectual properties.

In China, we are no longer far away from the world. International resources are available to us in digital formats. Our authors, editors, proofreaders and production team could be in different countries while we as the manager can still stay in control. Why is Nissan such a successful company worldwide?

Besides the general opportunities and threats shared by all publishers, we have to see some potential threats existing in the Chinese publishing industry. Our current asset value is constrained by money invested in unsaleable stock, low IP books and fixed assets. Almost all Chinese publishing houses have some unsaleable stock in their warehouses.

Somebody told me that the average printed value could reach 100 million RMB per publishing house. If we can not face the fact that those books are unsaleable and get rid of them, they will be there consuming our cash for storage. What is more important, we will not have a reliable balance sheet to plan our future activity.

Every book we publish is our intellectual property. We are after IP value in every book rather than purely the number of titles. We need to use our limited capital in our books to develop more intellectual properties which can make us money for over 100 years rather than building grand offices and warehouses. We are not property developers. As one of the largest academic publishers in the world, Blackwell is still in a rented building in Oxford, because they invest all their money into books rather than buildings.

There is always some policy uncertainty and it will not help publishers make long term plans if they are not sure what is going to happen.

Publishing groups have advantages in scale but lose out in specialized areas: this could be a threat for the future when the digital age requires a more personalized publishing industry.

3.3 Solutions

Changing the mindset is the key to everything. Initiative, financial competence, creativity and teamwork are equally important to publishers. More publishers will need to convert from skilled workers to professional managers. Chinese publishers need to learn to use international resources including overseas employees. The best opportunity is through international cooperative projects. As we work increasingly in joint ventures in the overseas market, we must learn from our partners.

Control of intellectual property will be challenged in the digital age. We need to produce more added values to keep our position as the key intermediary between writer and reader. Licensing books from other publishers will not add wealth for our future. We need to own more internationally marketable copyrights.

Let me be specific about a good strategy for entering the digital age. We need to learn new talents. Publishing houses, especially publishing groups can create an experimental environment for a group of employees, who will work on experimental, new projects for the digital age. They will help you prepare for the digitalization pressure as it comes in a few year's time. They can also re-explore your existing intellectual properties in new formats.

Finally, as the managers of the future publishing industry, it is your responsibility to get the concept of the digital age into every part of our business.

REFERENCES

Allen, Michael. *Grumpy Old Bookman: Essays and Criticism*. Kingsfield Publications. 1 Feb. 2005.

"Publishing in the Digital Age." <http://www.thebookseller.com/?pid=4&did=18338>

Copyright Infringement in Digital Publishing

Shay Humphrey

Copyright protection for authors and publishers of books and print works has a well-established history in the United States which continues to protect electronic works and the new technologies involved in digital publishing. Even at the founding of the country, the drafters of the U.S. Constitution gave the legislative body the power to grant to authors protection for their works in the useful arts and sciences through exclusive rights for a limited period of time (United States Constitution, Article I, Section 8). There has always been a desire to award authors (and publishers) exclusive rights in their works which rights are counterbalanced by the right of the public to have free and unfettered access to authors' creations. This balance has been largely regulated by the US Copyright Act, first enacted in 1790 and amended periodically to account for cultural changes and technological advances (17 United States Code, Section 101, et seq.). The primary purpose of the copyright laws is to protect copyright owners from unauthorized uses of their works, which is known as copyright infringement.

In the digital publishing world, the Internet allows great quantities of information to be published, searched and purchased through electronic means. The development of new digital devices also promises to make books and other textual information easily downloadable and portable (Rich 1). Encryption methods and other anti-circumvention technologies have assisted digital publishers in this regard but adequate legal protections must also exist to supplement protections to copyright owners. In the pre-digital age, limited technologies for copying and protective statutory law gave copyright owners a great deal of control over when, where and how many copies of their works would be sold. Copying now is easier, faster and cheaper in the digital world and nearly perfect copies can be made. The fear of publishers and authors is that the number of copies sold will be only one and that the sale of that one copy will allow access by everyone in the world without payment to the copyright owner for the use (Stefik 320). Due to this increased ease of copying in the digital world, additional protections are needed for copyright owners in the digital age including clarity as to what constitutes copyright infringement (Mtima 372). Despite this need, few legal solutions have been proposed or adopted in the US to address digital copyright infringement issues.

International Copyright

At this time, there is no international system of copyrights the way there is for trademarks under the Madrid Protocol, which has established a registration system in which 78 countries participate (WIPO Madrid Protocol 2006). Considering the impact of digitization on the world, it is appealing to imagine that such a uniform, international system could exist and there have been many international organizations meetings and treaties that have attempted to establish worldwide uniformity in the treatment of copyrights (Geller 245). The impediment to this globalization of copyright protection is that the notion of authorship, copyright and property ownership varies widely from country to country and is deeply rooted in each one's cultural heritage and historical development (Geller 261).

The US is a member of the Berne Convention, an attempt at establishing uniform, international treatment for copyright owners by treaty, which forced the US to recognize that copyright exists at the moment of creation of a work and requires the US to recognize authors' moral rights of attribution (the right to be credited as the author) and integrity (the right to object to derogatory treatment of the work) (WIPO Berne Convention 2006). Yet, the US still maintains a registration system for copyrights requiring the copyright owner to register each work with the US Copyright Office and deposit a copy of the work with the US Library of Congress before the author may bring a lawsuit for copyright infringement in the US or to gain the advantage of certain statutory damages (US Copyright Office, Cir.1). The US still does not recognize any meaningful moral rights for authors protecting the integrity of their works or to require attribution for authors, either by statute or in the courts (See Eldred; Seshadri). Even with international pressure, the US has refused to abandon its registration system or establish moral rights for authors. Based on the history of copyright protection in the US and the historic refusal of the US to change its copyright policies based on international pressure, it is unlikely that the US will protect digital works primarily through international laws or treaties.

The US Copyright Office

Not only has the US resisted any international harmonization of copyright laws as a method to handle the issues presented by the digital age, but even the US Copyright Office itself has not changed its policies or procedures to accommodate digital works. While the US Trademark Office has an entirely electronic method for processing trademarks including the submission of all necessary forms for filing a trademark, the US Copyright Office still requires paper submissions of copyright registrations (US Copyright Office, Cir.1). Also, the US Copyright Office has not developed any particular forms or methods for protecting digital or online content, including websites, software or electronic materials which differ substantially from printed works but require the same treatment by the US Copyright Office in terms of submission and application (US Copyright Office, Cir.66). The US Copyright Office is still utilizing print-based methods and forms for all materials, which forces digital works to fit into a print-based system. The US Copyright Office is in the process of establishing new methods for processing and registering digital content that will be better suited to the electronic mediums but such a system has not yet been formed or established.

The Digital Millennium Copyright Act

Digital works and technologies are not capable of comfortably fitting into the system of print-based laws and procedures and it is believed that new laws should be enacted by the US Congress that encompass novel ways of thinking about copyright and protection for copyright owners (Coale 763). For the most part, the US Copyright Act and other statutory laws have failed to address the unique copyright infringement issues presented by digital publishing. One exception to this is the Digital Millennium Copyright Act passed in 1998, although this legislation only addressed two narrow areas (DMCA; España 136). First, it criminalized the circumvention of anti-piracy measures built into commercial software. Second, it limited the liability for internet service providers (ISP) who merely transmit information over the Internet but do not review or screen the content of the information. While this legislation was important in protecting ISPs from a multitude of lawsuits and in placing an outer limit on what constitutes digital infringement, it shows the US desire to utilize the existing legal structure to address the digital era rather than crafting unique legislation to address these issues (Norris 1). Although the DMCA clearly criminalizes circumvention technologies and actions that seek to intentionally access, copy and distribute another's copyrighted work, the DMCA and the current state of US copyright law fail to clarify what other conduct constitutes infringement of digital works or electronic infringement.

Lawsuits and Case Law: Napster

The US legislature has not enacted widespread legislation regarding digital infringement, so copyright owners have turned to lawsuits in the US courts which will establish the primary and guiding body of law relating to digital infringement. The music industry, rather than the publishing industry, was the first to address digital copyright infringement in the Napster case. In an effort to challenge digital infringement, a lawsuit against Napster, a company that permitted individuals to download music for free from the Internet, was filed in the US by representatives of the owners of the copyrights in the music (Napster, 239 F.3d at 1004). The use by Napster was found to be copyright infringement and Napster was required to remit licensing fees to the copyright owners (Napster, 239 F.3d at 1017). This lawsuit also made an impact on the public perception about electronic copying by placing the public on notice that illegal copying will be monitored and actions will be taken against unauthorized users of copyrighted works. The Napster website still exists (through a successor company), but it charges customers for the music downloads, which are encrypted to prevent against unauthorized file sharing and use.

Fair Use

The Napster case used traditional copyright concepts of "fair use" to determine whether Napster was engaging in copyright infringement. Under the "fair use" doctrine, certain uses of the copyrighted work are permitted by the public without the necessity of obtaining permission for the use from the copyright owner (Coale 729). In a copyright infringement lawsuit, a court examines four elements, no one of which is determinative, in deciding whether a use is a fair use or is copyright infringement. First, the court determines whether the character of the use is "transformative" (i.e. uses for comment, news reporting, teaching, scholarship, and research) or whether it is merely the retransmission of the work in another form. Second, the court examines how much of the copyrighted work is used in the allegedly infringing work. Third, the court determines whether or not the use impacts negatively on the profitability of the work for the copyright owner and the market for the work and whether the alleged infringer was making a profit from the use. The fourth element is whether the copyrighted work is a work of fiction or a fact-based work, as works of fiction enjoy greater protection from fair use than fact-based uses (Coale 738). In the digital era, the same "fair use" analysis is used. In the Napster case, the use by Napster failed every element of the fair use test as the use was profit-based, negatively impacted on sales of the music by the copyright owners, merely retransmitted the copyrighted works in a different medium and the entire work was utilized, therefore the court found that this was not a "fair use" of the copyrighted works (Napster, 239 F. 3d at 1017).

The Google Books Library Project

The current controversy in the US publishing industry regarding digitization and copyright are the copyright infringement lawsuits against Internet search engine giant Google for its Google Book Search and Google Books Library Project. Google entered into agreements with the libraries at Harvard, Stanford and Oxford Universities, the University of Michigan, New York Public Library and the University of California to place their entire collections online in a searchable format for the public (American Libraries Online, 2005 and 2006). Google did not seek permission or licenses from the copyright owners of the works that will be included in this project. After the announcement of this Google Book Library Project, the Authors' Guild and the Association of American Publishers on behalf of McGraw-Hill, Pearson Education,

Penguin Group, Simon and Schuster and John Wiley & Sons filed lawsuits against Google for copyright infringement. In response, Google has offered the publishers an opportunity to opt-out of the project by informing Google of which works they do want included in the book project. This has been rejected by the publishers as they believe that it is a backwards approach to require copyright owners to request that third parties not infringe on their works (Band 244).

The court addressing the Google case will most likely utilize a "fair use" analysis balancing the research and educational aspects of the use against the potential damage to the copyright owner's profits if the use is permitted. In the Google lawsuit, Google is arguing that placing the collections in a searchable digital format is a fair use because it is using it for a scholarly purpose, Google will not make any direct profit on the use, the use is transformative in that the copyrighted works are being placed in a unique searchable database, that the ability to search the works will not negatively impact on sales of the underlying works and for copyrighted works, the searcher will only see a few sentences of the work that it locates through the search.

The publishers contend that Google: is a commercial venture; that they will make a profit on this use; that Google will be scanning the entire copyrighted work into the electronic library; that the work is simply being retransmitted in another medium (online) making it not transformative; and that users will not purchase the works if they are able to access them electronically for free thus negatively impacting the market (Band 243). This lawsuit is still active in the courts and it is being closely monitored to see how the courts will handle this balancing of public and private rights in the digital arena. Another recent case involving Google may provide some clue as to how the courts will rule and indicates that the courts may be willing to permit certain digital uses as "fair use."

Access vs. Copying: Field v. Google

An author of an online article sued Google because the article was included in Google's cache system, through which search engine users could locate and search the author's article (Field 1106). Although the article was not encrypted and was accessible to the public at no cost on the author's website, under traditional copyright notions, the use of the cache system by Google is per se copyright infringement as unauthorized copies are being made of the author's entire article without permission. Until the digital age, the balance between public access and author/publisher's rights to control and profit had been reached through a distinction between access and copying. While the public had access to the works for a fee, the author and publisher retained all rights to duplicate or copy the work. Conversely, all digital access of a work involves making a copy because, when you view a page on the Internet copies are automatically made to the remote computer, to the computer's memory and a copy to the screen (Davis 3). In a strict analysis, all digital access of a work is tantamount to copyright infringement because copies must be made to provide access. The Field v. Google court recently ruled that it is not copyright infringement for Google to copy websites, store the copies and transmit to users through the cache feature because the use serves a different and socially important purpose in offering access to copyright works through cached links (Field 1122). The court also utilized a fair use analysis in finding that the use by Google was transformative and did not negatively impact on the market of the copyrighted work. The court also noted that there was no real "market" for the work as the author had provided this article at no charge without encryption restrictions and that Google was operating its system in good faith. While the court used a "fair use" analysis it also recognized that copying alone would no longer be enough to constitute infringement in electronic mediums.

Conclusion

The digital age will make it increasingly more difficult for the US to protect the rights of copyright owners as digitization provides the public with increased access and ability to copy published materials (Mtima 372). The publishing industry is fearful that the same problems befalling the music industry will happen to digital publishing. Even after the Napster case, digitalization has altered the economics and structure of the record industry with sales of single digital music tracks up more than 1,700 percent in two years and total album sales down 19% and CD sales down 16% over the last five years (Rich 2). In order to provide enhanced rights to authors, the US has relied largely on self-help measures such as encryption and anti-piracy mechanisms while continuing to utilize existing statutes and case law frameworks to handle copyright infringement.

The decision in the Google Books Library Project case will be closely monitored to reveal whether a new framework is needed to strike the balance historically sought in the US between public and author, or whether the failure to take more aggressive measures to protect author rights will lead to a shift in favoring public access over private rights. A cultural shift away from private rights in the US seems unlikely as does the prospect of sweeping legislation or international harmonization of copyright law catering exclusively to the digital era. More likely, there will be a slow molding of legislation, case law and US Copyright Office procedures in the US to address copyright infringement in digital mediums. In the US, the upcoming years will be fraught with some legal uncertainty for authors, publishers and users of information as the law of copyright infringement and digital publishing is formed and analyzed by utilizing the US court system.

REFERENCES

American Libraries Online. "University of California Joins Google Books Library Project." Aug. 2006. <http://www.ala.org/ala/alonline/currentnews/newsarchive/2006abc/august2006a/newucgoogle.cfm>.

American Libraries Online. "*Publishers Group Sues Google over Library Project.*" Oct. 2005. <http://www.ala.org/ala/alonline/currentnews/newsarchive/2005abc/october2005ab/aapgoogle.cfm>.

Band, Jonathan. "The Google Print Library Project: A Copyright Analysis." *ARL Bimonthly Report* 242 (2005).

Coale, Ann. Fall. "Fair Use: Considerations in the Emerging World of E-Books" *16 St. John's Journal of Legal Commentary* 727 (2002).

Davis, Randall. "*The Digital Dillemma*" 44 Communications of the ACM 2. Feb. 2001.

Digital Millennium Copyright Act (DMCA). United States Code, Chapter 17, Section 512 (2003).

Eldred v. Ashcroft, 537 US 186, 260 (dissenting opinion).

España, Mauricio."The Fallacy That Fair Use And Information Should Be Provided For Free: An Analysis of the Responses to the DMCA's Section 1201" 31 *Fordham Urban Law Journal* 135 . Nov. 2003.

Field v. Google. Nev. 2006, 412 F.Supp.2d 1106 (D. Nev., 2006)

Geller, Paul Edward. "*Copyright History And The Future: What's Culture Got To Do With It?*" 47 J. Copyright Society U.S.A. 209 (2000).

Mtima, Lateef. "Tasini and Its Progeny: The New Exclusive Right or Fair Use On The Electronic Publishing Frontier?" *14 Fordham Intellectual Property, Media and Entertainment Law Journal* 369 (2004).

"Electronic Publishing Frontier?" 14 Fordham Intellectual Property, *Media and Entertainment Law* Journal 369 (Winter 2004).

Napster, Inc. adv. A&M Records, Inc., 239 F.3d 1004 (C.A.9 (Cal.), 2001). Norris, Alison M. 2006. "American Copyright Issues In the Pre-Grokster Landscape" 9 N.Y.U. J. *Legislation & Public Policy* 1.

Rich, Motoko. Jun. 2006. "*Digital Publishing Is Scrambling the Industry's Rules*", New York Times on the Web , Books. 31 Aug 2006 <http://www.nytimes.com/2006/06/05/books/05digi.html?ex=1307160000&en=a5abdb7fe3a0f48b&ei=5088>.

Seshadri v. Kasraian. 1997, 130 F.3^{d} 798 (CA7, Wis).

Stefik, M. "Shifting the Possible: How Trusted Systems and Digital Property Rights Challenge us to Rethink Digital Publishing," 12 *Berkely Tech.* L.J. 137 (1997).

United States Copyright Act, *United States Code*, Chapter 17, Sections 101, et seq.

United States Copyright Office (July 2006), *Circular 1 'Copyright basics'* 31 Aug. 2006 <http://www.copyright.gov/circs/circ1.html>.

United States Copyright Office (July 2006), *Circular 66 'Copyright Registration For Online Works'.* 31 Aug. 2006. <http://www.copyright.gov/circs/circ66.html>.

United States Constitution, Article I, Section 8 (stating "Congress shall have power . . . to promote progress of science and art, by securing for limited times to authors and inventors exclusive right to their respective writings and discoveries").

World Intellectual Property Organization (WIPO) *Berne Convention* (1886): summary. 31 Aug. 2006 <http://www.wipo.int/treaties/en/ip/berne/summary_berne.html>.

World Intellectual Property Organization (WIPO) *Madrid Protocol* (1989) <http://www.wipo.int/treaties/en/documents/pdf/madrid_marks.pdf>

Yu, Peter K. *The Copyright Divide*, 25 Cardozo L. Rev. 331 (2003).

New Frontier of Digital Publishing in the Domain of Creative Education

Chen Wuwei

Digital publishing comes with huge applause and expectations. Many people are optimistic about this evolutionary change and thinks it will bring brand new view for industry and learning. In the contrary, others take digital publishing as short-term technological blossom that can not interfere traditional publishing in the long run. It is indeed that digital publishing integrates with internet, new media and new technology. New Concepts are brought out by digital publishing which traditional publishing lack of.

Issues related to digital publishing are activated like chain reactions and there are key agendas we should research: copyrights, emphasis of intellectual properties, changes of business models, utilization of new technology, diverse concepts of digital rights between East and West, influences of related policies . . . , etc. How much do we understand about the current status of digital publishing ? what can we utilize from the non-linear knowledge flow formed by new technology and new media? In the red hot discussion of creative cultural enterprises, what constructive opinions can digital publishing propose in the aspect of education.

1. Observation of Digital Publishing

1.1 Statistics

Recent surveys categorize broadly the spread of information in China. The following are the approximate numbers: Web users are around 123 million, mobile users are around 440 million, newspapers print around 82 million copies daily the annual value of print products is 220 billion RMB, and annual value of audio/video products is 3,000 million RMB . . . etc. Facing such a huge population and market, how do we perceive the messages behind those numbers?

1.2 Status quo

Industries related to digital publishing in China nowadays are beyond our imaginations: In the field of emerging industries, new technologies and cultural-oriented innovative forms animation, gaming, digital contents . . . etc., are drastically integrating; Traditional media closely merge with internet to change ways of reading and combine mobile communication to reach new standards in terms of ubiquity and instantaneity. New milestone is being built by ground-breaking inventions of print-related technologies developed by domestic talents in China: Chinese digitization, laser photo composition systems for Chinese character typesetting, tele-transmission publishing systems, etc. Besides, the wide-spread of new mediums in reading is pushing the boundaries of software/hardware upgrading in educational institutions (e.g. digital library); The follow-up of digital publications also leads to the drastic growth of digital publishing. Founder Technology Group, Super Star Reader, Chinese all are the main digital publishers of China. According to the forecasting of media, the total amount of an e-book will occupy from 6% to 10% of digital publishing, and reach 50% in 2020. In 2030, 90% of books will have "e-book" edition according to the forecast. From the above we can understand the tight relationships between digital publishing and internet. The annual conference on digital publishing in China which has just rung down the curtain went one step further to include topics related to DRM (Digital Rights Management) which influence industry structure and management. It indicates that from content, technology to industry structure, digital publishing is undoubtedly of the most important topics of the next digital revolution.

2. Non-Linear Knowledge and Information Flow brought by New Technology and New Media

In the logic of traditional education, linear procedures exist between educators and disciples in terms of knowledge receiving. The coming of digital era challenges this linear order. Besides educational institutions, online resource websites, blogs and forums broaden the ways of learning. Some of the resources are even turning from the guest into the host and let the audience become writers, editors and publishers . . . etc. in order to provide information in a reverse way. In the meantime, the lead new technologies challenges the traditional medium. Products like Sony Reader present book contents by means of digital display, and transfer the books from physical to virtual formats. These factors not only make a statement of structural changes but also provide new reading experiences to audiences.

2.1 Role-changing between publishers and readers

In terms of the relationships between publishers and readers, new technology lowers the gate of publishing. New types of communication also forces the roles of traditional publishers back to the margin of the stage. Writers nowadays can present their work on multimedia platforms. Take the e-book as an example, Chapter/Indigo fully utilizes channels like podcasts, You Tube, Google to email web links of preview versions of new books to potential clients. Preview on the internet provides chances for readers to enjoy the benefit of flipping pages of desired books virtually. Services like this are no doubt a challenge to the marketing mode of traditional publishers. The role-play game of publishers and readers has upgraded to the next level.

2.2 Logic of non-linear knowledge flow

When the network era came, concepts of hyperlinks and hypertexts heralded the birth of new modes in knowledge aquisition. The calling of web 2.0 stimulates the utilization of POD (Print On Demand), online bookstores, web marketing . . . etc. On one hand these services lower the budget for printing. On the other hand, they broaden the format of publishing. One of the best known example is Barnes & Noble and its online bookstore, iUniverse. The Management modes of traditional publishers face the demand of evolutionary changes in stocks, time, promotion, marketing, . . . etc. The other example of this is the Wikipedia. The instantaneity and interactivity of this online encyclopedia edited by any potential user on earth challenge the long-time impression of time-consuming knowledge collecting and huge amounts of printing.

2.3 Role-play of new technology and new media

When asking readers how they know that "The World is Flat", they do not have to research the phenomenon of the capital market flow at present. All they have to do is to make a decision among the following choices: paperback for 35 dollars, multimedia CD for 40 dollars or 19.95 dollars for an audio book. This is the brand new role-playing game for new technology and new media in ways of reading. Technologies embedded in Sony Reader allow users to order e-books from Connect. HaperCollins and Simon & Schuster, Inc. combine the benefits of budget reduce in e-book and the reading experiences in traditional publishing. The E-Link technology also demonstrates the ability of image and graphic display. The integrations of technology, service and softwares completely emphasize the privileges of digital publishing.

3. New frontier of digital publishing in the domain of creative education

The other hot topic as digital publishing is the development of innovative cultural enterprises in China. This new trend combined with creativity and culture, industry and academy, official and folk, brings the new thoughts of changing. Innovative cultural enterprises, based on different historical developments in each individual area of the world, have diverse looks. Projects related to innovative cultural enterprises in these areas are also different. When taking a closer look to these areas, we find similar tactics among different approaches: enhance the connection among society, industry and culture, upgrade the structure and status of traditional industry, develop multi integration of horizontal alliances, the thoughts of globalization . . . etc. Digital publishing, which has similar thoughts of transforming from traditional publishing to new platforms of managing, also share the same visions as innovative cultural enterprises. By the cross look between digital publishing and innovative cultural enterprises, we can observe this revolutionary change that overwhelm our society in the near future.

3.1 Observations of communities in innovative cultural enterprises

The development of innovative cultural enterprises leads to the phenomenon of communities or clusters, and the related cultural preservation and utilization become important indexes for evaluation. Take the announcement that European Commission issued in 1996, which emphasized the importance of cultural and area corporation, development of cultural industry and preservation of culture and tradition. The area revolution lead by art, media and culture become the key position of related economy and industry. Take SOHO in UK as an example. This cluster formed by media industry has continuously absorbed related talents and enterprises in film, television and design since 1930. Coincidentally in the US, SOHO (South of Houston Street) in New York City also transformed the abandoned warehouses into the core for resident artists and galleries, and becomes the first example of listing factories to historical landmarks in world history. It is now creating the business phenomenon for related service industries never imagined in the very beginning. Factory 798, Dashanzi Art District, M50, Suzhou Creek . . . etc also utilized the abandoned factories and turned them into gallery spaces. CISV (Cultural Initiative Silicon Valley) in the US combined academy sponsorship, research and development, brought up the development of creative education and art of the community around local areas of Santa Clara County. CISV also presents the Creative Community Index that evaluates and integrate all together technology, education and culture.

3.2 Integration of digital publishing and innovative cultural enterprises

In the development of creative cultural enterprises based on communities, conflicts between business benefits and cultural values happen very often. Take the above industry cluster in China as an example; the confrontations of benefits often degrade the well-developed cultural communities into marketplaces and destroy the original idea of cultural development and preservation. Therefore, education itself carries the tasks of bridging integration and communication among creative talents, investors and habitants. Utilizing concepts like digital publishing in education to convey cultural contents and bring the perception of brand images will renew the cultural and historical assets and create new chances for corporation between diverse industries. One of the most effective ways to convey cultural contents is by art and design. Different forms of art like literature, music, architecture, drama, dance, photography . . . etc. and design-oriented industries like publishing, galleries, art trading, broadcasting and television, film, fashion and interior . . . etc. translate cultural contents into visual and sounds to shape the whole picture design of culture, tradition and industry.

3.3 Creativity, culture and learning

In the crucial moment that industries related to publishing call for reforms and changes, let us draw back from the above thoughts and rethink the future of digital publishing in the perspective of creativity and culture.

The global environment we are living has come to the crossroad of ever-changing and integrating. The cultural scenes exist and connect like flat and floating living form as a whole. Inside this living form, different parts reflect its individual face. How to keep the individual characteristic inside this living form becomes the common issue for all of us. Creativities in everyday life becomes the way to emphasize individual characteristics. Transforming our daily experiences into wisdoms and finding diverse solutions for questions become our unique culture context. This context has no way to be copied and reproduced for it come from the collective wisdoms varied of different regions of the world. Although this collective wisdom can not be totally copied or reproduced, we can still compensate with each other's advantages through means of education. Therefore, it takes creativity to shape culture and culture is inherited by education. Lives filled with creativity accumulate cultural contents with characteristics and transform into different forms of values. It is the process that takes time and experiences to fulfill and continuous efforts are needed in order to become mature industrial module in the common ground.

Conclusion

The coming era of digital publishing not only provide the industry, officials and academics more chances to make alliances and help the reform of the traditional industry, but also combine the channels of communication to provide brand new ways of receiving information. Furthermore, the development of innovative cultural enterprises has similar experiences and visions with digital publishing to refer to each other conceptually and methodologically. The care of cultural contents and industrial developments can be deepened into our next generation by education. Besides their own privileges of superior abilities in absorbing information, let them understand the importance underneath the economic development such as the health of the industry system, the protection of intellectual property and the preservation of cultural assets. It is crucial that we use the support from new media and new technology to consolidate the creative education so that the new generation will develop more abundant knowledge and visions. If we can convey the above messages efficiently through the reform of publishing and consolidate by education, it will help to influence subtly in the long run in terms of future development and communication of global information in China.

REFERENCES

China Book Business Report. <http://www.cbbr.com.cn/>

China Economy. <http://big5.ce.cn/gate/big5/finance.ce.cn/rolling/200610/22/t20061022_9077135.shtml> (accessed Oct. 22, 2006).

Creative Index Research. Home Affairs, Hong Kong Special Administrative Region.

CRI Online. <http://big5.chinabroadcast.cn/gate/big5/gb.chinabroadcast.cn/1321/2006/08/29/1569@1194769.htm> (accessed Aug. 29, 2006).

Cultural Initiative Silicon Valley. <http://www.ci-sv.org/>

European Commission. <http://ec.europa.eu/>

First Chinese Digital Publishing Trend & Technology Summit. <http://www.dpe.com.cn/>

Frankfurt Book Fair 2006. <http://www.frankfurt-book-fair.com/en/index.php?content=/en/presse_pr/tlp.html>

HarperCollins. <http://www.harpercollins.com/search/index.aspx?tab=author&kw=cidian&custCatName=&custCatId=0>

iUniverse. <http://www.iuniverse.com/>

Lin, Huaimin. Cultural development first, industrialization later—Looking at the feasibility of industrializing Taiwan's performing arts, based on the Cloud Gate experience.

Liu, Luna. Challenges and opportunities presented by globalization–Development of new cultural enterprises in Taiwan and lessons to be learned from Europe.

Ministry Of Information Industry of the People's Republic of China. <http://www.mii.gov.cn/>

publishing.com.hk. <http://www.publishing.com.hk/pubinfo/pubevents.asp?eventid=M&startyeara=19&syear=1980>

People Daily—IT—Opening of the First Chinese Digital Publishing Trend & Technology Summit. <http://it.people.com.cn/BIG5/42891/42893/3528170.html>

People Daily. <http://it.people.com.cn/BIG5/8219/50411/50436/3519590.html> (accessed Jul. 5, 2005).

Reference of Innovative Cultural Enterprises. R&D Center of Culture & Creative Industry of Communication University of China.

Power Law, Long Tail and Book Publishing

Lian Xiaochuan

Book Publishing Is a Niche Market Business

In his book *Making the List*, former Editor-in-Chief of Simon & Schuster Michael Korda recalled an anecdote. The publishing legend Robert Gottlieb once held an informal contest among his Simon & Schuster colleagues when they were on the train to the American Booksellers' Association convention in Washington, D.C.. The contest was to think of the most boring title anybody could imagine for a book; the winning title was *Canada, Friendly Giant to the North*. But the next day, Gottlieb and his colleagues actually found a book by that exact title at another publisher's booth in the convention. The moral of this episode is that, Korda says, book publishing is an industry "defiantly determined to answer the needs of everybody who can read, however special, strange, or odd their taste and interests may be."

This story catches the nature of book publishing—publishers strive to satisfy every imaginable human intellectual need and interest. No matter how obscure a book's subject is, its publisher always feels that somebody out there will buy the book. As a result, the book publishing industry perhaps produces more products than any other industry. According to R.R. Bowker, American publishers released 150,000 new titles in 2002, 175,000 in 2003, 195,000 in 2004 and 172,000 in 2005. On average, American publishers release one new book every half hour. R.R. Bowker's *Books in Print* database now contains over 2.8 million unique titles that are currently on the market.

Each title on the market can be seen as a unique product that is catering to a specific human interest and taste. Therefore, book publishing is inherently a niche product business—most books have only a narrowly defined audience and aren't intended to sell huge numbers of copies. Most books are not mass market products. In 2004, for example, 79% of the 195,000 new titles published in the U.S. sold fewer than 99 copies, another 17% sold fewer than 1,000 copies, only 2% of titles sold more than 5,000 copies. The average book in America sells only about 500 copies. With so many books on the market competing for readers' attention, it is a great challenge for publishers and booksellers to find readers for each of these books.

Based on this book sales pattern, if we plot sales per title as vertical *y*-axis and ranking of title as horizontal *x*-axis, we will have a sales curve which is heavy and short on the left side and low and long on the right side:

Fig. 1: Book Sales Curve

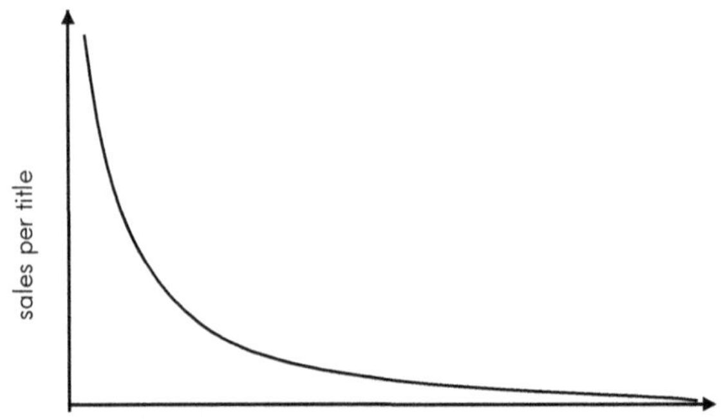

In statistics, this type of curve is called a power law distribution. Power law describes the phenomenon where, in a natural or social system, large elements are rare and few but small elements are common and many. Power law distribution has been found in many areas. Italian economist Vilfredo Pareto observed a power law pattern in wealth distribution where 20% of the population holds 80% of the wealth. Harvard University linguist George Zipf found that word usage follows the power law pattern, where a small number of words are used extremely often (such as *the, of*), a moderate number of common words used relatively often (such as *book, health*), and a huge number of low words are rarely used (such as *mitotic, bauer*).

Clay Shirky, a technology writer, observes that website traffic also obeys the power law distribution, with a few websites getting the majority of traffic. Shirky explains the characteristics of power law:

> The basic shape of power law is simple – in any system sorted by rank, the value for the N*th* position will be 1/N. For whatever is being ranked—income, links, traffic – the value of second place will be half that of first place and tenth place will be one-tenth of first place. . . . The power law distributions tend to arise in social systems where many people express their preference among many options. . . . As the number of options rise, the curve becomes more extreme. This is a counter-intuitive finding—most of us would expect a rising number of choices to flatten the curve, but in fact, increasing the size of the system increases the gap between the number one spot and the median spot. A second counter-intuitive aspect of power law is that most elements in a power law system are below average because the curve is so heavily weighted towards the top performers."

In the business world, including book publishing, power law is commonly known as the 80/20 rule which says 80% of the results usually come from 20% of work, or, to look at it another way, 80% of products do not sell and 20% of products usually generate 80% of revenue. Power law certainly applies to book sales. Market data has shown that book sales are heavily weighted toward a small number of bestselling titles.

Nielsen BookScan is a market research firm whose point-of-sales service tracks 1.2 million titles on sale in US bookstores and accounts for nearly 70% of all book sales in the United States. In 2004, BookScan's data revealed 87% of all book sales tracked by the company came from 7% of the bestselling titles, while 93% of the remaining titles generated only 13% of all sales. The 80/20 rule describes book sales so well that Jim King, Vice President of BookScan, joked that in 2004 the old 80/20 rule had become a 90/10 rule.

Dictated by the 80/20 rule, publishers and booksellers have adopted a "bestseller driven" business model and devoted their resources to bestsellers. They try to find the next *Da Vinci Code*. Since no one knows for sure how to produce a bestseller, publishers resort to the strategy of publishing more and more books and hope to get lucky and land a bestseller.

However, for most publishers, chasing the small number of best-sellers is like chasing a mirage. In 2005, only 0.2% new titles made it onto *Publishers Weekly*'s four weekly bestseller lists (Hardcover Fiction, Hardcover Nonfiction, Mass Market Paperback, Trade Paperback). The distribution of bestsellers among publishers also shows a power law pattern: the five largest publishing conglomerates—Random House, HarperCollins, Time Warner Book Group (now Hachette Book Group USA), Penguin USA; and Simon & Schuster—grabbed about 82% of hardcover bestsellers, and 77.6% of paperback bestsellers.

Publishers and booksellers are therefore facing a dilemma: a niche market business by nature (so many new books come to market each year) is dictated by mass market rules (focus on a few mass market bestsellers). The result is a vicious cycle; to increase the odds, publishers have to pay large advances to bestselling authors and rely on large print-runs to recoup the advances. But with an industry-wide return rate over 30%, it is getting harder and harder to break even for those bestsellers.

Recent statistics have shown a culture shift in the publishing marketplace. The Print-on-demand company Lulu.com has conducted a study for the life-expectancy of bestselling novels on the *New York Times* Bestseller List. The study shows that the number of weeks a bestselling novel on the list has declined by 50% within the last decade.

We can see from the study that back in the 1960s there were very few bestsellers, but they were on the bestselling list for several months at a time. In the 1990s and the 2000s, more books made it to the bestseller list but they stayed there for only a few weeks. Bob Young, CEO of Lulu.com, says the plummeting life-expectancy of a bestselling novel is part of a broad cultural shift, similar to what happened in the movie and the music industries. In 1950s, for example, more than 70% of American households watched the TV program "I Love Lucy" on any given evening. Today, the biggest hit on TV is "CSI," but it is viewed by just a bit over 10% of households. The future of publishing, Young believes, belongs to "niche-busters"—books targeting a niche rather than the mass market.

Fiction on the New York Times Bestseller List

	The Longest Stint at No. 1 Place (shrinking)	Number of Novels to Reach No. 1 (spreading)
1960s (average)	21.7 weeks	2.8
1970s (average)	13.9 weeks	4.4
1980s (average)	7.2 weeks	7.6
1990s (average)	5.5 weeks	10
2000-2005 (average)	3 weeks	18.2

(Source: Lulu.com)

Interestingly, BookScan data for 2005 also shows that the sales of bestsellers are decreasing. In 2005, total book sales increased 9.3% over 2004, but the share of the top 200 bestselling titles was down from 2004's 10.8% of total sales to 2005's 10.5%. Furthermore, comparing the top ten bestselling titles in 2004 and 2005 BookScan shows that five titles in the 2004 group sold 2 million or more copies, while the 2005 group had only one such title (*Harry Potter and the Half-Blood Prince).* In 2004 all the top ten titles sold more than 1 million copies, but only six titles of the top ten in 2005 achieved that level. Moving down the sales ranking further, in the 2005 list the 500,000-copy-mark occurred at number 34, in 2004 it occurred at number 32; and the 200,000-unit-mark appeared at number 148 in 2005, in 2004 it was at number 133—fifteen more titles sold at least 200,000 copies in 2005 than did so in the prior year. It appeared that the dominance of bestsellers was lessening and book sales were spreading to more titles.

Chris Anderson, the Editor-in-Chief of *Wired* magazine, studied the phenomenon that our culture is shifting away from the dominance of hits or bestsellers and came up with a hypothesis called the Long Tail theory, which provides a new framework for us to look at the 80/20 rule in the Internet age.

The Long Tail and Book Publishing

Chris Anderson has read Clay Shirky's article on the power law distribution of websites and expanded Shirky's findings to business models. He coined the phrase "long tail" to differentiate the power law distribution in the Internet era. Anderson noticed the "long tail" effect of the power law distribution when he was writing an article about Ecast, a digital "jukebox" company that supplies digital jukeboxes to bars and restaurants. Ecast stored 150,000 music albums online that subscribers can pay to download. During an interview, the chief executive of Ecast asked Anderson to guess what percentage of Ecast's top 10,000 tracks sold at least once per month.

Anderson knew very well that, based on the ubiquitous 80/20 rule, the normal answer would be 20%—that is, 20% of Ecast's tracks accounts for 80% of the sales. But Anderson also suspected that Ecast's equation might be a bit different, so he ventured that 50% of its top 10,000 tracks sold at least once per month. It turned out, however, Anderson's guess was way off. The answer was 98%—that is, 98% of Ecast's top 10,000 tracks sell at least once per month.

This percentage was astonishing and intriguing when compared with sales data from Wal-Mart. Wal-Mart is America's largest music retailer and accounts for one-fifth of all music sales in the country. Wal-Mart carries an inventory of 4,500 CD albums but gets 90% of sales from the top 200 CD titles (the "hits" or "bestsellers"). At Ecast, Anderson saw a long string of small sales from many less popular and older records that are normally known as "niche market products" but Anderson calls them the "long tail products" because these small sales are coming from the tail part of the power law curve, like in the following graph:

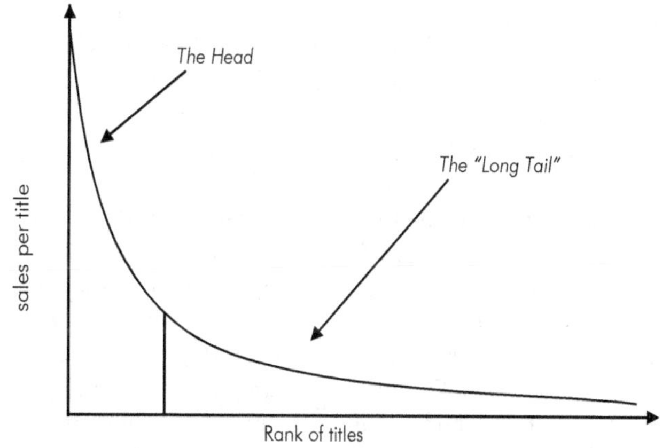

Anderson thought he had stumbled upon something worth further research. He studied other online companies such as Amazon, iTunes (an online music store), Rhapsody (an online music subscription service), and Netflix (an online DVD rental store) and found that these companies also have similar sales patterns.

The results of Anderson's research become the Long Tail theory and are detailed in his 2004 Wired magazine article "The Long Tail," his blog (http://www.thelongtail.com) and his new book *The Long Tail, Why the Future of Business Is Selling Less of More* (Hyperion, 2006).

According to the Long Tail theory, the head of the graph represents blockbusters, bestsellers or any popular mass market products; the tail represents all other less popular, niche market products with low volume and low demand. In the physical world, a bricks-and-mortar retailer faces two basic constraints: the limited shelf space a store has and the limited geographic area a store can serve. Since the shelf space is limited each product in a store must generate enough sales to pay for the cost of the shelf space it occupies. For example, Anderson's research shows that an average music record store has to sell at least four copies of a CD per year to compensate for the half-inch of space it takes up on the shelf. American movie theaters will not show a film unless they can attract 1,500 weekly customers, which is the minimal number to generate enough revenue to cover the rent of a movie screen. That is why only about 100 films each year get into movie theaters, but roughly 13,000 films are shown in various film festivals each year in the U.S. In a physical bookstore, according to Anderson, each square foot of shelf space needs two to three feet of aisle, checkout and open space, plus staffing, rent and other overheads; thus the average square foot of bookshelf space must generate between $100 and $150 of sales per month. Traditional retailers simply can't afford to carry products on their shelves that do not generate enough sales. In 2005 about 65,000 new music albums were released in the U.S., but only 700 of them made it into Wal-Mart. Wal-Mart has to sell 100,000 copies of a CD to make it worthwhile to put that CD on its shelf. While the US publishers release about 200,000 new titles each year and have 2.8 million books in print, a typical Barnes and Noble super bookstore can only carry about 130,000 titles. The largest independent bookstore can only carry about 40,000 titles. If a book is not selling quickly enough, it will be removed from the shelf.

At the same time, the demand for a particular product is limited by the size of a local consumer population that a physical store can reach or the distance customers are willing to travel. A movie theater, for example, can attract an audience from a 10-mile radius. A bookstore's service area is similar or even smaller. An audience, even if large in terms of absolute numbers but too thinly spread is the same as no audience at all, Anderson says. Each year, for example, India's film industry produces more than 800 feature films and there are an estimated 1.7 million Indians in the US. Yet the popular Hindi-language film, *Lagaan: Once Upon a Time in India*, showed on just two screens in the US because the Indian population is dispersed thinly across the country. Similarly, if a book has a potential audience of 10,000 readers but the readers are scattered across the country, a bricks-and-mortar bookstore is unlikely to carry that book on its shelf due to the lack of critical mass of local readers who may be interested in that book.

Prior to the Internet, the 80/20 rule emphasized the "short head"—the 20% mass market products and bestsellers. In the era of the Internet, the Long Tail business model emerges, which tells us that the 80% of the "non-bestsellers" in the "long tail" can be profitable as well. Anderson points out:

> Our culture and economy are increasingly shifting away from a focus on a relatively small number of hits (mainstream products and markets) at the head of the demand curve and moving toward a huge number of niches in the tail. In an era without the constraints of physical shelf space and other bottlenecks of distribution, narrowly targeted goods and services can be as economically attractive as mainstream fare.

A case in point is Amazon. Amazon is not restrained by physical limits in shelf space and geographic service area. It can then afford to aggregate huge supply and carry a book inventory of 3.8 million titles, making the long tail of non-bestseller titles available. As an e-commerce company Amazon also aggregates demand and can reach potential readers worldwide for any particular title in its vast inventory, increasing the chances that a niche title will be purchased by somebody somewhere. Netflix, the popular online movie rental company, is another long tail business example. While American movie theaters couldn't attract enough local viewers for Indian movies, Netflix is able to aggregate the scattered Indian audience online and, according to Anderson, rents out about 100,000 Indian movies a month.

To see how Amazon has broken the limit of physical shelf space and critical mass for the book market we can take a look at Amazon's book sales curve. Since a typical Barnes & Noble super bookstore offers 100,000 titles, we can use 100,000 as the cutoff figure to separate the head and the tail on the power law curve. With the top 100,000 ranked titles constituting the "head" and anything lower than 100,000 making up the "tail" portion, we then compare the sales from "head" to "tail." One study conducted by a group of researchers from MIT, Purdue University and Carnegie Mellon University calculated that 47.9% of Amazon's unit sales came from titles with rankings above 40,000 (since a large independent bookstore typically stocks 40,000 titles, it means that about 48% of Amazon's sales come from books not carried by independent bookstores), and 39.2% of sales came from titles with rankings above 100,000, which are the long tail books–books people normally cannot find in bricks-and-mortar bookstores. In other words, the shaded tail in the following graph represents a new market that does not exist in the physical world of bookselling.

An Amazon employee described the long tail business as follows: "We sold more books today that didn't sell at all yesterday than we sold today of all the books that did sell yesterday."

In his book and blog, Anderson estimated that the value of Amazon's long tail book sales (for titles ranked above 100,000) is about 25% of the total sales.

Share of Amazon Sales above Rank 100,000

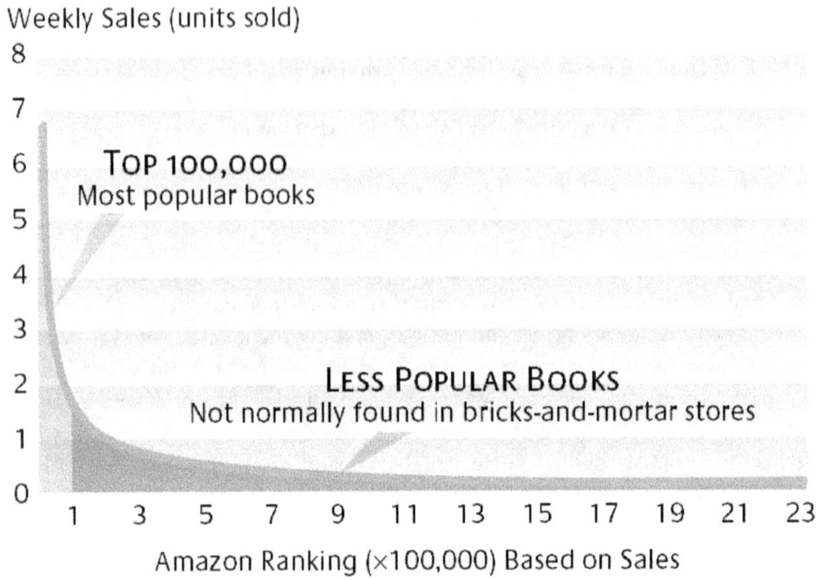

(Source: Brynjolfsson, Hu, and Smith, "Consumer Surplus in the Digital Economy")

But whatever the true percentage is, the long tail phenomenon is real. When companies move from the physical world to the online world all the physical constraints disappear. The cost of stocking "low demand, low volume" niche products is the same as the cost of carrying "hits" or "bestsellers," the long tail products start to have value. As a result, the Long Tail theory says that the profits found in selling millions of niche products, one or two at a time, can add up and overshadow the profits found in selling one or two products, millions at a time. Anderson quotes venture capitalist Kevin Laws as saying: "The biggest money is in the smallest sales."

The long tail phenomena is certainly good news for the book publishing industry, since by nature most books don't sell many copies and belong to the tail of the sales curve in the first place. But due to physical restraints, the bricks-and-mortar bookstores cannot afford to carry many "long tail" books. In an online environment, however, the bottleneck of distrbution no longer exists and more long tail books are sold than in a physical environment. To see the true effect of the long tail on books, we can compare the different sales curves between a physical bookstore like Barnes & Noble and an online book store with emphasis on both bestsellers and niche books like Amazon, and Abebooks, an online bookstore focuses mainly on long tail books. Abebooks has a virtual inventory of 80 million new, used, rare and out-of-print books from 13,500 independent booksellers.

Long tail comparison between different types of bookstores

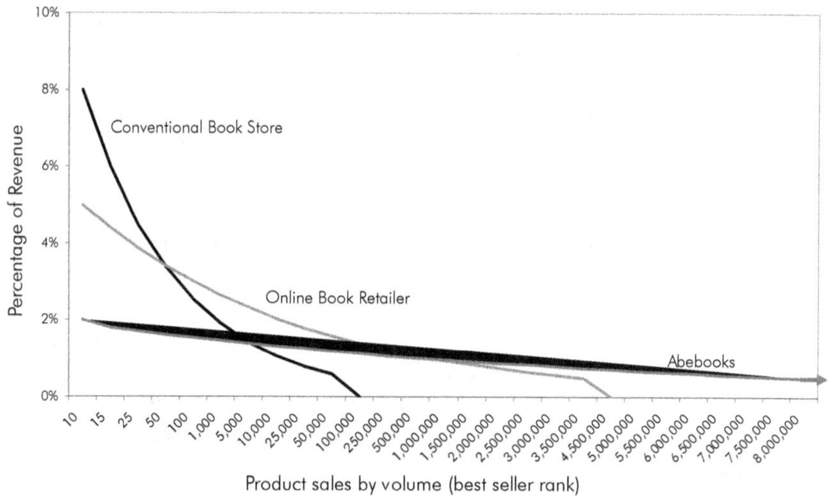

(Source: Boris Wertz)

A conventional bookstore has to rely on bestsellers and needs to keep the tail short; for online booksellers, on the other hand, the tail is getting fatter and longer. Abebooks has more niche books on sale than Amazon and therefore its tail is even longer. Abebooks reported that nineteen of its top twenty titles in 2005 were published prior to 2005.

How can the book publishing industry benefit from the long tail phenomenon? Book publishing by nature is a long tail or niche product business, but due to the physical constraints publishers and booksellers have been forced to stay away from the niches and focus instead on the "head". Only recently, thanks to the Internet, has the "tail" becomes economically viable and can be exploited as easily as the "head." "Hits" and "bestsellers" are still important, but now publishers and booksellers should not or cannot ignore the niches any more. Anderson lists two rules for a successful Long Tail business: first, *Make Everything Available*; second, *Help Me Find It.*

The Long Tail theory is based on the fact that in any market there are far more niche products than popular hits. The first thing a long tail business needs to do is to leverage the unlimited online shelf space and aggregate every niche product, no matter how small the sale volume is. That is why Amazon has a growing inventory of 3.8 million titles. For publishers, "making everything available" means keeping every book in print. With the development of short run printing and print-on-demand (POD) technology, this goal can be economically achieved.

Lightning Source is a POD company founded in 1997 by book distributor Ingram. Among its 4,200 publishing clients, 59% of them are traditional publishers, including Perseus Publishing Group, Cambridge University Press, HarperCollins and Simon & Schuster. Lightning Source now has more than 350,000 titles in its digital library. It has so far printed one copy at a time for 2.7 million titles and is printing more than 1 million books per month. The average print run at Lightning Source is 1.8 copies. Publishers set the retail price of a title typically at $24.95. After the 55% wholesale discount and printing cost of about $3.50, publisher will receive $7.73.

On Demand Books LLC is another POD company set up by former Random House editorial director Jason Epstein The goal of the company is to "become the first company to globally deploy a low cost, totally automatic book machine, which can produce 15 - 20 library quality paperback books per hour, in any language, in quantities of one, without any human intervention." In April 2006, On Demand Books installed its first Espresso Book Machine at the InfoShop at the World Bank in Washington D.C. When two high school students pressed the print-on-demand button, in 8 minutes each student received a copy of the 248-page *A Guide To the World Bank*. Printing can be initiated from the Espresso Book Machine itself or from any locally connected computer using a web browser. Two additional Espresso Book Machines will be installed at the New York Public Library and the Bibliotheca Alexandrina in Egypt. The retail price of the machine is less than $100,000.

Books by short run printing and POD are still more expensive than books by traditional offset printing, but the costs are continually coming down as the technologies continue to improve. Also, short run printing and POD can prevent lost sales and reduce inventory expenses and write-offs.

Many major players in the publishing industry are involved in POD development. In 2000, Random House invested $10 million to purchase 49% interest in POD company Xlibris. Barnes & Noble is the co-owner of POD company iUniverse and Amazon purchased BookSurge–another POD company, in 2005.

We never have a shortage of books; rather, people have been complaining that publishers produce too many books and the shortage has been with shelf space. Now that the Internet has eliminated this distribution bottleneck, we are facing another shortage: the shortage of readers' attention. As online inventories from publishers and booksellers grow, it becomes harder and harder for readers to select and find what they want. In terms of shelf space, the Long Tail theory argues that we are now moving from the economics of scarcity to the economics of abundance. In an economy of abundance, customers need filters to search and find niche products.

In the publishing industry, book search engines and digital book archives will be the next battleground in the digital and online world. With millions of books available online, the wisdom content is king is valid only if customers can find the content. The market power is shifting from companies who own copyrights of content to companies who own information *about* the content and who can help customers search and find content. Google doesn't own content, but readers go to Google to start their search of content. Two Google projects—Google Book Search and Google Library are hotly debated topics in the US publishing industry, not only because of copyright issues but also due to the possibility that content may one day become part of search engines.

The most advanced filtering algorithms are Amazon's (book selling) and Netflix's (Movie rental) recommendation systems. Amazon is the first U.S. company to create the position of "Chief Algorithms Officer" to enhance the search capability of its website. Netflix understands how crucial a filtering mechanism is to the long tail business model; it announced in October 2006 an open contest with an award of $1 million to the first person who can improve the accuracy of Netflix's current recommendation system by 10%. An improved recommendation system can help Netflix's customers find movies they want to see and in turn will certainly increase sales for the company.

In an online discussion in Harvard Business School's Working Knowledge Forum, Gerald Nanninga, Vice President of Retail Ventures Inc., summarizes the change of business logic in a digital world and long tail market:

> in an era when content is virtually infinite in variety (think of millions of books), the value in the supply chain is no longer created through producing content. Instead, value is created through the service of helping customers find what they want within the sea of choice (which can be seen as helping customers moving down the long tail). Those who can help customers manage choice and find the right product efficiently will be rewarded.

Conclusion

The Long Tail theory fits publishing and bookselling well since publishing and bookselling are long tail businesses by nature. With the development of the Internet and digital technology, publishers and booksellers finally can go back to their roots and have a new business model to explore the tail of the power law curve: to lengthen the tail (add inventory) and fatten the tail (increase unit sales). The challenges for publishers and booksellers are to make every book available and provide efficient search and recommendation mechanisms so customers can find books they want.

References

Anderson, Chris. (2006). *The Long Tail, Why the Future of Business Is Selling Less of More.* New York: Hyperion

Best, J. Kirby. Discovering Markets for the "Deep Backlist" and Small Sellers. <http://www.bisg.org/docs/MIP06_Best.pdf>

Brynjolfsson, Hu and Smith. "Consumer Surplus in the Digital Economy," *Management Science*. Nov. 2003.

Christman, Ed. "2005 Numbers Crunched." *The Book Standard*. Jan. 09, 2006.

Hafner, Katie, "And If You Like the Movie, a Neflix Contest May Reward You Handsomely." *The New York Times*. Oct. 2, 2006.

Korda, Michael. (2001). *Making the List: A Cultural History of the American Bestseller 1900-1999*. New York: Barnes & Noble Books.

Maryles, Daisy. "Bestsellers by the Numbers." *Publishers Weekly*. Jan. 9, 2006.

Rosenthal, Morris. "A Lightning Source Book Example." <http://www.fonerbooks.com/pod.htm>

Shirky, Clay. *Power Laws, Weblogs, and Inequality*. <http://shirky.com/writings/powerlaw_weblog.html>

Wertz, Boris. "How to Cost Effectively Sell Books to Micro-Markets." <http://www.bisg.org/conferences/biz3_presentations.html>

Wolf, Gary. "The Great Library of Amazonia." *Wired Magazine*, Issue 11.12, Dec. 2003. p. 4. <http://www.wired.com/techbiz/media/news/2003/10/60948?currentPage=4>

Digital Surviving and Developing for the Publishing Industry

Zhang Zengshun

The twenty first century is an age springing up new technologies. The multimedia technologies based on electronic publications have become more and more diversified and customized, and the Internet oriented net-publishing and e-commerce business model are changing to be more convenient and popular. POD (print-on-demand) technology strongly challenges the existing production model, and digital administration has gradually taken control instead of the traditional management system. Without any doubt, new technology is greatly impacting the publishing industry.

The swift development of the digital publishing industry can be credited to three elements, which are: the maturation of the market, the improvement of the technology, and the unique advantages of the digital content product. Dissemination through the Internet makes people accustomed to relying on it. Browsing the news, searching for data, and downloading music have become ordinary parts of our daily life. As of June 30, 2006, there were 1.23 million cyber citizens in China, which constitutes a solid and huge base for the digital survival of publishers. The application of Internet technology, the development of terminal equipment, and the popularity of 3G cell phones, e-reader, etc. all can diversify ways of communicating. Compared with traditional publication, digital publications are naturally endowed with the features of a great capacity of information, ease of copying and searching, and multi-media presentation models.

As digital publishing is ascending, international publishing magnates are snatching market shares by expanding their business areas, strengthening the digital content of their product, changing the original production models and developing value-added service models. Let's take Thomson Learning Group as an example. In 2005 its digital products, software and related services made 12% of its annual revenue, 8% higher than the total rate of increase. In 2001, McGraw-Hill promoted twenty five thousand digital teaching materials, which have all-round digital learning solutions, professional teaching websites that contain downloadable test books, online learning centers, supplementary teaching and learning resources, and a general course management system. As for Springer Verlag, in 2006 they made over 700 kinds of journals totally available through online publishing and distribution, and established a completely digital publishing system. Meanwhile,

Google, the giant in IT, is working with thousands of global publishers, including our Higher Education Press, and releasing an online book searching plan and then the Google Library. They want to make the largest online digital library and STM literature database. Consequently, Yahoo has made a team under the name of the " Open Resources Union" to make e-files for " all global digital products including multimedia contents."

In this network-oriented digital information era, where should we go? This is a serious question for all the Chinese publishers who view their publishing career from the traditional stance. In my view, I believe digitalization is the only way for our Chinese publishers to keep on surviving and developing.

HEP has raised the idea of relying on the technology to accelerate the development of our newly promoted "2006-2010 Developing Guidance." In recent years, HEP has made meaningful exploration in the construction of digital content resources. As a publisher mainly focused on the higher education and vocational education teaching material, we entirely grasp the opportunities brought by the new technologies to expand our range in digital educational publishing. We have divided it into 3 steps:

First: In late 2002, HEP raised the concept of "multidimensional education materials," which includes electronic teaching plans, course software, or "courseware," and online material that supplement classroom paperwork. The purpose is to form a comprehensive set of publications, such as education materials, teacher's books and student's guide books, as well as supplementary materials to further solidify the core content. This supplementary material is made up of various forms of media, such as paper publications, audiovisual productions, electronic productions and online content. By now, HEP's "Multidimensional Education Materials" project has built almost one thousand kinds of publications, and HEP's representative product, "Experiencing English", is one product of the idea. The "multidimensional education materials" have sped up the pace of the modernization of the course system and contents of colleges and universities.

Second: In 2004, based on the "multidimensional education materials," we created a new concept of "integration teaching solution." The purpose was to further adjust to the demands of education, and fully utilize digital technology and Internet technology to satisfy the growing demand for individualized and specialized education. We have built eleven teaching resource repositories to provide teachers with appropriate teaching plans that would meet their individual demands. Currently, HEP has successfully built seventeen different integrated course material plans. Two of our information repositories, "Higher Mathematics" and "College Chemistry," have gained a favorable reputation among teachers and students.

Third: In order to provide teachers with integrated services and digital content more effectively, HEP launched a project called "content management system" (CMS) in 2005. The content management system uses standardized methods and scientific classifications to digitize and sort the content resources that were originally divided amongst different departments into one single system for administration. Thus, the same content resources could be reused in book publication, on-line publication, electronic publication, and specialized websites, essentially allowing content to be used easily and quickly. Meanwhile, we developed a co-editing network platform for authors, editors, cover designers and typesetters to communicate and work on it, which are totally different from the traditional publishing work. Now CMS has been taken into the "Digitalization Project" of HEP launched this October.

While considering the construction of the digital content resource, HEP also did well in the digital administration process. Back in October 2002, after 8 months of discussion, HEP signed contracts with SAP and Price Waterhouse Coopers to buy and apply the SAP R/3 System, which began to run in applications on May 12, 2003 with seven modules including PS (Project System), PP (Production Planning), MM (Materials Management), SD (Sales & Distribution), FI (Financial Accounting), CO (Controlling), and HR (Human Resources). The launching of ERP system symbolized that HEP had begun to transfer ourselves from the "partially using, self developing" model to the " wholly integrating, standaradized and customized developing" model. With the implementation of the second-phase and third-phase ERP, HEP has basically fulfilled the digital administration of the supply chain of the whole publishing press.

In a word, HEP is aiming to be an educational resource integrator based on digital administration. Consequently, surviving and developing under this digital environment need a great deal of talents with digital publishing abilities. I sincerely hope that our universities and colleges devote themselves to cultivating more and more publishers familiar with digital technologies. And I also hope our friends in the international publishing industry can make efforts with us in establishing a good resource platform and explore a whole new Chinese publishing education model.

Friend or Enemy: The Developing Trend of Popular Magazines in the Digital Era

Li Jianwei

Chinese traditional media began to establish a relationship with the Internet on January 12, 1995, when the digital version of a Chinese magazine named *Shen Zhou Xue Ren* could be read online. At the very beginning, it was generally predicted that, with the booming of the Internet, traditional printed media would suffer catastrophic devastation. Several years later, we can see that the Internet brings traditional media new opportunities for development instead of such predicted devastation. Some newspapers have comprehensive websites, which take news as their main content and make the newspapers more competitive. However, the interacting speed and scale of popular Chinese magazines and the Internet is obviously slower than that of newspapers and TV. Does the digital era bring popular magazines chances or challenges? Is the Internet their friend or enemy? It seems there is no obvious answer for popular magazines.

On July 19, 2006, the China Internet Network Information Center (CNNIC) issued *The 18th Statistical Report on China's Internet Network Developing Status* in Beijing. The statistics indicated the re-acceleration of China's Internet development, the tendency of vigorous growth in various aspects and the embracement of a fast-developing time plan. As of June 30th, China's web-using population had reached 123 million, earning a growth of 19.4% compared with last pervious year's statistics. Meanwhile, there are a total of 788,400 websites in China. Moreover, 30 million among the 200 million Chinese students in primary and secondary schools have web-using experience; 15.4% of them have access to the Internet and half of Chinese high school students surf the Net. This report also reveals the growing frequency of Chinese people using Internet. In this survey, Chinese web-using people spend 16.5 hours on average on the Internet, which sets a new record. From these statistics, it can be concluded that China has entered the digital era. For popular magazines, no matter whether the Internet is their friend or enemy, they are going to develop against the background of the digital era.

1. The advantages and disadvantages of web magazines

As a new medium, the Internet is quite competitive. Compared with traditional magazines, the Internet, the fourth medium in the digital era, enjoys several advantages. Chinese academe currently does not have a uniform name and definition for those magazine-websites. The web magazine in this paper refers to the digital magazine on the Internet. It is a kind of digital magazine that relies on computer technology, network support and electronic communication and is published and distributed via e-mail and hypertext transferring. Popular magazines here refer to those traditional printed magazines.

First, the Internet is not limited by time and space. The Internet changes this world to a real village. All those traditional magazines have a certain distribution scope and the government has various regulations for their domestic and overseas distribution. However, in the digital era, as long as the magazines are available online, they can be read at anytime and anywhere when necessary equipment such as a computer and an Internet connection are provided. The transferring of messages is no longer restricted by time and space, which means as long as the message is available online, the Internet can make it reach every corner of the world immediately and anything happening anywhere and any web-user's opinion in any country can be obtained.

Second, mass information. The Internet combines all the computers and networks in the world together, establishing a giant database. Traditional magazines can only be read issue by issue, while each issue is ready to be chosen and read in web magazines. Web magazines that are set up by traditional media have much more information. For example, *Cosmopolitan*'s website (http://trendsmag/com) provides various other information and columns besides the digital version of *Cosmopolitan,* supplying information services in every possible aspects.

Third, mass media. Traditional printed magazines transfer information via letters (characters) and pictures. The development of computer technology makes the Internet have more means, such as letters (characters), pictures, sound and videos, to convey messages, providing its users with more options for receiving messages.

Fourth, interactivity. The traditional media's conception of communication has a strict division between message disseminator and message receiver. Disseminators voluntarily send off information and receivers passively accept it. The inevitable barriers in the communication process make such communication slow and ineffective. However, such division is not obvious on the Internet. Message receivers are entitled to choose what to accept and anybody is able to express an idea or opinion on the Internet. When readers have questions or suggestions concerning web magazines' content, they can declare their opinions at anytime.

Fifth, audiences with specific interests. With rapid social development, people become more interested in pursuing a distinct personality; therefore, they are in great need of the information that satisfies their specific interests. The mass information on the Internet covers every possible aspect of our society and the personalized services provided there help users gain deeper understanding of specific information. Web-users choose what they need on the Internet while ignoring the information they are not interested in.

Many people are afraid that those free, professional web magazines offered to web-users will attract most traditional magazines' readers and advertisers. However, in terms of the recent development of printed magazines in such a web era, these features of the Internet listed above, to a certain extent, restrict the growth of commercial web magazines.

The general conception of a magazine defines it as a sequential publication with a certain interval, whereas web information requires instant message transferring. For professional web magazines, how to attract an audience to keep visiting their websites and reading the magazines is a very difficult question. In addition mass information on the Internet and its hyperlinks always lead readers to other interesting topics, which make them forget what they originally were looking for. If web magazines intend to make a profit, a certain number of loyal readers should be guaranteed, but these limitations of the Internet make such loyal readers almost unavailable. Therefore, even though the Internet enjoys very fast worldwide growth, the development of web magazines is still quite slow. Most web magazines are sent to readers via e-mail and are a kind of advertising event aiming to promote the website they are attached to.

2. Opportunities for traditional printed magazines in the digital era

Though web magazines develop slowly and have an unknown future, we cannot conclude that the digital era and the Internet are the opponents or enemies of traditional printed magazines. On the contrary, if traditional magazines can make full use of the Internet for self-development, they will embrace new chances for further development in the digital era.

First, the Internet is traditional magazines' necessary complement, and not an enemy but a friend. Compared with web magazines, printed ones enjoy strong competitiveness and advantages. Traditional popular magazines are printed on paper, easy for reading and carrying around and the letters (characters) and pictures are finely printed, which all please their readers. Printed magazines can be seen and bought almost everywhere and most of them have a long history of distribution, which guarantees a certain size of loyal audience. It is known that reading web magazines requires the necessary equipment. Compared with the cost of such equipment, the expense of traditional magazines is much less. Therefore, the low cost of traditional magazines attracts more potential readers.

According to the development of web magazines and traditional ones in recent years, it is believed that traditional printed magazines are inevitably going to begin their journey on the Internet. It seems impossible for the traditional magazines to have their own comprehensive websites as the newspapers do, but they can take the Internet as their complement to promote their influence and reputation.

There are two kinds of printed magazines whose digital versions are available online: one is magazines establishing their own websites, such as *Cosmopolitan*, and the other is magazines publishing their contents on some famous websites; for example, *Southern People Weekly* relies on the websites named "Sina," "21cn," etc., for content publishing. "Tencent," a famous Chinese website, has hyperlinks to *Ray*, a fashion and beauty magazine. Therefore, printed magazines have every reason to make full use of the Internet to expand content for reading. It not only promotes magazines' circulation and influence, but makes magazines more profitable.

Second, the magazine's web version can extend its printed version's content. For printed magazines, some articles or details need to be omitted because space is very limited. If a magazine has a web version, it can put the website address on the printed version in order to remind readers to visit its website for more information and details. For news magazines, this method works quite well. Further, websites can be used to attract web-users' attention, encouraging them to subscribe to the printed version. Many readers are first attracted by some magazines' websites and then begin to look for the printed version of the magazines. Because the Internet has some unique characteristics, such as hyperlink and interactivity, web-users are more likely to learn about some magazines while net surfing. Websites can also invite experts to chat with web-users about something they are interested in and these experts can answer their questions. In this way, magazines can keep their readers' interest while attracting new readers as well as offset the lack of mutual communication of printed magazines.

Nowadays digital technology connects the magazine and the network and shortens the distance between printing magazine and cyberspace. Many magazines put web links at the end of articles. Sometimes the addresses are so long that it is inconvenient for readers to search for them. A new scanning facility can help readers with this problem. Once the address is scanned by this facility and input into the computer, the computer will automatically find the webpage for readers. These facilities haven't been popularized until recently, but the development of technology will finally bring them to every family, like computers.

Third, the Internet can help magazines give full play to their social functions. Popular magazines undoubtedly play an important role in leading social trends. By reviewing Chinese magazines' development history, we can see that many magazines, such as *New Youth* and *Fiction Monthly*, exerted tremendous influence on Chinese social development. In the contemporary era, some magazines concerning people's daily life, such as *Readers' Digest* and *Woman Friend*, influence people's life in every possible aspect. In recent years, some magazines focusing on fashion and beauty have become young people's instructors on lifestyles and views. *Cosmopolitan* and *Ray* are two famous examples. Many people dress as *Ray* tells them and believe *Ray* is their fashion guide. Thus, as printed publications, popular magazines lead many people's view of social trends, whereas the Internet provides people with more convenience to follow such trends. For example, many websites for shopping sell what *Ray* recommends. Many BBS always have discussions concerning some magazines' content, attracting more web-users' attention and participation. These all bring magazines' functions, such as guiding consumptions and leading social trends, into full play.

Fourth, the Internet brings economic profits to magazine publishers. The first reason is that the development of e-business makes it convenient for readers to subscribe to and buy printed magazines online. Like *New Weekly*, many Chinese magazines' websites provide online subscription services. The second reason is plenty of popular magazines establish a cooperative relationship with different merchandise manufacturers. For example, manufacturers' web addresses can be printed on magazines and their hyperlinks can be included on magazines' websites, which attract readers' attention to manufacturers' websites. Moreover, the application of new digital technologies draws printed magazines and cyberspace much closer, as with the scanning technology mentioned above by which a web address can be immediately found by scanning a page. Last, but not least, the increase of web users and the development of Internet companies attract more advertisers for printed magazines, thus bringing them more profits. In addition, the further opening of China and the growing of the Internet industry make it possible for large websites to invest in and start printed magazines.

In the digital era, the Internet has every reason to be a friend of traditional printed magazines and it will definitely provide more opportunities for magazines' further development.

References

China Internet Network Information Center. <http://ww.cnnic.net.cn>.

Dominick, Joseph R. Cai Qi, tran. *The Dynamics of Mass Communication*. Beijing: Renmin University Of China Press, 2004.

Xiang, Sa. "A Discussion on the Restraining Factors to the Web Magazines' Development." *Journal of Zhengzhou University*. 6 (2004).

Zhang, Haiying and Teng Quian. *Fundamentals of Web Communication*. Shanghai: Fudan University Press, 2004.

COMPARATIVE ANALYSIS OF CHINESE AND AMERICAN PUBLISHERS' WEBSITES

ZHANG ZHIQIANG & XING PENG

1. Preface

Negroponte has said: "When every industry looks itself in the mirror and asks, 'What is our future in the digital world, in fact, their future entirely depends on whether their products or services can be transformed into digital form." According to this principle, the publishing industry, whose core business is providing content, has become the darling of the digital age. From editing, and then printing, to distribution, from market research, then publicity, to terminal sales, every step is stamped by digital technology. Moreover, digital technology has created a new publishing form, net publishing, to provide entirely new publications. Digital waves come and go, and the publishing industry, which is at the forefront of changes, also experiences a lot of setbacks. Construction of websites is the epitome of publishers at home and abroad joining the digital reformation.

Publishers' website construction is a pragmatic work and relavant research has been focusing on empirical observation and investigation. Ge Tang and Zhiqiang Zhang (1999), pioneers in the analysis of publishers' websites, have constructively designed website evaluation criteria. Lei Wang (2003) has clearly presented the defects of publishers' websites in Mainland China, such as "the lack of features and multi-language versions, the shortage of interaction, and immature online book sale services." Ling Li and Hua Jin (2004) have made a regional study of seventeen publishers' websites in Chengdu, Sichuan province. However, according to the current research, scholars have not yet made a comparative analysis of the publishers' websites on the basis of investigation.

Comparative analysis is an important method of publishing research. In publishing studies, effective use of the method can bring many benefits. Faced with the complexity of publishing materials and publishing phenomena, researchers will be at a loss. If we can distinguish the differences from similarities or the similarities from differences, we can not only grasp the similarities and differences, but also be able to more clearly see things for their own characteristics, and can tap them more profoundly. The construction of publishers' websites is pragmatic work, and we need to learn from experiences. Through the comparison of many different websites, we can seek their characteristics, grasp their laws, and this will be beneficial to the construction and development of China's publishers' websites.

This paper will compare the construction of American publishers' websites and China's, because the United States has the most developed publishing industry in the world with a large number of publishers, each of which has its own characteristics. Meanwhile, the United States is also the birthplace of networks, e-commerce, and online bookstores; further network stocks on the NASDAQ stock market have become the barometer of the global network economy. In this comparative analysis, the authors will pay more attention to describing characteristics of American publishers' websites. The aim is to show domestic publishers the strategies and advantages of their foreign colleagues' websites, as a point of reference.

2. The General Situation of American and Chinese Publishers' Websites

There are about 28,000 book publishers in the United States now, but only 4,000 can maintain their businesses in a situation where more than one book is published in a year. Publishers started to establish their own websites when the network began to be used by the public: in 1993, Time Warner Book Group established its website, and it can be said that it was the first publishing house with a website in the United States and in the world. Later, Random House and Simon & Schuster, Inc. also set up their websites. According to statistics, as of early 1999, the United States had more than 7,700 websites related to the publishing industry. According to a website devoted to a survey of publishing marketing, publishers with websites in early 2000 in the United States had reached 80%, e-mail usage reached 100%. Seventy-six percent of the websites were book promotional websites. By 2003, according to the authoritative media's statistics, 99% of American publishers had connected to the Internet. After the financial industry, the publishing industry is the second largest industry in the application of the Internet.

China is one of the world's largest publishing countries, and the pace of the publishers' construction of websites in China has not lagged behind. Back in 1993, Chinese publishers had access to the Internet, when Tsinghua University Press used the e-mail function of the Internet to contact and negotiate with foreign publishers about copyrights. In September 1995, the Electronics Industry Publishing House (www.phei.com.cn) launched the first domestic publisher home page on the Internet. In August and September 1996, 10 publishers such as Science Press and Chinese Encyclopedia House also created their spaces online, followed by many other publishers. In December 1998, 78 of all of China's 528 publishers set up websites on the Internet, accounting for 14.8% of the total. Just two years later, this figure had doubled to more than four-fold. At the end of 2000, China had a total of 565 book publishers, and 374 had online businesses, a rate of 66.2%. Among them, there were 182 publishers of the 219 central-level ones that had online businesses, a the rate was

83.1%; 192 local publishers of a total 346 were online, with a rate of 55.5%. In 2004 and 2005, the authors used Google to search publishers' websites in China, and used the Publishers Association of China's directory as a reference; the conclusion was: there were 231 publishers who had set up their websites on the Internet by March 2004, and 252 in March 2005.

Compared with their American counterparts, Chinese publishers are slow in creating their websites. Despite its pickup in the recent past two years, it shows that the publishers sense of the information is relatively lagging behind, and they don't understand what the website really means to a publisher, this is an important reason for the ebb and flow of publishers' website construction. (See Figure 1)

Figure 1: Chinese Publishers' Websites Development Trend Chart

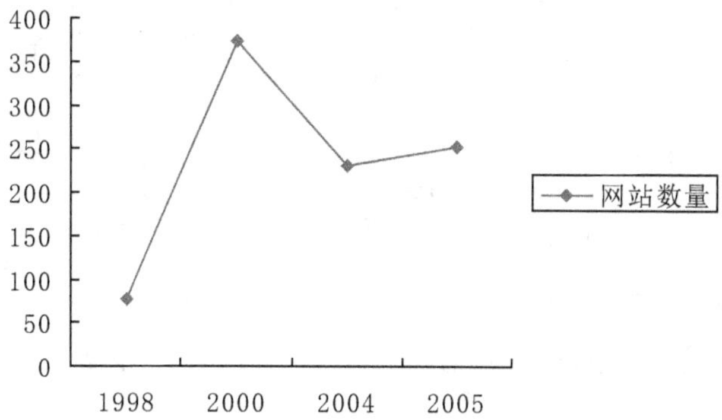

3. Investigation Method and Content

Comparative analysis must be based on facts and data. This paper will make a sampling investigation of the two countries' publishers' websites. There is a huge number of American publishers, and no authoritative statistics on publishers' websites. On the principle of combining science with flexibility, the authors made an equidistant sampling from 252 publishers' websites in China, gaining 52 samples; with the same sampling method, the author selected a list of 52 members who have websites from the Association of American Publishers (AAP) for comparison. As the number of American publishers' websites is much greater than the number of Chinese publishers' websites, this paper mainly makes a comparative analysis from the perspective of the relative proportions. Therefore, all the data in the tables in this paper are divided into two parts. Data in brackets are the numbers of websites meeting the specific requirements of sampling investigation, data out side brackets are the proportions of the number of required websites to the total samples. In the following tables, CPW represents Chinese Publishers' Website, and APW represents American Publishers' Website.

The investigation occurred from March 1, to March 15, 2005. The investigation is divided into the following two parts: First, the services provided by the websites, including information, inquiry, marketing, value-added and interactive services. Second, the quality of services provided by the websites, including the updating frequency of the websites, pseudo services, copyright and privacy protection.

4. Comparisons of Service Content Between CPW and APW

4.1 Comparison of Information Services

Information services include publisher introductions, dynamic news, book recommendations, etc. According to the relative proportions, CPW and APW have a similar performance in basic information, dynamic news, new and forthcoming books, because these are the basic elements that a publisher's website should have. The Book Review has nearly no differences in the data, but CPW or APW has its own characteristics of the book review. CPW prefers including book reviews as a separate section; although APW has a similar feature, they are more inclined to integrate the book review with the introduction of book contents. The typical approach is to extract the significant phrases from the book reviews, then mark the names of the book critics in bold and locate them in a striking place in the book's introduction. (See Table 1)

Table 1: Comparison of Information between CPW & APW

	Basic Information	Dynamic News	Coming Book Report	Bestseller Recommendation	Book Review
CPW	100% (52)	90.4% (47)	98.1% (51)	96.2% (50)	71.2% (37)
APW	100% (52)	86.5% (45)	90.4% (47)	88.5% (46)	76.9% (40)

Hyperion Press has great ingenuity in book introductions. Every book has Reviews, a Reading Guide, Excerpts, and Audio Reading. The Reading Guide is particularly meticulous. It carefully integrates the author biography, discussion, and commentary. The following figure shows a book titled *The Five People You Meet in Heaven*, and the publisher provides 20 reading topics for discussion. (See Figure 2) In China, Beijing Normal University Press has a similar provision for book introductions, but the columns contain nothing.

APW has a commendable advantage in book introductions. When clicking on a page for a book introduction, the website will also list relevant books about similar subjects, or written by the same author. If a reader bought a book from the publisher's online bookstore, the website will automatically list the other books consumers have bought. About 81.8% of American publishers' websites used this publicity skill.

Figure 2: Hyperion Press Book Introduction

4.2 Comparison of Inquiry Services

Inquiry services include book classification, simple inquiry and advanced inquiry. Book classification will divide all the publisher's books into a number of major categories, then subdivide them into subcategories, and, finally, provide lists of various categories of books, so that readers can search gradually. Simple inquiries can approach books by author, title, date, ISBN or other external characteristics alone. Advanced inquiries integrate the items of writer, book name, and so on, thereby improving the accuracy of search results. In this context, CPW and APW have a consistent performance, as shown in Table 2.

Table 2: Comparison of Inquiry Service between CPW & APW

	Book Classification	Simple Inquiry	Advanced Inquiry
CPW	94.2% (49)	82.7% (43)	51.9% (27)
APW	90.4% (47)	75% (39)	63.5% (33)

CPW has a better performance of simple inquiry and book classification, but the advanced inquiry is 11.6% lower than APW, and the latter is much more effective than the first two, and this shows that our publishers have failed to take full advantage of information technology to serve readers. CPW should take the advantage of APW's "fuzzy inquiry" form. Using this form, the website can output all the matching results according to an arbitrary keyword, such as author name, book name and so on. "Fuzzy inquiry" and advanced inquiry have roughly the same degree of technological difficulty, but the former is easier for readers. Therefore, websites with "hybrid" inquiries are more user-friendly. In this investigation, 17 APWs used the "Fuzzy inquiry" form, 32.7% of the total samples. Part of CPWs also provides this service, but no introduction to the users. Incidentally, it should be mentioned that both CPW and APW have attached great importance to the service of book classification, but the methods, influenced by local culture, reading habits and other factors, are different.

4.3 Comparison of marketing service

The comparison of this type of service can be made nearly without doubt, because America has a well-developed credit system, and the logistics are smooth. The development of its electronic commerce leads the world. Relatively, China's credit system is undeveloped, and the e-commerce level is not high. Statistics have proved this point. (See Table 3).

Table 3: Comparison of Marketing Service between CPW and APW

	Offline Order	Online Bookstore	Member Register	Copyright Trade
CPW	92.3% (48)	57.7% (30)	57.7% (30)	23.1% (12)
APW	90.4% (47)	80.8% (42)	80.8% (42)	11.5% (6)

In this investigation, 30 of the 52 CPW samples have the online sale function. However, only two have online payment functions. All the APW samples, which have online sale function, provide online payment function with a credit card, and many of them announce in the shopping guide that the online payment services are provided by "Geo Trust," "Geo Trust" is a world-renowned supplier of digital certificates; it has an outstanding reputation for identity authentication and credit services, so that readers can buy the books with peace of mind.

It's worth mentioning that some publishers, such as the Inner Ocean Publishing, outsource their online sales service, and include Amazon, a professional online bookstore, which has a good reputation, a large number of readers, and extensive experience in logistics and distribution. This phenomenon is a little puzzling, because America's e-commerce is very developed. And in China, e-commerce is not ripe at all, so publishers who have tried this are still new to the process.

It can be said that the widespread online bookstores in the United States were mainly due to the good macroeconomic environment, but the publishers' understanding of e-commerce and attention of integrity also plays an important role.

4.4 Comparison of Value-added Service

The first three items of value-added service are close, only a difference of less than 10 percentage points. However, in regard to the characteristic functional service, APW is far ahead. (See Table 4)

Table 4: Comparison of Value-added Service between CPW and APW

	Online reading	Resource downloading	e-book/ magazine	Characteristic function
CPW	50% (26)	53.8% (28)	11.5% (6)	32.7% (17)
APW	55.7% (29)	57.7% (30)	7.7% (4)	61.5% (32)

We define value-added service as a free service available to readers. The data in the table can reflect the publishers' marketing awareness, but it may also reflect how much the publishers think of the readers. APW is about 5% higher than CPW in the fields of online reading and resource downloading. Taking the commercial level of publishing into account, the data can be accepted. The resources provided by CPW and APW for downloading are basically their own bibliographies. More than 90% of CPW's bibliography files are in "Word" or "Excel," format and the content is nothing more than a set of the external characteristics of books (for example, title, ISBN, price). Some American publishers characterize their bibliographies according to the focus of the books. The format of the files is usually PDF, and digital book covers are attached. These files not only have the basic data of a book, but also carefully chosen comments. As described above, this is the peculiar way of APW's book publicity. Such bibliographies are simple but brilliant, and they are there to move readers and book dealers.

Setting up Readers Clubs is the main characteristic function of APW (27.3% of the total samples), organizing readers to read or select books, or announcing the schedules of some forthcoming authors and some books' publicity tours, or inviting readers to participate in activities. Some publishers have special services aimed at authors (22.7%). For example, through the website, the publisher tells the author which kind of manuscripts are considered, what kind of norms the manuscripts should follow, and so on. The "Author Guide" on Cornell University Press's website is a 30-page electronic file. Some other publishers fully use their resources to provide readers with services (9.1%). For example, the column "Parenting A-Z" on Zero to Three Press's website introduces "A-Z" parenting knowledge to parents. Knowledge in every area comes from one kind of book the press has published. It is a win-win situation. These three forms also appear in our country, but the popularization is far from enough.

Their excellent marketing sense strengthens American publishers' attention to readers and authors. Understanding and grasping their own resources make a contribution to the situation: 61.5% of characteristic services, which is nearly 30 percentage points higher than Chinese publishers'.

Table 4 also reflects a similarity between APW and CPW. There are not many publishers' websites involved in e-books or other related businesses. Although the website is the e-book release platform, there are only 10% of publishers' websites that have e-books or magazines.

4.5 Comparison of Interactive Service

CPW has an overwhelming advantage in these services, except email, the most basic interactive way of communication. Forums, chat rooms and online surveys are almost non-existent on American publishers' websites. (See Table 5)

Table 5: Comparison of Interactive Service between CPW and APW

	Email	BBS	Forum	Chat Room	Online Investigation
CPW	100% (52)	72.7% (37)	31.8% (21)	1.9% (1)	31.8% (13)
APW	100% (52)	7.7% (4)	0% (0)	0% (0)	3.8% (2)

American publishers mainly rely on mailing lists for interactive marketing promotions, and 23 publishers' websites of the total 52 samples have that function, with a rate of 44.2%. There are only two websites in China that have mailing lists. This interactive form is not popular in China, because using mailing lists to contact customers would fall into the "spam" traps, and the energy and resources invested by publishers into the websites is relatively small in our country, so publishers are powerless to deal with the negative impacts at that form. Spam is also rampant in the United States, but there is relevant legislation. Interactive publicity through mailing lists has many obvious advantages; for example, it is able to be sent in large quantities, it is informative, and it has clear targets. These advantages attract investments from publishers for book publicity in the U.S.

5. Comparisons of Service Quality between CPW and APW

5.1 Comparisons of Service Quality

In our investigation, if the content of the website was last updated in March 2005, we call it "prompt updating." If it was between January 1, 2005 and February 28, 2005, we call it "timely updating." If it was before 2005, it is called "lag updating." As interactive services, the comparison of service quality has emerged as a one-sided trend, but this time, it is on the side of American publishers' websites. Over 80% of American publishers' websites are concentrated in the "prompt updating" category, and the number of "lag updating" websites is only half of the number of Chinese "lag updating" websites (See Table 6).

Table 6: Comparison of Updating Frequency between APW& CPW

	Prompt Updating	Timely Updating	Lag Updating
CPW	36.4% (19)	45.5% (17)	18.2% (16)
APW	84.6% (44)	5.8% (3)	9.6% (5)

5.2 Comparison of pseudo service

Pseudo service means that the services the website has promised have not been fulfilled. For example, many websites provide channels for resource downloading, but if you click one, you will find that it is empty and only mistakenly reports the availability of the download. This investigation defines pseudo services by analyzing empty and unavailable links. Empty links are hyperlinks that do not have any specific content. Unavailable links can't display the content they are supposed to have, for which are two main forms in the Internet Explorer browser: 404 errors and server mistakes. The performance of APW can be called perfect in this aspect; only two websites had empty links, and there were no unavailable links. (See Table 7)

Table 7: Link Situation of CPW & APW

	Empty Link	Unavailable Link	Both
CPW	30.8% (16)	28.8% (15)	13.5% (7)
APW	3.8% (2)	0% (0)	0% (0)

When empty links and unavailable links exist must be eliminated, some technical means are needed to check them, but sophisticated technology is not indispensable. Relatively speaking, the level of frequency of updating of the website depends entirely on the degree of attention paid by the publisher's managers to the websites. In a short, the service quality is determined by the attitude of the publishers.

5.3 Comparison of Copyright and Privacy Protection

According to the statistics, CPW and APW are close in terms of copyright protection. 82.7% of Chinese websites have copyright statements; in the United States it is 86.4%. The difference is that parts of the American websites in this aspect are far more detailed: 40.9% of the websites add hyperlinks of "Copyright" or "Terms of Use" at the bottom of the page as detailed notes of the website's ownership, content, purpose, warnings and so on.

Meanwhile, 54.5% of American publishers' websites have privacy statements, because the viewer's personal identifiable information (PII) will be collected, retained and used by the website. For the purpose of protecting the privacy of the individual, at the bottom of the home page, there is an additional "Privacy Policy" link, and the website will make a note of the measures taken to ensure the security and transparency of PII. Publishers' websites in our country usually neglect the protection of individual privacy, because they are at the stage of book publicity where they rarely collect personal information from visitors to carry out customer relationship management.

6. Conclusion

The above comparisons highlight the differences between CPW and APW, according to which many conclusions can be derived, such as that the good e-commerce environment in the United States contributes to the publishers' websites' online sales and online payment, American publishers' commercial operations in book publicity and bibliography design make them place greater emphasis on sales techniques than Chinese publishers, and so on. We believe the most important conclusion is that Chinese publishers do better in the aspect of website technology applications than their United States counterparts, while the latter do even better at construction awareness and innovation. This is a surprising discovery, because the United States is the birthplace of information technologies, but the publishers' websites are typically without a lot of technological applications, as shown in Table 5. Although a number of technologies are integrated on Chinese publishers' websites, the updating is slow, and privacy protection is usually neglected, and some technologies have even become ornamentation and have no content. Obviously, the technology has not brought innovative characteristics. However, the websites of American publishers are rich in innovative characteristics, which should be attributed to the publishers' emphases on website design and construction. After China's Renmin University Press realized its information reform, an article by that press figured out that the difficulty of publishers to realize financial management information is due neither to technologies nor funds, but to the change of management ideology and the updating of management philosophy. Only when publishers emancipate their minds and treat the construction of websites seriously can they break the misunderstanding of the blind use of technologies, and put themselves onto a track of normal development. The best measure is to place the construction of websites into the publisher's development program, while actively attracting talents, and thereby strengthening the reserve of information professionals.

In building websites, Chinese publishers seem to have experienced a lot. However, the information about the publishing industry has just started to be analyzed and every outstanding publishing staff should make every effort to combine national conditions and the publisher's characteristics, raise awareness and introduce talented personnel; then, a unique path of the information of the publishing industry can be opened up.

REFERENCES

Chen, Zhen. "Diversified Functions of Foreign Publishers' Websites." *China Book Business Report.* Jun. 2003.

Li, Ling and Jin Hua. "A Regional Research of Internet Publishing: An Investigation of 17 Provincial and Civic Publishers' Websites." *China Publishing Journal.* (2004): 57-58.

Negroponte, Nicholas. Hu Fan, tran. *Being Digital.* Haikou: Hainan Press, 2003.

Wang, Lei. "Chinese Publishers' Websites: Status In Quo, Problems and Perspective." *Editor's Friend.* (2003): 18-21.

Wei, Longquan. *The Structure and Marketing of USA Publishers.* Beijing: Chinese Economy Press, 2000.

Publishing Education Within the Environment of Digital Publishing

Zhang Wenhong

With the development of modern science and technology and their widespread utilization in the publication domain, digital publishing already has become a topic of great concern for the publishing circle. Digital publishing is one kind of brand-new publication idea and mode, which sprouts within the environment of new medium technology. It refers to the method of publishing carried out through the participation of binary digital technology, and involving the publication contents, attributes, processes, management, and so on.

Within the new technical environment, there are another two concepts along with the concept of digital publication: network publishing and electronic publishing. Network publishing refers to publication carried out by means of the Internet. Electronic publishing means the making and communication of electronic publications. From the angle of technical analysis, digital publishing has included the digitization of text content, the editing process, duplication and printing, sales release, as well as consumption by readers and the like. Therefore, from the technical angle, some people also generally take network publishing and electronic publication as digital publication.

With the arrival of digital publishing related research and development has exploded. This includes not only the study of the new types of publication media such as network and cell phone, but also the study of innovation in relation to publication, for example, the research, development and application of computer proofreading software, two-dimensional bar code technology, a Chinese character input system, metadata software process and input technology, a new digital reading acceptor, digital copyright technology, as well as electronic paper research applications, and so on.

We can say that new technology represented by digital publishing provides a beautiful prospect for the publishing industry throughout the world. Firstly, digital technology will realize the maximized savings of natural resources and meet the demands of environmental protection, reducing the consumption of natural resources to the minimum. As the technologists expect, digital paper and digital reading machines will totally take the place of traditional paper in the future. Secondly, digital technology brings about new spaces for the development of the publishing industry, meaning that new technology can expand productive scales, enhance the efficiency of publishing and dissemination, and realize technological reform in every aspect of the publishing industry. Digital technology will realize fast profit modes of publishing resources, and publishing operators may gain considerable financial benefits.

Meanwhile, digital technology has brought about huge challenges and uncertainties for the traditional publishing field. As Yu Yongzhan pointed out at the Beijing International Books Exposition Forum in 2006, new technology makes a lower access criterion for the publishing industry. New dissemination methods lead to the marginalization of traditional publishing roles, and digital publishing forms challenges to the traditional book market; new technology also creates new implications for the golden rule of "content as king" in the publishing industry. Who has stronger intensive integrating abilities on content resources? Who can win stronger power to control the market? The free resources on the Internet greatly impact the publishing industry based on content profits. More importantly is that the quick development and extensive application of new technology in the publishing field has enormously shocked publishing education that operates within the traditional publishing environment.

As a teacher of publishing education, I believe that digital technology has brought opportunities and challenges for publishing education. Publishing education is facing a systematic and overall reform of every aspect, such as educational opinions, goals of professional education and education plans, curriculum design and practical methods, etc., rather than something like trivial complement. While digital publication is becoming an irresistible general trend, there are several problems of publishing for education in our country.

Firstly, the process of publishing education ignores the needs and demands of the field. Some bad things exist widely, such as no market investigation and blind development of schools or only according to which teachers they employ. In the past twenty years, publishing education has quickly become a more popular major in many universities than ever before. Until now, publishing education has grown greatly. According to investigations into the conditions of many universities, many of them are going adrift, starting this major with very limited educational resources. In these universities, either education publishing is affiliated with Chinese language education, or with news dissemination, or with information management education, and the curriculums are designed only according to what teachers they have. For instance, in some universities, publishing education is affiliated with the departments of Chinese language, where only some courses publishing are given by several Chinese teachers, without any knowledge of publishing practices. And in some other universities, publishing education is affiliated with news dissemination colleges, lacking relevant professional teachers, ignoring publishing practices, and only focusing on the education of news dissemination students.

Secondly, the idea of publishing education cannot keep up with development in the digital age. In the first place, the construction of professional teaching materials for publishing education falls behind. Some materials relevant to instruction in publication practice are out of date. Teaching materials are still at the stage of traditional print editions, as well as delivery. Even if digital publication has been included with them, it is a small amount. Due to the limitations of textbooks and their knowledge structure, some teachers from the traditional print media environment are not able to make up new content, causing them to fail to combine the taught contents with the reality of digital publication development, let alone guide the practice of the new technique. Secondly, the publishing education pattern in our country has been out of date. As far as the specialty of the subject is concerned, publishing is a subject affected greatly by the times and practice. It is very important to study the reality of publishing, explore the discipline, research publication theory and put them into action. According to our present publishing education pattern, although there is a publishing major in some of the comprehensive universities, no outstanding pattern of publishing education as been come into being. It is very common for them only to copy traditional teaching patterns, to focus on the study of theory, ignoring the practical educational link.

Thirdly, as for the pattern of skill cultivation, there is a blur of "professional", "intelligent", and "erudite" skills. The target for cultivation is not clear enough in the undergraduate, double-degree, master's, and doctorate courses. And the knowledge system is blurry for all levels of skill. To begin with, publishing education is a very special subject, so in the lowest layer students from the technical academy and the ones with double degrees should equip themselves with the basic knowledge and professional, practical skills. At the same time, students in the middle layer need not only some basic knowledge, but also excellent quality of professional practice. For the master's and doctorates, they should master all-around knowledge, enforce their studies relevant to edition and publication in order to further their research and activities in this field. At present, there are not many differences among the terms of course setup, the selection of teaching materials, and skill cultivation for the undergraduate, double degree and master's education. The doctoral publishing program is new in China and has not been reorganized by the Ministry of Education as a stand alone discipline; therefore a doctoral publishing program is often affiliated with other recognized disciplines such as Library Science. There is a lack of exact ideas and set patterns for skill cultivation.

Considering the developing trend of new technology and the above questions, we must break through the present framework, adjust our idea of publishing education, formulate the program to keep pace with the times in order to develop publication skills, and then complete the intelligence support in order to greet the time of globalization in digital publication which will soon arrive.

First, concerning digital publication development, we should open the school gate to manage publishing education. Under the concept of "big publishing," technology education should act as the important segment and development space of publishing education, and should be an important part its content. Opening the school gate manage publishing education means that publishing professionals may enter the publishing education classroom by any path. Therefore, experts from the fields of culture, economics, and technology pass on ideas, instruction and explanation, which means cultivating students' abilities for open thought and a publishing concept that is advancing with the times, which, further, allows for testing and verification of the knowledge and techniques of students in practical publishing situations. Network publishing and computer proofreading techniques should be obligatory courses for publishing education.

Second, the teaching materials system of publishing education should be perfected. We should write a series of teaching materials for publishing education that merge with digital publishing, and then update and perfect the mode of publishing education gradually. Teaching materials are the core of publishing education; they are also the transmitter of new ideas about publishing education. Under the new technology environment, publication production and communication have showed the trend of integration between traditional paper media and digital media. The categories and quantities of mobile phone, newspapers, e-books and digital magazines increase quickly by a hundred times or a thousand times every day. If teachers explain publishing in accordance with the traditional technological processes of publishing and plan teaching materials in accordance with the traditional publishing processes, students will lose enthusiasm because of the out-of-date knowledge. Following the full spreading of the new technology in the publishing industry, it is imperative to explore the new mode of publishing education. It is a fundamental point for present publishing education to combine digital publishing with publishing theory, publishing technology and publishing practice.

Third, on the basis of the background of diverse subjects and specialties, we should subdivide personnel training, and build up a personnel training pattern for different levels and fields. Within the digital publishing environment, the cultivation of the skills in digital publishing application and digital publishing research should be enforced. At the meeting for the twentieth anniversary of China's publishing education in 2004, Wu Qidi, the Vice-Minister of Education, said, "Editing and publishing, as a special industry, requires the students to be provided with the basic knowledge, basic theory, basic skills relevant to this major as well as knowledge and theory in other fields. We need talents who are not only special and intelligent but also all-round knowledgeable and erudite. So we should explore the all-round skill cultivation mode in terms of double majors, double degrees and postgraduate." In the digital age, as an editing/publishing major student, he should not only have composite cultural and professional knowledge of the liberal arts, but should also master information technology, digital publishing processes and its publishing characteristics.

References

Song, Muwen. Development of editing and publishing major in China and some advices on its construction. *Publishing and Distribution.* 2005 (11).

Yu, Yongzhan. The future of publishing industry and new technology. *The Network of China book and publishing.* 2006.

Education in the Editing and Publishing Specialty Based on Solid Humanity, Market and Technology

Li Xinxiang

In recent years, the education of editing and publishing science in our country has been developed at a high speed. Presently over fifty universities in the whole country have established undergraduate specialties in editing and publishing science. This is certainly in close relation to the social demand, but the main driving force is probably from the higher educational institutions themselves, including the enlargement of enrollment size, and regulation of specialty structure. But it is insufficient to rely only on the enthusiasm of the higher educational institutions themselves for supporting the education of editing and publishing science. We are also confronting the problem of transforming the education ideas of editing and publishing science, and increasing teaching and learning quality to fulfill social demand in real terms. How to realize the transformation of editing and publishing education from "high speed" to "high quality" has become a topic of concern among the related persons. In our opinions, the specialty of editing and publishing science is interlaced by multiple courses to train innovative and composite talents, so we should excel in the digital media surroundings, put much emphasis on "basic theory, systematic specialty, broad knowledge and innovative capability," and actually realize the organic unification of solid education containing humanity attainment, market planning and technological application.

1. Means of Implementing Specialized Education in Editing and Publishing Science of Solid Humanity, Market and Technology

1.1 Achieving Comprehensive Development of Humanity and Training "Perfect Talents" in Modern Advanced Education

The comprehensive development of humanity is the final pursuit of Marxism, and is the intrinsic requirement of socialist society. The targets to establish a harmonious society include economy, politics, culture and sustainable development, and are fundamentally the targets of comprehensive development of humanity. To carry out the specialty education in editing and publishing science of solid humanity, market and technology, and to train comprehensively developed talents who have high humanity attainment, powerful market planning capabilities and a high level of technological application skills are not only one of the important elements in advanced education reform, but are also the basic requirements of deepening education reform and promoting quality education overall. The target of advanced education should be to train "perfect talents" who have both humanity and scientific attainment, but not to train "scholars" who have knowledge of humanity only but lack market consciousness, or to train "businessmen" who have market consciousness only but lack knowledge of humanity, nor to train "craftsmen" who can operate techniques only but lack humanity attainment or market consciousness.

1.2 Integrating Fundamental Elements in the Specialized Teaching and Learning System of Editing and Publishing Science

Structure is the manner of mutual contact and mutual relation for all fundamental elements in a system. Any system is the summation of fundamental elements, a certain relation exists between fundamental elements, and the united integration, which is formed by these summations, has a function. The specialty teaching of editing and publishing science is the system that is formed by many types of fundamental elements including intelligence, time, recognition, information and training. Research has indicated that the more rational the structure is, the more harmonious it will be for the interaction among all fundamental elements, and the more easily will teaching and learning enter the best state. necessary. As for the function played by the system, it is necessary to help students form the capability of planning, processing, marketing and spreading the spiritual product of human being, and such a comprehensive capability is a kind of solid quality of humanity attainment, market planning and technological application. In teaching and learning, "humanity" should be used as the basic stand and to state the development patterns of editing and publishing, "market" should be used as the practical background to explain the demand mechanism of publishing, and "technology" as the basic requirement to process the operation of publishing propagation.

1.3 The Necessity of Teaching Reform in Editing and Publishing Science.

Taking a wide view of present specialty teaching in editing and publishing science, no matter if it is for the positioning of courses, or training targets, or the design of the curriculum, they are basically following the existing teaching model and teaching personnel; either importance is attached to humanity, or to marketing, but generally the importance attached to technology is insufficient. As a result, students have a defect in capability, and cannot accommodate demand from society, and even cannot lead the development of the editing and publishing course. Therefore, bold reform must be conducted on the specialty teaching of editing and publishing science to embody modern teaching philosophy of solid humanity, market and technology.

2. Principles of Implementing the Specialty Education of Editing and Publishing Science of Solid Humanity, Market and Technology

2.1 Trust Principle

First, it is necessary to believe that students have basic study abilities. Many students do not study their specialty well; first of all, it is not a problem of low intelligence, but non-intelligent psychological behaviors and behavior obstacles, such as lack of study interest, unstable attention, weak will, and lack of study habits. Second, it is necessary to believe that students have the desire to study from the start. They have great malleability; their curiosity and desire to learn are not as strong as when they were younger, but that desire can be revived. Third, it is required to believe that students are the main body of study, they should be regarded as persons with independent dignities, sufficient development space should be offered to them, and teachers of the specialty should create an atmosphere for the course that protects students' principal status as students.

2.2 Understanding Principle

First, it is necessary to understand the actual base of knowledge of the students. Only by starting from the actual base can progress be made. Second, it is necessary to understand the self-accusatory psychology and inferiority complex of students in the event that they have failed to accomplish the study task well. And then it is necessary to understand the students' motivation and their desire to actively show their own expertise.

2.3 Encouragement Principle

First, encourage students to set up positive and practicable targets: "Take a leap and pick the peach." After becoming aware of the benefits from their efforts, students will concentrate on studying with greater enthusiasm. A kind of democratic, and relaxed surroundings and atmosphere should be created in the specialty education. The individual particularity of students should be fully respected, and each should be encouraged to have his own principal ideas different from others. Encourage them to open their wings with ideas and make them aware that being a unique person, they are not secondary terms of ideas, feelings, imagination, and creation. Second, encourage students to achieve, and even for very minor achievements, the teacher should be good at encouragement and praise to make them experience the delight due to success. More importance should be attached to those students who are not mature but their particular judgment has been determined by themselves. Constructive and innovative recognition or views should be especially cherished without criticism of insufficiency. Words of encouragement that express sincere expectations should be used more to make students release greater potential energy of passion.

2.4 Development Principle

Educationist Cyxomjnhcknn once said, "At the bottom of people's hearts, there is a kind of fundamental need, and this is the right to hope that he himself will be felt as a discoverer, researcher, and explorer." Originating from the individual growth process of students, never ignore the student's present grasp of specialty knowledge, capability of achievement, or even the formation of individual particularity, and attach more importance to his development potential and would-be progress.

2.5 Difference Principle

First, as for the set contents of courses, teachers should make appropriate "cuts" in the teaching materials. As for what should be cut, what should be maintained, or if it is necessary to add or delete some parts, proper arrangements should be made in accordance with the actual situation, never blindly following the agenda made by specialists of the course who ignore the particular teaching situation and the vivid "human." Especially, teachers must deepen and enlarge the connotation and extension of the courses for the specialty in line with students' interests, hobbies and particularities. Second, as for the specific individual student, teachers should treat in different manners a student's academic performance requirements according to his past specialty base, and find apt and specific ways to solve problems, so as to ensure the individual's best enthusiasm level in the study of his or her specialty.

3. Education Methods for Implementing Specialty Education in the Editing and Publishing Science of Solid Humanity, Market and Technology

3.1 Make Students Love the Specialty of Editing and Publishing Science, Obtain Pleasant Feelings from the Specialty Study and Enrich Their Inner World

One of the age-old malpractices in the specialty education of present editing and publishing science is that students receive passively; they lack delight, lack experiencing the feelings of personal success and satisfaction that are obtained through the study of the specialty, and lack tasting the pleasure of life through the study of the specialty. Students are under high pressure and the individuals exist in colorless surroundings. Therefore, our education of the specialty must concern the inward world of the students' feelings, make students learn to be active, vivid, and flexible, to be with true sentiment, real delight, and faith, and make students' lives full of vigor and vitality. First, it is necessary to activate the internal drive of students' feelings and train their interests in studying the specialty. It is necessary to actually establish students' principal statuses in study activities of the specialty and constantly awaken students' dormant subject consciousness to form long-lasting internal drives of feelings, and, thereby, it is beneficial for the students individual self-study, self-development and self-realization. Passive and instilling education during teaching should be changed;

instead, importance should be attached to the student's self-understanding and experience of feelings, to the arrangement of exploration and research activities rationally, to solving problems in an innovative manner, to improving the recognition structure gradually, to promoting the self-realization of students, and to tasting the delight of success in such activities. Interest is one of the important psychological qualities of studying well the specialty in an innovative way, and practice has shown that when students have the interest, they will consciously spend time, make efforts, use their heads and study actively. With interest, a strong appetite for knowledge will be formed. Students will study with good motivation and can "study in delight" to win "the fruits from study." Second, it is necessary to enrich the spiritual world of students, and dig into the connotation of the specialty. It is necessary to link textbooks with social practice, integrate the activities inside and outside the class as a unit, and enlarge students' horizons. Further, it is necessary to enhance the organization to guide extracurricular reading, and lead students to appreciate and experience excellent works first hand so as to enrich students' knowledge and capabilities in editing and publishing.

3.2 Make Students Obtain Wide Knowledge and Enhance Capabilities Through the Study of the Specialty and Create a Basis for Lifelong Study

Importance should be attached to the understanding of inspiration and self-expression, and to train various abilities of students to meet with modern society. Then attention should be directed toward students' potential, encourage them to study what is happening in the publishing industry, so as to incorporate fresh materials in their publishing education. And then it is necessary to train the consciousness of innovation, develop innovative abilities and lead students toward keeping pace with the pulse of the times.

3.3 Develop Teaching Contents and Reform Teaching Methods

In order to implement the specialty education of editing and publishing science of solid humanity, market and technology, it is necessary to arrange the three parts of pre-class, during-class and post-class with an overall plan for giving lessons. In traditional views, the parts of pre-class and post-class both serve during-class, and during-class is the most crucial and most important part. Actually, viewed from the specialty characteristics of editing and publishing science, the new idea that both pre-class and during-class parts serve post-class should be set up. Before class, it is necessary to prepare well, make arrangements well and select well the important materials for key points in the class. During the class, beyond teaching some basic theory and knowledge, it is more important to activate the appetite of the students to study actively and make pads and guide well for the practice after class. In the case that the teaching in class has been carried out very successfully, but after listening the students of the class fail to actively study and practice, then the case cannot avoid falling into the traditional study stereotype of some specialties. The teaching and learning pattern that "students take notes in class, copy notes while doing assignments, and recite notes before examinations" is not suitable for the specialty study of editing and publishing science.

4. Implementing Specialized Education of Editing and Publishing Science of Solid Humanity, Market and Technology

4.1 Transform the Educational Idea of Unilaterally Pursuing Utility

We should, at once, embody the value that advanced education improves human nature, increases attainment, and improves dignity, and realize practical value of training humans, grasping technology and learning to seek skills. Teachers should think in the manner that puts themselves in the positions of students: how should the teachers teach so that I can understand? What kind of language, tone and facial expressions should the teacher use to attract my attention? What should the overall image of the class be like to, jointly, activate our motivation and accomplish the teaching task in class? What is needed in the digital age is applicable talents who not only have high humanity attainment and powerful professional techniques, but also have high comprehensive qualifications and potentials. Therefore, in class teachers are not only required to instruct regarding knowledge of the specialty, but also required to include something about philosophy, or literature or moral education that is in line with the content needs at the proper time and in the proper manner, so that students may grow up faster and more healthily under the double cultivation of teacher's direct instructions and potential influences.

4.2 Establish Well the Standardization of Curriculum with Clear and Definite Targets

Training targets are the specification of educational targets. In order to comply with the needs of education of the editing and publishing specialty of solid humanity, market and technology, specific teaching targets, teaching contents and the ratio of courses and class hours must be made, and assessment standards and teaching evaluation criteria must be normalized to form standard teaching guide documents. In ancient times, the schooling tenet was "to deliver a sermon, impart knowledge and to make trouble shoots." Now, the training target is the all around development of moral, intellectual, physical, aesthetic and labor education. So, it's undoubtedly necessary to regulate the curriculum settings of the existing specialty, and distribute rationally the ratio of the three parts in terms of humanity attainment education, marketing education, and technique application education in the specialty teaching plans.

4.3 Establish Solid Teacher Resource Teams with Constructive Teaching and Learning

Teacher resources are the most important guarantee of education quality. If there is only advanced education philosophy but without excellent teacher resources, the philosophy will never automatically convert into reality. To implement the education of an editing and publishing specialty of solid humanity, market and technology, first of all it is necessary for teacher resource teams that engage in education of the specialty to embody the solid feature. Of course, this does not require each teacher to be a comprehensive body of humanity scholar, market operator and technology expert, but requires that the overall team structure should embody the solid feature. There are professors who are proficient and profound in academic virtues, also there are practitioners who are from the community of editing and publishing, and there are experts who have proficiently mastered the modern technology of editing and publishing as well.

4.4 Create Modern Educational Surroundings

The science of editing and publishing is a young one, and should embody modern features. Either the education of humanity attainment or the training in market planning capability requires for study a particular kind of surroundings. The education atmosphere in schools speaks to the schooling traditions and the spirit of school control that have been accumulated for a long time. It also refers to the campus cultural space of the students' studies and lives within the school and refers to the internalized world of feelings of the school internalized members as well. No matter whether it is a famous school with a long history that is traditional or a young college without very much history, it needs a kind of educational surrounding that is in close pace with the trend of the times for developing the specialty education of editing and publishing science.

4.5 Establish Practice-based Experimental Teaching and Learning Surroundings

Fundamentally speaking, to implement the specialty education of editing and publishing science of solid humanity, market and technology, it is also necessary to establish practice-based experimental teaching and learning surroundings. Only by keeping pace with and surpassing the practice can the education of an editing and publishing specialty obtain sound development. With the rapid development of information technology and the course of news and publishing, the technology of news gathering, editing and publishing is under development in the areas of digital, intelligence and network. In the traditional work of news gathering, editing and publishing, the links in terms of information gathering, editing and proofreading, typesetting and sampling, publishing and circulating are independent of one another, and there is definite work distribution in the overall and mechanical work system. But with the rapid development of computer technology, and technology of network and digital video frequency, the integrated network of interviews, writing, editing, design, typesetting, publishing, storage and searching have been widely applied in all levels of news and publishing institutions.

In order to cope with the challenges from newly developed media and apply new communications technology, the news and publishing community has made endeavors to restructure business procedures, and establish digital information processing platforms one after another to enhance work efficiency and efficiently integrate resources. With the establishment of digital platforms, editors select necessary content according to the media features of different patterns, and, respectively, edit into the version of plain communications, the version of broadcasting and TV communications, network and mobile communications, as well as value-added service versions of professional data analysis. Newspaper agencies have been converted from the institutions of gathering and publishing print into the ones who supply professional news and related information content, and are not purely for page gathering and editing news information in print any more; publishing houses and journal houses have been converted from institutions of planning and publishing books and journals into ones that supply professional information and knowledge contents; they are not purely the makers of paper media any more, and they can also serve other network and mobile communications.

Correspondingly, such trends rely more highly on the techniques of editors and journalists, such as newspaper agencies requiring journalists to master the existing technique of distributing news dispatches on the spot and rolling distribution of news dispatches. Publishing houses require editors to master the typesetting technique of newspapers and periodicals, and the circulating institutions require members to grasp modern circulating technology. So it is necessary for the specialty education of editing and publishing science to keep pace with the situation, and abandon the teaching model of "focus on theory but ignore practice." The basic work is to enhance the building of laboratories and conduct experimental teaching and learning so that students have the platform on which to obtain practical training.

On Publishing Graduate Education in the Digital Era in China

Huang Xianrong

From the 1980s, under the support of the Ministry of Education, the press, and publication administration, China's editing and publishing education made notable achievements in nurturing talents and scientific research through the efforts of teachers. This has contributed a lot to the development of publishing undertakings and to the construction of socialist spiritual civilization construction. However, with the influences of the market economy, the digital technologies, and, additionally, the defect of education system, there are still some problems in editing and publishing education. For example, the scale of publishing education has developed too extensively. Many schools do not have qualified faculty to support publishing education. There is no national unified editing and publishing education coordinated mechanism so the development of the whole country's editing and publishing education is a bit blind. Meanwhile, the levels of schooling do not fit the actual requirements. Undergraduate education is indiscriminate, while the double BA degree and postgraduate education seem too weak. According to this, I will try to give some advice on graduate publishing within the digital environment.

1. The Emphases of Editing and Publishing Education Should Be Graduate Student Education

The foundation of our country's publishing education is undergraduate education. Since the Central Industrial Arts Institute been an undergraduate specialty called Book Binding and Design in 1956, publishing education could be said to have a fifty year history. Since the establishment of the Beijing Institute of Graphic Communication in 1978, or since the first undergraduates whose major was Book Publishing at Wuhan University in 1983, the history of publishing education is at least over twenty years. According to incomplete statistics, our country has more than seventy schools that have set up undergraduate specialties in editing and publishing. In addition to so many correspondence, internet, and special certification classes, more than 5,000 students in editing and publishing graduate every year.[1] Editing and publishing undergraduate education developed very fast especially after changing the undergraduate education enrollment catalogue in 1998. According to a report in the *China Book Business Report*, an average school which offers the specialty of editing and publishing may have at least fifty undergraduates, and possibly even more than a hundred undergraduates. In 2003, colleges and universities enrolled more than 2000 undergraduates. There are currently more than 5,500 students at school. These all result in more undergraduate job hunters than graduate job hunters. Since the Ministry of Education determined that the editing and publishing science is a subject subsidiary to journalism and mass media science, the scale and the enrollment of publishing graduate education has greatly improved. On the basis of incomplete statistics, there are twelve universities that have established editing and publishing science and nurtured postgraduates. At present, Beijing University has educated graduates for over ten years, and Wuhan University has educated over 200 master's and doctoral students.

However, when referring to the absolute quantity, the number of graduate students is still very few. This educational pattern cannot meet the developing requirements of the publishing industry in the digital age. First, the publishing industry cannot be replenished with enough qualified persons, especially the people who have specialized knowledge and editing ability. This will hinder the development of publishing in China. A person who is engaged in editing should have a master's degree or double BA degree education. These days, "some publishers do not recruit graduates whose major is editing and publishing directly. They always aim at the postgraduates or doctorates whose major is not editing and publishing. This means that the required education level is higher and higher." The difficulties in undergraduate employment show indirectly that the emphasis of editing and publishing education should be postgraduate education. Second, some colleges that have established an editing and publishing specialty can hardly provide professional teachers in time. The teachers in many specialized publishing schools are from other specialties; and they are unfamiliar with the publishing industry. This situation could be understood when the publishing specialty was established in the early days. However, even employees must study to keep up with the changes and the developments of the publishing industry. Teachers in an institute, should be even more active in renewing knowledge and keeping up with the occupation.[7] So, the development of publishing education needs to replenish teachers who are young and professional on one hand; on the other hand, it needs professional postgraduates or specialists to supplement the teacher team. We find that postgraduate education should be the emphasis of editing and publishing education. In the twentieth anniversary of the founding of the editing and publishing speciality, WuQidi, who worked at the Ministry of Education, pointed out that our country's editing and publishing core members should have political minds, professional abilities, high qualities and management abilities. Not only should they have pioneering talent, but also they should seize opportunities in international competition. To nurture these talents, we should mainly rely on the postgraduate education, especially the postgraduate degree.

2. Editing and Publishing Science Should Produce People with High Abilities and Broad Concepts of Publishing

Now, as for "Editing and Publishing Science," the standard name only exists in the Common Higher Education Undergraduate Specialty Catalogue in China, where it was defined by the Ministry of Education in 1998. However, there are not any subjects or specialties related to publishing science such as 'editing' or 'publishing' in the "Doctoral, Master's Degree and Postgraduate Subjects and Specialty Catalogue" which was issued by the Subjects Discussion Team of the State Council Academic Degree Committee in 1997. It only sets up two second-class subjects, "Journalism Science" and "Mass Media Science," which are subsidiaries of the first-class subject "Journalism and Mass Media Science." We cannot find "Publishing Science" or "Editing Science" either. The Subjects Discussion Team of the State Council Academic Degree Committee only defined the subjects or specialty catalogues, but did not define the "specialty direction" which is subsidiary to the specialty. The specialty direction is defined by the institute itself, according to the reality of the situation. So some universities set publishing science subsidiary to "Library, Information and Archives Management Science" (such as the Information Management Institute at Wuhan University). Some universities set editing science or publishing science subsidiary to Journalism and Mass Media Science and enroll postgraduates (such as the Publishing Department at the Beijing Printing Institute and the Literary Institute at Henan University). Some universities even enroll postgraduates related to publishing in the "Chinese Contemporary Literary Institute." The Ministry of Education took a flexible approach to constructing postgraduate subjects and specialties in 2002. This stipulated that the institute that had the authority to construct the first-class subject could establish the second-class subject by itself, and could enroll master's and doctoral students in the second-class subject. (Incidentally, the second-class subject should be reported to the Ministry of Education to make records.) Then, Wuhan University established the doctoral and master's degrees of "Publishing Science, " which were subsidiary to the first-class subject "Library, Information and Archives Management"; and China Media University also established the postgraduate degree "Editing and Publishing Science," which was subsidiary to the first-class subject "Journalism and Mass Media Science. " After that, Beijing University and Fudan University established the doctoral and master's degrees of "Editing and Publishing Science," which were subsidiary to the first-class subject "Journalism and Mass Media Science" in the same way.

So, there are only two editing and publishing postgraduate education programs which are approved and recorded by the Ministry of Education in China: One is "Publishing Science," which is subsidiary to the management subject "Library, Information and Archives Management;" and the other is "Editing and Publishing Science," which is subsidiary to the art subject "Journalism and Mass Media Science." However, these two names are not scientific enough. No matter whether in the publishing industry or in publishing academic circles, the concept of "Big Publishing" has already formed. And the concepts of "editing," "editing and publishing," "publishing and issuing," or "issuing" are all subordinate to "Big Publishing." Therefore, the subject positioning should conform to the high caliber requirements of the integration of editing, printing and publishing. Editing and publishing postgraduate education should be positioned within the "Big Publishing" arena. The education should be adapted to the concept of "Big Publishing," but not be restricted to one sector such as editing, publishing or issuing.

3. The Chief Goal of Editing and Publishing Postgraduate Education is Ability Training

Ability, means the capacity to accomplish a task, including the specific ways and psychological characteristics of completing the task. Ability is based on physiological quality. It is formed and developed by educating and by adopting the masses' wisdom and experiences through practice. The chief goal of editing and publishing postgraduate education should be ability training, including practical ability, innovative ability and managing ability.

Practical ability mainly indicates social practice ability. As for editing and publishing postgraduates, practical ability indicates the ability of doing practical jobs such as editing, publishing, printing or issuing. Now our country's editing and publishing postgraduates are mainly graduate students. From undergraduates to postgraduates, they studied at school for seven years (three years in master's degree study) or six years (two years in master's degree study). Except for the internship, which was arranged by the school, students seldom have contact with society and seldom engage in actual editing, publishing or issuing jobs. Therefore, some graduates are fastidious but incompetent; some grasp skills very slowly. So, some famous publishers do not want to employ the graduating postgraduates whose majors were editing and publishing. They want to employ people who have work experience, especially the ones who have "three or five years of work experience related to publishing." This shows that, to a certain extent, publishers have high practical ability requirements for the graduating students. In view of this, universities could make students visit publishers, presses or printers to learn about the process of editing and publishing, to grasp some basic publishing knowledge. Universities could also make students practice in those companies in their spare time, so as to improve their actual operating ability.

Innovative ability is required both in scientific research and in practical work. Firstly, compared with undergraduate education, postgraduate education emphasizes the ability of scientific research. It requires postgraduates to develop innovative ability during the process of scientific research. Not only are the postgraduates the tutors' helpful assistants, but also a vigorous research team. They are brisk, innovative and pioneering. They do the scientific research in their own subject field with the tutors' direction to promote research in publishing science. Secondly, postgraduates should be pioneering and innovative in their actual job should do their jobs creatively. Academician Kejun of Beijing Science and Technology University said that, the next twenty years is an important strategic period to develop our country's economy and society. We must be independent and sustained in innovation. To construct a resource-saving and environmentally friendly society, the first thing is to train innovative postgraduates. The postgraduates we are training now will play a positive role in the next twenty to forty years. How they will develop depends on the present direction of education.

Organizing and managing ability means the ability to coordinate and organize each factor effectively by using various ways flexibly to achieve goals. This includes the ability of human resources management, coordinating relationships, of effective execution, and so on. Organizing and managing ability is the external, synthetic manifestation of one person's knowledge, quality and some other basic factors. Modern society is a huge and complex system; most jobs need people's cooperation. So, in a sense, everybody is an organizer and manager; everybody undertakes some managing task. After graduating, not every postgraduate could do some managing work as a leader, but everyone may use some managing talent to a certain extent in their future work. This is the new requirement posed by the modern society. Postgraduates whose majors are editing and publishing must pay attention to developing managing ability. Postgraduates should pay attention to developing abilities of leadership, communication and coordination, as well as abilities of execution. Postgraduates should be good at choosing the best execution path, optimizing the distribution of executive resources, expanding the efficacy of execution. Developing responsibility is the first step. Responsibility is a cohesive force. It is an attitude of doing every task well. No matter what jobs, no matter what things, with basic responsibility, one has confidence in doing things well, and is willing to accept the results. This is a basic factor in assessing whether a person has managing ability.

4. The Training Mode of Postgraduate Study in Publishing Science Should Pay Attention to Integrating Theory and Practice

According to our country's actual circumstances, the training theory of postgraduate education in editing and publishing may be divorced from practice to an extent, such as the sources of the postgraduates, the training mode, the curriculum and so on.

Firstly, the main sources of postgraduates in editing and publishing are still graduating students. Graduating students do not suspend studying, and their English and special courses are much better. So the proportion of graduating students admitted will be much greater. Almost every graduating student lacks work experience. They are unfamiliar with the business of publishers, book stores and printers. Their opportunity for social practice is also very limited. Meanwhile, most teachers who are engaged in publishing education have never worked in publishing. However, publishing science is a highly practical subject. In the international world, especially in America, universities that have publishing master's specialties pay much attention to the students' skill training, such as New York University, Pace University and Emerson College. Though there are some differences in the curriculum, study period and study content in these three universities, they all offer some editing and publishing skills courses. Their curriculums are practical and operational so the trained students are fit for the requirements of the publishing industry. Under our country's actual circumstances, on one hand, we could invite some publishers as part-time professors, making use of their rich work experiences to counteract the weakness of publishing education. On the other hand, we could enroll more cadres in a postgraduate program. This could make the education more focused, enhance the contact with publishing industry, and help integrate the publishing education and publishing development closely and promote the development of postgraduate education in editing and publishing.

Secondly, after postgraduates enter the university, they will choose their tutors. This training mode has its advantages, namely, the possibility of entering a special field early; postgraduates can do their research under their tutors' directions. This is significant in training special talents. However, this mode can not meet the developing requirements of the publishing industry under digital circumstances. In digital times, editing has extended to the first step and the last step of the publisher's work; editing has infiltrated the process of the author's creation and book marketing in advance; and publishing also needs the employees to not only know about books, but also to know about the market. If the special field is too narrow, the preparation of common basic knowledge is inadequate, and innovation will be restricted. To solve this problem, we could adopt the method of a direct team to train postgraduates. That is to say, training postgraduates could regard one tutor as the chief tutor while many associate professors make up a direct team. The team should contain at least one tutor, who has a different research direction, or invite at least one publisher to act as a part-time professor. We should bring in people with high caliber abilities and improve the postgraduates' innovative abilities by using ways of integrating theories and practice.

Thirdly, the proportion of theoretical courses in over editing and publishing training system is very large, but the practical courses are few. Some colleges do not pay attention to the postgraduates' practical training, some even neglect it. We think that practical training is an essential step in the editing and publishing teaching process. Practical training is a benefit for students to learn about the publishing business. It could help students aquire the knowledge to solve practical problems, and find a research topic conformed to practical requirements. Among them, the internship for a master's should be six months or one year. But as for the two to three year flexible educational period in some colleges' postgraduate training, the period of internship will be restricted. So, "studying publishing" through "doing publishing" should be a good training mode. We should advocate case study and discussion in the teaching mode. For three year postgraduate programs, six month, or one year internships could be guaranteed. Students trained by this mode could meet the requirement of "having practical experience" proposed by the publishing business, and be fit for the development of the publishing industry.

REFERENCES

Cai, Kenan. "Editing science and editing teaching." *Publishing Science.* 2006 (3).

Chen, Lifei. "Where is the block in publishing education." *Editing Journal.* 2005 (2).

Chen, Yan, Wenyan Zhang and Jianhong Shen. "Observing and thinking about the present situation of editing and publishing graduate education in China." *Publishing Research.* 2004 (1).

Chen, Yan, et al. "The investigation of occupation situation and factors about 2005th editing and publishing students in part of the schools in China (I)." *Publishing Research.* 2005 (10).

Deng, Leicang. "Self-examining the awkward of editing and publishing science." *Publishing Research.* 2005 (11).

He, Hao. "Discussing the publishing high education." *Publishing Science.* 2005 (6).

Li, Yuan. "Editing and publishing teaching in universities: trudging on the road" *China Bookseller Newspaper.* 2005-7-22.

Liu, Yongjun and Hongkui Li. "Track back the 20 years development of editing and publishing science." *Publishing Research.* 2005 (2).

Wu, Qidi. "Promoting the sustained and healthy development of editing and publishing education initiatively." *China Editor.* 2004 (6).

Zhang, Zhiqiang and Jing Wan. "Briefly discussing the American publishing graduate education." *Editing Journal.* 2005 (6).

Four Mechanisms that Should Be Introduced into Chinese Publishing Education in the Digital Age

Yao Lei

Since the 1990s, computer technologies, especially digital technology centered on the Internet, have developed rapidly and changed all aspects of social life at a noticeable speed. The publishing industry has also been affected by this revolution. The characteristics of Internet technology, that it is not restricted by time and space, influences every aspect of publishing activities and traditional modes of releasing, distribution, promotion and reading. With the impact of the Internet, some celebrated publishing houses in developed countries are exploring their opportunities with the development of networks and some switching to other businesses. For example, *Encyclopedia Britannica,* which has been categorized as an information product with the most abundant contents, tried to transform its product from paper to Compact Disc, and then to the Internet. Many domestic publishing houses have established their own websites, whose main functions are news issuing, bibliography downloading and enterprise drumbeating, instead of making networks looked at as new opportunities for their businesses. The whole publishing industry distinctly realizes that the Chinese publishing industry is facing both crisis and opportunity in the digital age. In the process of transformation, skill training becomes one of the key factors. As mentioned in the "National Outline of News and Publishing Talents Management from 2005 to 2010," designing and progressing to any reformation and innovation needs the support of talents. Observing the recent situation in China, I insist that there are four mechanisms that should be introduced into publishing education.

1. Innovation

In the process of economic globalization and the later transition period after China joined the WTO, it is a basic strategy of the development of an economy and society to boost independent innovative capacity. As a knowledge-intensive industry, publishing plays an important role in the innovative system of our country. In the past twenty years, publishing education has nearly formed an intact curriculum system and a correspondingly integrated education system. It has given great support to the publishing industry. Trained by the current Chinese publishing education system, students have superior skills in basic theories, but they are lacking innovative capabilities. Compared with those specialties that are familiar with new technology and marketing, people who are familiar with the traditional publishing industry stressed the quantity: there are more people who can master single media than multimedia; there are more people with editing skills than management skills; and there are more people who know about the domestic market than about both domestic and foreign markets. Especially in the digital era, publishing innovation is a complicated and creative job which not only contains the innovation of publishing mechanisms, modes, patterns, structures, and contents, but also includes the innovations in publishing organization, system, management and so on. However, the talents training under the current education system can not take on these important tasks.

In order to promote the development of the publishing industry, the innovative reforms of publishing education should contain four aspects. The first is the training target. The target of higher education in our country has been changed from professional training to general education and to fostering compound talents, which has become a trend of higher education around the world. In the digital age, the training target of publishing education must meet the need of multimedia development. To be exact, it is to train knowledgeable and skillful students who can master modern technologies such as IT and do a good job in every part of publishing, including teaching and researching creatively.

The second is subject construction. We should put publishing education under the same circumstances as "Big Publishing," rather than only certain segments, such as editing or distributing. Moreover, to meet the various needs of the publishing industry, different levels of personnel training should be verified, too. For example, we can promote postgraduate education on the basis of undergraduate education. In addition, while determining curriculum, we should arrange new courses which can keep step with society, industry and technology on the basis of the essential theoretical courses and central courses. What's more, students would not only pay attention to their studies but also the development of practical skills and investigating and researching abilities.

The third aspect is teachers' cultivation. None but a creative and highly qualified group of teachers will have pioneer students. Teacher training is the guarantee of the quality of education. And there are two training modes: one is "sending out," and another is "inviting in." "Sending out" is to send out young teachers to related fields of the publishing industry to learn actual strategies and to avoid them teaching blind. "Inviting in" is to employ experts and scholars in the publishing field as part-time teachers to keep the publishing education system vital.

The last one is school management. The mode that combines the education, industry and research department is a double-win pattern, which on the one hand may lighten the economic pressure of school and improve the quality of education, and on the other hand may improve the quality of the workers and gain plenty of talents. In the changeable and competitive digital age, this kind of education model needs to be strengthened and popularized.

2. Carving Out

The concept of Carving Out was brought forward by Collin Bore in the "Twenty-First Century International Education Forum," which was held by UNESCO (United Nations Educational, Scientific, and Cultural Organization) in November 1989, and was then widely disseminated. Compared with fundamental education and professional education in normal universities, Carving Out education is becoming a third passport for university students and the target of world education. Under the new circumstances of the digital age, Carving Out education has great significance. To begin with, Carving Out is an important means of lightening the pressure of employment, as the employment of university students becomes a serious problem. Secondly, carving out education focuses on training students' creative capacities and is good for the formation of independence and the development of integrated qualities in students. Thirdly, new modes will inject energy into the whole publishing industry and promote competition in innovation. Moreover, the programs that were instructed by tutors were done with a good vision and can be adapted to publishing enterprises through negotiation. They help both to provide more funds for education and to establish the students practice base.

The coming of the digital era brings new opportunities for students to carve out their own businesses. Firstly, the Internet lowers the threshold of entering the publishing business. Although many publishing operations, which have a high political threshold, must be checked and approved strictly nationally, the development of network technology creates new opportunities for students to participate in any capacity, such as designing, typesetting, proofreading, typewriting, subject selecting, editing, distribution and so on. Secondly, applying network technologies decreases or escapes some costs generated by the traditional publishing operation, such as printing, storing and transportation, lowers the risk of carving out business, and improves efficiency by cutting down on some procedures. Lastly, the development of digital technology makes possible any creative idea when carrying out publishing business. New technology creates lots of new publishing media and develops new markets with huge business opportunities.

Therefore, the Carving Out mechanism should be introduced into publishing education. There are three ways to achieve this goal. At the beginning, we should cultivate students with the idea of carving out business under appropriate circumstances. For example, we can invite some successful businessmen or investors to give lectures to stimulate the students' consciousness and abilities in carving out business. Next, we would add courses to teach the knowledge and skills of Carving Out the curriculum, such as operation and management, negotiation, decision-making, market forecasting and financial management. Moreover, students are encouraged to join in the social practices. In the past, most practical bases have been publishing houses or Xinhua Book Stores, while few are private enterprises. Henceforth, we should increase the opportunities for practicing in private businesses to find out the strengths and difficulties. This is useful for our carving out business in the future. In addition, we should provide opportunities to students to experience carving out business. To be specific, we could set up a Carving Out foundation and form some groups. Each group, which would be instructed by a teacher and composed of several students, would submit their carving out project to the foundation. After a bid presentation that explains the design, cost and expected profit, the members of the foundation would fund the most promising project. During the running of the project, the foundation would check upon the implementation of the project, such as the management and financial situation. The project that runs poorly would be suspended from funding. The imitation can teach students a more practical knowledge of Carving Out.

3. Talents Customization

Since China's reform and opening to the world, the number of universities that develop publishing education has increased from several at the beginning to forty recently. According to the statistic, more than 5,000 professional publishing students of different levels are brought into the industry every year and the number is still increasing. However, publishing houses still complain that they cannot find the talents they urgently need, and even some argue that they don't want to recruit students from publishing majors. Pressure from employers pushes schools to reform the mode of education, and they unaminously believe that "cooperation between school and enterprise" is an ideal mode. But having reviewed the whole industry, we find that this mode hasn't been widely spread: "there is an estrangement between education and industry, which results in misunderstanding of each other." As for the problem that education ignores practice, we hold that businesses should be charged with part of the responsibility. The publishing industry should back skill cultivation in school education and participate in education. They should customize talents rather than ask for talents from schools.

Recently, some publishing houses have begun to try the method of talents customization. For example, in light of the press development strategy and the orientation of publishing, the Huazhong University of Science and Technology Press looks out for talents among students who have passed the postgraduate entrance examination and whose majors accord with the publishing field. If the candidate is interested in working at the press, he or she will be a postgraduate who is customized by the press and his or her education fees will be paid by the press. During the studying period, besides the compulsory courses of the major, the candidate must accept the practical courses arranged by the press, and the press assesses the candidate by the standards of a formal staff member. This method benefits the three parts, the press, the students and the school. Firstly, from the viewpoint of students, it helps to decrease the pressure of finding employment. Further, the intentional curriculum and practice improve the efficiency of their study. Secondly, if the press doesn't use the method of customization, it is very difficult for it to find suitable, talented people who have both professional knowledge and publishing knowledge. Nowadays, most of the students in publishing majors have a background in liberal arts, and it is hard for them to be familiar with or master a special subject quickly, especially, engineering, science, medicine and so on. Even if the press can recruit students from certain majors, it will spend at least half a year to train them. The students whose study has been customized can fling themselves into work as soon as they graduate, which improves the efficiency of human resources. Lastly, as for the education department, they look forward to cooperating with the publishing enterprises. On one hand, enterprises can provide some funds for education; on the other hand, the practical courses can make the curriculum lively and more effective.

4. Evaluation and Supervision

In the 1990s, Chinese traditional higher education was challenged by the market, and the western educational evaluations mechanism was introduced into China. Later on, the Chinese followed a the policy of increasing recruitment to popularize higher education and many problems were generated. Against this background, Zhouji, the current Minister of Education, holds that evaluation is an important means of improving the quality of higher education. We believe that the development of publishing education depends not only on the evaluation system of the whole university, but also that it should have its own evaluation mechanism.

Firstly, let's take the Publishing Center of Oxford Brooks University as an example to provide a review of the evaluation mechanism in western countries. To ensure the quality of education, a quality evaluation and supervision system was introduced. At first, students are asked to evaluate the class verbally or by writing at the end of each teaching module, and then teachers summarize their evaluation in the lesson report and render it to the faculty. Next, the Course Committee, which is composed of representatives of teachers and students, will hold regular meetings, checks the situation of the class, and resolves problems during the semester. Otherwise, stylebooks of the students' homework and the teachers' suggestions are supervised by an expert from the outside. In addition, there are other types of supervision. For example, representatives of teachers and students will evaluate every curriculum annually, and submit the suggestions to the Education Quality Supervision Committee. And schools will invite experts from the outside to check all curricula every five years. The Education Supervision Bureau will examine the quality of curricula every six or eight years and publish an evaluation report. If the results are unsatisfactory, the government will withdraw the investment.

There are four principles that should be followed in the evaluation and supervision mechanism. The first principle is openness and clarity of, which can avoid formalization and help to resolve problems in education. The second is the dynamic principle. We should check the education problems with our eye on developing, and improve problems while evaluating, rather than maintaining the original states. The third is the scientific evaluation index. A reasonable standard, which is based on research and surveys, is one of the key factors of an evaluation. The last one is enterprises' participation. At present, compared with publishing industry culture, education culture is more active, whereas its counterpart is reluctant. Although the leaders of publishing houses announced publicly that they would support publishing education, there are few jobs vacant for students who have majored in publishing. The reason behind the phenomenon is their misunderstanding and underestimation of the publishing education. Hence, the culture of education should invite enterprises to take part in evaluation and supervision. During the evaluation, schools may learn the needs of the market, and enterprises may have a chance to know the real situation of education and transmit practical information to schools. Nothing but working together can make publishing education cultivate eligible talents and could help the Chinese publishing industry develop.

REFERENCES

Ai, Guanghui. "The Evaluation of Higher Education Call the Leading of Culture." *Journal of Xinjiang Finance and Economy Institute.* 2006.

Huang, Xianrong. "The history and Creative Trend of Publishing Education in China." *Publishing Research.* 2001.

Liu, Yongjun and Hongkui Li. "Track Back the 20 Years Development of Editing and Publishing Science." *Publishing Research.* 2005.

Richardson, Paul. "Publishing education in the UK." Translated by Hongjun Xu and Zhonggeng Xu. *Journal of Ningbo University,* (2) Vol.24 (1). 2002.

"The Survey of Employment Situation and Influencing Factors of Publishing Science in Some University in 2005." *Publishing Research.* 2005.

Wang, Bo. "Review the Cultivation and Employment of Publishing Talents from Three Aspects." *A Vast View on Publishing,* (1). 2004.

Wu, Guohua. "Discuss the Regular Professional Training." *A Vast View on Publishing.* 2004.

Wu, Jingxue. "The Second Training of Publishing Talents." *Publishing Research.* 2006.

Xu, Hongjun. "Discussion on Publishing Creation." *Publishing Science.* 2001.

Zhang, Wenwu. "Discuss the Significance and Implement of Publishing Education." *Adult Education in China.* 2006.

The Actuality, Problems, and Countermeasures of Editing and Publishing Education in China

Liu Canjiao

Compared with flourishing publishing industries in many countries in Europe and America, China is just a big publishing country now, but is far below the standard of a strong publishing country. The important reason is that the total quantity of publishing talent is incompatible with the rapid development of the publishing industry, and that the overall quality of publishing talent is incompatible with the high quality required. In short, the talent problem has already bottlenecked the healthy growth of the publishing industry in China. Whether or not enough excellent publishing talents can be provided quickly not only concerns great-leap-forward development of the publishing industry, but also concerns the further building-up of comprehensive national strength. In this sense, to evaluate the position and role of editing and publishing education in any way won't be excessive. To use little to get much, the writer analyses the status quo of editing and publishing education and puts forward his "two cents."

1. The Status Quo of Editing and Publishing Education in China

Compared to the long history of editing and publishing in China, editing and publishing education is very young. Formal higher education large in scope began to form in the 1980s. The Library and Information Science School of Wuhan University first set up the specialty which was called "book issuing" in 1983. Peking University, Fudan University and Nankai University set up the specialties which were called "editing science" at Comrade Hu Qiaomu's suggestion in 1984. In 1998, the Ministry of Education compiled the lately-revised Common Higher Education Undergraduate Specialty Catalogue, which combined two specialties into one specialty that was titled "Editing and Publishing Science." Reviewing the process in the past more than twenty years, it's worthwhile to sum up the experience of editing and publishing education. During this time, Chinese editing and publishing education made notable achievements. Which can be summarized as follows:

1.1 The Discipline Position was Established, and the Scale of Publishing Education Developed Gradually

Over the past twenty years, as an emerging specialty of higher education, editing and publishing education has played an irreplaceable role in nurturing scientific research and promoting the development of the industries, universities and research institutes. In 1998, the Ministry of Education adjusted the catalogue of undergraduate specialty, and classified editing and publishing science as a subject subsidiary to the first-class subject "Journalism and Communication Science." In recent years, editing and publishing education has made enormous progress. According to incomplete statistics, by September 2004, our country had 131 schools that had set up specialties of editing and publishing. By July 2005, our country has 31 schools that had set up graduate specialties of editing and publishing.

1.2 The Educational System Has Already Taken Initial Shape

In the construction of specialties and the teaching process, the different universities become different types according to their own characteristics, manpower, and the demands of the industry. There are three types of curriculum of editing and publishing specialty: book publishing and issuing, the editing science, and editing and publishing science. Our country already has an educational system of various disciplines (including editing science, publishing management, printing, book issuing, book design), of various education levels (including the doctorate, master's, double bachelors degree, undergraduate, specialty, professional certificate of the college, technical secondary school, skill school, vocational high school, etc.), of various education modes (including formal school education, teaching by correspondence, evening university, vocational university, etc.), and whose characteristic is "various disciplines, various levels, various modes, various channels."

1.3 The Content of Courses Has Gradually Matured and Stabilized

Editing and publishing has already formed a characteristic teaching system during the past twenty years. The teaching plan and development projects of many schools have been gradually stabilized. There are more than ten professional basic courses and core courses, and several tens of elective courses. Corresponding publishing of teaching material and learning monographs also have made great progress. According to the statistics, there are more than 100 kinds of relevant teaching materials and learning monographs in the editing and publishing field.

1.4 The Teacher Team is Growing Up and Strengthening

More than twenty years ago, there were large numbers of editors and publishers whose practical experiences were rich in the publishing industry, but no expert who was engaged in publishing education. Through the practice of teaching for several years, there are large numbers of professors and scholars who are engaged in publishing education now. The seniors can be called the founders of the higher education of publishing in China, and have fostered a lot of undergraduates and graduates. Following their lead, many young and mid-aged teachers who are determined to be engaged in the higher education of publishing have sprung up. They have high academic qualifications, are good at foreign languages and modern technology, and have the pioneering spirit and innovative consciousness. We can see in them the future and hope of editing and publishing education in China.

1.5 Editing and Publishing Education and Scientific Research Developed Synchronously

The 1980s was a period both when publishing education rose and when publishing research started. There was an obvious phenomenon that these two fields were in perfect harmony, and advanced side by side over more than twenty years. The professional teachers and the students and publishing industry's experts made great achievements in the publishing of academic monographs, in theses, and in the exploitation of academic position and fostering of academic troops by common effort. In the last more than twenty years, they have announced thousands or hundreds of academic theses and comments, which have played important roles in pushing theories and research, initiating hot research topics, organizing academic discussion, and promoting discipline construction.

2. The Problem in Editing and Publishing Education in China Currently

From the 1980s, after innovation and development for more than twenty years, China's editing and publishing education made great progress in scale and performance. However, in the face of these pleasing phenomena, we have to pay attention to the inherent crisis in editing and publishing education. There are many problems in most academies and schools which set up this specialty in different degrees, such as the inaccurate discipline position, unpopular training targets, and theories of teaching and researching which are separated from practice, and conditions of employment that are not optimistic. These problems need to be resolved urgently, or they will face elimination in the violent competition.

2.1 The Discipline Position is Inaccurate

The name of the discipline is unreasonable. There are still significant differences in the comprehension of "editing and publishing science" in teaching practices and theoretical research. Professor Wang Zhenduo of Henan University put forward that editing and publishing science means two independent disciplines of editing science and publishing science. Is publishing science subsidiary to editing science, or is editing science subsidiary to publishing science? If it is the former, they may as well be divided into editing science and publishing science, respectively. If it is the latter, this is too narrow, obviously, which goes against the discipline construction. Professor Huang Kaiqing of Wuhan University thinks it more suitable that the specialty name should be called "publishing science" because "editing science and publishing science" should be a general concept, and its discipline construction should carry on research on all processes of publishing activity and all factors of publishing work. Editing is a business link in big publishing, so it shouldn't be the main content of the specialty's construction. It is not suitable to emphasize the editing characteristic of the specialty apart from the social need and the employment of students.

2.2 The Training Target is Unpopular

Many unprecedented changes appeared in the development of information communication technology (ICT), publishing industry. From the traditional publication process of the numeral turn retail system and way of reading the numeral turn, the application of new technology makes the publishing industry face an unprecedented challenge and opportunity. In the Common Higher Education Undergraduate Specialty Catalogue, the higher education publisher thinks of the business training target of editing and publishing science as "high-level specialized personnel who have systematic principles and skills of editing and publishing, have wide cultural and scientific knowledge, and can engage in editing and publishing, issuing business and management work, and teaching and research in books and periodicals, news publicity and cultural educational organizations." This is a basic guidance document, and also an important basis for setting up and adjusting the specialty, training talents, etc. If the regulations which the Ministry of Education made training targets of professional talents of editing and publishing in 1998 represented the total request of the publishing and issuing field at that time, after eight years, in the digital age, we must have new understanding towards training targets, and also must deepen its content.

2.3 Theory of Teaching and Research is Separated From Practice

It is inevitable that theories lag behind practice and are separated from practice because editing and publishing science is an applied discipline. In a survey report from the editing and publishing specialty of Peking University, concerning the most important quality requisite of teachers of this specialty, fifty-five percent of classmates think they should "have relevant practical experience." But "spoon-feeding" teaching methods in great proportions is a common problem in editing and publishing education in China. Each course has long been in the traditional teaching mode of "classroom teaching- academic; exercise-apprentice and practice." The student studies the theories without practice first, then practices without theory. Teachers over-emphasize theory infusion and neglect practice in their teaching. There is no "agency" link which combines theory with practice in the curriculum. So the students of editing and publishing specialties spend a great deal of time and energy on studying theory courses at school, forget them after examination, and can't apply theories to solve actual problems and still handle affairs with experience. With the reform of editing and publishing education, many universities arrange editing practice, press practice, bookstore practice, printing house practice, graduation practice, visits and investigations in order to reform traditional teaching methods, but these practice lessons in the schools are still separated from practice in the publishing industry, and still lack concrete arrangement, so the practical teaching cannot achieve the anticipated result.

2.4 The Condition of Employment is not Optimistic

The booming development of the publishing industry in the new era has already made a greater demand on publishing talents. Graduates can't adapt to the demands of the publishing industry completely, which is another problem in editing and publishing education in China. There is currently an interesting unfortunate phenomenon in the publishing talent market: on the one hand, there is heavy demand on publishing talents in the publishing field; on the other hand, the supply of graduates of publishing and issuing specialties exceeds the demand. From this paradox in the talent market, it is not difficult to conclude that the amount and level of skills all can't satisfy effective demands of the publishing industry's development. On the one hand, although most universities set up the editing and publishing specialty, they laid more emphasis on courses in editing science in the actual teaching process, so the professional structure is heavily focused on only one area of publishing knowledge and skills. On the other hand, most universities can't train high-level talent in editing and publishing independently. Currently, publishing education mainly concentrates on the undergraduate level or in part of a second academic degree, and there is not only effective demand on various specialties (such as publishing economics, publishing management, and publishing information technology), but also a more and more urgent need for high-level talent that has the master's or Ph.D. degree in editing and publishing.

3. The Countermeasures of Editing and Publishing Education

3.1 Make the Discipline Positioning Clear

To do well in the education of editing and publishing, the first thing is to make the discipline definition clear. The editing and publishing specialty is not a single specialty, but includes several specialties, such as editing science, book issuing and publishing management. As far as we know, most universities in the western, developed countries just set up publishing specialties, and seldom divide into publishing, editing, issuing and printing. Publishing science is a theory of knowledge in the discipline of publishing science, and reveals the principles of all publishing activities and the relation of publishing activity to social economic culture and ideology. Publishing science plays a guiding role in all disciplinary branch of publishing science. Therefore, publishing science is more appropriately named as the first-class subject of editing and publishing specialty.

3.2 Increase the Units Granting Master's Degrees and Doctorates and Making High-level Skill Training Formal

Famous American publisher J.P. Desol put forth: "All editors in the publishing industries should hold a master's degree." As shown by the experience of the development of the domestic and foreign publishing industry, strengthening editing and publishing education that trains high-level talents is the objective, and demands that the modern publishing industry develops and participates in international competition, which has become one of the key problems urgently needed to be resolved in the development of the publishing industry in China. But, there were no units granting master's degrees in editing and publishing in the specialty catalogue in 1998; the Academic Degrees Committee under the State Council just approved a publishing department at the Beijing Printing Institute and the literary institute of Henan University recruited postgraduates whose major was mass media science, and whose research focus included editing, publishing and issuing. So there were no formal units granting master's degrees and doctorates. Some universities made this specialty subsidiary to other units granting master's degrees and doctorates. This kind of teaching method is hard to develop on a large scale and cannot win enough funding. To a great extent, it limits the high-level talent training of editing and publishing. Therefore, the educational circles should win the support of the Academic Degrees Committee under the State Council actively, and set up "Editing and Publishing Science" in the "Doctoral, Master's Degree and Postgraduate Subjects and Specialty Catalogue." Some experienced departments with a long history and a strong teacher team can adjust the training target, improve training levels, change direction to mainly train postgraduates supplemented by the undergraduate education, and transport more high-level and high-quality talent around the country.

3.3 Develop Multi-level and All-Directional Cooperation of the Industries, Universities and Research Institutes

Editing and publishing higher education and the publishing industry should mutually support one another and work closely together. The universities should win the support of the industry actively, develop multi-level and all-directional cooperation with it, make use of human resources, and take advantage of practice bases of publishers to improve the quality of higher education. As far as we know, the publishing specialties of many universities in the United States establish a specialty advisory committee which consists of a famous writer, an experienced editor and a chief executive officer of the publishing industry, who regularly assemble to aid the development of the specialty, and to shape the course to the latest needs of the publishing industry. In the meantime, they give necessary personal advice to the students through faculty and staff. Some domestic universities also are trying to do this. For example, the editing and publishing specialty of Peking University and Peking University Press, and that of Wuhan University and Hubei Provincial Publishing Administration have built up a good cooperative relationship. Publishing outfits support publishing higher education actively, and provide a base and instruction for students' practice. These two publishing outfits, respectively, have established scholarships or teaching prizes, and the managing director, and editors-in-chief worked with the teachers to contribute to talent training. At the same time, the universities should also work in alliance with institutes to train the graduates. For example, the University of Shanghai for Science and Technology and the China Research Institute of Publishing Science are uniting to declare a Master's unit. These cooperative ways are worth spreading.

3.4 Train Publishing Talent to Meet the Needs of Industry

For various reasons, there is a problem with the separation between the training of universities and needs of society. If the graduate of an editing and publishing specialty cannot be engaged in publishing work, it is a waste of educational resources, which influences the student's enthusiasm for study. It also influences the brand image of a university, and, as a result, the publishing industry doesn't concern itself with the training of publishing talent, and it is more difficult to train publishing talent. The Program of National Journalism and Publication (Copyright) Talent Work in 2005-2010 points out: "More personnel who are skilful in traditional journalism and the publication business, fewer professional and technical personnel who understand new technology and market; more personnel who are skilful in a single medium, fewer personnel who can adapt to multimedia management; more personnel who are skilful in the editing business, fewer senior personnel who understand management; more personnel who understand the domestic market, fewer personnel who can keep their hold on home and overseas markets.[7] Therefore, editing and publishing higher education has to make great efforts to adapt to the development of the publishing industry, adjust specialty structures and talent training modes according to the special needs of the development of "big publishing" industry. It must make an intensive study of the teaching plan of the editing and publishing specialty and the specialty focus which it covers, build up a new teaching system which can meet the needs of the publishing industry in the twenty-first century with the spirit of reform and innovation, and train "leadership" and "highly-skilled talent" for the publishing industry.

REFERENCES

Fang, Qing. 2005. "Speed up the Step of Talent Training through Apprehending the Spirit of *Programme*." *China Publishing* 2005 (11).

Feng, Zhijie. 2003. "Training the High Quality Publishing Talent." *Journal of Editing Science* 2003 (1).

Huang, Kaiqing. 2000. "The Discipline Construction of Editing and Publishing Education." *The Friend of Editor* 2000 (4).

Huang, Xianrong, Tao, Li. 2004. "The Development Trend of Editing and Publishing Education in China." *Publishing Science* 2004 (6).

Shao, Yiwen. 2005. "Editing and Publishing Education Need to be Concluded and Improved." *Publishing Science* 2005 (5).

Xiao, Dongfa, and Xu, Huan. 2004. "Concerning Argument and Investigation and Analysis of the Editing and Publishing Education." *The Journal of Hebei University* 2004 (5).

Xiao, Dongfa, Yang, Lin. 2005. "The Change of Publishing Industry Calls the Development of Editing and Publishing Graduate Education." *University Publishing* 2005 (3).

The Cultivation of Publishing Talents in the Context of Digital Publishing

Liang Chunfang

1. The Influence of New Technology upon the Publishing Industry in China

In the face of economic globalization, media internationalization and publishing digitalization, the rapidly advancing new technology brings profound, revolutionary change to the publishing industry in China. Regarding the ten year development of a global publishing industry, we find that the influence of politics, economy and society is indubitably crucial, but the most important and immediate factor is technology. Surveying the developing history of the publishing industry, each grand progress was the direct effect of a new technological development. The main stages are, firstly, the application of laser phototypesetting in the field of publication; secondly, digital publishing techniques. China's transformation from traditional publishing to digital shows a promising future.

What is digital publishing? There are various terms, including net publishing, desktop publishing, electronic publishing, game publishing, cell phone publishing, and, finally, digital publishing. With the unceasing development of new technology, multimedia publishing is getting closer and closer to the essential digital publishing. Mr. Liang Gang, vice director of the Digital Book Research Center and simultaneously the CEO of the Tongli Corporation in China, said that the former concepts presented mostly a certain flow or a medium application, and none but digital publishing, for the first time, generalized the entire publishing process with more essentially technical attributes. For the moment, his definition of digital publishing is the one most approved of in the field of publication: "If only a binary system is employed for the operation of the whole publishing process, we regard it as digital publishing, ranging over the digitalization of original works, editing, printing and reproduction, issuance and reading consumption." This definition clarifies genuine digital publishing, which spreads traditional publishing resources by taking advantage of multimedia.

Then, we can agree that it's a misunderstanding to assign paper publication to the traditional publishing field and electronic publication to the digital publishing field. This is for the reason that paper publication is one part of digital publishing; no matter what the terminal reading medium is, as long as the content recorded in the medium is recorded by digital methods, this kind of publication is digital.

From the point of view of publishing practice, digital technology is achieved through the publication's carrier, communication means, management methods, promotion schemes and methods of payment. For instance, the information application in publication distribution, digital publishing, printing on demand, internet bookshops, internet marketing and the like, have been accelerating the revolutionary effects on the traditional publishing industry. Proof of this can be found in the following statistics:

Purpose. "*Statistical Reports on Internet Development in China*" shows that, for the 94 million netizens, searching information, recreation, and learning are the three main purposes, accounting for 83.2%. Those three factors are tightly related to digital publishing, and are the most lively markets on the seven seas.

Quantity of netizens and cellphone users. In July 2006, netizens in China reached 0.123 billion; cell phone users exceeded 0.44 billion. Thus, the interaction and amalgamation between traditional media and internet mobile communication is impelled effectively.

Net sites and net practitioner number. There are 35,000 thousand web sites referring to internet publishing in China; the number of publishing houses holding we publishing service is more than 400; the number of net practitioners beyond 0.1 million. The data suggests that web publishing in China is stepping into a new industry shaping gradually.

Statistics on e-book selling. By the end of 2004, 805 million e-books were sold in China. Until April 2005, 148,000 e-books titles were in circulation, more than any other country in the world. Now, beyond one thousand digital museums are in use in China. With the technical advancement and the participation of traditional publication, mobile reading devices will be more diverse and user-friendly; and the content of e-books will be more abundant. E-books have an immeasurable future.

E-book developing trend. According to Microsoft's forecast, it's not until the year 2020 that 90% of book varieties will be issued both by paper and electronic means. In 2008, upwards of 50% of internet bookshops in China will list e-books in their booklists; in 2015, the sale of e-books in China is predicted to reach 10 billion, accounting for half the profit of all books.

Statistics on net publication selling. By the end of 2004, the gross income of web publication in China came out to be 3.5 billion yuan, increasing 50% annually, bringing along related industries, and increasing production value to about 25 billion. Figures show that, by 2020, the sale of net publications in China will account for half of the entire publishing industry; the year 2030 will see 90% of books are e-books.

The rate of online reading. The Chinese book-reading rate has been declining for six years successively, meaning less than 50% of people read books for the first time. Simultaneously, the rate of online reading is growing rapidly, from 3.7% in 1999, to 18.3% in 2003 and rising up to 27.8% in 2005 going up 7.5 times in 7 years, with an average rising rate of 107%. Presently, the Internet has been the way for 60% of netizens to approach books.

Readers' demands. Since July 1999, CNNIC (China Internet Network Information Center) added the item of 'What listed below cannot meet your demands?' in its survey. Thirty percent of the interviewees chose books, which ranked third that year. Among the 10 surveys carried out from July 2000 to January 2005, e-books ranked first of all the choices.

Obviously, digital publishing not only enriches the content and format of traditional publication, but also diversifies its production and selling, together with the consumption of ideas. The burgeoning, growing economic point the interaction of different media, which has arisen through digital publishing techniques shows a bright future.

2. Challenges of Digital Publishing in Publishing Education in China

New technology requires new knowledge, new skills, new wisdom, new marketing strategies and new management means. Compared with traditional publishing chain, digital publishing has a remarkable characteristic in that that every step of digital publishing is highly techinical, such as the techniques of content criterion and copyright protection; distributed websites' selling skills and museum management techniques; instant printing and displaying techniques. The digital publishing age brings forward more demanding and special standards for publishing workers.

Few people in traditional publishing have the required new knowledge and skills for digital publishing. Some traditional publishing houses don't keep pace with the digital publishing trend, failing to refresh ideas and to cultivate and absorb comprehensive skils, thus resulting in a series of tough problems like unenlightened ideas, digital technique deficiency, pirating, funds shortage, brain drain, and lack of skilled workers.

It's obvious that to apply new technology in the publishing field in China is very hard. The basic work of digital publishing in China is transferring paper books into e-books, and persons with good command of the required skills are limited. We can find another convincing example in website establishment and maintenance. Since workers mastering a general knowledge of publishing, digital techniques and management are badly lacking, it's a ubiquitous fact that, except in some certain large-scale publishing corporations, publishing houses face technical problems such as untimely information updating, inconvenient net interaction, limited operation functions and immature client service. It's chilling to find that some websites don't make any sense. To solve all these matters, skill support and professional education will be indispensable and crucial factors. We can reach the conclusion that training comprehensive, high-quality publishing talents is a really pressing issue.

In China, under the active system of higher education, publishing education has disadvantages such as homogeneous skill training methods. Undergraduate publishing education, to a different extent, fixes more on arts and less on science; more on knowledge acquisition, less on ability training; more on classroom teaching, less on practice; more on copy-editing, less on management; more on traditional publishing, less on multimedia interaction; more on standard traditions, less on unconventional ideas. The fact that both unmarketable skills and very marketable skills co-exist in the market reflects that the idea of skill cultivation lags behind the digital age, structure remains unbalanced, and methods are homogeneous. In addition, disadvantages can be found in professional education's targeting, orientation setting, courses and teaching methods. It's painful for talents trained by this method to adapt to the digital publishing trend, and consequently, the publishing industry in China is badly restricted.

It makes clear to all that in the digital publishing age, publishing is an information producing and serving industry that considers creativity its content, is stimulated by new technology, and takes the Internet as the channel and information management as the measure. Therefore, traditional publishing needs reforming. It should establish new cultivation goals and meet the demands of digital publishing, instructing needful, creative, skillful and competent professionals.

Considering the fact that publishing education has failed to catch up with digital publishing in China, how to build up a new idea, a group of instructors, establish new course systems and set up a new cultivating mode become new tasks for publishing education to study and work out urgently.

3. Effective Approaches to Cultivating Digital Publishing Skills

Publishing education in China has gone through a weather-beaten history during the twenty years. To our great joy, with the endeavor of publishing educators and people in the same camp, China's publishing education has achieved great growth. Now, it is demand-oriented, shunting from planned economy to market economy, combining content publishing with management knowledge, paying equal attention to both theory teaching and practice. In publishing education, a cross-link between arts and science is made to train comprehensive talents, copy editing becomes multimedia editing, education level upgrades from academy and undergraduate levels to master's and doctorate education; horizons are broadened from homeland to the whole world, publishing mode is changed from traditional to digital.

However, it's an acknowledged fact that publishing education in China doesn't yet make adequate preparations to cater to the huge market needs. Owing to the composite impact of several factors, it's difficult for actual publishing education to get acclimatized to the development demands of digital publishing. Unenlightened ideas, knowledge deficiency of the instructor's group, improper course systems and inadequate construction of a practical foundation are responsible primarily for that worrisome actual state. Measures should be taken to found new skill-training methods.

3.1 Conversion of the Publishing Education Concept

Educational concepts guide skill cultivation, which directly influences the final effect. With the introduction of new technology into the publishing industry and the interaction and amalgamation of multi-media, firstly, we should form a brand-new, adaptive concept—a concept of macroscopic publishing. In addition to the field of doctoral traditional publishing, we should emphasize more digital publishing, aiming at training high-level students of research and students of skillful practice. Only in this way can we instruct advanced professional students who can adapt to the demands of the modern publishing industry and the digital publishing age in China.

3.2 Course Setting Reform

Ji Baocheng, principal of Renmin University of China, pointed out that the homogeneity of course settings is worth concern. Blind sameness wastes educational resources, declines educational quality, and is not beneficial for graduate employment.

According to incomplete statistics, there are more than 130 academies and universities offering majors in editing and publishing in China, with a certain number of spots for master's and degrees. We have formed a professional education system of multiple specialties, levels, channels as well as specifications. In answering to the pressing demands of digital publishing, a few colleges have commenced carrying out digital publishing education, and subjects on modern publishing techniques have been set up in some universities. Take Peking University, Wuhan University, Beijing Institute of Graphic Communication, Hebei University, and Zhejiang Gongshang University, for example. Digital publishing has been brought into their undergraduate publishing courses; at the same time, due to various factors, a variety of courses on digital publishing technology are rather limited, and cannot satisfy the need of digital publishing development in China. The following classified table demonstrates the main courses of editing and publishing majors in the universities mentioned above, referring to Power Point of *The Establishment of a Core Course System of Editing & Publishing in China*, authored by Yanxiang Wang and Yunyan Yang, Department of Publishing, Beijing Institute of Graphic Communication.

A course system of 'subject + module' is adaptable, namely, regarding human sciences, social sciences, and natural sciences as basic subjects, and taking editing theories, communication theories, digital technology, operation and management, 'symbol' editing, law and regulations as modules, which achieves the integration of arts and science. Based on the recent demands of like digital publishing market and the respective features of publishing majors in universities, we can give prominence to the module of 'digital technology' to fulfill the pressing need of skilled workers with technical abilites.

Table 1: Main courses in the universities mentioned above.

University	Communication Theory	History	Editing Theory	Distribution	Management	Law & Regulation	Literature	Copyright Trade	Publishing Technology
Peking University	News Communication	China History of Editing and Publishing	The Outline of Editing	Basics of Publishing Distribution	Press Management	Basic of Book Law	Modern Chinese	Copyright and Book Foreign Trade	Modern Technology of Publishing
Wuhan University		China History of Publishing	Theory of Editing	Basics of Publishing Distribution	Book Enterprise Management	Basic of Book Law		External Book Trade	Modern Technology of Publishing Distribution
Beijing Institute of Graphic Communication	Communication	China History of Editing and Publishing	Editing	Distribution	Press Operation and Management	Publishing Law and Regulation	Modern Chinese	Copyright and Copyright Protection	Multi-media Publishing
Hebei University	The Outline of Communication	History of Book Publishing	The Outline of Editing and Publishing		Publishing Operation and Management	Publishing Law and Copyright Trade	Modern Chinese Culture	Publishing Law and Copyright Trade	Electronic Publishing Technology
Zhejiang Gongshang University	The Outline of Communication	China History of Publishing	The Outline of Publishing	Basics of Publishing Distribution	Press Operation and Management	Book Law and Regulation		Book Copyright Foreign Trade	Internet Editing

In addition, the teaching plan should be optimized to offer more opportunities for the students to participate in the practice, from which they can enhance their skills and actual operation abilities; required courses should be cut down while electives should be increased to leave more learning space for the students to choose by themselves. This amended teaching module will be good for cultivating professional, comprehensive and creative talents.

3.3 Strengthen the Construction of Instructor Groups in Digital Publishing Education

Teachers play the leading role in education; therefore, to cultivate digital publishing talents, a new-type of digital publishing instructors are indispensable. The selection of instructors of high quality is vital for establishing the cultivating module, carrying through the teaching reform, and enhancing the effects of digital publishing education.

At the present time, the structure of publishing education teaching in universities is mostly traditional. Teachers with comprehensive knowledge in education, publishing and digital techniques are extremely limited. Now, publishing talents with a high-level diploma are found to be experientially deficient in their education, publishing, digital technology, or practice, which leads to difficulties in carrying out courses on digital publishing technology. The effect of teaching is incomplete. To satisfy the demands of digital publishing teaching, it's really pressing to strengthen the quality of the digital publishing teaching group.

In our recent situation, two ways may be adopted to ease the problem of teaching group deficiency. On the one hand, giving attention to the training of digital publishing: for example, the Information Management Institute of Wuhan University offers advanced classes. On the other hand, absorbing the sophisticated techniques and latest information in the development of worldwide digital publishing and then introducing them to classrooms. It's helpful to train the student's ability to change digital content to digital publications, and the practical ability of multimedia interaction and amalgamation.

3.4 Reinforce the Construction of Digital Publishing's Practical Foundation

The major in editing and publishing requires social practice, which plays a crucial and indispensable part. It's beyond argument that social practice teaching is an effective way to deepen publishing theories, upgrade professional quality, and strengthen practical skills. Therefore, in the process of digital publishing talents training, we should highlight practical education, encouraging students to take part in practical activities to heighten their skills and research abilities. In this way, the competitiveness of carving-out and employment in digital publishing will be boosted. From this point, we can conclude that it's essential to strengthen the construction of digital publishing's practical foundation.

For the moment, through many years of hard work, the major of editing and publishing in China has achieved great progress—it is market-oriented, combined with the publishing industry, education and research, supported by enterprises and government-sponsored institutions, and a refined and steady digital publishing practical foundation has been set up. Publishing houses associate with society to cultivate eligible publishing talents. However, due to the persistent influence of the traditional publishing education concept, practical locations are mostly in publishing houses or distributive divisions, aiming at the training of literal and distributive capabilities, while practical locations for digital publishing, for example, websites and electronic presses, are not common enough, which reflects that publishing education pays inadequate attention to the instruction of digital skills.

With the transformation of publishing methods, digital publishing education in China should make amendments, focusing on social practice in digital publishing, extending the construction of practical foundation to digital publishing houses, offering new operational locations and training chances for digital skills cultivation.

At the same time, we should make full use of intramural facilities and resources. At capable universities, practice rooms can be opened to build favorable environments for digital practice education. Then, students can absorb, comprehend and apply digital publishing theories and techniques; students can be aroused to employ the facilities and resources to research and develop new technical items in digital publishing. Their practical, creative and operational digital capacities can be intensified.

To sum up, digital publishing is newly-emerging. As a new subject, there are many matters waiting for us to research and discuss more deeply, like the teaching concept, cultivation module, instructor group construction, teaching methods, social practice, teaching material betterment, accreditation as well as individual development. We should be level-headed enough to know that digital publishing is an inexorable trend. Digital publishing is the mainstream of the future publishing industry. So, we should explore new issues, new ways of thinking, conceive new modules and bring forward new solutions to provide powerful talents for the development and construction of digital publishing, and to make contributions to the cultural development of the publishing industry in China.

REFERENCES

2005. Digital Publishing Industry Waits For Transformation. *Economic News Daily.*

2005. "Four Barriers to the Development of Digital Publishing." *Communication Industry Newspaper.*

Feb. 15, 2006. Digital Technology Cause A New Publishing Conformation. E-book sale turns out to be 148 thousands. *Renmin Daily.*

Gang, Liang. 2005. DigiBook Upgrades Domestic Digital Publishing. *Sina Cartoo.*

Qu, Jinfan. 2006. Ready or not, Book Industry in China? *China Book Business Report.*

Yu, Yongzhan. 2006. New Technology VS Publishing: Blessing or Baffle? *China Book Business Report.*

Zhen, Xihao. 2005. Report 2004 of Digital Publishing Industry Development. *Sohu Digital World.*

On Editorial and Publishing Talent Development

Wu Ping

What type of editorial and publishing talents do we need in the twenty first century? How can university publishing education satisfy these needs? There are currently many theories on these issues in China. Each theory has its own set of requirements, conceptions, goals, and methods, and each has its own merits. It is worthwhile to analyze the situations and challenges facing the publishing education. Publishing students will enter a field where commercialization and civilization, traditional publishing and modern editing, creative thinking and technology are intertwined.

Since 1978 when China adopted the reform and opening policy, the publishing industry in China has made tremendous progress along with the development of Chinese economy, culture, and education. With 570 publishers and the vast Xinhua bookstore network around the country, the Chinese publishing industry is now releasing nearly 220,000 titles a year, with a total of 400,000 titles in print. New publishing concepts and practice, such as online bookstores, supply chain management, ERP, digital publishing and print on demand, are also taking hold in China. Still, the Chinese publishing industry has a long way to go.

Entering the twenty first century, the Chinese publishing industry will face fierce international competition; the demands for new technology, new ideas and innovation are stronger than ever before, and these all require high quality talents. Competition in twenty first century publishing is also the competition for creative publishing talents. College students are the product of higher education; they also reflect the quality of their alma mater. The publishing industry is in urgent need of innovative talents. To educate and provide publishing talents, university publishing education must know its goals as well as the means to achieve these goals.

1. The Three Components of Publishing Talent

1.1 Theoretical Component: Having Sound Editorial and Publishing Knowledge

Theories are always the guide for action. Theoretical knowledge helps students acquire the capability to analyze things thoroughly and scientifically; it helps students solve problems and find solutions; it also helps students confidently seek truth, and carry out work creatively. There are some people who think practice and hands-on experience are the best way to develop talent, but without theories, a publishing professional sooner or later will face productivity limitations, and those limitations can't be solved without the help of theories. So systematic theories are indispensable for students majoring in publishing and editing.

What kind of theoretical knowledge do the publishing talents need? In addition to philosophy, methodology, and management science, publishing talents also need to be knowledgeable in the following fields: publishing laws and regulations; theories about culture and cultural development; economics and marketing; logic and linguistics; the history of books and publishing; art, humanity and sociology; theories on public relations and psychology which are certainly helpful in advancing one's career; knowledge of international etiquette and commerce; knowledge of science and technology. All of these are the basic foundation for doing publishing and editorial work, and they are also the groundwork for the future editorial and publishing talents.

1.2 Technological Component: Familiar with Advanced Publishing Technologies

Publishing students should understand, acquire and master modern publishing technologies, especially digital technology. Digital technology has revolutionized traditional publishing in the areas of production, distribution, management and marketing. Technology can not only increase efficiency, reduce cost, and boost growth, but also improve the efficiency and management of the entire publishing industry. For many major U.S. and European STM publishers, the majority of revenues are now coming from digital and on-line products. For example, 70% of the income the Reed Elsevier group comes from their online service. According to the latest report given by the Association of American Publishers, "the total book sales in the U.S. increased 6.5% in 2005, and the sales electric books have increased 44.8%." New technologies bring enormous potential to publishing industry; a publishing professional will not be able to do a good job nowadays if he or she does not possess enough technological knowledge and skills. Technology-savvy talents will also raise the level of technology and management for the publishing industry as a whole.

1.3 Innovative Component: Being Creative

Since the late twentieth century, with the rapid development of science and technology, economies are increasingly globalized. Innovation becomes the driving force for a country's growth, and is the core of a country's competitive advantage. The Chinese government also emphasizes the strategic importance of innovation. The Chinese publishing industry has made great progress since the country adapted economic reform, but the Chinese publishing industry is not as strong as its Western competitors, especially in the area of innovation. There are not many Chinese books which have an impact by offering new thoughts and ideas, scientific discoveries and management theories. Therefore, it is the duty of the Chinese publishing industry to publish more high quality books and improve its competitiveness; the current situation also calls for publishing education to focus on the innovative component of talent development.

To sum up, the goal of publishing education is to provide professional talents with both theoretical knowledge and practical skills. The goal requires that the talents should have solid theoretical foundation as well as practical skills.

2. Creative Education as the Means of Achieving Talent Development Goals

Zhou Ji, the Chinese Minister of Education, said: "Compared to the graduates from top foreign universities, our college graduates are relatively weak in innovation and creativity, we are unable to educate enough top talents. It seems that our education system is unable to stimulate innovation, and our students don't have enough practical skills when they graduate." To change this situation, we must be more creative in publishing talent development.

2.1 Emphasizing All-round Talent Development

Creative editorial and publishing talents should first be all-round talents. The innovative and critical-thinking aspect of a talent is closely related to one's other qualities. The emphasis on theoretical knowledge does not mean it is the only important thing; on the contrary, a one-dimensional knowledge structure could not support a successful publishing career. A country's higher education should create an atmosphere for the development of all-round students, provide students with knowledge of various fields and satisfy their learning needs, which is in accordance with the concepts of "all-round man" of German philosopher Karl Jaspers, and the concepts of "complete man," "man as a man" and "free man" of American educator Robert M. Hutchins. For example, Harvard University's mission is "To advance Learning and perpetuate it to Posterity," and the university places great importance on the development of all-round talents, who should be highly and insightfully educated and fully developed both emotionally and intellectually. By 1998, 35 Harvard University faculty members and thirty eight of its graduates had won the Nobel Prize. Consequently, it has become one of the most successful universities in the world in educating creative talents, and provides a model for talent development in higher education.

Creative education is comprehensive and all-round. The emphasis on theoretical knowledge does not mean that students should become traditional learned scholars, but ones who are capable of seizing current opportunity and have an understanding of the problems of the publishing industry, and therefore are capable of solving them. Editorial and publishing work surely ask for various backgrounds of expertise, such as selecting and editing manuscripts. But at the same time there is also a need for the editors' insight reflecting the outcomes of China's creative activities. In developing the Chinese publishing industry and establishing an open, competitive and orderly cultural market system, we need more comprehensive and all-round editorial and publishing talents. Higher education should not only teach students theoretical knowledge, but also the quality of being a true citizen.

2.2 Following the Trend

The development of modern society takes place in an unprecedented international and domestic environment. Consequently, higher education for publishing should cultivate creative talents in accordance with the needs of the time. In the past twenty years since China's economic reform, the publishing industry has undergone tremendous change. However, it should be noted that the Chinese publishing industry's competitiveness is still behind its international counterparts.

Take scientific journal publishing for example. Currently, European and American journals account for over 96% of international core journals and Western publishers control almost all professional and scientific publishing. To compete with them, China should also have plenty of publishing talents who understand the rules, the global market, and possess the latest marketing and management knowledge and skills. The Hong Kong publisher Sino United Publishing (Holdings) Limited has been exploring the overseas Chinese book market for years and has succeeded in doing so. The company is now recognized as a major Chinese book distributor in the international market. Mainland Chinese publishers need to learn from such examples and work on a winning international strategy.

As another example, digital technology poses a challenge to traditional paper-based publishing. This trend is further supported by readers who embrace the new technology. Digital publishing is a major theme for publishing in the twenty first century. To meet the challenge, the Chinese publishing industry should step up its technology innovation and creative talent development.

Every industry has its own challenge at any given time; the Chinese publishing industry in the twenty first century will face a sea change in industry structure, publishing concept and technology. The change will provide enormous opportunity and potential for publishing talent development.

2.3 Emphasizing Talents with Hands-on Experience

Creative education should combine the reality and theory of the industry while higher education in this area should provide students opportunities to take on real tasks in the industry, such as doing internships in publishing companies, bookstores, studios and private publishing firms. The focus of these activities is to let students become familiar with difficulties and challenges in the real world, and test their theoretical knowledge in a hands-on process. They will see first hand the issues and problems facing the industry, such as the facts that many Chinese publishers rely heavily on the business of study-aid materials, too many books copy each other, are poorly edited and shabbily published. This experience will hopefully intrigue the students' critical thinking.

The approach of capability development through hands-on work breaks the traditional model of education, which separates the education environment and real world, disconnects theory and practice, and distances talents from the market. The new approach will lay the foundation of connecting publishing education with the industry.

Science and technology help to forge the competitive edge of the publishing industry, and human resources are always the key factor. Presently, as new technologies such as digital publishing and online book selling become part of the publishing industry, editorial and publishing professionals should be versatile and have strong scientific and technological backgrounds. Creative education requires students, future editorial and publishing professionals to have both science and humanity qualities, as well as the capability of being innovative and forward-thinking, mastering technologies of the trade, all these are also in accordance with the goals of creative talent development.

References

Liu, Yandong. "Innovation Is a Basic Function of the University." *China Education* 1 Sep. 2006: 3.

Wu, Shulin. "Build a New Nation, Grow the Publishing Industry." *China Book Business Report* 20 June 2006: 2.

The Multi-Facet Mode of Publishing Human Resource Development in the Digital Age

Sun Fan

The Chinese Publishing Bureau, in the newly issued *Guideline of Publishing Human Resource Management 2005–2010*, points out that "Significant achievements have been made in developing publishing professionals. The overall volume, quality and composition of publishing human resources have undergone great changes. However, the current situation calls for further development in team building and working mechanisms." There is an urgent shortage of senior professionals who are acquainted with both publication and management across media, and who are familiar with both the domestic and the overseas market. Therefore, the development of publishing human resources must be given enough attention, and much effort shall be directed to build an elite publishing human resource pool.

Besides, the Digital Age has also brought unprecedented challenges to publishing education in universities. It calls for the development of publishing professionals who have more than one expertise and who are able to deal with the global market in a creative way. The discussion of the mode of publishing education is of great importance in both the academic field and in real practice because it will decide the future direction and the wellbeing of the publishing industry. This essay, based on the experience of successful publishing entities both at home and abroad, creatively brings forward a multi-facet education mode which integrates resources within the university, the enterprises, and worldwide resources.

1. Mode A: Integrating Resources within the University

The development of publishing human resources shall be supported by advanced education philosophies and a flexible education system. It should make full use of the various resources in the university as well as in its schools. Cooperation should also be fostered across schools in order to cultivate professionals with more than one expertise.

Students in a publishing major should be encouraged to take courses offered by other schools as well as compulsory courses offered by their own school. As publishing is a business, students should also take courses relating to finance, statistics, sales and marketing, management, commercial law, etc. Some overseas publishing schools even send their students directly to the Business School to receive related training.

Publishing undergraduates shall be recommended or encouraged to go to the schools of other majors to further their studies, in the form of graduate studies or dual-major studies. The priority should be given to those majors which are in great need of recent years, such as economics, management, journalism, law, foreign languages, and computer science. The dual major can take the form of "3+2": 3 years to study publication, and 2 years to study other majors.

Senior students of other majors should be encouraged to take publishing science as their minor or as their major in their graduate studies. The practice of the New York University is highly recommended. When recruiting students for its MA class in publishing, it chooses students with either an arts or sciences background. Its curriculum includes both a systematic survey of publishing professional knowledge, and the latest trends of scientific development related to the publishing industry. The globalization of the publishing industry is also given much attention. Therefore, getting approval from the administration to register publishing science as a minor for students of other majors is a priority at present.

Senior students of the publishing major and other majors should be encouraged to take the annual "Certifying Examination for Publishing Professionals." If more college students graduate with both a university diploma and a professional certificate, the overall situation of the publishing industry will improve. Heilongjiang University is a good example in this case. It introduced the certifying examination into its entrepreneuring workshop in 2004. Many undergraduates and postgraduates have taken the training and the exam.

2. Mode B: Integrating Resources of Universities and Enterprises

Universities and enterprises should join forces by integrating their human resources, information and equipment. The cooperation pattern could be universities and publishing entities such as publishing houses, news agencies, and bookstores; universities and the administrative authorities of the publishing industry; universities and the publishing societies. As to the cooperation between universities and enterprises, there are plenty of successful cases both at home and abroad.

One successful case comes from MIT in the USA. Its publishing school initiated a six-week workshop in which students were not only given all-round training about the process of publishing and distributing as well as the specific techniques involved, but also were introduced to experts in this field. Students listened to lectures given by those experts, and also cooperated with those experts in the "Publishing House Simulation Lab." In this way, students gained first hand experience in close-to-life practice as well as necessary professional knowledge that will enable their future success in this field.

The pioneer to advocate this mode of education in China should be Wuhan University, the Xinhua Bookstore, and the Journalism and Publishing Bureau of

Hubei Province. With the joint efforts of the three, China's first degree in publishing science came into being in 1984. And then, many universities and enterprises followed suit, with Peking University pairing with Peking University Press, Beijing Normal University with its university press, and Suzhou University with its university press. Specifically, Heilongjiang University has been working successfully with Harbin Xuefu Bookstore, Jinghua Bookstore, the Heilongjiang Publishing House, the Harbin Publishing House, Heilongjiang Morning News, Beijing Youth Newspaper, Heilongjiang Journalism and Publishing Bureau, and Heilongjiang Publishing Research Institution.

These universities and enterprises have supported each other and created a win-win situation. The enterprises provide the universities with internship opportunities, lectures by professionals, and employment opportunities for university graduates. On the other hand, the universities offer on-the-job training and further education to enterprise employees.

All the experiences from China and other countries of the world have proved that bilateral cooperation between universities and publishing entities is a good mode of education, beneficial to both sides. It has been proved to be an effective way to develop human resources for the publishing industry in the Digital Age. Its future perspective is rosy, and many attempts to upgrade this cooperation are underway.

2.1 Employing Part-Time Professors

It has been proved to be a successful practice to employ senior publishing professionals with rich pertinent experience as part-time professors in the university. Besides giving lectures, the part-time professors should also be invited to get involved more in curriculum drafting and revision, project application, and internship arrangement. Their suggestions should be given due attention since they are working in the real market.

2.2 Encouraging Publishing Professionals to Further their Education

Mid-term and long-term career plans should be drafted for publishing professionals. They should be encouraged to further their education in various ways, such as certificate studying and night school training. They should also be given priority when universities evaluate applicants. Therefore, the development of human resources for the publishing industry relies both on the education of students in universities and on the on-the-job training of current publishing professionals. Only in this way can the overall quality and the composition of the publishing professionals be elevated.

2.3 Establishing an Internship Base

Establishing an Internship Base at the publishing entities will not only improve students' hands-on experience, but also facilitate the research work conducted by teachers. It will thoroughly overthrow the traditional approach to publishing education which emphasizes theories in books while neglecting practice. In this way, both students and teachers will be able to update their knowledge in the publishing industry and prepare themselves better for the job.

2.4 Setting up Joint Labs

The "Publishing House Simulation Lab" of MIT could be taken as a role model for Chinese universities. Chinese universities may consider setting up such labs as "Publishing House Simulation Lab," "Bookstore simulation lab," and "News Agency Simulation Lab." These labs may be newly set up with the university budget, or utilize the established training base in the publishing houses, bookstores and news agencies. In this way, the resources within universities and enterprises will be put to full use.

2.5 Integrating Research, Education and Production.

By joining hands in human resource development, the cooperation between publishing education institutions and publishing entities will be enhanced. This integration will speed up the evolution and innovation of research, education and production in the publishing industry.

2.6 Awards and Scholarships

Publishing entities may set up awards and scholarships for teachers and students who have made significant contributions in this field. For students, they may act as an encouragement; for teachers, they will supplement the research budget; for enterprises, scholarships and awards may give them an opportunity to find potential qualified employees.

2.7 Joining Hands in On-the-Job Training

The publishing societies and big publishing companies in European countries and Japan conduct training courses of all kinds each year. Since the introduction of the Chinese National Certifying Examination of Publishing Professionals in 2002, a great number of teachers are needed in face of the increasing number of training courses for this exam. Thus, the cooperation of universities and publishing enterprises are called for. Many provinces and cities have taken the first step and reaped early rewards. Heilongjiang University joined hands with Heilongjiang Journalism and Publishing Bureau in 2006, and they are expecting success.

3. Mode C: Integrating Resources at Home and Abroad

With the globalization of the publishing industry, modern publishing companies are in great need of professionals who understand both the market and the latest techniques, and who are able to introduce Chinese companies to the world. Integrating resources in China and in other countries in publishing education has become an irreversible trend.

3.1 Setting Up a Staff-Training Center

Editing and Publication is a newly emerged major in which most university teachers do not have the necessary education background. Their unfamiliarity with modern technologies brought about by the Digital Age seems to cause even more confusion in their teaching career. Therefore, a national staff training center is greatly needed where teachers may receive formal training in a systematic way from there.

3.2 Establishing a Publishing Research Network

The Digital Age calls for creative ways to upgrade teaching practices. Networking is obviously one option we should take into consideration. In China, a national publishing research network should be set up to facilitate communication between teachers, students and professionals. With the help of the network, people could keep track of the latest trends in publishing development, the change in publishing policies, the availability of training opportunities, and so on. In this way, the publishing industry could be upgraded as a whole.

3.3 Globalizing Publishing Education

It is a necessity for the Chinese publishing industry and education to step onto the global stage. The first step is to strengthen the relationship with the world famous universities which also offer publishing courses. These universities include Stanford University, University of California at Berkeley, New York University, Pace University, University of Chicago, MIT, University of Denver, Baltimore University in the USA, and several universities in Britain and Japan. The bilateral communication can be achieved through staff and student exchange programs, short-term training sessions, and seminars. In this way, Chinese universities can absorb the advanced education philosophies and experiences related to publishing education, and be able to develop publishing human resources that are able to adapt to the world publishing market in the digital age.

The department of editing and publishing of Heilongjiang University is located at the north eastern part of China, bordering Russia, Korea, and Japan. It should utilize its geographical advantags to step out of China and seek cooperation opportunities with the universities and publishing entities in those developed countries.

All in all, the advancement of the Chinese publishing industry depends on a large group of elite editors, publishers and distributors who are able to progress with time. However, the development of such a group is a time-consuming systematic project. It requires generations of publishing educators and administrators to take a strategic perspective and to devote all their efforts to achieve. Therefore, we should broaden our vision and explore new modes of education, in order to gain a competitive position in the fierce competition for publishing talents.

REFERENCES

Deng, Benzhang. 2005. The Strategic Goal and Approach for Publishing Professional Development. *Editing and Publishing Study* (11).

Liu, Yongjun and Li Hongkui. 2005. A Survey of Chinese Editing and Publishing Education in 20 years. *Editing and Publishing Study* (2).

Song, Muwen. 2005. An Overview of Editing and Publication Education in Chinese Universities and Suggestions on Improvement. *Editing and Publishing Study* (11).

Xiao, Dongfa. 2003. Thoughts on the Chinese Editing and Publication Education. *Editors' Companion* (1).

Yu, Youfa. 2005. Human Resouce Development of Modern Publishing Professionals in China. *Editing and Publishing Study* (12).

Yu, Youxian. 2003. Modern Publishing Education and Human Resouce Development. *Publication Reference* (5).

Yu, Youxian. 2004. Publising Industry and Human Resouces. *Modern Publishing Industry.*

Comparison and Contrasts in Sino-American Talent Development for Publication

Lin Yuyin

1. Comparison in Historical Developments

1.1 Undertaking Talent Development for the Publishing Industry in the U.S.

U.S. publishing talent development can be traced back to the early years after the Civil War. For example, a printers-editors training class was given by Washington & Lee University in 1869. After that, the training of employees mainly appeared in the way of apprenticing, thereby, the knowledge and skills for publication were not systematic and could not be advanced. Many novices bumped into this business without any training; many of them had never even known about the publishing industry.

The specialized development of talents for publishing started in the 1970s and then increased. With the status of the publishing industry rising and business competition growing sharply, more and more importance was attached to talent development. A report titled "Professionals By Chance," issued in 1977 by the Educational Commission of the Association of American Publishers (AAP), explained the necessity and importance of developing skills, and called on AAP members for increasing investment in it. Henceforward, publishing companies strengthened employee training.

The McGraw-Hill Company, for example, set up a professional training center, which was in charge of the regular or irregular training of employees. And the tradition has been kept up.

Meanwhile, many U.S. universities started publishing specialties or curriculums. Most of the universities and publishers' associations still held various short-term training classes. According to an incomplete statistic, there are so far more than ten universities and colleges in the U.S. that have started publishing specialties, such as Pace University, Columbia University, New York University, the University of Denver, the University of Chicago, Stanford University, and Syracuse University. Further, many higher institutions have publishing curriculums, such as George Washington University, "Books World" in Pacific Rim University, and Northwestern University that are systematically provided for regular students, or advanced students, and also there are lectures provided at night for employees working in the business.

In the U.S., the development of publishing talents has made stable progress since the 1970s. And it notably shows a trend of internationalization.

Firstly, on the one hand, expression of this trend is found in the globalization of publishing educational entities. Now the IAPE (The International Association for Publishing Education) has been set up between America and Canada, Britain, Australia, and France, with the idea of promoting and strengthening the international information exchange between professional organizations, individuals and academic institutes that are related to education and publishing. On the other hand, there are more and more publishing and education companies in the U.S. cooperating with their counterparts in other countries all over the world. They aim to develop common talents for their businesses.

Secondly, the trend is expressed through the internationalization of developing subjects. In the U.S., there are more and more publishing and education organizations starting to recruit overseas students.

Thirdly, the trend is expressed in the globalization of curricular contents. Most organizations have newly added contents such as international publishing industry, international publishing cooperation, international copyright trade, and international book exhibition.

1.2 The Historical Retrospect to the Development of Publishing Talents in China

There is a history of over 2000 years of publishing activities in China, but for a long time the community of publishing was lacking a scientific grasp and editorial and publishing theory. So it is no surprise that there was a controversy about "whether there is a theory in editing or publishing" existing in the community. The controversy led to a delayed construction of the publishing and editing subject, which directly influenced the development of publishing talents. And that issue was not on the routine agenda for a long time.

In 1983, Hu Qiaomu submitted to the Ministry of Education a proposition to offer an editing theory curriculum on a trial basis in some universities. In 1984, the Ministry authorized Beijing, Fudan, and Nankai University to establish an editing theory specialty. After that, Qinghua and Chinese Technology University were permitted to set it up, and it also was offered in Henan University, Shanghai University, as well as Sichuan University. Furthermore, Qinghuan and Wuhan University set up a second bachelor's in publishing education.

So far, according to an incomplete statistic, there are forty colleges and universities all over the country that have offered the specialty of publishing, editing, or distributing. In addition to those mentioned above, they still include Beijing Printing College, Beijing Normal University, Northeast Normal University, Nanjing University, Inner Mongolian University, and Guangxi University For Nationalities, and many short training programs.

From 1999 to today, publishing skills education has been developed so strongly that the current community brings forth two different opinions on it. One is a view of regulating progress which has figured that moving too fast in the progress of publishing education, with too many publishing programs, and too much student recruitment will lead to a graduate supply that exceeds the demands of the market, thus making it difficult for graduates to find a job. The other is a view of expansion which has figured that we should establish and hold new concepts of "big publishing" and "big editing" to develop talents suitable for all media systems such as books, newspapers, magazines, broadcasting, film and TV, video, electronic and Internet.

1.3 Findings

Comparison of the historical and existing statuses of publishing skill development between China and the U.S., leads to these conclusions:

1. In the U.S. skill development has an early start and stable advancement; in contrast, in China it was late, but has developed quickly.
2. In China and the U.S. publishing skills went from being neglected to having importance attached to it.
3. In the U.S., it grew from apprenticing inside companies to training in business organizations and to internationalizing development; whereas in China it turned from master-apprentice learning inside a publishing house to mainly relying on education in colleges and universities; however, what we have done in the training of international publishing students is not good enough.

2. Comparison in the Form of Skill Development

2.1 Talent Developing for Publishing in the U.S.

There are several ways in which talents are developed for the publishing business in the U.S. Briefly these include:

1. Master's level Education: for example, MS in publishing at Pace, New York University; MA in Emerson University; MS in journalism in the School of Journalism, Northwestern University, and Columbia University.
2. Education in regular college courses, for example, the publishing specialties at Pace, Stanford, Chicago, and Queens University; in technological and educational specialties at the University of California; and in editing design and plate-making specialties at Syracuse University.
3. Training in Summer College: summer training classes are set up widely in Stanford, Denver, Columbia, and New York University. They provide two-to-six-week training for incumbent staff or employees who wish to enter the publishing business. The form of training includes the training of publishing certificates, regular college courses, or even postgraduate diplomas and non-diplomas.
4. Reinforced course seminar, also called advanced publishing management seminar. Aiming as some special topic or subject such as book exhibition or copyright trade, it provides a reinforced training, such as Stanford and Northwestern University's seminars.

5. Various training classes held by publishing associations; for example, by the Educational Commission of Association of the American Publishers (AAP).

6. Training classes held by publishing companies. These were popular in the 1960's and 1970's; however, some publishing firms such as Macmillan/McGraw Hill and the Chicago University.

The six forms described above can be generally divided into two major kinds: diploma or regular education, which includes numbers one and two; non-diploma or irregular education, 4-6; only 3 mixes diploma and non-diploma education.

2.2 Talent Development for Publishing in China

There are also various forms for developing talents for the publishing business in China. These include:

1. Doctoral degree: at present, there is no doctorate in publishing per se. But some universities have recruited doctoral students majoring in publishing in other doctoral programs such as Library and Information Science. For example, a doctoral degree in this major has been offered at Beijing University, Chinese Media University, and Wuhan University.

2. Master's degree: so far, publication theory is still not listed under the specialty category for the master's degree. But the Ministry of Education has authorized Beijing Printing College and Henan University to recruit and develop students for master's degrees majoring in publication. In addition, master's students in this major have been enrolled under related specialties in Beijing University, Wuhan University, and Nanjing University.

3. Regular college courses: since the publishing major has been categorized as a regular college course, there are more than forty universities, such as Beijing, Fudan, Nankai, Qinghua, Wuhan, Henan, Sichuan, and Shanghai University that have opened the education program.

4. Adult continuing education: mainly includes correspondence specialties, evening school, and refresher classes, as well as qualification training classes aimed toward employees held by governmental departments. The latter form has seen rapid growth in recent years.

Similarly, the forms of numbers 1-3 can be viewed as diploma education; 4 blends diploma and non-diploma education.

2.3 Findings

1. There is no single form of talent development in both China and the U.S., and there are many arrangements, from non-diploma (or irregular) education to diploma education, from undergraduate courses to master's degree courses and even doctoral degree education.

Notably, doctoral education has appeared in China, but not in the U.S. Why does it not appear in the U.S.? If students will study publishing from the perspective of culture, they should enter schools of liberal arts, departments of social science, or media departments at a university; if students will study publishing from the perspective of modern technology, they should major in an Information doctoral degree. A person with a doctoral degree should not engage in routine work. A professor, Bench, of New York University said that doctoral graduates are better suited to enter institutes for research or universities for teaching. If we want a deputy manager general of publishing, he or she needn't have a doctorate; it's enough for him or her to hold an MBA or master's degree.

2. The institutions engaging in this kind of education are all schools, whether in China or in the U.S. The difference is that in the U.S., in addition to schools, business associations and publishing firms also hold a great number of training classes; whereas in China, specialty training beyond schools is mainly held by governmental departments.

3. As to the period of development, short-term training prevails in the U.S., whereas long-term education is popular in China. In the U.S., the training period is generally several weeks. Even if it is a diploma education at a university, the courses will focus on specialty knowledge and skills, not occupying three or four years; but in China, diploma courses are the main form, which will occupy three or four years and will include specialty courses, plus theory, philosophy, politics, liberal arts, etc.

3. Comparison in Development Goals

From Bench's remarks mentioned above, we learn that in the U.S., Americans view publishing theory as a subject of strong application, and they pay special attention to the development of ability and capacity. Their goals focus on practical talents, on vitalizing talents, and on problem-solving ability. In contrast, Chinese publishing education attaches importance to handing over knowledge, and the goal of development is to build a publishing student of high scholarship.

Many domestic universities hold firm to such a goal: this specialty will develop special, advanced publication talents who grasp basic theory, have basic knowledge of the Chinese language, have systematic publishing theory knowledge and skills, and are able to engage in the editing, publishing, and distributing business, as well as in teaching and research work, in such fields as book publishing, journalism, or cultural and educational departments.

From there, we can easily see that our goal is mainly aimed at theory-led or scholarship-led skill. It impressed me that Bench said his impression of Chinese publication and education is that publication is taken as a special knowledge or subject and not a commercial activity.

4. Comparison of Curriculum Design

Owing to the different goals of China and the U.S., curriculum design is consequently different.

In curricular arrangements in China, the theory courses occur prior to skills courses, and the publishing specialty, set up in the school of Liberal Arts, is always inclined toward courses in literature and language. Take the publishing curriculum design for class 2005 in Guangxi University as an example. Such courses as the Common Required Theory course, General Education, and the basic course for Chinese Language and Literature, totally take 84 credits, accounting for 52.5% of the required 160 credits. The basic major courses include classical literature, modern and contemporary literature, as well as foreign literature. So real major skills courses are only a part of the curriculum.

In the U.S., the major course design is characterized by practicality and skill-led courses. Furthermore, the credit aims generally are not high, thirty or forty credits for graduation, compared with over 100 credits in China.

From the design of a ten-week publication course for postgraduates at Emory University, we can learn that Americans pay very much attention to practical education.

In the first week, students take some article as an example to discuss what kind of writing can be published and to learn how to revise articles.

In the second week, students learn how to deal with periodicals and how to choose a suitable way to contribute articles.

In the third week, students cover what the magazine editor expects.

In the fourth week, students learn some problems related to book publication.

In the fifth week, students learn some problems related to book printing.

In the sixth week, students learn some problems related to book publishing.

In the seventh week, students work out of the manual of the workings of examine and revision.

In the eighth week, students learn new means available to authors and publishers.

In the ninth week, students visit a printing works.

In the tenth week, students submit complete projects.

5. Comparison in Teaching Approaches

In the U.S., publication teaching focuses on a heuristic approach and the learner's initiative. In class, students get used to discussing with teachers as an equal. Teaching is closely interconnected to practice, and so employs intuitional instruction and simulation teaching. For example, the class usually enters a publishing company, a printing works, or bookstore and ends up with an intuitional approach.

On the other hand, New York University and Hartford University always adopt the latter approach. They organize students to build a publishing house and let students learn everything from practice.

It is an approach of cooperation between schools and the publishing community. The university provides a workplace, equipment, and teaching faculties, while the publishing community offers capital and teachers. They mutually build a school for this major. This mode is employed very commonly in the U.S.

In contrast, publication teaching in a Chinese classroom, because of many theory courses, high credits, and urgent teaching time, mainly consists of teachers' lecturing; what's more, most teachers are novices in the practice of publishing. Meanwhile, due to lack of capital and time, there is less practicing in class.

To sum up, there is a common ground in publishing talent development. But owing to different social and economic systems, as well as cultural traditions, there are also many differences. We cannot simply make judgments. It needs a dialectical aptitude to view them and benefit from them.

REFERENCES

Lu, Benrui. *Introduction to Foreign Publication.* Shenyang: Liaohai Publishing House. 2003.

Xu, Lifang. Close to American Publication Education. *China Book Trade* (7) 22. 2005.

Hu, Qiaomu. *A Letter to the Ministy of Education on Opening Publication Major on Trial in Universities. Modern Chinese Historical Materials (modern part).* Volume III. Shandong: Shandong Education Publishing House. 2001.

Xiao, Dongfa and Xu Huan. Thinking and Exploring for Education of Publication Theory. *Journal Seek* (1): 37-39. 2003.

Application of a Task-Based Model in the Teaching of Digital Publishing Technology

Wang Qiuju & Wang Hongmei

Introduction

In the history of the development of the publishing industry, the advancement of technology plays a very important role in pushing the industry forward. In recent years, with the fast development of multimedia and network technology, there is a trend of high-speed increase in the digital publishing industry represented by digital games, books, newspapers, magazines, etc. which has become an important new growth point of the publishing industry. The position and influence of digital publications have become established by their advantages. Many universities in China have begun technology of digital publishing courses for students majoring in editing and publishing. Compared with other courses, these are highly practical, creative, and up-to-date. In the process of teaching, the teacher can promote students' learning by using appropriate teaching models. As part of the teaching system design, teaching models provide a blueprint for teaching and exercise by their important theoretical and practical functions. The writer applies a task-based teaching model to the practice of teaching the technology of digital publishing and has obtained good results.

1. Brief Introduction of Task-Based Teaching Model

Teaching models refer to steady structures and forms developed in the process of teaching in certain pedagogical settings, under the guidance of certain theories of pedagogy. They are summaries of those teaching thoughts, teaching methodologies and teaching forms. They are instruments and methodologies of teaching process thinking from an overall perspective. The task-based teaching model is based on the learning theory of constructivism and changes from the knowledge-imparting teaching theory to problem-solving and task-completing, a multi-interactive teaching theory. It changes reproduction teaching to exploration teaching and puts students in an active learning position. In the process of learning, learning activities are combined with tasks and students' learning interests and motivations are initiated and maintained through exploring problems. In the real teaching setting, students learn with a real task and, therefore, have the initiative to learn, while the teacher's role in this process is to enlighten and encourage students. In task-based teaching model, the whole process of teaching revolves around several specific tasks; the introduction and learning of basic knowledge and skills are conducted through the process of completing the tasks. For example, while teaching sound information editing, the content of teaching can be divided into such specific tasks as the adjustment of the order of sound materials, the connection, mixture, and deletion of sound materials and the addition of special effects. Students can learn the knowledge and skills of sound information editing through the process of completing the tasks.

The important point of task-based teaching is the design of learning tasks. Students' learning is done in the process of exploring the tasks, and their desire for the knowledge and skills of the technology of digital publishing is created also in the process of exploration. The teacher arranges the knowledge to be learned to be one or several tasks, and students find the solution to the problem through analysis, discussion, self-exploration, cooperation and with the help of the teacher. In the process of accomplishing the tasks, students reconstruct the knowledge to be learned. For example, the organization of the information in network publications is non-linear and can be realized by hyper-links and different links are created differently. While teaching this part, a teacher can take the knowledge to be learned, such as the creation and management of hyper-links and MAP technology, into several tasks and students can learn the relevant knowledge in the process of finishing the tasks. In the learning process, students' learning is not simply a transfer of knowledge from the outside to the inside, but rather a process of active reconstruction of knowledge and experience. The theory of "learning by doing" and "learning while doing" should be advocated. Students master the skills of designing and creating digital publications during the process of accomplishing the tasks.

From the students' perspective, task-based learning is a method with specific learning objectives, and is applicable to the learning of operational knowledge and skills. An a certain stage of learning, students can immediately see the results of their learning, experience the pleasure of success and strengthen their confidence in learning by actually finishing a series of tasks revolving around a specific objective. From the teacher's perspective, task-based teaching is a model based on the teaching theory of constructivism, and is applicable to foster students' overall ability in practice.

2. The Different Levels of Tasks Designed in Teaching the Technology of Digital Publishing

In designing tasks, the differences of the students as well as the characteristics and the degree of difficulty of the knowledge should be considered. In general, the tasks should be designed in three levels as follows:

Basic tasks. The requirements for these tasks are very clear. They contain the knowledge and methods to be learned. The teacher gives a specific example and the students do the tasks according to the teacher's requirements. As long as the students can do the tasks according to the teacher's requirements, they have almost mastered the knowledge and skills required to do these tasks. Tasks on this level, such as the creation of different types of network multimedia magazines, are mainly suitable to students who are still new to the knowledge and skills and can be conducted in class.

Higher-level tasks. The teacher only gives part of the detailed requirements for these tasks without any specific examples. Students are given the space for free development. They are allowed to have different styles and methods and are encouraged to create their own original works. Tasks on this level, such as the making of network animation, are suitable for students who can carry out some creative activities after finishing the basic tasks.

Open tasks. The teacher only gives a few requirements for these tasks and the content and form are to be organized and arranged by the students themselves. These tasks are more suitable to the comprehensive exercises of modules in activity classes. Take the comprehensive exercises of the technology of digital publishing for an example: students can be asked to design a digital newspaper or a digital magazine, which should contain navigation, pictures, texts, art characters, columns, sound, image and animation, etc. The content and the layout can be completely decided by the students.

3. The Relationship of the Different Instructional Elements in a Task-Based Teaching Model

Learners vs. the Teacher

The application of the task-based teaching model has, to some extent, smashed the trammels of traditional teaching and changed students' and teachers' traditional roles in class. The task-based teaching model has changed the teacher-centered, one-way knowledge-imparting teaching into a two-way, cooperative development teaching in which teacher initiates and students explore. The application of this model has changed dramatically the teacher is and students' role in class with the teacher becoming the organizer, instructor and encourager of the students. The teacher's leading function is not mainly reflected in class, but rather reflected before class in preparing for the class, doing such homework as designing learning materials, selecting teaching models and designing tasks, etc. Students have become the subject of cognitive learning, information processing and the active constructors of knowledge and meanings.

Learners vs. Learners

3.1 Partnership

In order to finish a task, learners become partners. In the process of learning, they cooperate with and help each other. They divide the task and share each other's individual thoughts and wisdom. The communication among students can help them obtain knowledge from different perspectives and, therefore, develop students' thinking abilities. In the learning process, students need to express their solutions accurately and, therefore, their expressive abilities can be trained. The communication among students can build their solidarity and foster students' awareness and abilities of cooperation, which is beneficial to their development. Effective learning can not be dependent merely on imitation and memory. Self-exploration, personal practice and cooperative communication are some of the most important ways for students to obtain the basic knowledge and skills of the technology of digital publishing. Students of different cognitive levels and learning abilities are put into small groups and they collectively finish a learning task through helping and encouraging each other. The construction of a media network requires the cooperation of many people and individual endeavors always turned out to be inadequate. Therefore, teachers should consider how to foster students' awareness of cooperation while designing their courses. For example, students can be asked to design and create different types of publications, like a digital newspaper or a magazine, in groups. They have to first decide the theme of the publication, the structure, the arrangement and format and finally create a draft. These tasks can be divided among students according to their interests, cognitive levels and learning abilities, one module each, and accomplish them jointly.

3.2 Competitiveness

Competitiveness exists when learners have to finish the task divided individually. For example, after an explanation of the method of making network multi-media digital magazine, the teacher assigns the tasks to be finished individually, leaving the content to be decided by the students themselves. The learning result can be graded in four levels, with 10% of A, 20%of B, 40%of C, 20% of D and 10% of E. Competitiveness can help improve students' initiative in learning and efficiency. In the learning process, some students lack the awareness of self-exploration because of the influence of a long-time habit; some students do not have a strong sense of self-study, they don't have a habit of independent thinking, they intend to obtain knowledge directly from the teacher instead of solving the problem themselves. All these problems affect the overall result of teaching to some extent. Therefore, teachers should pay attention in order to elicit and guide students in the course of teaching and actually improve their abilities to obtain knowledge on their own initiative through the training of abilities.

Conclusion

The practice of teaching indicates that, through the process of accomplishing tasks, by debating, supplementation, and modification of different ideas, students can deepen their understanding of current problems, observe and understand problems from different aspects and come up with many different solutions to the same problem. They can be guided to participate in creative activities and foster their creative abilities. The application of a task-based teaching model can not only enable students to master firmly most of the necessary knowledge and skills, but also improve their ability to solve problems. When the learning process is finished, students can not only strengthen their confidence in learning, but also be able to conclude and express the knowledge and methods using their own language and styles. They are able to apply the knowledge to solve variant problems. Based on the analysis of the statistics of a questionnaire, this teaching model can solve some of the problems existing in traditional teaching, arouse student's enthusiasm and initiative in learning, foster student's coöperative abilities, promote students learning and improve the efficiency of teaching in class.

REFERENCES

Gao, Wen. 2002. *Models of Teaching.* Shanghai: Publishing House of Shanghai Education

Guo, Shandu. "Explorative Teaching Model and Modern Education Technology." *Network of Education and Science Studies.* http://www.edu.cn/20010827/209290.shtml

He, Kekang. "Constructivism—the Theoretical Basis for Traditional Teaching Reform." *Information Network of Chengdu Education.*

Hei, Kekang and Li Wenguang. 2002. *Education Technology.* Beijing: Publishing House of Beijing Normal University.

Xie, XinZhou. 2002. *Technology of Digital Publishing.* Beijing: Publishing House of Beijing University.

Digital Era Expedites the Naissance of "Reading Studies"—A Basic Course in Editing and Publishing

Gao Hong

The twenty first century is a digital era, a knowledge explosion era. The speed of knowledge renewal redoubles; only by advancing with the times can the publishing industry meet readers' needs for spiritual products, therefore, the publishing industry is going to step into a digital publishing era.

In the digital publishing era, great changes will take place in each link of the publishing chain. Here we just take editing as an example.

First, facing enormous numbers of book submissions, we must sift through them when selecting a topic suitable for the market; quantity of reading will increase by ten tor even a hundred times, and it will be very difficult for us to finish reading with traditional reading methods. Second, enormous first drafts need to be checked and approved in order to determine whether they are acceptable or not, which will also be very difficult to do using traditional reading methods. Third, enormous book manuscripts need to be processed. When processing the manuscripts, the key factor affecting the processing is reading speed, and it is quite unpractical for editors to complete the task of manuscript reading of digital publications with traditional reading methods. Fourth, enormous proof sheets need to be processed, and obviously, it is unpractical to use traditional methods. Fifth, exchanges with outsiders (for instance, the authors, readers, booksellers) must increase. Traditional reading methods cannot meet this requirement. Finally, the editors must keep updating their own knowledge based system, and must learn new knowledge and new skills through vast reading, and this won't work with traditional methods.

Facing these changes occurring in the publishing industry, how shall we cope with them?

First of all, we should be fully aware that the advent of the digital era has affected the human race itself. Mr. Deltuzos, director of the MIT Laboratory for Computer Science has said: "the fourth revolution aims at comprehending the human race itself—the rarest resource on earth. Each day in the twenty first century, you must accept many new things, new changes and new concepts, and its headstream is technology. Humans, from the outside to the inside, will be technologized. And then, what is important is no longer the technology itself, but its speed that changes the society, the speed of a natural person being turned into a skilled person. In the twenty first century, the strongest technological revolution is the revolution of humans." This human revolution takes the change of human thinking mode and values as a guide, the transformation of human knowledge and competence structure as the focal point, and technology as the impetus, accordingly, to realize the transformation of the "human" in itself. Without these changes, we cannot cultivate a team of editing talents of international standards who are embracing the digital era. Therefore, we should first help students construct a rational knowledge and competence structure, and in this regard, the emphasis should be put on cultivating the reading ability of university students in the editing and publishing major, since reading ability is the basis for all other abilities. In my opinion, we should offer a basic (compulsory) course—"Reading Studies" in the undergraduate editing and publishing specialty.

1. To Improve Reading Speed is the Need of the Digital Era

Digital publishing is the outcome of the information era, and its impact upon the traditional publishing industry is obvious. "Magnanimity" is one of its relatively remarkable characteristics. "Magnanimity" results in the change of traditional editing forms as well as that of the working conditioning of editing in itself. To say it directly, this sort of change is the change of speed, and the unusual acceleration makes it difficult for traditional editing means to adapt to such changes. The key to the adaptation is reading speed. With original reading speed, each day, one can only finish reading a book with approximately 100,000 words; however, digital publishing requires editors to read publications, manuscripts or data of hundreds of thousands of words or even one million words each day. If the problem of reading speed is solved, other problems will be readily solved. How to improve the reading speed of present editors as well as that of would-be editors? The course "Reading Studies" can solve this problem; it enables one to finish reading a book with approximately 300,000 words within one hour, besides also enabling one to grasp the main ideas of the book. Therefore, the establishment of the "Reading Studies" course can help university students in the editing and publishing major to improve their reading speed so as to adapt themselves to the needs of the digital era. Therefore, the advent of the digital era expedites the naissance of "Reading Studies"—basic course of the editing and publishing specialty.

"Reading Studies" is one of the age-old disciplines in China. According to historical data, it can be traced back to the Period of Spring and Autumn and Warring States. At that time, people were able to apply "Reading Studies" proficiently. In the long river of Chinese history, many people who mastered scientific reading methods read extensively, became erudite scholars, and left their deep footprints in history. In modern times, especially in the contemporary era, our fellow countrymen almost forgot this discipline, a discipline with a long history and which has great influence upon knowledge acquisition. Reading ability is a problem that should have been solved in the elementary school phase; however, up until the college phase, it remains a problem that urgently needs to be solved. In the middle of the twentieth century, people from Easter Europe began to research Reading Studies, and they soon put it into use. A person, who has never learned a foreign language, can learn by heart 1,200 foreign words and master their usages, with a one-time memorization rate reaching over 95%, which has aroused great responses around the world. Scientists from many countries, such as the United States, former Soviet Union, Great Britain and France, have devoted themselves to its undertaking with great enthusiasm, and, before long, its application in these countries had achieved great success. Our near neighbors, Japan and South Korea, have also studied and researched "Reading Studies," and it has been playing an important role in their study and work. However, in China, there are few universities that offer this course.

The data of ancient China as well as that of other countries, it shows that people who have studied "Reading Studies" can transform their instinct reading speed into scientific reading speed, and after completing this transformation, their reading speed can be increased by five to fifty times, and their reading efficiency can be improved by three to thirty times.

Publishing in the digital era requires editors to improve their reading speed and efficiency to a great extent, by about ten-times; namely, the workload of an editor suddenly increases by ten. To accomplish the changed workload, editors have no other choice but to improve their reading speed and reading efficiency. Therefore, it is the digital era that expedites the naissance of "Reading Studies"—a basic course of the editing and publishing specialty, making this old tree burst new sprouts.

2. To Master Study Methods is the Foundation for Learning to Learn

Alvin Toffler, an American writer, predicted in his book titled *The Third Wave*: "In the future, the illiterates are no longer the analphabetic, but those who don't know how to learn." From this, it can be seen that the importance of learning to learn. But if one has to learn to learn, one must learn to read first. Wenliam D. BeiKerr, a German reading expert, pointed out: "Eighty-five percent of the whole knowledge of a person is acquired through reading." Therefore, we can say that reading is the typical form of learning; the reading is the main activity of a learner, and reading is the most important skill of learning to learn.

Therefore, each learner must master correct reading methods. Whether the reading method of a learner is correct or not determines his studying proficiency, his lifelong success or failure. We may say: Reading is the mother of study, reading may change one's life.

College students who have correct study methods can read the maximum amount of relevant books within the shortest period of time. Furthermore, they can basically master the knowledge of the books they need and can integrate them into their knowledge system; they can use them very fluently, and without any obstruction. They cannot only finish their studies remarkably, but also can easily achieve excellent results in each discipline. Furthermore, they can smoothly complete the study of their second degree.

The case will be otherwise for college students who have incorrect reading methods. Slow reading speed and low reading efficiency greatly restrict their study, and it has become a bottleneck of their knowledge acquisition. Each day, they feel they don't have enough time; they have tried hard, however, with un-ideal study methods. Thus it can be seen, whether the reading method is correct or not, is the key for college students to know how to learn.

Therefore, offering "Reading Studies" and enabling college students to master correct reading methods are the foundations for helping them know how to learn.

3. Reading Ability is the Essential "Passport" for International Talents

In the digital era, the publishing industry is calling for international talents. What qualities should the international talents possess? They should be qualified and compound talents who possess a global view and are familiar with international regulations. They must also possess ten kinds of modern consciousness, namely: moral consciousness, subject consciousness, innovation consciousness, foresight consciousness, consciousness of going all out, competitive consciousness, effectiveness consciousness, cooperative consciousness, market consciousness, and global consciousness.

They must also possess the following basic qualities of modern people: devotion to work, mastery of operation, erudition and extensive knowledge, one specialty and many kinds of abilities, information sensitivity, thinking acuity, be diligent and hardworking, brave in innovation, collaboration and mutual help, youth and vigor.

Among a good many qualities, people attach more importance to foreign language competence and computer competence. The two competences are often called the second "passport" and the third "passport" for international talents. In my opinion, the most important competence an international talent must possess is reading ability. This ability should be their permit and necessary "passport" for entering the international community. Reading ability is the most basic ability whether in improving your diathesis or your ability. Reading is the precondition, if reading ability is improved, other abilities will be improved naturally. Just like the examples of foreign language study mentioned above, the improvement of reading ability helps to improve computer application competence, since with the improvement of their reading ability, their typing speed will be greatly quickened.

How to cultivate reading ability?

3.1 To Set up Chinese "Reading Studies" and to Form a Scientific Curriculum

"Reading Studies" is a kind of course that studies how to improve reading ability. It is a kind of learning with very strong practicability, and is an independent discipline with a complete system. Although "Reading Studies" in China started early, we lagged behind afterwards. We lagged behind not only in theoretical study, but also in application. In particular, in the teaching of reading there are great differences between China and foreign countries. In these countries, for instance, the United States, reading has always been regarded as the foundation for education in standard schools, from elementary schools to universities, and there are relevant reading courses. They even popularize reading courses in infant education and adult education. However, the level of domestic reading teaching still rests on the level of Chinese teaching in junior high schools. There is almost no relevant high-level research and at present, the research on modern "Reading Studies" is still in a state of early development.

The research on "Reading Studies" from other countries in the world started in the late 1960s, and has made great breakthroughs. Such countries as the United States, Germany, France, Austria and Bulgaria, take the lead in the research on reading studies. First, the University of Chicago in the United States put forward the index system of reading; then, the International Institute for Children's Literature and Reading was set up in Vienna by UNESCO; the enlightenment period of the research on reading studies started in terms of reading testing standards and children's reading. In the late 1970s, the reading research in other countries of the world reached another climax, with Germany making breakthroughs in theoretical reading research, reading skills study in Japan and South Korea, and reading studies application study in France and Great Britain. At present, the research on reading studies in the world is about to enter a third stage; its focus is to improve the reading level of all humans. Facing the differences with the advanced countries, we must attach great importance to it, strengthening the input of manpower and material resources as well as research strength. We must use as reference the advanced reading studies research results from other countries, and to organically combine it with the reading methods in ancient China, to carry out comprehensive study with the use of multi-disciplinary theories, to introduce theories, such as physiology, psychology, brain science, ophthalmology, philology, communication studies, and informatics into the whole course of research, so as to create a set of scientific methods adaptable to Chinese reading, to set up reading studies in China and to form a scientific curriculum. To apply these advanced and practical research results to the teaching of reading so as to improve the reading ability of Chinese people once and for all.

3.2 To Offer the Basic Course for Students in the Editing and Publishing Major—"Reading Studies"

At present, in setting up college courses, the attention paid to College Chinese is far more than that to College English. People often overemphasize the importance of cultivating the listening, speaking, reading and writing abilities of English, but neglect those abilities of Chinese. Especially to cultivate reading ability, they think that our fellow countrymen have inherent mastery of their mother tongue, and there is no need for them to spend time learning it. However, what is the real situation? The examination-oriented education implemented for so long a time makes students accustomed to utility reading, which results in a narrow knowledge scope, poor writing ability and the lack of humanistic spirit, all, the results of lacking good Chinese reading ability. At all times and all over the world, there are innumerable reading practices, and there are innumerable reading experiences; however, the science of reading studies and humanistic values always been disregarded, and the set-up of reading studies courses also is given a "cold shoulder." Reading and writing are originally twins in human cultural activity. "Writing Studies" has stepped onto the lecture room of colleges for quite a long time, and has been regarded as one of the important courses. However, except for very few colleges that have offered "Reading Studies," it has not yet had a niche in the college hall lecture room. To analyze from a logical perspective, reading should come before writing; reading is the foundation for writing. Therefore, we must give "Reading Studies" a niche in the college lecture hall to impart its theories and skills of to editing and publishing majors so as to improve their reading ability. Therefore, I myself plan to set up a basic professional course in the editing and publishing specialty of colleges—"Reading Studies".

3.3 To Guide Reading, to Cultivate Students' Reading Interest and to Improve their Reading Abilities

One of the reasons why university students have poor reading ability is that they are not interested in reading. Impacted by TV and the internet, there are fewer and fewer people who are interested in reading. In particular in the digital era, reading has become a problem of the whole country and even a global problem. The second reason is that they lack reading practice. From elementary school to college, they are accustomed to listening to the teachers and to doing large numbers of exercises, they seldom read independently, and therefore, they have not fostered good reading habits. Scholars from Hong Kong think the theme of "Reading and Human Development" will become a new development trend in Chinese teaching. To guide reading is a very important issue. The emphasis of teaching is gradually transferring from the joint reading of teachers and students to students' independent reading. One way to solve these problems, on the one hand, is to combine theory with practice, and to apply the reading research results to teaching practice; on the other, teachers should guide students to read, letting the students experience the enjoyment and gains of reading in their reading practice, and accordingly, cultivating the students' reading interests and reading habits, gradually developing it into a kind of ability.

3.4 To Construct a Rational Knowledge System, and to Build a Team of Editing Talents with International Standards

Reading is a kind of important ability and it is very important both to our study and work. Especially in the digital era, it is a basic ability a person must possess. It is more important than foreign language competence and computer, and is the foundation for basic ability. The aim of education and course reform is to improve teaching quality and to cultivate compound talents with high diathesis. To take "Reading Studies" as a basic professional course editing and publishing majors is a requirement of higher education reform as well as for building a team of talents with international standards. Through the study of reading theories and practical courses, students will master scientific reading methods and skills, improve their reading levels, know how to learn, and achieve twice the results for half the effort; this is the scientific value brought out by reading. Under the guidance of the teachers and through a vast amount of reading, the students can not only construct a rational knowledge system, but also can learn how to behave and how to become useful people; this is the humanistic value brought about by reading. The author points out in the preface of a book titled *How to Teach Reading*: "The reading level of a person determines the amount of his knowledge; the total amount of his knowledge determines his working quality." Therefore, to improve reading level, construct rational knowledge systems and to increase the total amount of your knowledge is the only way build a team of editing talents with international standards.

REFERENCES

Hu, Youmu. *Large View of Talents*. Beijing: China CITIC Press.

Toggler, Alvin. *The Third Wave*. Trans. By Zhu Zhiyan et al. Beijing: Joint Publishing, 1984. p. 28.

Zheng, Xiangqin and Han Xueping. *Reading Research Abroad*. Henan Education Publishing, June 1992, p. 132.

——. 1992. *Foreign Reading & Study*. Henan Education Press.

Zheng, Xiangqin. 2003. *Reading changes one's Life*. Qingdao: China Ocean University Press.

Zheng, Xiangqin and Han Xueping. *Reading Research Abroad*. Henan Education Publishing, June 1992. p. 44.

Digital Technology Promotes China's Publishing Industry

Huang Kaiqing & Zhou Guobiao

In the twenty first century, we are entering into knowledge-based economy and the age of information. The birth of the Internet in the twentieth century triggered the e-commerce boom, and offered us enormous opportunities for the development of our society. Digital publishing is the result of combining computers, Internet, information technology, multimedia technology and print media. Before the 1980s, no one could expect that digital technologies would bring tremendous changes to the publishing industry, or would have such a remarkable impact on its development. Today, print media generally benefit from the application of digital technologies, while publishers also consider how to deal correctly with the new digital publishing, and how to take advantage of opportunities for the development of traditional publishing.

1. The Publishing Industry Cannot Grow without the Support of Digital Technology

Digital publishing technology is the basis of the informatization of publishing. Mastering the technology in electronic and internet publishing and in e-commerce is important in raising the level of publishing skills.

Internet publishing was previously called online publishing. It was developed in the America in 1960s and refers to the use of Internet technology in publishing. When the Internet was widely used throughout the world in 1996, readers from all over the world started to realize the convenience and quickness of accessing online publications from anywhere at any time. As a result, publishing and selling books by using the Internet have attracted a lot of attention. The Internet is becoming the best way to attract potential readers.

Electronic commerce started in the 1970s. At present, over 95% of the world's 1,000 largest companies are using e-commerce. In developed countries, e-commerce is widely used by businesses, but in China, there are only a few companies in this field, and even fewer in the field of publishing. This fact has negatively affected the competitiveness of Chinese publishers in the international market. There's no doubt that digital publishing represents the trend in the twenty first century. Internet publishing, electronic publishing and electronic commerce are the main forms of digital publishing. Digital publishing not only brings a revolution in publishing industry, but also reflects the strength of the knowledge economy and information society.

2. Technological Innovation Brings in New Economic Mode

The Science and Policy Research Centre of Sussex University in the UK developed a theory in 1988 which says technological innovation changes economic mode, and can even smooth economic cycles. According to this theory, the development of information technology created the Internet, and the Internet in turn made e-commerce possible, which then became a new economic mode. We can see that the Internet will surely lead to changes in economic mode, increased productivity, and offer more business opportunities. In the publishing industry, Amazon pioneered in online bookselling, followed by many other companies in Internet publishing, electronic publishing, blog publishing and online games. Today, traditional publishers and bookstores rely heavily on the Internet in their daily workflow; many information technology companies and venture capital firms are also investing in digital publishing technologies. A digital publishing revolution is well under way.

In his 1962 book *The Logic of Scientific Discovery,* American scholar Karl Popper argues that scientific research has its own system of core values and judgment standards, and its own operation mode and rules; Popper calls this a model. When the old scientific method cannot solve new problems, a new model will be created. Popper's model system is widely applied by businesses around the world and is built into some profit-generation model. Based on Popper's theory, we believe that the digital publishing revolution is happening in two areas: new publishing format and new profit model.

Traditional publishing pays a lot of attention to controlling cost, quality and price as a way of maximizing profit. The new digital publishing calls for speeding up the distribution process, creating industry standards and realizing the core value of publication. Obviously, these two publishing modes reflect two different operating philosophies, different ways of thinking and game rules. The traditional publishing mode focuses on individual products, and organizes the publishing process around the product. The new publishing mode is first considering how to meet the needs of all readers. In other words, the traditional mode emphasizes the production and organization efficiency of the tangible products while the latter emphasizes maiming the intangible value of the new digital products. In the new mode, companies are using new technologies such as the Internet to look for target groups of readers in the market, and to design a complete scheme to meet the needs of these readers (including production, marketing, selling, and customer service). Facing fierce competition in the publishing market, publishers pay great attention to providing good service to readers and improving their ability to obtain constant profit. Compared with the traditional publishing mode, the new publishing mode has potential to bring in more profit to the company. How to make better use of the digital technology to create a new mode and get more profit becomes an important and practical issue for publishers.

3. The Achievements of Digital Publishing in China

In Publishing Houses

The application of modern technology in Chinese publishing enterprises has brought good results, especially in those major state-owned publishing houses, national newspapers and magazines, such as Electronics Industry Publishing House, Posts and Telecommunications Publishing House, Machine Industry Publishing House, Higher Education Press, People's Daily, Guang Ming Daily, and Rayli magazine. The new technologies in Chinese publishing enterprises are mainly used in composing, processing, and production management, and the application of modern technology in information service etc.

The informatization in composing, processing and producing mainly refers to: the composing of words, charts, images, sounds and animation by using computers and related software; then transferring them to publishing houses through email, MSN, QQ etc; editing and processing the manuscripts through software such as HuaGuang, Fit and WPS; processing the materials through all kinds of image and sound processing software; checking and correcting proof sheets through Chinese or English proofreading software; marketing through publishers' websites.

The informatization in production management mainly includes: the collecting, preserving, and utilizing author information in order to better select publishing projects; using computers and networks to identify good book subjects and improve the management of subject resources; using computers and local area networks to manage book production schedules and control production process; using modern technology to control and manage contracts, control costs and quality of publications; using digital technology in typesetting, plate-making, and digital printing; using digital devices to digitize traditional book inventory, which is an important part of digital publishing; using professional software to computerize accounting and financial management; using modern devices to manage the logistics and inventory; establishing e-commerce websites to improve the efficiency and quality of customer service; deploying HR management systems, CRM systems and ERP systems etc.

In Bookstores

Applying digital technologies in bookstores is one of most important issues and it has attracted the attention of many state-owned bookstores. Xinhua bookstore, the biggest state-owned bookstore chain, began to use computers in 1985. At present it has had good results in distribution management, financial management, store management and e-commerce applications. The following table shows survey results about the phase of information application.

Table 1: The Information system status of large chain bookstores in China

Bookstore Name	Beginning Time	System Status	Update Times
Beijing Xinhua Bookstore	1986	Bayankala company RCM, NVC system software	4
Northern Book City	1995	Oracle large-scale database management software	3
Jiangxi Xinhua Bookstore	1990	Bayankala NVS2000 chain system software, Taiwan EXCEED logistics management system software, UF financial software UF	2
Hunan Xinhua Bookstore Group Ltd.	1988	Headquarters complex business management system software, office automation system software, VPN software	4
Jiangsu Xinhua Bookstore Group Ltd.	1986	business system software of Beijing Zhongqi,NJU Sotheby's special " Jiangsu Xinhua issue chain management system" software, financial software UF	4
Zhejiang Xinhua Bookstore Group Ltd.	1986	Zhejiang Jingwei "Zhejiang Xinhua Bookstore system" software (GBIS)	4
Sichuan Xinhua Issue Group	1984	Bayankala BIMS chain of system software, Sichuan emerging smart-management system software (ZNX 2000), small bees financial software	3
Chongqing Xinhua Bookstore Group	1985	Bayankala BIMS business system software, Bayankala NVS, TOPS chain system software, the financial software of CDs	4
Shanghai Xinhua Bookstore Group	1987	Management system software developed by Shanghai Qiming and South China Computer	4
Wuhan Xinhua Bookstore	1995	NJU Geminsai "Xinhua Bookstore information management system" software	3

The table shows that the information systems in the large bookstore chains have experienced three to four systematic updates. It can be summarized as having three phases.

The first phase was from 1985 to 1992. In order to improve efficiency and speed up book selling, some provincial bookstore chains used software to manage and analyze inventory and delivery, and automate the billing process. The goal of information application in this phase was to satisfy the wholesale business management of the bookstores.

The second phase was from 1993 to 2003. In this phase, the application of the information system expanded to other areas, including retail bookstore, finance, procurement, materials, and logistics management. At present, most bookstore chains' information systems have achieved the functions mentioned above.

The third phase started in 2003, and was a phase of integration. Large chain stores have been exploring integration software to manage chain-wide bookstore businesses, and to share information with financial and logistics departments. It indicated that large bookstore chains now have even higher requirements for the digital and information technologies.

REFERENCES

Bao, Jianyong and Chen Baixun. *The Strategy to Success in E-Times*. Shanghai: Fudan University Press, 2001.

"Focus on the Informatization of China Bookstore." *Publishing Research*. 2005: 9.

Huang, Kaiqing. "Speed up the Informatization of Press without Any Delay." *China Computer Information*. 9 Jan. 2006.

Jin, Xia. "Accelerate Informatization Construction of Publishing Industry." *China Book Business Report*. 12 Dec. 2003.

Qin, Biyu. "A Study on Integrating Information Systems with E-Commerce." *Publishing Research*. 2005: 2.

Tendencies of the Book Industry Under Media Industry Convergence

Wang Songmao

1. Convergence and Development of the Industry

The media industry is one of the fastest changing industries of the past few decades all over the world. The development the of media industry is fuelled by technological transformations. This main driving force not only changes the industry, but also promotes the industry convergence.

There are many meanings attributed to the term convergence, consisting of several layers into which we can divide convergence: device convergence, network convergence, service convergence and industry convergence. Industry convergence has become the prevailing trend in some industries. It is especially related to technological convergence as different industries are heavily adopting information communication technologies.

The nature and speed of this convergence has posed new challenges to relevant industries. First, the former distinct industry boundaries are now blurred; we can no longer clearly point out which product belongs to a specific industry. Second, it has also meant that traditional industry structures have changed. As we know, on January 10, 2000, America Online announced plans to acquire Time Warner for roughly $182 billion in stock. The merger, the largest deal in history, combined the top new media service provider with the world's top traditional media conglomerate. The industry structure changed dramatically.

With the high rate of penetration and diffusion, convergence has aroused the special interest of academia. The phenomenon of convergence is relatively new, and the future of convergence is uncertain. There is a range of different views on convergence. There is broad agreement that convergence is creating the potential for a new approach to providing traditional services and for completely new services. There is less agreement on how much the convergence will change existing industries and over what timescale. Some consider that convergence will lead to the complete and rapid transformation of existing industries in such a way that these currently separate kinds of industries will merge into one another.

2. Media Industry Convergence

Convergence is a megatrend shaping the whole of media industries. Since the traditional media industries are operating in a very mature and declining market, there are generally few growth opportunities, once new technology has been introduced. Traditional media enterprises seem to have tried almost every workable business model. But any business plan targeting the new technology is based on insecurity. There are few sources to draw knowledge from, and entering the market consequently becomes virtually impossible if one is not willing to use a "try and fail" strategy. Similarly, it did not initially seem clear how one could make a profit from the convergence. They had to try several different models, sometimes even at the same time.

At first, publishers and newspapers transformed their print publication to electronic content, targeting traditional readers. In the 1990s, they began to tentatively go into the chilly rapids of cyberspace, trying the new product and new channel, but they still can't quite figure out what to do with the convergence and how to make money. Finally, they are starting to see the Internet as central to their future. And there is proliferation of non-print production that combines traditional book and other media; for example, the new genre of mobile novels is now distributed on mobile phone networks, while other mobile devices are used in new business models, such as the Apple iPod for audio books.

Evidence of such convergence has been mounting in recent years with the development of the Internet and with the increasing capability of existing networks to carry new media services. Newspapers are expanding their digital footprints, providing more ways to attract customers, with the introduction of a range of multimedia products. More than 1,500 North American daily newspapers have launched websites worldwide; there are more than 5,000 daily, weekly and other newspapers online. Most of the dominant news websites are run by old media- the traditional news organizations such as daily newspapers, newsmagazines, and network and major cable television outlets. In the book industry, electronic publishing takes on a new look, including online downloading, packaged products such as CD-ROMs and DVDs, and small-volume on-demand publishing of discontinued titles.

In China, newspapers own most of the top online news and information websites, and publishers have set up websites to provide electronic books. On June 8, 2006, China Mobile purchased 19.9% of The Phoenix New Media and then became the second shareholder of Phoenix TV. This collaboration is very significant. China Mobile offers the best channel for Phoenix New Media to release its content on mobile devices, now we can see the coming of new a convergence.

3. Book Publishing Industry's Convergence in China

The rapid economic development and per capita GDP growth have contributed to the vigorous development of the media in China, and book publishing industries. But the trend of convergence forces the publishing industry to rethink its development strategies.

3.1 The Convergence of Books

Traditionally, a paper-like book is composed of content and structure. The content of a book means the main text with a few different types of heading; the structure of a book is only a simple hierarchical division into sections and subsections. The development of technology allows for the convergence of traditionally separate media, including book and audio-visual product into a single product, putting together text, sound, video and voice.

With the book converging with other mediums, its contents may include figures, images, photographs, formulas, music, videos, and lots of other forms of communication. The structure of a book may include the relationships of various kinds and pieces of contents with each other and with the contents and structure of other books or other media products. The various elements might each have their own style of presentation. Moreover, the same book may take on different forms: sometimes the book is in an all-electronic mode, sometimes in traditional forms, sometimes combined; some may even take on a new form that we don't know now.

The key to the future of the book is the effort to build a broad portfolio of products around the core product, the traditional book, and to connect with both general and targeted readers. Publishers across the country have established their presence on the Web and are aggressively developing additional online products. They are launching niche publications and reaching out to new readers, particularly minorities. We can also regard the book as one of a mixture of media types to achieve synergistic effects. Content is communicated not only through books, but also through TV shows, movies and newspaper, as well as through video games.

3.2 The Convergence of Book Producing

Since the birth of publishing, the publishing houses have gradually created a linear production flow. Authors provided manuscripts; publishing houses edited and published them. Once prepared, the publication is reproduced in some sort of mass production, i.e. identical copies are issued. Originally, the paradigm was adopted for obvious economic reasons. It was necessary to issue publications in thousands or even millions of identical copies. The role of the consumer is to take it or leave it.

Before the 1990s, development in the book industry lay in the new technology adopted in the production flow. In China, the book industry has been using new technology for more than twenty years. At first, authors typed their manuscripts using word processing software and submitted them to book publishers by e-mail; publishers edited and set type with advanced machines, but the production flow remained the same.

Now the production paradigm has been challenged by convergence. The roles of author, publisher and distributor seem to be converging. There are quantities of free online materials on an open access basis, without fees or restrictions. Everyone can be an author, such as in the popular online encyclopedia Wikipedia that anyone can edit. In addition, the contents of a publication may vary, since the author may update it quickly and the book can be versioned with slightly different editions for different products, geographic reasons, or demographic targets. And the reader may customize the contents. Thus, the author, publisher and distributor have to change their roles in the flow, and pay attention to the whole flow to some extent. For example, the author should not only create the content, but also know how to publish and distribute; the publishing house should know not only how to organize the authors, but also know how to use different modes of presentation, such as visual and other external expressions of the contents, and how to meet the readers' different preferences. The publishing industry deals with a massive number of titles, with as many as 128,578 new titles added each year, about 222,473 titles in 2005. Some titles sell several million copies, while academic publications may sell only a few hundred copies. Many people want to publish their own books, but not always with the aim of sales or profit. They only need to publish a few dozen copies, or maybe even just a single copy. There are blogs and podcasts, so such features will become very important in the industry, and they raise interesting questions on the roles of authors, readers and publishing houses.

Rather than printing thousands of these types of books and warehousing them, publishers can retain the digital content and produce only as many books as might be required for a period. That is a print-on-demand option for books, the just-in-time fulfillment model. The very short run and very quick turnaround necessary in print means that the print process no longer is an independent component of the production process, but a part of marketing.

Traditional distribution channels for book are the physical distribution networks through which books, CDs, or DVDs are distributed to the retailer. In China, the Xinhua Bookstore is the biggest state-owned book distribution enterprise. As protected by policy, it has enjoyed some seventy percent of the market share. Retail sales methods are diversifying in response to the collapse of the conventional sale system and distribution structure and the increase in Internet sales. In addition, the advent of electronic publishing has enabled publishers to distribute directly online. More recent distribution channels are mobile telephone networks and the Internet. Any future mode of publishing must almost inevitably include some form of electronic distribution. It will improve distribution efficiency and speed up the service provided to readers, and be one of the key elements to keeping this cost to serve low and, thus, maintaining discount levels.

3.3 The Change of Chinese Book Market Structure

In China, there were 573 publishing houses in 2005. Their releases are printed and bound at printing companies, forwarded to distributors, and sold at over 159,000 bookstores and other retailers across the nation. Due to historical reasons, publishing houses have long existed as public institutions rather than companies. Under the wing of the government, publishing houses could easily survive without participating in market competition, many of them long used to a comfort zone of high demand resulting from the country's large population.

Due to the change to books and book producing, traditional book producers in China are facing increasing challenges. The technology convergence has broken the boundaries of traditional books. Mutual penetration of the traditional media, blending of traditional and new media and trans-regional media are becoming an inevitable trend of development. Now authors themselves can publish their material in the form of an e-book. According to the Annual Internet Development Report of China in June 2006 by the China Internet Network Information Center, the number of internet users in mainland China reached 123 million by June 2006. There are twenty eight million blog writers. Because of the lower costs of publishing, books will be produced in ever-greater numbers by small publishers, private corporations and companies, colleges and universities, and individual authors. These might include full-color picture books for children that can be personalized with a child's name, hard-copy editions of blogs, hobbyist books, personal travelogues, family histories, and fiction. The publishing houses are losing their core competitive advantages to authors- editing.

Under China's WTO commitments, the Chinese government has been loosening control over the publishing industry, because of which competition will become fiercer with the introduction of international competitors who are more advanced in terms of marketing and management. Under such circumstances, they have quickly come to realize more attention must be paid to factors that affect the market, specifically consumer preferences. The publishing houses are losing the market barrier that defends their high profits.

Moreover, new media has attracted a share of the book markets. The number of netizens in China has exceeded 123 million and the younger generation is increasingly dependent on the Internet, while more and more readers of books transfer to the Internet. Data from the government show that the readership is kept declining and now below 50%. In that sense, new media attracts some traditional book readers. The publishing houses have to face a declining market.

According to statistics provided by the State Press and Publication Administration, in 2005, 222,473 books were published nationwide with 63.228 billion Yuan fixed price. But the inventory value is over 40 billion Yuan. Due to competition and the drifting away of profits, the value chain of books is being stretched by exterior production and distribution units. In the past, a book was a complete value chain with profit mainly coming from content creation and editing. However, the chain is expanded today, with the profit being shifted outward. The content of books is relayed and re-developed by websites and search engines. With production and transmission being expanded, the profit focus of books is silently shifting downward. The single profit mode, a given company's hold over the primary input at the top of the value chain of the book, which company then distribute it, is curbing the industry's growth.

In the 1990s, the Chinese book market was characterized by fixed prices; the effects of the transition gradually emerged in the form of increased price competition and structural changes in the market. Despite the increased price and sales channel competition, the number of publishers begins to decrease to the extent that specialization dominates in some fields. There are many publishing houses of varying sizes. Most publishers and distributors are small, mid-sized enterprises and sole traders. In 2004, only about thirty publishers published over 1,000 titles. Half of the publishers published 100-500 titles per year. A development toward increased collaboration between publishers and different forms of chains has also taken place. Concentration of ownership within Chinese book publishing emerged.

In China, to enhance the book industry's competitiveness, the Chinese publishing industry initiated the process of setting up publishing groups as early as March 29, 2003, when the Liaoning Publishing Group totally divorced from the local government publication authorities and announced its establishment, ending decades of confusion that had existed between the government functions and business management in the publishing industry. The newly founded publishing group is made up of all the publishing companies including the Printing Corporation, distribution group and publishing houses that used to fall directly under the government authorities. In 2001, a Chinese TV-radio broadcasting group, which is made up of China Central Television (CCTV), China Radio (CNR) and China Radio International (CRI), was set up. So was the newspaper and film groups. What is particularly new about these groups in the media industry is the search for not only the traditional economies of scale, but also the search of economies of scope. Vertical and horizontal integration may be a natural outgrowth of competition in the converging book industry.

In early 2004, the General Administration of Press and Publication announced that about 570 state-owned publishing houses were to be restructured and transformed into companies in the next three to seven years. Though restricted by the harsh policies of the book industry, more and more enterprises began to enter the market through different mergers, acquisitions and reorganizations. It is expected that more companies will access the book industry through reorganization, coupled with mergers and acquisitions.

In conclusion, the Chinese book industry has undergone considerable changes over the last 20 years. The Chinese book industry is becoming a market-oriented industry and a converging industry. But it should be emphasized that the future of convergence is very uncertain.

References

Cui, Baoguo. *Report on the Development of China's Media Industry.* Beijing: Social Science Academic Press, 2006.

Domonick, Joseph. *The Dynamics of Communication: Media in the Digital Age.* Beijing: McGraw-Hill Education and China Remin University Press, 2003.

Fidler, Roger. *Mediamorphosis: Understanding New Media.* California: Pine Forge Press, 1997.

Green Paper on the Convergence of the Telecommunications, Media and Information Technology Sectors, and the Implications for Regulation. Towards an Information Society Approach. Brussels: European Commission, 1997.

Greenstein, S. and T. Khanna. "What Does Industry Mean?" *Yoffie. Competing in the Age of Digital Convergence.* 1997.

"Japanese Economy Division, Japanese Publishing Industry, JETRO." *Japan Economic Report* (2006).

Mueller, Milton. *Telecom Policy and Digital Convergence.* Hong Kong: City University of Hong Kong Press, 1996.

Zhang, Xiaoming. Hu and Huilin. Z. Jiangang. *Report on Development of China Cultural Industry.* Beijing: Social Science Academic Press, 2006.

Digital Supply Chain: A New Platform for the Chinese Publishing Industry

Zhang Meijuan

In the 1990s, with the reform of the Chinese publishing industry and the large scale development of the publishing economy, Chinese modern publishing logistics experienced great development in terms of efficiency and scale. After a rapid growth period in 2000 when many big warehouses and distribution centers were built, Chinese modern publishing logistics began to use digital network technology to improve delivery and customer service, and experimented with applying digital supply chain techniques and management.

1. The characteristics of digital supply chain

The digital supply chain, as a new concept, means to use network technology in the publishing supply chain, to improve the efficiency of the whole publishing process.

Compared to the traditional publishing supply chain, the digital publishing supply chain has the following characteristics:

- Information flow: the digital supply chain stresses the important role of information flow in modern logistics.
- Digitalization: the digital supply chain stresses the important role of information and network technologies in the managing of logistics.
- Standardization: the digital supply chain stresses the sharing and standardization of information, especially communication between the partners in the supply chain. By improving the efficiency of the whole supply chain, the cost of the logistics will be reduced and the service and the efficiency of the supply chain will be improved.

2. The current Chinese publishing supply chain

In recent years, the book market in China has had rapid growth. In 2000, total books sales were 84.79 billion RMB, in 2002 it was up to 99.39 billion RMB, and in 2004, it broke through 100 billion RMB. The average book supply chain cost in China is 25% of sales; we can therefore imagine the huge saving potential of improving the efficiency of publishing logistics. Meanwhile, the Chinese publishing industry currently has more than 40 billion RMB worth of book inventory which reflects inefficiency in the supply chain. If we combine other publishing logistics, such as magazine and audio video publishing, the potential of improvement in the publishing logistic market will be very attractive.

According to China's commitments to the WTO, controls of book and magazine distribution has ended and restrictions on foreign investment in publication distribution were lifted in 2004. Now foreign companies can operate in both retail and wholesale levels of the publishing supply chain in China, and they will get the same treatment as any state-owned enterprises.

On the one hand, the business opportunities in the Chinese publishing supply chain are huge; on the other hand, as foreign investments enter China, competition in the publishing supply chain market is heating up. Facing this challenging, Chinese companies in the publishing supply chain should first analyze the current situation as well as the main problem publishing logistics.

2.1 The present condition of Chinese publishing logistics

- The market structure of the publishing supply chain. In terms of ownership, there are 3 types of logistic enterprises: the state-owned, the shareholder-owned (for example, a distribution center funded by a publishing group, the logistic system of provincial and municipal Xinhua bookstore chains, the post office logistic system etc.) and the private-owned.

- The majority of elhi textbooks and study-aid materials go through Xinhua Bookstore's logistic system: This business alone accounts for more than 80% of Xinhua Bookstore chain's revenue. The private-owned publishing logistic systems have gained considerable market share and become more competitive.

- Technology: Since 2000, the publishing industry in China has greatly accelerated the construction of mega distribution centers, publishers and provincial Xinhua bookstores invested heavily in building super distribution centers and warehouses, equipping them with advanced logistic technologies. As a result, the designed capacity is far more than the present business needs.

- Management: the current publishing logistic system has basically completed the transition from planned economy to market economy. The market-oriented system has greatly stimulated the enthusiasm of the workers and enhanced the efficiency of publishing logistics. More attention has been given to quality of management, and many enterprise management systems have been gradually established.

2.2 Major problems facing publishing supply chain

Despite the achievements of our publishing logistics in recent years, there are still some problems that hinder its further development.

- Due to its technological and financial strength, Xinhua Bookstore's supply chain system is still the backbone of China's publishing logistics. However, Xinhua Bookstore's supply chain system is divided and confined by each province, resulting in redundant construction and the lack of coordinated resource planning and management.
- Book return rate is still growing and inventories are swelling.
- Book distribution costs are high. In the current decentralized publishing logistic system, a large amount of equipment in often idle in those super warehouses and distribution centers, but many small and medium-sized distributors have no access to that idled capacity and have to set up their own logistic systems, which greatly adds to the burden on the public transportation system.
- Lack of logistics information sharing: each logistics information system in China has its own standard, does things in its own way, and cannot talk to others. The poor information sharing greatly affects the efficiency of the existing supply chain system.

3. Construct a digital publishing supply chain

The two main causes for the above problems are the following: the publishing industry is still in the transition stage and is hindered by residues from the planned economy; and poor information sharing between companies in the supply chain.

It is very difficult and time consuming to solve the first problem because it depends on changing the entire publishing industry. But the digital and network technology can be utilized to improve information sharing relatively easily.

The digital supply chain is the general trend of logistic development. We should make good use of these digital network technologies to establish a platform where people can share publishing information. The platform should be built based on the Internet and have the ability to display and integrate logistic services of all players in the chain.

The digital supply chain platform is just like a virtual marketplace where people can not only exchange all sorts of publishing logistic supply-and-demand information but also develop many-to-many exchange activities with logistic agents by registering on the Internet. As one essential part of the supply chain in a system, the existence of logistic agent (a middleman between publishers and bookstores) is an important sign of a developed logistic market. The logistic agent transfers the logistic enterprise from a distributor of real goods to an entity providing an integrated logistic market information service. Through the integration of logistics supply chain management, these logistic agents become a central point for information sharing, serving upstream publishing companies and downstream retail bookstores, and provide other publishing logistic services.

On this platform, publishing houses can check inventory information and stock on hand at various sales points, which is reflected on the network platform, and therefore detect the sales tendency of each book. This platform is valuable to bookstores as well. Bookstores can make more informed decisions when ordering books, and thus reduce book returns. Even for the returned books, publishers use the information from the digital supply chain platform to redistribute these books and extend a book's life cycle.

More important, this virtual platform of publishing logistics can bypass the bottleneck of geographical fragments caused by provincial government administrations. It will integrate all resources of the Chinese publishing logistics market, and boost the development of the publishing supply chain.

4. Obstacles in establishing the digital publishing supply chain

The above blueprint is promising, but to realize it, we need to fully understand the obstacles and difficulties in the way.

- The investment will be huge. To realize the value of information flows in the digital supply chain, we must use the current information generated by the physical supply chain as its source. Therefore, whether the physical system can produce and share information in a timely manner will be key to the success of digital logistics. In order to achieve that, vast investment is needed for a network of computers and processing terminals. This should be treated as strategic investment and is crucial for the industry's sustainable growth. The efficiency improvement in information sharing from participating in the digital supply chain could provide scale benefit to all players in the publishing industry.

- Standardization is the foundation of valid operation and value realization of the digital platform. Currently there is no industry-wide information standard in the Chinese publishing supply chain; different distributors use different hardware and proprietary software, and cannot share information among each other's systems. Due to the high cost of industry-wide standardization, we suggest the government takes the initiative and provides policy support to promote information standardization in the publishing supply chain.

REFERENCES

Hu, Zhaojie and Guan Zhongliang. "Framing Digital Logistics System Based on Information Technology." *Value Engineering* 2003: 1.

Li, Qing. "Making use of the Information Technique and Framing Digital Logistics." *Computer Knowledge and Technology* 2006: 11.

Publication Yearbook of China 2001. Beijing: Publication Yearbook of China Publishing House, 2001.

Sun, Hong, Li Yifan and Li Guanghui. "'Digital Logistics': The Soul of the Modern Logistics." *Chinese Logistics and Purchase* 2003: 6.

Wang, Hua, Bo Zikang and Wang Bing. *The Viewpoint of Improving University Publishing Logistics.* Shanghai: University Publishing, 2003.

Zha, Xianjin. "The Statement of Publication Logistics' Manpower Development of Electronic Business." *Publishing Issue Study* 2003: 3.

Zhu, Quan. "Publishing Logistics: Need set up Decisive Standard Urgently." *Publishing Reference* 2004: 7.

On Fostering Magazines' Core Competency in the Digital Age

Zhu Jingwen & Sun Jue

With the development of digital technology, there are great changes in magazine publishing. Digital technology has not only given rise to some new ideas in magazine publishing, developed new operating models, improved marketing methods, and reduced cost, but also has brought the digitization of content. The influence of digital technology on magazine publishing is increasing; therefore magazine publishers should re-think how to maintain their unique core competency.

A magazine's core competency is its unique competitive advantage acquired through a longterm development process and being incorporated into its intrinsic quality, which is reflected in the value of a magazine, the distinctiveness and the influence of its content, the number of its readers as well as its adverting revenue and core advertisers. The value of a magazine is essential to its core competency; the value includes readership value and advertising value; the distinctiveness or uniqueness of content is the main characteristic of a magazine's competency, which is beyond imitation by its competitors.

1. The digitization extension of brand

Nowadays, with the influence of digital technology gaining momentum, the formation of a magazine's core competency depends on whether or not the traditional brand can extend to the Internet. A magazine's brand refers to the unique and outstanding quality of its editorial content as well as its cultural taste, which is recognized by the public and the magazine industry. Traditional magazines have the advantage of superior content and publishing talents. Many traditional magazines in China have started to digitize their contents and distribute them through the Internet. Combining their high quality contents with digital technology, many online versions of famous traditional magazines are quickly recognized by the public and become popular on the Internet. In 2006, for example, the 7th issue of *Trends Shine*—an online version of the *Trends* magazine—recorded nearly 1.6 million downloads.

At present, there are 1,500 to 2,000 content providers in China 143 of them use the Xplus platform, and these content providers have created a boom in digital magazines. For example, the digital interactive magazine *Wowzine* has excellent digital contents, and interactive columns such as "Drawing Board" and "Network Scene

Drama". The goal of branding is to attract new readers, retain existing readers, and keep customer loyalty. To form a longterm branding strategy, a magazine needs to consider how to connect to the Internet, such as whether it is necessary to publish an Internet version of its print magazine or create a new online service in order to attract a new reader group.

2. Establishment of new reader-relationship

The Internet not only provides a long lasting subscription channel, but also establishes a new interactive reader-magazine relationship. Although print magazines are convenient to carry, the reading process of print magazines is one-dimensional, without interaction between magazine and the reader. The Internet has overcome this shortcoming of print magazines. The time when readers can only communicate with editors through "letters from readers" has gone. Communication between editors and readers can now be conveniently achieved online through various digital methods such as cell phone messages, e-mails, blogs and so on. For instance, a reader can respond to a poll by a magazine through sending back a mobile phone message; a piece of writing and a segment of video offered by magazines is easily available on a mobile phone; the desired and customized contents of a given magazine issue can be sent to a given reader; through online community, especially via blogs, readers can give their instant feedback regarding magazine contents. However, it does not necessarily mean that the Internet is grabbing readers from traditional magazines; on the contrary, the Internet has made magazines more multifunctional and has helped magazines expand their market. Making use of the easy accessibility of the Internet, traditional magazines can, by building up a domestic and international online community, provide a platform where people can exchange ideas and comments after reading a magazine; thus a magazine can better serve its readers.

3. Online Subscription

With its low cost and high speed, the Internet provides a brand new distribution channel. With online subscription, billing and customer service are automated.

Currently, many magazines have developed new readers by offering subscription online and by posting selected contents online to attract attention of those readers who are not their traditional consumers. Two magazine networks, *Browse* and *China Magazine,* have established such an online distribution service. The digital magazines at *Browse* network, for example, keep the same format and advertisements of their print editions, but the digital editions can be delivered directly to their customers via e-mail, and thus publish simple digital magazines at no additional cost. In addition, online magazines can increase the sale of traditional print magazines. Although there are not many online subscribers switching to print magazines, a magazine can promote its print subscription, develop new readers through various online promotion methods, such as pop-up ads, embedded ads and e-mail. Magazine distributors can, without jeopardizing the sale of print magazines, encourage renewal of print magazines by offering selected and customized online contents to potential subscribers.

4. Digital advertisements

For most consumer magazines, advertising is the main source of revenue. Digital advertising on the Internet has various advantages compared to print media, such as interaction among readers, advertisers and contents. For instance, digital ads can be delivered to a targeted audience unobstructed. Mixing entertainment with information, the interactive nature of online advertising can stimulate consumers' interest and desire; the degree of popularity and the quality of advertisements can be instantly and accurately measured by the number and time of mouse clicks; those are characteristics of digital ads valued by advertisers. Online technologies also help advertising sales. Instead of carrying thick magazine samples, ad sales people can just conveniently go through the Internet and show clients the most suitable columns for their advertisements. Utilizing the Internet, advertisers and advertising agencies can review magazine samples, advertising price lists and monitor sales reports online.

With the demand for digital magazines increasing, the online magazine business model in China will gradually mature. In China, we can see two trends forming in online magazine publishing: subdivision and integration. With the increasingly refined subdivision of work and operation in an individual magazine, the online operators of magazines should distinguish themselves by focusing their publishing resource on the specialties in certain areas. Those who pursue the publishing model of big and comprehensive will most likely be the loser in fierce competition. On the other hand, the industry is going through a process of integration in which Internet service operators, technology providers and traditional magazine publishers are working together to provide online magazines. The Internet service providers with online operation experience and a valid business model will seek contents from magazine publishers, and thereby integrate Internet technologies, resources and contents; thus all stakeholders of digital magazines can complement each other.

REFERENCES

Ding, Hegen. *Media Competitive Power—Core Strategy of the Chinese Medium Development.* Shanghai: Fudan University Press, 2005.

Lei, Shegyuan. "Periodical's Core Competitive Power." *Editors Bimonthly Magazine.* 2005: 4.

Li, Pin. *Report on the Development of Chinese Magazine Industry.* Beijing: Social Sciences Academic Press, 2005.

Liang, Hao. "Xplus: Electronic Magazine Subversive Future." *Discovering Value.* 2006: 1.

Lu, Taihong. *Report On The Chinese Consumer Behavior.* China Social Sciences Press, 2005.

Tan, Haiyan. "Discuss on the Profit Pattern of Multimedia Carrier." *China Book Business Report.* 28 March 2006: 7.

Tan, Haiyan and Peng Peng. "The Traditional Media Make Transition to the New Media." *China Book Business Report.* 1 Jan. 2006: 3

Wang, Jingui and Jing Shan. "The Development of Network Publishing Industry Needs High Quality People of Online Publishing." *China Publishing.* 2004: 11.

Wu, Feng. "Review of Distribution by Magazine for 20 Years." *Media.* 2005: 10.

Xu, Ruobing and Liu Chang. "The Periodical Core Competitive Power is a Kind of Joint Power." *Editors' Friend.* 2003: 4.

Zhou, Weihua. "Analyze on the Publishing Enterprise Core Competency." *Editors' Friend.* 2003: 1.

———. "Digitization Magnify Magazines' Marketing Opportunities." *China Book Business Report.* 2 Jun. 2006: 4.

———. "Economy Development and Media Tendency in Globalization Time." *China Book Business Report.* 17 Jun. 2005: 15.

———. "The New Readers' Relationship under the New Media Circumstance." *China Book Business Report.* 3 Jan. 2006: 7.

———. "Magazine Publishers Get Benefits from the Digitization." *China Book Business Report.* 30 Jun. 2006: 7.

———. "Six Great Technologies Change Magazine Publishing." *China Book Business Report.* 15 Jul. 2005: 15.

Research on Tourism Magazines in the Digital Environment

He Yun

Nowadays, digital technology plays an ever more pervasive role in society, especially in the publishing industry. Magazine publishers have recognized that the new digital technology will make the way magazines are sold absolutely different. What is the difference before and after using the new technology?

1. Survey of Digital Tourism Periodical Publication

Digital technology initially was used to transmit content and to support mobile phones and websites.

1.1 How Digital Technology Come to be Used in Magazines

The digital magazine can be divided into two major types: one is called the common electronic magazine, which is related to the electronic hardware, the soft diskette, CD, etc. It saves magazine information by carrying the electronic version of the publication. The other is called the network magazine; it is an electronic magazine that makes use of networks such as the Internet.

The first is usually used for storing the content of the magazine instead of the paper medium. As we all know, paper is not durable and is prone to decay or destruction from a variety of sources. With the use of the soft diskette and CD-Rom, magazines can be kept for a long time. Besides, the electronic magazine can classify automatically, which can save the reader's time in finding writers and titles of articles.

The second is making a totally new way of operating magazines. In the old days, making a magazine at least needed an editor, some writers, a print factory and some deliverers. As the network magazine appeared, all of this work could be done by one person. People can read these magazines directly on a website as soon as it is ready. The writer can also be the editor by using some editing software.

In 1992, Chongqing Offset of Chinese Science and Technology Information Institution published the Chinese Science and Technology Periodicals CD Database, which signaled that electronic magazines began to flourish in China. The first Chinese network magazine, *China News Digest,* appeared in April 1994. Created in January 1995 and operated by the China Education Ministry, *China Scholars Aboard* was the first electronic magazine published in Mainland China through the Internet, and published throughout the world with the CERNET.

Henceforth, Internet electronic magazines began to grow profusely and quickly in China, including *The Internet World*, and *The China Computer Users* in the IT category, S*trategy and Management*, *Modern Insurance*, and *Capital* in the financial category, and *The Traveler* and *China National Geography* in the tourism category.

1.2 Survey of Digital Technology Application in Tourism Magazines

The tourism magazine has a unique characteristic among magazines. Nowadays, the standard of living and the quality of life rise continuously, allowing people more holidays and leisure time, so they pay more attention to traveling than before. People who like traveling and leisure activities here become the main targeted readers of tourism magazines. The main body of a tourism magazine is photos, so the paper quality requirements are strict. Due to this, most traditional tourism magazines are thick and heavy, which make delivery and storage difficult and expensive. Therefore, the new digital technique is more useful for tourism magazines than any other type of magazine.

By using the first type of new digital technology, the traditional tourism magazine was changed into the common electronic magazine. The thick and heavy original one turned into a small and portable CD format. When readers read it, they just need to place the CD in a computer.

But by using the second type of technology, network technology, the traditional magazine has changed into a network magazine. Such magazines are different from the former ones, and no longer need CD-ROMs; readers can read the articles and browse the photos from the websites operated by the tourism magazines directly.

Take the world famous tourism magazine *National Geographic* as an example. In 1990s, it expanded its products in the digital field, such as photos collection CDs, video collection CDs, maps and some specialized equipment used for photography or exploration of the wild. Further, readers can also subscribe to both the paper type and web type of *National Geographic* online. Based on the unique character of *National Geographic*, it is also a scholarly journal. Data from its articles can be used in research papers, therefore, another revenue source for *National Geographic* is to sell its database in its online shop. This database also has two types: one is a hardcopy database (CD, etc.); the other is a digital database, only provided to members.

2. Impact of Digital Technology on Tourism Magazine Publishing

Digital technology affects magazines by making them into two types: common electronic magazines and network magazines. This just concerns the magazine operation of the magazine, but how does digital technology affect the circulation of the magazine? Taking the tourism magazines as an example, something has changed after using the new digital technology in publishing.

2.1 Digital Technology Spurs Circulation Growth

The traditional tourism magazines are always printed on coated art paper in order to keep the photos and maps as intelligible as possible. On this ground, the postage fee is higher than for other types of magazines without images, because the tourism magazine is heavier and thicker. Because the cost of the magazine is high, the circulation of tourism magazines is limited.

When using digital technology, the cost can be reduced by large-scale production of CD's or video diskette cards. And with computers and PDAs widely available, people will tend to read on screen instead of on paper.

Before the Internet appeared, magazines usually put their subscription advertisements in the post office's subscription catalog or on television or in other magazines. The magazine operating costs consisted in great part of this advertising fee. But when the network magazine appeared, all advertisements could be put on the website, and the magazine did not have to pay a lot of money for advertising. The saved money can be used in the production of the magazine and can decrease its price in order to increase circulation.

The network broke the boundary between regions that existed before the Internet was widely used. Some magazines can be only read and subscribed to where they are published; however, by using the network a magazine is available to readers all over the world.. This also helps the travel magazines to expand their sales in the domestic and international markets. For example, once *National Geographic* could be read in the United States only; now crossing over national boundaries, people can subscribe to and read it on its website directly. And they also can order related products on its website, such as equipment for exploring the wild, maps, etc.

2.2 New Publishing Ways Appear

Before the wide use of the Internet, almost all magazines depended on the post office or advertisements on television, radio or in other paper mediums; certainly tourism magazine were of no exception.

After network magazines and electronic magazines appeared, sales of the magazine had an additional mode besides the two types mentioned above. The magazine website also had an online order function; readers could subscribe to the magazine directly from the website and could choose the one which they liked most instead of subscribing at least a quarter before. Some magazines have a network version, where readers can read articles directly online for free, or use an email box to subscribe. If the reader subscribes to a magazine via their email, the magazine agency will periodically send the magazine into the subscriber's inbox, and the subscriber can pay the fee by using a credit card or online-bank paying systems.

Traditional magazines generally could be sold once, but in the new digital technology-supporting era, magazines can double or even triple sales.

The so-called second-time sales mean both the network magazines and the electronic magazines have huge supporting databases. Generally the reader can acquire information from the magazines which he purchased or to which he subscribed. If he wants to acquire any information beyond the magazines he has, he needs to purchase these issues. Now, the magazine agency can select and sell the database or digital magazines that the reader needs. And when some professional organizations and research institutions want to buy the data, maps or photos they need, the magazine agency then can sell the whole database to them.

The third-time sale means pictures, articles, maps the image documents that have been used in out of date magazines, which can be sold again to television stations or publishers who professionally publish maps. These things can be sold in the form of real objects, and also can be established as large subscription on-line databases, and carry on online sales.

3. Ways that Digital Technology Helps Tourism Magazines Increase Income

The main income of most consumer magazines is not dependent upon circulation but on ad revenues. For magazine publishers, advertising sponsors are as important as readers. Under general circumstances, fashion publications acquired the highest advertising revenue of all types of consumer magazines, but after digital technology became widely used, the advertisement sum of tourism magazines also grew greatly, and advertising sponsors acquired profits from them that more directly compared with fashion magazines.

3.1 Bringing More Advertising Patrons

Take the United States, one of the most developed magazine publishing countries, as an example. The top advertising revenue is from the magazine *Travel Week*, instead of from the best-welling magazines such as *TV Guide* or the well-known *Time.*

Why do tourism magazines have more advertisements than other magazines? There are many reasons, one of which is that tourism magazines have a unique character. Their readers are more flexible and extensive, for many people only like one type of sport or music, but almost everyone likes traveling and leisure, and so they can take more types of advertisements than any other magazines. The second reason is that tourism magazines usually introduce some travel destinations and include photos of them in the magazine, which is like a free advertisement for the travel destination, and some travel publishers will pay money to the magazine agencies in order to have an article or some pictures in the magazine.

During travel, tourists often need additional equipment or information, for example, a mariner's compass, airline information, hotel information, etc. All of these are good business opportunities; they can bring profit to the travel agency and other related companies. Hence, these companies or organizations will save the tourism magazines advertisement expenses and other service charges in order to have their product appear in the magazine.

3.2 Providing Online Payment Services for the Target Readers

People are all trying to differentiate themselves. More and more people choose different travel routes from others. But the preparation of corresponding products and the drawing up of itineraries all need a professional person to carry this out. Therefore, the tourism magazine has become a good data provider and a good adviser.

When people decide where to go, most of them will follow destinations that the tourism agencies have recommended or suggested before. But more and more young people will choose to consult experienced travelers or explorers, and then tourism magazines can provide a network platform, letting common tourists and professional experts chat online or exchange information. Then they charge them a service fee.

Some tourism magazines will adopt the form of a membership system; the traveler only needs to hand over certain expenses, then he or she will become a member of that magazine. The members can acquire some benefits such as the use of magazine databases or attending tour groups. Even more, when the member is traveling or driving in open country, they can use the Internet to learn their position and the information from satellites can be sent to the member through GPS, so that the member can conduct his journey safely.

REFERENCES

Huang, Pei and Chen Junfang. 2003. *The Theory, Method and Practice of Business Model.* Beijing: China Standard Press, 2003.

Li, Ping. 2003. The Public Magazine Operation. *Beijing: Encyclopedia of China Publishing House,* 2003.

Woll, Thomas. *Publishing for Profit.* Beijing: China Renmin University Press, 2005.

http://www.trendsmag.com/

http://www.cng.com.cn/

http://www.nationalgeographic.com/

Application of Digital Technology to Newspaper Publishing and Distribution

Jiang Ling

Since the 1990s, digital technology has developed quickly, which is characterized by processing, delivering and receiving information in the form of bits. Now, it has penetrated every field worldwide. During this digital revolution, newspapers are enduring the most profound change in their form in history.

1. Influences of Digital Technology on Newspaper Publishing and Distribution

The onset of the digital era leads to boosting information display modes in the direction of diversification and high-production. Digital technology has influenced every part of the whole process.

First, traditional newspapers base production management on digital technology. According to a survey from *China Media Science and Technology*, journalism has almost carried out fully digitalized management. Second digital technology has become a useful help to editors and journalists. If they are not able to grasp digital technology skillfully, they are not qualified for publishing. Third, as the representative of advanced productivity, digital technology will bring the reform of the newspaper industry, which can be reflected in the concept and form of newspaper publishing. Different from traditional newspaper publishing and distribution, it has transformed to cross-media publishing. That means the information can be tailored once but communicated in multiple forms and distributed in traditional or online commerce.

2. Some Examples of the Application of Digital Technology in the Newspaper Industry

Owing to computer technology, the newspaper industry leads the way in saying goodbye to the typing and offset printing age. With the rapid development of laser typesetting, the pre-print production of colorful newspapers has arisen, and colorful newspapers are a popular phenomenon. Further, increasingly mature page-transmission technology has broadened the market coverage, allowing a newspaper to be published at the same time in different areas.

2.1 Computer to Plate (CTP)

CTP's advantages coincide with the high quality and exact timeliness of newspaper printing. For example, CTP saves the plate-making time, streamlines production techniques, reduces pollution and boosts productivity. Facing fierce competition, the CTP system can shorten the publishing cycle, which is favorable for the publication of evening newspapers. With a fixed print time, the news deadline can be delayed in about half an hour. CTP was first introduced in the trade show *drupa* in 1995, since then many newspaper offices have adopted the technology. In 1998, the *Yangcheng Evening News* from Guangzhou was the first to introduce AGFA flat-plate plate making, arousing a warm response in the newspaper circles. As of 2004, China's newspaper industry owned 58 CTP equipments. Now, there are some newspaper print factories which have adopted full-scale CTP instead of traditional techniques. Undoubtedly, CTP has shown a promising future.

2.2 Digital Proof

Considering the increasing popularity of colorful newspapers and stricter advertisement requirements, digital proof has become widespread in the newspaper industry. Digital proof has redefined the proof standard on the basis of CIP3/CIP4. With the help of computers and related equipment and software, it reproduces colorful graphs and character information from RIP data on the same page and controls print the quality of the whole process. In 1995, digital proof entered the Chinese market. Now it has been gradually accepted by newspaper circles and over 150 digital proof machines used in China. *China Youth News* has used digital proof into the advertisement, publishing and printing departments. It has been an important means to control and manage colorful newspaper production.

2.3 Digital Print

Digital print is a print technology that uses a pre-print system to input all information to a digital printer through the Internet. It brings print to such an effective operation mode that from input to output, the whole process can be controlled by one person no matter time or distance; so it suits POD (Print on Demand) particularly well. Especially now, the newspaper market needs POD, because POD can not only satisfy multi-type, multi-edition and mini-circulation requirements, but also can finish any task on demand in the shortest time. Under digital print conditions, newspapers can go another way to distribution first and then publish and print. The Canadian website "Newspaper Direct" publishes and delivers 400 newspapers from sixty eight countries in thirty nine languages. Through worldwide distributors, the web service has been realized in eighty five countries. The newspapers are delivered to corresponding customers with limited sales locations such as hotels, embassies and educational institutions.

2.4 Digital Workflow and Criteria

Digital workflow integrates and manages all information from pre-print, print and post-print to ensure digital information circulates completely and correctly. In order to specify the whole workflow information, some related technical criteria have been posed. In 1995, some famous pre-print, print and post-print producers (three P's) organized the CIP3 Association, dedicated to vertical integration of pre-print, print and post-print processes. In 1999, AGFA, Heidelberg, Manroland and Adobe organized the JDF Association and also developed the JDF format. The JDF format is an open data format, which has introduced the CIMS (Contemporary Integrated Manufacturing Systems) concept to printing. In July 2000, CIP3 and JDF were united as the CIP4 Association, plus the process on the basis of three P's. Recently, some producers have developed workflow systems based on JDF.

2.5 Digital Publishing and DAM

When newspaper offices have digitalized all press releases and then print through digital print flow, that is digital publishing. In essence, digital publishing makes the content and process digital. During the process, a great deal of information such as news releases, pictures, websites and pages are stored. These are digital assets. DAM (Digital Assets Management) can organize and manage the digital assets effectively. In this way, it can establish newspaper office databases, save production costs, and carry out cross-media publishing, which is attractive to more and more newspaper offices.

2.6 New Media Technology

Under the conditions of new media, newspapers have extended to the Internet, mobile phones and other media, changing the style of reading and distribution.

2.6.1 Online newspapers

The Internet is regarded as the fourth medium. In the 1990s, many newspapers witnessed the attractive potential of the Internet, so they went online. In October 1995, *China Trade Newspaper* became the first to connect to the Internet. After nearly twenty years, online newspapers have developed a particular design and editing process from newspaper to information paper. What are the prominent characteristics of online newspapers? They are the advantages of all-round and unlimited communication. Recently, several online newspapers websites became key news portals while some local newspapers established local news websites. In general, online newspapers fall behind news portals.

2.6.2 Mobile phone newspapers

Mobile phones as a new medium become more popular with the development of the Internet. The newspaper news can be sent to a customer's cell phone through a wireless platform, and then the customer will read the latest news in time on his or her cell phone. This it helps newspapers establish good relationships between readers and advertisers. In 2004, *China Women News* started the first mobile phone newspaper in China. As of February 2006, there are more than thirty newspapers that have cell phone editions.

2.6.3 Electronic paper

At the first China Digital Publishing Expo, the electronic paper, invented by Philips, attracted many visitors' attention. Electronic paper can also be called digital paper, which combines paper and electronic apparatuses. Compared with traditional paper, electronic paper can be carried easily and read comfortably. In 2004, Philip together with E-Ink applied a screen of electronic paper into a Sony electronic reader. In the future, it is likely that electronic paper will be a mainstream medium of the Internet.

Digital technology has pushed the newspaper industry to develop along the digital track. There are enormous innovations in editing, printing and other aspects. Newspapers are transforming to digital mediums. At the same time, newspapers have taken more than one form. Readers can receive and consume them from different ends. Meanwhile, newspaper offices are being improved as a new platform to offer digital content.

REFERENCES

Li, Baoqiang. 2005. The Modest Proposal for Newspaper Print Digitalization. *Print Technology* .2005 (1).

Miao, Miao. 2005. E-newspaper arised for use of Digital Publishing. *Publishing World.* 2005 (7).

Min, Dahong. 2006. The course and Forcast of China Newspaper Digitalization. *Media.* 2006 (3).

Newspaper Direct. http://www.newspaperdirect.com (visiting date: 08/24/2006).

Wu, Dingyong. 2006. Where is the newspaper future: mobile newspaper or e-newspaper. West-south University For Nationalities Transaction (Art and Social Science).

Which Plays the Dominant Role: Content Resources or Technical Resources?

Xiao Lei

Introduction

The publishing industry has experienced two technological revolutions so far. One is the innovation of an electronic composition system; the other is the appearance of digital publishing technology. The former resulted in a revolutionary change in the publishing and printing industry. The system is characterized by its low cost as well as high efficiency. However, this technology is just an improvement on printing. It still relies on printed media, and there is not a substantial material improvement in how to make use of the information efficiently. Digital technology has changed this phase. It gets rid of the limitations of paper; the new technology not only realizes permanent storage without deterioration, but also quickens the speed of transformation and searching of information. Digital technology has a great influence on the Chinese publishing industry where, in the early 1990s, it was widely applied. The innovation of the digital CD impelled a whole level of audiovisual publishing. With the development of multimedia technology, digital publishing becomes more and more popular. Along with the development of new digital information technology, the publishing industry is entering a new era.

The development of digital publishing is the emphasis of "the eleventh five year" progress program. The Annual Conference on Digital Publishing in China was held in Beijing on October thirteenth, 2006, and lasted three days. Three hundred delegates from the press and publication institutes, libraries as well as high and new-technology industry enterprises attended the conference this year. Their discussion concerned the tendencies of the digital publishing industry, standardization, protection of digital copyright, among other issues.

The Development of Digital Publishing in College Press

Nowadays traditional publishing still plays the dominant role; however, printed media fuses with electronic media. Take college presses, for example. There were ninety eight presses in 1994, which accounted for seventeen percent of the total 572 publishing houses. They have various publishing rights of both books and audiovisual publications; 34 own the copyrights of books and electronic books; another twenty two hold the copyrights of both books, audiovisual and electronic books. Many of them have participated in digital publishing.

The Shanghai Foreign Language Teaching Press, which was founded by Shanghai International Studies University in 1979, is one of the most authoritative publishing houses for foreign language books and e-books. In order to accommodate the digital era, the publishing house added an Electronic Publication Newsroom. The press also introduced the new edition of *College English*, which includes the textbook, videotape, a multimedia CD, network system and a collection of exercises that give convenient English study. Requested by the Ministry of Education, they explore the "new idea college English online teaching system," which is composed of four parts: online courses, supplementary teaching resources, online tests and managing support. Based on advanced information technology, this new system focuses on individuation of teaching, and provides an environment for self-instruction. The "new idea college English online teaching system" is one of the greatest multimedia teaching systems using advanced technology, which provides a good environment for college English study and breaks through the limitations of textbooks and classes.

The Higher Education Press was founded in 1954, and is the largest and most prominent publisher of educational books in China. With the development of science technology, the press established an "Audio-visual Publishing Centre," "Electronic Publishing Centre," "Multimedia Publishing Centre" and created the "Higher Education Electronic and Audio-visual Press" in 1999. During the past two decades, its publication scope has been significantly broadened. Never confining itself to paper printing, the Higher Education Press also develops a great amount of audio-visual, electronic products and online teaching materials today. United Learning Software Technology Company is a subsidiary of the Higher Education Press. The company bases itself on the development of educational information and campus digitalization. It focuses on the creation of good educational resources for home use. In virtue of the network, the company produces educational software and develops various educational services. In the past five years, they have emphasized development of digitized management and content resource building, and this attempt has been very fruitful. Furthermore, the press put forward the idea of "developing the press by making use of new technology" in its program for the next five years. They regard digital technology as the impetus of further progress.

Content Resources and Technical Resources

In the digital age, technology is a great essential: The golden rule "content is king," is endowed with new meaning. Meanwhile, the publishing houses are facing challenges. The sticking point consists of searching for related technical support according to their own content resources, and dealing with the relationship between content and technology correctly. On the one hand, content is the key resource.

We should strengthen our acquisition abilities, and in this case, we can handle the market; on the other hand, the traditional publishing industry centering on content resources has difficulties keeping pace with digital technology. Firstly, online publishing demands the centralization of publishing resources, but the resources owned by printed media publishing are inadequate to sustain online publishing operations. Secondly, the application of new technology is costly, with serious risks and long cycles. It is unreasonable to develop a new information system alone. Due to this, traditional publishers and technology providers should establish cooperate, instead of competing or being adversaries. Both sides need to enhance communication and interaction in order to drive the upgrading of our industry. For example, Beijing Founder Electronics Co., Ltd, ChineseAll, DigiBook and Tsinghua Tongfang all are IT technology providers. The Apabi product family is widely used in online bookstores, school libraries and publishing houses. The "Online Anti-Pirate Alliance" sponsored by ChineseAll is an important component of anti-piracy online.

In this cooperation, the publishing house should hold the initiative. It is necessary to persist in a suitable price standard and distribution portion when sending digital content to others. In addition, the ultimate task is to foster the development of people with abilities and enhance the capabilities of independent innovation. To achieve this goal, our government and publishing companies should launch related forums or training courses so as to improve overall competitiveness and optimize the industrial structure. Additionally, we need to change our teaching program by adding some new research directions and enhance theoretical research.

The Future of Digital Publishing

Owing to the advancement of global information, the digital publishing industry will have a bright future. According to research by GAPP, the total revenue of online publishing reached 3.5billion RMB in 2004, and it also drove the income of some related industries (IT, communications, media, education etc.). It mentions that the sales volume of e-books was 8.05 million in 2004. It is forecast that the portion of online publications will increase to fifty percent of the total revenue by 2020. What is more, ninety percent books will be online editions after ten years.

In Germany, most publishers hold an optimistic attitude toward the future of digital publishing. It is calculated that its profit only amounts to 5% of the total turnover now. Nevertheless, the publishers suggest that the proportion will increase to 15% in the following ten years. In October 2006, Bertelsmann Media Worldwide announced their launch of a venture foundation Bertelsmann Digital Media Investments. The investment area emphasizes digital media, and the fund totals fifty million euro. Digital publishing turns out to be an international tendency.

REFERENCES

Hou, Yi. "DigiBook Surges the New Tidal Wave of Digital Publishing." *Chinese Publishing* (2006): 1.

Liu, Zhipeng. "Developing in Virtue of Technology, and Building a Digitized Enterprise." *China Book Business Report* (2006).

Liu, Chao. "Drawing the Outline of Digital Blueprint in Xiangshan." *Publishing Today* (2006).

Social Science Research and Ideology and Politics Department, Ministry of Education of PRC. *Report on the Development of College Press in China 2001–2004.* Beijing: China Renmin University Press, 2005.

Open Access Publishing: The Game Playing among Researchers, Libraries and Publishers

Fang Qing & Tao Li

Technology is always the basic motive for the evolution of the communicative mode of scientific information. With the development of technology, the communicative mode of scientific information is ever changing. Scientific information has been traditionally communicated via mainstream channels such as books and journals. With the arrival of the 1990s, open access publishing, which is based on the Internet and digital technology, has brought about the "revival" of informal scientific communication and the "return" of rational scholarly publishing. Nowadays, open access has already become an important new scientific communication, which has greatly influenced traditional academic communication mode and aroused widespread attention from research organizations, research supporting organizations, publishers and libraries.

In December 2001, the Open Society Institution (OSI) held a small meeting in Budapest, at which the Budapest Open Access Initiative (BOAI) was released. BOAI offered the popularly acceptable definition of open access. Up to early March, 2006, 3,998 individuals and 343 organizations have signed on in support of this idea. On April 11, 2003, at the headquarters of the Howard Hughes Medical Institute in Chevy Chase, Maryland, the people interested in open access of scientific literature gathered together and drafted the Bethesda Statement on Open Access Publishing, which clearly pointed out two necessary conditions for open access publishing. During October 20 to 22, 2003, initiated by Max Planck Society of Germany and with the participation of many research centers and funding bodies from lots of countries such as Germany, France, and Italy, the Conference on Open Access to Knowledge in the Science and Humanities was held in Berlin. At this conference, the Berlin Declaration on Open Access to Knowledge in Sciences and Humanities was signed in accordance with the open access spirit put forward by Budapest and Bethesda in order to encourage scientists to make public their papers in open access format. Since that moment, the range of open access has extended from the natural sciences to the humanities and social sciences.

Through the three important manifestos of Budapest, Bethesda and Berlin, relevant individuals have a relatively clear and complete understanding of the denotation and connotation of open access. The governments of many countries, such as Great Britain, the U.S., Canada and Australia, have already shown their approval for open access. Some international organizations like the United Nations and the International Federation of Library Associations (IFLA), also have taken a positive attitude toward the development of the open access movement. With the prosperous development of open access journals of the non-profit organization Public Library of Science (PloS) and the for-profit organization BioMed Central (BMC), some traditional academic publishers like Oxford University Press (OUP) started to cultivate their open access publishing business. Some scientific research funding and charity organizations, such as the Howard Hughes Medical Institute and the Welcome Trust, promise to pay researchers for their papers publishers financially for moving in the direction of access journals. Moreover, some government organizations like the Joint Information Systems Committee (JISC) financial compensate publishers to move in the open access. These policies and movements strongly advocate the evolution of the open access movement.

However, suspicions have come from authorities in academic circles and the publishing field. The British Royal Academy, which issued the first peer-reviewed scientific periodical (still in publication) in the world in 1665, announced that "open access journals and open archiving would bring 'disaster' to the scientific publication." Some publishers emphasized that the reformation of the current academic system would mean a devaluation of current academic qualities and standards, which would transfer higher publishing fees to the scientists and scientific research organizations and finally damage the whole course of scientific research course. The typical opinion is, as the Vice President of Professional and Scholarly Publishing at the Association of American Publishers, Barbara Meredith, pointed out, that AAP was not against open access, while it did disagree with the government interfering with the free market principle via deciding how to publish research output.

Then how about the prospect of open access publishing? This depends on the game playing among the three players. This article takes Open Access Journals as an example and briefly articulates the game playing among researchers, users and publishers from the perspectives of scientific research impact as well as cost sharing.

1. Researchers: Widespread Influence vs. Increasing Publishing Cost

The researchers are the author resource of scientific publishing. With roles both as content providers and publication users (this article only focuses on the role of content provider), their attitudes toward open access decide the pace of its development to a great extent.

1.1 Widely Obtaining Information and Greater Influence of Scientific Payoffs

As providers of content, researcher's while they are choosing a journal to contribute to, would consider factors such as the journal quality, authority, influence, publishing frequency, as well as whether it is abstracted or indexed. First, open access removes the obstacle of high fees to access to academic literature, which positively enlarges the influence of the researchers' outcome. This has been proved by research on the open access conference paper in the computer science field (Lawrence 2001), and by similar research in wider scientific fields (Antelman 2004). With the help of electronic technology, open access publishing enhances the rapidity of academic publications. Meanwhile, in open access publishing, the restrictions on the users of academic documents are far fewer than in the traditional mode. As to the open access publications, the researchers mainly hold the "spiritual" rights, such as contribution right and right to maintaining the integrity of the works. And they usually allow the users to read, copy, share, store, print, index, connect and search through the whole paper without restrictions. Without any doubt, this results in more quotations and enlarges the influence of the scientific output. Due to the particular purpose of academic publishing, this copyright transferring ensures the maximum of influence and the maximum of application of research output; it also ensures the balance between publishers and the public users.

Therefore, most researchers take the view that open access publishing symbolizes a comeback of the core values of academic research, i.e. open access removes the barriers to academic communication, and accelerates the development of academic research. (Key Perspectives 2004). The result of a study about university authors conducted by the Coalition for Networked Information (CNI) in 2004 reveals that eighty seven percent of informants considered that the most attractive point of open access publishing is the equal public access opportunities for all readers and hence the wider circulation of the paper (Schonfeld 2004).

1.2 Licenser-paying Mode Increases the Academic Publishing Cost

Under the mode of open access publishing, researchers have to pay to publish their papers. The American Physiological Society rules that if the writer paid $1500 to *Physiological Genomics*, the writer's paper could be freely obtained; but if the writer did not pay, readers have to gain the paper through subscription or after a 12-month embargo. As of 2004, about ten percent of writers have agreed to pay (Crawford 2004a). Blackwell's Open Online system regulates that the writer-paying open access papers can be published in the print journals or can be obtained freely via the online platform Blackwell Synergy. During the experimental time, the fee for the writers settled to $2,500 or $1,500 per paper.

Concerning the mode of copyright-owner payments, there are many people shaking their heads, alleging that this mode "brings a new barrier to obstructing knowledge communication." The British Royal Academy suggested that this economic barrier has more profound influence on researchers who are short of funds, and that scientists in their early career stages or researchers from developing countries are all included in this echelon.

However, the advocates of open access have reasons to revolt against this fallacy. Although the writers have to pay for the published papers in the journals, most writers would solve the funds problem through research funds or relevant organizations; for researchers under economic stress, many open access publishers are willing to cut or decrease the fees; as a result, open access publishing modes are quite acceptable for the authors. What's more revolutionary is that this mode breaks through the traditional restriction of using academic literature fairly, hence it spreads the research result more widely, which is of great benefit both to researchers and to the public.

2. Library: Decrease in Cost of Obtaining vs. Shaking of Academic Status

In the environment of open access, libraries are quite likely to lose the importance that they have through the traditional academic communication system. When the authority, completeness and currency of the provided academic information are challenged by other communication modes, how can the advantages of library information services be explained?

2.1 Open Access Publishing Greatly Cuts the Cost of Obtaining Library Collections

The traditional scientific publishing mode started to cause a "serials crisis" in the 1970s. The "big deal" strategy of journal sales binds the libraries in the passive position where several publishers monopolize academic publishing. Through bundle selling, the publishers bind an abundance of subordinate journals with a few core publications, and the libraries cannot select their necessary publications flexibly nor purchase the journals from other non-profit publishers due to their limited funds. Open access publishing breaks this monopoly in some sense. The libraries are not confined by various restrictions such as high prices or technological protections while they are acquiring research literature. The licensing mode frees libraries from economic problems, which makes them the greatest beneficiary and strongest supporters of the open access movement.

The supporting practice began in the 1990s, and, recently, many world-renowned libraries and library associations have started to encourage and initiate open access publishing. The Scholarly Publishing and Academic Resources Coalition (SPARC) has nearly 300 organizational members, with a lot of cooperative publishing organizations and open access publications, such as DOAJ, PLoS, BMC, E-Print Network, *Economics Bulletin* and *Journal of Machine Learning Research*. In February 2004, IFLA published the *Announcement about Open Access of Academic Documents and Research Files*, which promised to promote the widest availability of research information via powerfully supporting the open access movement and open access publications. In June of the same year, the British Columbia Library Association officially announced it would dedicate itself to the open access movement in its *Resolution on Open Access*. Just after that, in October of the same year, the cooperative company of the National Library of Scotland, the Scottish Science Information

Strategy Working Group, drafted of the *Scottish Declaration of Open Access*, which got published the next March. Further, individual libraries, such as the libraries of Harvard, Yale, and Washington University in the U.S., introduced the open access communication on their homepages. The National Book and Information Center for the Institute of Semiconductors of the China Academy of Sciences also established a column called the "open resource center" on their home page, organizing and uncovering popularly used open access resources for the researchers.

2.2 Open Access Publishing Changes the Libraries' Status in Scientific Communication Systems

The core of open access lies in the fact that the readers can freely read, download, copy, transmit, print, search and connect to the full text of research output, which breaks through the academic communication mode that was once controlled by monopoly publishers. The original open access journals are mostly initiated by individuals who use the servers of organizations such as universities for free and offer edited works voluntarily. With the increasing number of topen access journals, more and more libraries have begun to offer open access services. In 2002, responding to the proposal of the First Nordic Conference on Scholarly Communication, the library of Lund University undertook the task of sponsoring and maintaining DOAJ, which is a complete list dynamically covering all peer-reviewed open access journals in all languages.

Articles in open access journals are also self-archived, that is to say, besides open access journals, readers can find the article stored in the subject-specific repositories, institutional repositories or on the author's homepage. Meanwhile, some IT companies with insight also notice the potential value of an open access publishing mode. For example, Google enriches itself with open access files, in order to increase the number of users and visits. In November 2004, the Google Scholar website opened, and provided all the users with availability to academic articles and documents, including journal papers, degree theses and technical reports. Google encourages writers and publishing organizations to offer their academic papers and indexes for free. The users can get relevant documents indexed by writers' names, publication titles, publishing dates and article titles, and the search results are listed in order of the degree of relevance. Apart from that, there are some other influential open access projects, such as the Open Content Alliance co-operated by Yahoo and Microsoft, as well as the Million Book Project launched by the European Union, the Library of Congress and Amazon.

Therefore, both open access information collecting activities by individuals and open access projects invested in by IT companies challenged the open access service provided by libraries. Can libraries maintain their authority as information providers in the new academic communication system?

3. Publishing Organizations: Profit from Market vs Profit from Resource

As for the publishers, open access is a challenge too. If the traditional business model changes to the open access publishing model, the previous high profits depending on sales would not exist. It is undeniable that the existing profit margin under the traditional publishing mode would be cut.

3.1 The Profit of Traditional Academic Publishing Comes from the Monopoly Market

According to the statistics of the British government's Committee of Science and Technology, Reed Elsevier predominated in the 2003 global STM journal market with a 28.2% market share, following other commercial publishers such as Thomson, Wolters Kluwer, Springer, John Wiley, Blackwell Publishing, and Taylor & Francis. The only non-profit publishing organization entering the top eight is the American Chemistry Society (ACS) with a 3.6% market share. The statistics above prove that commercial publishers are still the controllers of the academic journal market.

Several reasons contribute to this situation: First, due to the particularity of their content, substitution between homogenous journals is not strong enough. Hence, the elasticity of the academic journals' prices is weak, i.e. the users are not sensitive to the prices of academic journals. Second, academic journals are in a increasing convergence trend, which is led by commercial behaviors like mergers and acquisition on the one hand, and on the other hand, many academies and societies choose to cooperate with publishers and commit the manufacture and sale of journals to them, in which way the monopoly of academic publishing also gets enhanced. The points mentioned above decide that the price-bargaining system does not exist in the academic publishing market and creates the monopoly conditions.

The feature of price elasticity and the structure of the monopoly market determine the existing space for the high profit of traditional academic journals. Nevertheless, the open access publishing mode changes it a lot. Most publishers still keep a suspicious eye on open access publishing and unceasingly resist it. Some of them emphasize that the reform of the current academic publishing system means the wholesale devaluation of academic qualities and standards, which would transfer the higher publishing fees to the scientists and scientific research organizations and finally damage the whole course of scientific research. Others advocated the point of view that due to the lack of capital, their creativity in academic publishing would be suffocated, or that would even keep them from fulfilling their basic functions. The small publishers with marginal profit would be the most anxious ones about this situation.

3.2 New Profit Mode and More Open Academic Communication

In 1987, a postgraduate at Syracuse University, Michael Ehringhaus, initiated a free, peer-reviewed e-journal *New Horizons in Adult Education*, which nearly included all the elements of today's open access journals. The invention of the World Wide Web in 1991 generated the exponential increase of electronic information, with which more and more free, peer-reviewed e-journals came about. Meanwhile, open access did not affect academic publishing substantially until a number of open access journals were published by some non-profit organizations like PLoS and for-profit publishers like BMC. In October 2000, a group of scientists supporting open access established the nonprofit organization PLoS in San Francisco, U.S.A. In the summer of 2001, PLoS had the idea to initiate its own open access journals in order to compete with the commercial academic publications. With the donation of $9,000,000 from theGordon and Betty Moore Foundation, PLoS gave birth to the most significant open access journal, *PLoS Biology,* in October 2003. This journal is a complete open access journal focusing on biological science at the highest level. It is ruled by strict peer-review, and boasts the high rejection rate of 90%. As of September 2004, over 400 papers of this journal have been indexed by ISI (McVeigh 2004). In order to maintain the basic operating fees, *PLoS Biology* employs the author-pays model, and the price for each research paper is $1,500. PLoS pointed out that the leading rule to judge whether a paper can be published or not is its quality instead of the ability to pay. Therefore, for writers from developing countries or ones without research funds, *PLoS Biology* will cut the publishing fees. Besides, *PLoS Biology* is also actively looking for a new paying mode such as charging the organization members. In the following two years, PLoS established several other journals like *PLoS Medicine* and *PLoS Computational Biology.* All PLoS journals have both an online and a printed edition. The online edition can be accessed for free on the Internet. Take *PLoS Biology* and *PLoS Medicine*, for example: the subscription fee for both was $175 in 2006.

With the growth of high-quality open access journals, more and more higher education organizations, research institutes and fund organizations offer writers funding to publish in open access journals. The publishers are also changing their attitudes toward exploring new profit sources. Even those publishers who held negative views of open access in the past are on the fence now. Some traditional academic publishers, such as Oxford University Press and Springer Publishing have begun to partially adopt the open access behaviors. Some government organizations like JISC offer funds to help publishers change to open access publishing. These policies and movements powerfully support the development of the open access trend.

4. Conclusion: Game-Playing and the Trend of Open Access Publishing

The prospect of open access depends on game playing between the researchers, the users and the publishers.

Researchers are the driving force of scientific publishing with the double roles of content provider and literature user. Their attitudes to open access decide the developing pace of this new scientific communication mode. The only reason for researchers to support open access with increasing research cost is that open access journals should maintain their advantages—they are more conveniently obtained, have wider authorization and higher quality.

Generally speaking, libraries providing open access journal service could maybe get temporary relief from the subscription fees, but they have to do more work for information collection and classification. Meanwhile, because of the quick updating speed of open access publishing, in order to maintain the links and hyper-links dynamically, libraries have to renew and maintain the information frequently. In the past, as the major subscriber and the academic information center, libraries decided the types and numbers of the journals to buy according to their financial situations; meanwhile, for the libraries providing open access journal services, what decides the scale of the libraries is the ability to collect and maintain academic information. Notwithstanding, under the environment of open access, the libraries are facing challenges from other information providers.

The traditional publishing mode not only means a paying and profit mode, but also means a relatively stable reliance between different players. The publishers play both the role of predators of high profit and the role of quality controllers of publications who push forward academic development in their own way. Most traditional publishers will carefully brace for the open access publishing mode with a paradoxical mind: on the one hand, they are worried that it will threaten their financial income; on the other hand, thanks to the latent readers all around the world, their open access journals would draw more advertisements than before, which will turn into extra income

There is also game playing between the new and old profit modes. The result is that more and more publishers take the flexible way. They insist that open access publishing should be confined to research articles; in the meantime, they actively offer the writers the options of the traditional publishing mode and the open access publishing mode. For instance, Springer's Open Choice gives writers the choice of the traditional model based on subscription and the author-pays model based on author fees. Even the most negative publisher, Elsevier, has changed its attitude toward open access subtly. It claims that open access would offer convenience for the publication of various prejudices, which would possibly put in peril the quality of academic publications and sabotage the public belief in science; on the other hand, it admits open access favors the public. One of Elsevier's prestigious journals, *The Lancet*, is also trying open access publishing partially. The sales manager Elsevier in the Asian-Pacific region, Pascal van den Nieuwendijk, says, as to open access, "we are just sitting on the fence."

Different players have different concerns: the focus of the researchers' concerns is how to efficiently enlarge the influence of their research output; libraries concentrate on elevating their authority in information service with limited funds; publishers hope to find a feasible commercial model. Both the traditional academic publishing mode and open access mode incur some costs and produce some effect, so the key point lies in the balance between the players who bear the costs and share the effects. Theoretical analyses and practices prove that for academic publishing, the researchers are not the only beneficiaries, so they would not be the only carrier of costs. As long as libraries and readers benefit from this system, they have to pay for the relevant costs. Therefore, although open access publishing is possible and reasonable, it still cannot substitute for the traditional way of academic communication. Libraries and publishers should be continually searching for a balance between traditional academic journals and open access journals.

REFERENCES

Antelman, Kristen. "Do Open-access Articles have a Greater Research Impact?" *College & Research Libraries* vol.65 (2004): 372-82.

Budapest Open Access Initiative. 5 March 2006 <http://www.soros.org/openaccess/view.cfm>.

Crawford, Walt. *Cites and Insights.* 4 Jan. 2004 <http://cites.boisestate.edu/civ4i13.pdf>.

Fang, Qing. "Theories and Practices of Information." *The Revival of Informal Communication in Internet Environment* (2002): 4.

"First Nordic Conference on Scholarly Communication." 17 Feb. 2006 <http://www.lub.lu.se/ncsc2002>.

Key Perspectives Ltd. *JISC/OSI Journal Authors Survey.* 4 Jan. 2006 <http://www.jisc.ac.uk/uploaded_documents/JISCOAreport1.pdf>.

Mikhailov, A. И. *Science Communication and Information Science.* Beijing: Scientific-Technology Document Publishing House, 1980.

Nieuwendijk, Pascal van den. "Ever-progressing Publishing Industry: Point of View on Open Access." *Institutional Repositories and Technology Exploration* (2005).

Schonfeld, Roger C. and Kevin Guthrie. "What Faculty Think of Electronic Resources 2003: Project Briefing." *Spring 2004 Task Force Meeting.* 4 Jan. 2004 <http://www.cni.org/tfms/2004a.spring/abstracts/PBwhat- guthrie.html>.

Wu, Li and Liu Ziheng. "A New Academic Publishing Mode: Research and Analysis on Open Access Publishing Mode." *Journal of Library Science in China* (2004): 66-69.

Open Access: From the Publishers' Perspective*

Xu Lifang & Xu Qi

After more than three hundred years of effort, publishers have established a science communication system based on numerous amounts of monographs and, especially, scholarly journals, which contributes greatly to the global development of science and technology. Meanwhile, with the advent of Information and Communication Technology (ICT), traditional publishers have found themselves in a very delicate situation. On the one hand, as greedy profit-oriented businessmen in the public eye, publishers were blamed as one of the main causes of the "Serials Crisis," which triggered the open access movement directly in 1990s. On the other hand, the enthusiasm and collaborative spirit of researchers involved in OA efforts was not, alone, enough to offer viable competition for traditional subscription-based delivery channels (Bo-Christer Björk, 2004). Some sober-headed open access advocates realize that the "green road" permitting post print archiving by authors may be the fastest and surest way to reach immediate OA, whereas its achievement largely depends on the publishers' agreements with authors. So it is important to perceive the publishers' real attitude toward open access publishing to date.

1. Traditional Publishers' Attitude Toward OA Publishing

One of the two main goals of the open access movement is to remove the price barrier, which means to cancel the subscription fee. It is almost an overturning of the existing scholarly publishing system for it ruins the lifeline of the industry. So it was imaginable that most traditional publishers held negative opinions about open access. However, with more popular support gained by the open access movement, publishers' attitudes are becoming more rational, and many of their queries have to be answered by the furthering of open access.

1.1 Is Open Access Publishing Sustainable?

The question that the publishers are concerned with most is: is open access publishing a sustainable model to try? From the financial point of view, scholarly publishing is a huge market of billions of dollars. It is impossible for it to depend solely on social subsidies and funds in the long term. As to governments, library budgets have seemed to overburden taxpayers already (in fact, budget decreases are another main cause of open access). It is not feasible for governments to establish a special system to facilitate open access publishing. For example, in the planned economy era, the Chinese government stipulated low prices for academic publications; publishing houses did not care about the bottom line at all, for the surplus had to be handed over to the government, and if there was some loss, the government would offset it. As a result, the system was inefficient. So China learned from advanced countries and is migrating to an academic publishing system controlled by the market instead of by the government. However, Chinese scholarly publishing has not become independent and strong yet because it lacks both competitive experience, such as trade publishing has, and thorough protection from the government, such as educational publishing, especially el-hi publishing, gains. In market economy countries, overthrowing the current system of Scientific, Technical and Medical (STM) publishing should be viewed with caution if public funds could only partly support open access (Elsevier, 2004).

To sum up the above analysis, open access publishing needs enough money generated by itself to support its development. So many open access journals charge authors fees to cover the cost. But usually the fee charged by open access publishers is $1,500 per article, which covers only about 40% - 60% of the estimated total costs to publish an article of the quality that researchers are used to today (Elsevier, 2004). And the issue is more severe for those super journals for they receive many more submissions than they publish. For instance, Nature has a high unit cost per paper published, because for every article published more than ten have been reviewed and not selected. Under an author-pays model, the actual cost per paper published would be in the region of £10,000- £30,000 (Nature Publishing Group, 2004). It is estimated that the remaining costs would range from £1 billion - £2 billion for the STM publishing industry globally if author fees are charged as mentioned above (Elsevier, 2004).

Even the daily operation is difficult to run; it would be impossible to update facilities and to adopt new technology in time. But with the digital era changing with each passing day, deep technology troubles remain hidden that might break out sooner or later. This is easy to understand if you consider the fact that there are few PCs today that can read a 5-inch diskette.

In fact, money and technology are not the only things that influence the sustainable development of open access publishing. Taking most open access journals, for example, they are created, managed and maintained by volunteers. With their job mobility, changing interests and age reasons, the journals could stop publication suddenly. A lot of subject repositories face the same problems. So undoubtedly, sustainable development is a serious issue for open access publishing to resolve.

1.2 How about the Quality of Open Access Publications?

After hundreds of years of evolution, the subscription model could ensure the high quality of published articles via independent peer review, rigorous editorial process and the like. So publishers are qualified to inquire about the quality of open access publishing.

First, in the publishers' opinion, a system based on revenues from authors and their sponsoring institutions may inevitably lead to lower standards, because it is obvious that the one that pays would have more influence, and even control. Some of them would seek to impact the editorial decision, e.g. letting the journal accept articles that are unqualified to be published; or forcing the journal to publish papers and ideas that they favored more. That is a little bit like the familiar influence exerted on consumer magazines by advertisers. Such kinds of influence might not be as unavoidable as the publishers claim, but really should be given attention.

And the more troublesome thing is that the open access publishers also have an inner motivation to publish more research papers in order to increase revenues, for only accepted papers generate revenues. It would potentially compromise the independence and the rigor of the peer review processes. Thus, it would finally risk undermining the public trust in the integrity and quality of scientific publications that has been established over hundreds of years (Elsevier, 2004).

Another quality issue is not related to the research articles directly; it is more about the functionality and usability of open access publications. Due to the lack of enough investment in technology innovation, open access publishers usually cannot afford to add advanced functionality such as searching, cross-linking and profiling to their publications. Failing to take advantage of the capacity of digital publishing, it would in turn impair the access to STM publications as a whole.

1.3 Unfairness Brought About by Open Access Publishing

As the subscription model favors richer reader; the author-pays model inevitably favors richer authors, richer institutions and richer countries. So in the publishers' opinion, the transition from a traditional publishing model to an open access publishing model is just allowing one kind of unfairness to replace another one, and it is difficult to say which one is better.

Furthermore, the open access model will lead to a very tricky situation. Namely, it seems to punish instead of encourage creation by charging authors for each article that has been accepted for publication. Open access publishing transfers the costs of publishing from institutions like commercial corporations and libraries that serve readers, to researchers and their sponsors such as universities, governmental funding agencies and foundations (Elsevier, 2004). A typical example is from the UK. While Britain's spending on journal subscriptions currently amounts to 3.3% of the world's total, UK researchers contribute a much higher 5% of all articles published globally. As a result, the UK government, foundations, universities and researchers could together pay 30-50% more for STM journals in an open access system than they do today. Thus, this is supposed one of the reasons that the UK government finally rejected the Science and Technology Committee's recommendations about open access publishing (see 2.1.2). Further, individual institutions like Cambridge University that are relatively prolific would pay more under an open access system, too. By contrast, commercial organizations that subscribe to many journals but contribute relatively few articles each year would pay substantially less. It is more or less against fairness and social benefit (Elsevier, 2004).

2. Open Access Publishing: Threats or Opportunities for Traditional Publishers

It should be said that publishers do not prefer open access, but there are so many environmental factors that force publishers to embrace it. Meanwhile, regarding open access as a new publishing model and author fees as a new income resource, it seems unreasonable for publishers to reject it completely.

2.1 Threats

Publishers, first of all, regard open access publishing as a big threat, for it puts such great pressure on them.

2.1.1 Pressure from libraries

The "serials crisis" made it difficult for academic libraries to fulfill their primary mission—to provide access to academic literature. So, unsurprisingly, most of them have been supportive of moves towards open access publishing.

Individual libraries such as those of Yale University and Lehigh University and so on have established websites with information about open access publishing for their academic staff and students; meanwhile, the library alliances are more powerful at facilitating open access publishing. In February 2004, prior to the release of the UK report, the IFLA (International Federation of Library Associations) issued a "Statement on Open Access." In early 2002, an ARL (Association of Research Libraries) task force recommended that the association promote "open access to quality information in support of learning and scholarship." The ACRL (Association of College and Research Libraries) has written to both the NIH and the US Congress in support of open access reforms. The Special Libraries Association (SLA), the Medical Library Association (MLA) and others have released statements regarding open access, too.

Most worthy of mention is SPARC (Scholarly Publishing and Academic Resources Coalition), which was established under the auspices of the ARL in the late 1990s in response to the continuing escalation of serials prices. It takes a very flexible combining strategy of encouraging low-price journal alternatives, open access business models (both open access journals and institutional repositories), and open archiving to boost "a more competitive scholarly communication marketplace in which prices are lower, quality is enhanced, and publisher responsiveness to market needs is rewarded." SPARC has a number of open access partners including PloS, BioMed Central, Economics Bulletin, Algebraic and Geometric Topology, Documenta Mathematica, eScholarship, the Journal of Insect Science, the Journal of Machine Learning Research, and the New Journal of Physics. With over 200 members and huge purchasing power, SPARC's movement should be taken into the publishers' account when they finally decide whether to transfer to OA publishing.

2.1.2 Pressure from governments

The governments' actions bring great pressure on publishers, too. In fact, during the first several years of the new millennium, the UK, US and EU have all investigated models for publishing scholarly research results. The Science and Technology Committee in the UK concluded that the current model for scientific publishing is unsatisfactory and that the author-pays publishing model could be viable. Nonetheless, the government finally rejected its recommendations, including that the Research Councils each establish a fund to which their funded researchers can apply if they wish to pay to publish.

The case of the US is different. In September 2004, the National Institutes of Health (NIH) released a draft plan for open access for materials from NIH-funded research no later than six months after publication in a research journal. The US Congress affirmed its support for this proposal in November. Then a bipartisan bill called the American Center for CURES Act of 2005 was formally introduced in December, which mandated OA for the bulk of federally-funded medical research, which goes beyond the NIH public-access policy in several important ways. For example, it requires free online access and does not merely request it; it requires deposits at the time of acceptance by a journal; it extends the OA policy beyond the NIH, and so on.

2.1.3 Pressure from universities and research institutions

Unsatisfied with the existing scientific communication system, lots of universities hope to reshape the marketplace in which scholarly ideas circulate via new models such as open access publishing.

The University of Southampton is one of the first institutions in the world to provide core funding for its Institutional Repository and establish it as a central part of its research infrastructure. Meanwhile, the university required that all its academic and scientific research output should be freely available. Since then many universities and research institutions have carried major OA policies or resolutions in different countries, especially in 2005. For instance, the Columbia University Senate claimed to support the principle of open access for the fruits of scholarly research and passed the Resolution Concerning Open Access on April 4, 2005. It urges the scholars of Columbia University to play a part in open access endeavors in their various capacities as authors, readers, editors, referees, and members of scientific boards and learned associations, by: (1) encouraging and collaborating with publishers' efforts to advance open access, (2) retaining intellectual property rights in their own work where this will help it become more widely available, and (3) remaining alert to efforts by publishers to impose barriers on access to the fruits of scholarly research.

Other universities and research institutions adopted stronger self-archiving policies and even mandated OA for their research outputs, such as Queensland University of Technology, University of Minho, University of Zurich, the University of Southampton Department of Electronics and Computer Science and the world's largest particle physics center, CERN. For example, CERN policies presented were: (1) implement a policy to require their researchers to deposit a copy of all their published articles in an open access repository, and (2) encourage their researchers to publish their research articles in open access journals where a suitable journal exists and provide the support to enable that to happen. Moreover, practical measures to reinforce these policies have also been prepared.

2.1.4 Pressure from authors

Researchers usually strive to publish their work in journals with high impact, because this is one of the main things that relate to their promotion, tenure and grants. So, most researchers will continue to publish in traditional non-open access journals at least for the time being. But besides these realistic considerations, letting the most readers possible have access to the research outputs is the ultimate objective of scientists and scholars, so many of them took up OA naturally.

In October 2000, nearly 34,000 scientists from 180 countries signed an open letter to encourage scientific publishers to make the research literature available for distribution through free online public archives such as the US National Library of Medicine's PubMed Central. They expressed in the letter that, beginning in September 2001, they "will publish in, edit or review for, and personally subscribe to only those scholarly and scientific journals that have agreed to grant unrestricted free distribution rights to any and all original research reports that they have published, through PubMed Central and similar online public resources, within 6 months of their initial publication date."

And open access publishing is gaining more acceptance among scientists and scholars. In a survey for academic authors that was conducted by the Joint Information Systems Committee (JISC) and the Open Society Institute (OSI) between November 2003 and January 2004, most (53%) had published at least one article in open access journals; 33% had published 2 to3; 8% had published 4 to 5; 1% had published 6 to 7; and 2% had published 8 or more. Six percent of respondents had published in open access journals for more than four years. Somewhat more (16%) had published this way for three to four years and larger numbers (38% and 41%) had published in open access journals for one to two years, and in the last year only, respectively. This result is probably much as expected by most OA adherents, since it is clear that open access journals are rapidly increasing in number and in influence.

2.2 Opportunities

Though OA puts much pressure on publishers, what they get from the movement is not only threats but also opportunities. At least, it offers them another business model for publishing research results. As the ICT develops, most publishers have reengineered or are reengineering to operate both in the marketplace and the market-space. Since open access publishers like BioMed Central have abandoned their no-subscription-fee approach and adopt hybrid models that incorporate a subscription component, it is sound for traditional publishers such as Blackwell to admit that the open access model is one of a number of different models that should be tried and tested.

And the better thing about open access publishing is that, although there is still some anxiety about publishing in open access journals, a few funding bodies have already started to pay for their grantees to publish in open access journals. For example, Cancer Research UK has paid for many of its units to be members of BioMed Central. JISC has taken an active interest in open access to subscribe to the major commercial open access publishers on behalf of its members. From a positive point of view, open access publishing is becoming a more accessible model for publishers because it ensures more guaranteed revenues.

3. Traditional Publisher Experiments with Open Access

Though some publishers are sympathetic to open access initiatives, only a few of them are willing to experiment with the new business model. The amazing thing is, most of them have adopted some measures in common to do open access publishing.

3.1 Some Open Access Trials

Leading STM publishers such as Springer, Blackwell and Oxford University Press (OUP) are some pioneers who are trying open access publishing.

3.1.1 Springer Open Choice

Although believing in the value and longevity of the subscription-based model, Springer, a publisher of 1,250 scientific journals, took a step toward open access publishing by offering its authors the Springer Open Choice model as early as 2004. Open Choice is designed to give authors the choice of how to have their research published in the same Springer journals to which they usually submit. Namely, Springer journals will contain a mixture of Springer Open Choice articles and articles published under the traditional subscription-based model. Authors may choose to pay a fee of $3,000 to have their articles freely available to readers through its online platform, Springerlink. There is no difference between Springer Open Choice articles and the more than 100,000 articles Springer regularly publishes each year. All articles will be peer-reviewed, professionally produced, and available in both print and electronic versions via SpringerLink. While Springer Open Choice articles are freely available for anyone to read, download, or print from SpringerLink, the others should be paid for by readers.

Springer evaluates its journal subscription prices on a yearly basis based on a number of factors, including the amount of subscription-model content being published. For instance, if the number of articles published under the traditional model in the previous twelve months is less than the twelve month period before that, then subscription prices will decrease accordingly; and vice versa.

3.1.2 Blackwell's Online Open

Blackwell Publishing is the world's leading society publisher, partnering with more than 600 academic and professional societies. It publishes over 750 journals and 600 text and reference books annually, across a wide range of subjects.

With the calls for open access publishing, Blackwell decided to offer a range of options from which authors and readers can choose, including author-pays, self-archiving, and subscription-based information. In February 2005, Blackwell announced Online Open via its online journals platform, Blackwell Synergy. It's a two-year trial of hybrid publishing optional front-payment OA on an article-by-article basis. Authors of accepted articles may choose to pay a fee of US$2,500, €1,850 or £1,250 which ensures that their article is made freely accessible to all audiences. Online Open articles are published to exactly the same high standards as Blackwell's subscription-based articles, following the full peer-review process and benefiting from the same production procedures and online features. Subscription prices for journals in the trial will be adjusted based on the number of "author-pays" articles expected. Online Open articles also appear in the print edition, but they are excluded from the price calculation, as their costs have been paid by authors or funding bodies already.

Most of Blackwell's 79 initial journals in the trial are in biology or medicine, subjects where there is likely to be funding for the author-pays model to eliminate financial barriers to open access publishing.

3.1.3 OUP's Oxford Open

Oxford Journals, a division of OUP, has announced an open access initiative, Oxford Open: an optional author-pays model for authors of accepted papers in participating Oxford Journals titles. Oxford Open is a further development of OUP's open access projects, including Nucleic Acids Research (NAR).

For each of the forty seven journals that offers an optional open access model, authors of accepted papers will have the option of paying an open access publication charge to make their paper freely available online immediately via the journal website. The charge will depend on whether the corresponding author is based in an institution with an online subscription to the journal. For an author based at a subscribing institution, the regular charge is £800, $1,500 or €1,200; for an author based at an institution that does not subscribe, the regular charge is £1,500, $2,800 or €2,250. Otherwise special charges including special rates and waivers will apply to authors from developing countries. Authors based in over 60 "List A" developing countries may apply for free charges; and those based in over 70 further "List B" countries may apply for deeply discounted rates. Lastly individual journals may offer variable charges depending on the paper type.

The Oxford Open initiative has been designed to explore the viability of the open access publishing model across a variety of different journals within different subject areas. During the first half of 2006 the amount of open access versus non-open access content in each journal will be analyzed, and this will impact the 2007 online subscription prices. Generally speaking, the more open access content published in a journal during the first phase of this initiative, the lower the 2007 online subscription price will be.

3.2 Common Ways to Do Open Access Publishing

Just like the open access advocates, publishers pursue almost the same goal of maximizing access to scientific information; but their concerns about financial sustainability, and even profit, make them take more realistic attitudes and actions to achieve the goal. So it is unsurprising that several pioneering publishers adopted some measures in common to try the open access publishing model.

3.2.1 Optional pay model

In the current funding climate, where many authors may not be able to cover the full costs of publication and not all authors' funding agencies are fully prepared to fund open access publications, a model that utilizes a mixture of funding sources including publication charges, subscriptions, advertising revenues, etc. is more realistic. So almost all of the publishers mentioned above give authors the choice of whether to pay a publication fee in order for their article to be openly accessible to all readers or not.

3.2.2 Self-archiving

Authors who choose to participate in the open access publishing initiatives and pay to have their paper freely available online are entitled to deposit a post-print of their accepted manuscript and/or the finally published version of the article into an institutional or centrally organized subject repository, immediately upon publication. Most publishers require being identified as the original publisher.

According to actual practice, many think publishers' experiments are not real open access publishing, for authors have to get permission from the publishers first, and open access is confined only to the articles that have been paid for by the author. But for publishers, these are substantial steps toward open access publishing.

3.2.3 No commercial reuse

Many publishers stipulate that no articles can be reproduced for commercial purposes without the prior consent of the original publishers and payment of any appropriate fee. In the publishers' view, this provision has several benefits: open access publications can continue to act as a central point of contact for commercial reuse requests; it would be easier to protect the original author and the journal from misuse of published content; revenue resulting from such permission requests will be used to supplement publication charges for authors, thus helping to keep these charges as low as possible; and publishers will be able to monitor commercial re-use that could directly harm their business interests.

3.2.4 Maximizing access

Lots of publishers offer free or low cost access to libraries in the poorest countries through projects such as HINARI, AGORA, INASP and related initiatives, e.g. OUP's Oxford Open initiative. Another way to attain universal access is for publishers to continue to make articles available in multiple media formats, at least both in paper and online versions, for only 11% of the world's population uses the Internet and print publications are still used by many scientists around the world (Elsevier, 2004).

As analyzed above, publishers are experimenting with open access publishing actively; however, they prefer the advantages of an evolutionary to a revolutionary change in access models, which might be the more feasible way to do things.

* This paper is a research result of the project—Digital-Publishing-Based Scientific Communication System's Mechanism Innovation, which is sponsored by Chinese National Social Science Fund. (Project No. 06BTQ010.)

REFERENCES

Continuing CERN Action on Open Access. 18 May 2006 <http://doc.cern.ch/archive/electronic/cern/preprints/open/open-2005-006.pdf>.

Framing the Issue: Open Access. <http://www.arl.org/scomm/open_access/framing.html>.

Key Perspectives Ltd. *JISC/OSI Journal Authors Survey Report.* <http://www.jisc.ac.uk/uploaded_documents/JISCOAreport1.pdf>.

Open Letter to Scientific Publishers. <http://www.plos.org/about/letter.html>.

Suber, Peter. *Open Access Overview.* 17 Jan. 2006. <http://www.earlham.edu/~peters/fos/overview.htm>.

——. *SPARC Open Access Newsletter.* 5 Jul. 2006. <http://www.earlham.edu/~peters/fos/newsletter/01-02-06.htm>.

An Expert-Assessment Model for Internet STM Publications*

Liu Jinhong

Being open and free, the Internet has given rise to such fresh problems as information overload and pollution while providing users with plentiful information; meanwhile, readers nowadays are faced with "the conflict between limited information processing capacity and information complexity." Compared with the traditional setting of printing publications, on the one hand, the openness of the Internet makes it rather easy to release and publish STM publications through the Internet; on the other hand, serious problems exist regarding the overall quality of what is published. For these reasons, in Internet settings, it appears quite necessary to design and establish scientific and reasonable expert assessment models for Internet STM publications.

Assessment is a form of understanding based on certain criteria. It is a rational judgment made by the cognitive subjects on the value of objects being appraised, which is based on some specific value yardsticks· Assessment of Internet STM publications should be carried out from different perspectives and with different orientations, such as discipline development, academic values and philological significance. Assessment carried out by craft brothers, as the most widely employed method for publication assessment at present, has attracted considerable controversies, which center on its objectivity, impartiality and reliability, as well as its inadequacy in supporting innovation and interdisciplinary aspects. There didn't exist better choices for academic assessment until the concept of expert assessment was put forward by the American Committee of National Science, Project and Public Policy in the report *Evaluating Federal Research Programs: Government Performance and Results Act*, which was published in 1999.[4] While not being equivalent to each other, assessment by peers brothers is embodied in expert assessment, with the biggest difference between them being that the choice of experts for the latter is not confined to peers, but includes the users of the objects being appraised, scientists and management experts in related fields. In this way, "inbreeding" can be avoided, thus making the results of the assessment more objective, impartial and reliable. By carefully selecting assessment indices for Internet STM publications, the present paper endeavors to set up simple and practical expert assessment models for Internet STM publications, which aim at further improving Internet STM publications' quality in both publication and application and consequently promoting our country's scientific growth.

1. The Construction of Indices for Expert Assessment Models

It has been practically proved that it is insufficient either only to quantitatively appraise Internet STM publications with such indices as times visited and rates of being quoted, or only to qualitatively appraise them with user opinions. Only by integrally combining these two methods can we establish relatively more impartial and reasonable assessment criteria. While referring to traditional publication assessment indices, it is necessary for us to take into consideration factors such as the unique characteristics of Internet STM publications, their organizational manners and operational patterns, and to select both quantitative and qualitative indices for expert assessment models.

1.1 The Construction of Quantitative Indices

Integrating the characteristics of Internet STM publications and referring to the quantitative assessment indices for traditionally-printed STM publications, we construct the following seven quantitative indices for Internet STM publications.

1.1.1 Number of visits

The number of visits, as one of important indices for assessment of Internet STM publications, refers to how many times an Internet scientific publication is browsed and visited within a period of time after being published. Generally speaking, to keep statistics about visits, entails keeping data about the time of being clicked as well as the number of pages being read. Something worth noting is that, while examining the frequency of an Internet scientific publication being visited, it is necessary to set the time range first, which is suggested to be a period of time immediately after the publication, for data gathered in this way can be relatively more impartial and objective.

1.1.2 Number of times quoted

The number of times quoted, as one of the basic indices for assessing the quality of publication from the perspective of information feedback, refers to how many times an Internet scientific publication is quoted by other authors since its publication. The academic influence of the publication can be measured by the number of times it is quoted, which, from a historical perspective, directly reflects the role the Internet scientific publication has played in scientific development and literature exchanges. Theses more frequently quoted are generally believed to enjoy research depth, theoretical value, originality and guiding significance for academic research to some extent, and consequently are of higher quality.

1.1.3 Number of times downloaded and printed

Number of times being downloaded and printed, as one of the important indices for assessing Internet STM publications, refers to how many times an Internet scientific publication has been downloaded and printed by readers, including the overall number of time the publication has been downloaded and printed as a whole, or part of the publication and the tables of contents has been downloaded and printed. If the publication is downloaded and printed by readers, it indicates that it is of use to them. With a positive correlation between the times a publication is downloaded and printed and its significance, the more frequently it is downloaded and printed, the more significant it is.

1.1.4 Number of times transferred

Number of times transferred refers to how many times an Internet scientific publication has been transferred as a whole or in part by other websites, magazines or other media. Theses more frequently transferred are supposed to be of better quality. In the context of paper publications, while evaluating the academic quality of a publication, the number of times and rate of being transferred have been considered as important indices, and to appraise Internet STM publications, the number of times being transferred remains an important index.

1.1.5 Number of quotations

The number of quotation refers to how many quotations an Internet STM publication has made from other references. To write a publication of high quality, the author must be very familiar with the field of the publication and be well acquainted with the latest developments as well as classical research findings in the field. Accordingly, a publication with few quotations from other sources may arouse suspicion about the author's comprehensive knowledge of the field of the publication; by the same token, the number of quotations is critical for assessing the publication. More quotations from other sources indicate that the author has consulted many references and has a more comprehensive knowledge of the publication subject; in this way the publication is supposed to be of better quality.

1.1.6 Number of links

The number of internal and external links of an Internet scientific publication is an indicator of its significance. The number of internal links, referring to the number of mutual links between different web pages within the same publication, plays an important role in browsing and searching for deeper web pages; the number of external links, referring to the overall number of links from other websites or web pages, is directly related to the number of times a publication has been visited and the rank it assumes in search engines. Generally, the more links from other websites or web pages to the website or web pages of a certain Internet scientific publication, the more significant it is.

1.1.7 Number of awards for research findings related to the publication

The number of awards for research findings related to the publication refers to the number and level of awards given to research findings related to the publication in question after its publication, which is an index directly reflecting the academic significance of the publication. The more and the higher level those awards are, the greater the academic significance of the publication is.

1.2 The Construction of Qualitative Indices

Generally speaking, quantitative assessment is superior to qualitative assessment in terms of objectivity, concreteness, precision and maneuverability; however, to achieve an objective and impartial assessment entails a good disposal of the relationship between qualitative and quantitative assessment. Based on the unique characteristics of Internet STM publications and integrating the assessment index system of traditional printed literatures, the present paper has constructed 13 specific qualitative assessment indices for Internet STM publications, which can be classified into the following five broader aspects: authority, precision, originality, comprehensiveness and facility.

1.2.1 The index of authority

Authority refers to the degree of influence of an Internet scientific publication, which includes the authority, prestige and degree of influence of the source website, the sponsor and the author. The index of authority is an important index in measuring an Internet scientific publication's quality, credibility and reliability, which can be further analyzed into three concrete indices. The first concrete index is the authority of an Internet scientific publication, which can be revealed by whether the publication has a solid academic background and whether its academic quality is recognized and supported by celebrated experts and scholars, and for a paper-printed publication in its simple electronic form, we have to focus on the authority of its source magazine. The second concrete index is the authority of the author, which can be first evaluated based on whether the author has provided means of contact, if so, whether it is true and valid; more important is to measure the academic status of the author in the discipline and field of research as well as the author's social influence. The third concrete index is the authority of the website publishing the publication in question, which includes the condition of the website and, for the publication transferred and re-published, the condition of the source website also needs to be scrutinized; in addition, the sponsor of the website, its professionalism and development should also be a focus of assessment and scrutiny.

1.2.2 The index of precision

Precision refers to the accuracy of an Internet scientific publication's contents, format and source. Index of precision is one of the important indices for assessing traditional theses, which includes the following three subordinate indices: the accuracy of the publication's contents, the accuracy of its format and the accuracy of its source. Scrutiny of the first should focus on whether the author has employed adequately convincing facts or experiments to support his argument, and it is consequently necessary to examine whether its viewpoints are objective, whether the data and facts cited are accurate and whether the statistical tables and graphs are clear and readable. The second subordinate index focuses on examining the accuracy of the publication in grammar, spelling, punctuation, notes for references or citations, whether there is an abstract, and whether the key words are accurate. The third subordinate index focuses on whether information about the issuer and author is accurate, whether information about the source magazine is accurate if the publication in question is the electronic form of a publication from a traditional magazine, and whether the contents are accurate against the source magazine.

1.2.3 The index of originality

Originality refers to whether there exists novelty and uniqueness in the theme of an Internet scientific publication, in the viewpoints which the publication has put forward or on which the publication bases its argument; originality and uniqueness in its research subjects, angles, instruments, etc. should also be taken into consideration, for "the value of academic theses lies in putting forward ideas which haven't been put forward, researching into subjects which haven't been researched into and studying in manners which are different from others." The index of originality includes two subordinate indices, one being the originality of the subject and contents of a publication and the other being the recentness of the publication's dates of composition and publication. The former focuses on whether the subject of a publication is unique and novel, whether its viewpoints, contents and research methods are creative, and whether the research findings are original, and the latter mainly examines whether the publication is recently written, uploaded to the Internet, modified and transformed into electronic form, or whether the publication was released lately.

1.2.4 The index of comprehensiveness

Comprehensiveness, as one of the important indices for assessing Internet STM publications, refers to whether or not an Internet scientific publication has discoursed upon its theme and viewpoints comprehensively and whether or not it has reflected different factors and relationships of an object. While assessing the quality of comprehensiveness, the following two aspects need to be considered. The first concerns the comprehensiveness of its contents, which aims at examining the depth and width of its theme as well as its readers, the second is the comprehensiveness of the publication forms, whether it is only published in the native language, whether such functions of online interaction such as BBS are provided by the website publishing the publication to facilitate reader interaction, whether it is published in varied formats and whether multimedia publication is employed.

1.2.5 The index of facility

Facility refers to whether or not an Internet scientific publication is in line with the users' actual needs and whether it is convenient to be used, which is an effective indicator of an Internet scientific publication's user-friendliness, because while the content of Internet resources is important indeed, form is a factor in need of scrutiny. The scrutiny of facility can be done with the following three main indices. The first index is the user interface's friendliness, which can be further examined by whether there exists such helpful information as user guidance to facilitate user consultation, whether the publication can be printed and downloaded in various formats, whether the internal and external links are sufficient, valid and rational, whether the information transmitting speed is fast, and whether the website runs stably. The second index is the retrieval function, which intends to examine whether the publication has the retrieval function, and if so, whether the retrieval approaches are complete, whether retrieval interfaces are varied, whether such advanced retrieval methods as Bull Retrieval are provided, and whether the retrieval results are accurate, etc. The third index is Internet safety, which mainly examines whether there are special servers for important information, whether technological measures have been taken against hacker attacks and viruses.

2. Quantitative Processing of Indices for Expert Assessment Models

Despite their advantages, qualitative indices, when used in assessing a publication, only give rise to rather obscure results in the form of being "good," "moderate" or "inferior," while results produced by quantitative indices are quite precise. The purpose of assessment is to reduce the obscurity and enhance the precision of assessment results; consequently, in an assessment system with both quantitative and qualitative indices, if qualitative indices are not quantified, the practical value of the system cannot be ensured, for it becomes impossible to obtain assured assessment results without combining qualitative and quantitative assessment indices. The focus of quantifying assessment indices should be fixing on the proportions of different indices, which is often found to be empirical since they rely to a great extent on the subjective feeling and experience of the person working out the index system. To make the proportions of all indices more scientific and reasonable, the expert assessment model has constructed a quantitative process that is concise and normative:

2.1 The Design of a Questionnaire

Questionnaire design should focus on dividing all indices into five scales of different importance, with K1 denoting very important, K2 rather important, K3 important, K4 not very important, and K5 unimportant. The five different numerical values of 9, 7, 5, 3, 1 are assigned to them, respectively, representing their relative importance. Based on the five scales, a questionnaire is designed concerning the twenty indices discussed in the preceding section.

2.2 The Selection of an Appropriate Expert Sample

Following the principles of the expert assessment model, a certain number of experts from related fields should be selected to constitute a sample for the investigation, which is supposed to be diversified, including experts both within and beyond the research field of the publication in question.

2.3 The Completion of the Questionnaire

Send the questionnaire and the answer sheets to these selected experts in person or by email. Directions for finishing the questionnaire should be detailed so that they can accurately and objectively answer the questions it, and then collect the questionnaire after they are finished.

2.4 The Calculation of Different Indices' Scores in Terms of Importance

In the first place, the validity of questionnaires should be analyzed. Questionnaires which are not finished as required and, therefore, invalid should be ruled out; in the second place, valid questionnaires should be analyzed carefully, and each index's scores should be computed in terms of its importance, the formula for which is as follows:

$$Bi = K1Ci1 + K2Ci2 + K3Ci3 + K4Ci4 + K5Ci5$$

Here, i is a variable, denoting i^{th} index (i=1,2, . . . 20)
Bi denotes i^{th} index's scores in terms of importance (i=1,2, . . . 20)
Ci1 denotes the number of valid questionnaires in which the expert regards i^{th} index as very important
Ci2 denotes the number of valid questionnaires in which the expert regards i^{th} index as rather important
Ci3 refers to the number of valid questionnaires in which the expert regards i^{th} index as important
Ci4 refers to the number of valid questionnaires in which the expert regards i^{th} index as not very important
Ci5 refers to the number of valid questionnaires in which the expert regards i^{th} index as unimportant
Finally, the scores of all the indices should be added up in terms of their importance, for which the formula is as follows:

$$B = \sum_{i=1}^{20} Bi$$

2.5 The Calculation of Proportion of Each Index

The proportion of a certain index refers to the importance of the index in the whole index system, which is the proportion of the scores of each individual index to the total scores of all indices, the formula for which is as follows:

$$Xi = Bi / B$$

Here, Xi denotes the proportion of ith index in the index system (i=1,2, . . . 20)
Bi denotes the scores of ith index in terms of importance (i=1,2, . . . 20)
B denotes the total scores of all indices

3. Implementation of the Expert Assessment Model

Internet scientific publication is the main vehicle of scientific and technological communication, and an important means of gathering scientific information and promoting the development of science and technology. In order to effectively develop and utilize Internet STM publications, and to establish a superb and effective assessment system, it is necessary to establish a set of practical and effective assessment models at first. Taking into consideration the advantages and disadvantages of various approaches to assessment employed by scholars at home and abroad, the author of the present paper maintains that an "expert assessment model" be adopted for Internet STM publications. To ensure accuracy and impartiality of assessment under such a model, its implementation process is as follows:

3.1 Defining the Objects of Assessment

While assessing Internet STM publications, it is essential to make sure which theses are to be appraised. The selection of assessment objects can be active and passive. Passive assessment refers to assessment trusted by others, in which the objects are provided by others, while active assessment refers to assessment in which objects are actively selected according to the particular needs of an organization where the assessment personnel work.

3.2 Defining Expert Panel of Assessment

Related experts and scholars should be selected to form the expert panel, which should be in line with the characteristics of the objects being appraised and the requirements of the "expert assessment model." To ensure its impartiality and justice, special care should be given in selecting experts and scholars from different areas and different organizations.

3.4 Inviting Experts to Grade the Objects

According to the table of the index system for the Internet scientific assessment, experts should be invited to appraise and score all indices of the object one by one, and put the scores in the corresponding table for future analysis.

Table 1. Table of Proportions of indices for Internet scientific assessment

<table>
<tr><th colspan="3">Types of Index</th><th>weight coefficients Xi</th></tr>
<tr><td rowspan="7">Quantitative Indices</td><td colspan="2">Time of being visited</td><td>X1</td></tr>
<tr><td colspan="2">Time of being quoted</td><td>X2</td></tr>
<tr><td colspan="2">Time of being downloaded and printed</td><td>X3</td></tr>
<tr><td colspan="2">Time of being transferred</td><td>X4</td></tr>
<tr><td colspan="2">Number of quotations</td><td>X5</td></tr>
<tr><td colspan="2">Number of links</td><td>X6</td></tr>
<tr><td colspan="2">Time of awards</td><td>X7</td></tr>
<tr><td rowspan="13">Qualitative Indices</td><td rowspan="3">Index of authority</td><td>Authority of publication</td><td>X8</td></tr>
<tr><td>Authority of author</td><td>X9</td></tr>
<tr><td>Authority of website</td><td>X10</td></tr>
<tr><td rowspan="3">Index of precision</td><td>Precision of contents</td><td>X11</td></tr>
<tr><td>Precision of format</td><td>X12</td></tr>
<tr><td>Precision of sources</td><td>X13</td></tr>
<tr><td rowspan="2">Index of originality</td><td>Originality of date</td><td>X14</td></tr>
<tr><td>Originality of contents & theme</td><td>X15</td></tr>
<tr><td rowspan="2">Index of comprehensiveness</td><td>Comprehensiveness of contents</td><td>X16</td></tr>
<tr><td>Comprehensiveness of format</td><td>X17</td></tr>
<tr><td rowspan="3">Index of Facility</td><td>Friendliness of user interfaces</td><td>X18</td></tr>
<tr><td>Function of Retrieval</td><td>X19</td></tr>
<tr><td>Internet Safety</td><td>X20</td></tr>
</table>

3.5 Analyzing the Data

To begin with, we have to calculate each expert's final scores for every object, for which the following formula can be employed. Supposing the number of experts taking part in the assessment is *n*, and the number of objects evaluated is *m*, then the scores of mth object given by n^{th} expert in the expert group can be worked out with the following formula: (supposing *n*=30, *m*=20):

$$Snm=\sum_{i=1}^{20} XiPnmi$$

Here, Snm denotes the scores of mth object given by nth expert (*n*=1, 2, 3, . . . 30, *m*=1, 2, 3, . . . 20)

X*i* denotes assessment object's proportion of ith index (*i*=1, 2, 3, . . .20)

P*nmi* denotes the scores of ith index given by nth expert (i=1, 2, 3, . . . 20)

Secondly, the total scores for each object should be calculated. After having computed each expert's scores for a certain object, add up the scores of all experts and get the total scores Tm for this object, the formula for which goes as follows:

$$Tm=\sum_{n=1}^{30} Snm$$

Here, T*m* denotes total scores for mth object (*m*=1, 2, 3, . . . 20)

S*nm* denotes the scores for mth object given by nth expert

Finally, the final evaluation results should be worked out, which are obtained by dividing the total scores by the number of experts, the formula for which is as follows:

$$Am = Tm/30$$

Here, A*m* denotes the final results for m^{th} object (*m*=1, 2, 3, . . . 20)

T*m* denotes the total scores for m^{th} object (*m*=1, 2, 3, . . . 20)

3.6 Composing the Evaluation Report

The final assessment results for each object should be ranked in order of the overall scores; in addition, assessment reports can be composed, which should be presented to users for their future use.

3.7 Collecting User Feedback

If users are rather satisfied, then the assessment can come to an end; if not, further modification and verification are called for on data or facts employed during the assessment, or expert opinions which have been consulted, so that re-evaluation can be carried out until the needs of users are answered.

At present, the approach of literature metrology is more and more widely accepted, under such circumstances, within academia. It is generally acknowledged that it is necessary as well as of practical significance to probe into a more scientific and maneuverable assessment model for Internet STM publications, which can make the assessment results of academic research findings more convincing. By adopting the "expert assessment model" to appraise Internet STM publications, different factors affecting the quality of a publication can be taken into consideration, thus avoiding the insufficiency of subjective judgment, which is quite common in assessment. In this way, objectivity, applicability and operational facility in assessment can be better ensured. The purpose of this paper is to cast a brick to attract jade, so that more concern from peers can be called upon to carry out further research into assessing Internet STM publications in a more profound and effective way.

* This paper is a research result of the project—Digital-Publishing-Based Scientific Communication System's Mechanism Innovation, which is sponsored by Chinese National Social Science Fund. (Project No. 06BTQ010.)

REFERENCES

Chen, Wenjing and Chen Yaowei. "A Research Review of Appraisement on Internet Information Resources." *Journal of Sichuan Library.* (2004): 1.

Fang, Jinqiu. "Principles for Academy Periodical's Orientation and Censoring." *Journal of Dalian Education University.* Vol. 18 (4 Dec. 2004): 1.

Liu, Yangshu and Fang Ping. "Research into Index System of Appraisement on Internet Information Quality and Its Acquireability." *Journal of Information.* (2006): 1.

Xu, Lifang. "Changes in Readers' Needs and Their Influence on Publishing Industry." *Document, Information and Knowledge.* (2002): 8.

Yang, Zhengxian. "On Appraisement of Value Orientations and Value Cognitive." *Journal of Tian Jin Normal University.* (2006): 2.

Ying, Jun. "Methods and Standards for Professional Internet Information Appraisement." *Chinese Journal of Medical Library and Information Science.* (2004): 3.

The Development of Open Access Repositories

Niu Xiaohong

1. Brief Account of Open Access Repositories

1.1 Concept of OA Repositories

Open access (OA) repositories are free online resource databases which not only provide free deposit services for authors but also free index and download services for users. In this sense, OA repositories are a real OA publishing method. The articles in the OA repositories, including both preprints and post-prints, are those which are not evaluated by others in the same fields and are stored by self-archiving. The documents in the OA repositories include journal papers, conference papers, research reports, academic works and even multi-media teaching courseware. According to statistics from the Registry of Open Access Repositories (ROAR), there are all together 754 OA repositories registered as of Oct. 18th, 2006. At the same time, according to the statistics of the Directory of Open Access Repositories (DOAR), there are altogether 798 OA repositories, involving 29 scientific fields and 42 countries, with more and more OA repositories being constructed.

1.2 Types of OA Repositories

OA repositories can be divided into subject-based repositories and institutional repositories.

1.2.1 Subject-based repository

A subject-based repository (also called a topic-based repository) is organized based on subjects or topic fields and the services are open to all researchers of a certain subject or many subject fields, providing a free document deposit and access service, so as to promote the mutual sharing of academic information in the subject.

The earliest subject-based repository was established by scholars in natural science fields, including physics, computers and astronomy, so as to solve the "lag time" of academic publishing under the traditional publishing mode and share academic scientific research results. The best known one is arXiv preprints Archives. At the beginning, most OA depositories were subject-based depositories and developed unbalanced among subjects, only limited to natural science fields. In recent years, some depositories of social science studies and humane studies have emerged gradually.

1.2.2 Institutional repository

Institutional Repository (IR) is a new concept that has emerged in recent years. A seminar entitled "IR and its Influence on Publishing" was held in London on June 24th, 2004. The seminar inquired into the functions of IR, its influence on academic publishing and came to an agreement on the definition of IR, regarding institutional depository as a service based on institutions and should be in charge of the deposit, assimilation, management and supervision of the contents of those depositories. Institutional depositories are generally established and maintained by colleges and universities, college libraries, research institutions or government departments, and carry out the OA publishing of all its academic outputs.

Institutional depositories started a little late and were a new type of OA depository since the emergence of subject-based depositories, but the concept developed very fast. The best known one is the D-Scholarship Depository, established and maintained by the library of Florida State University. Since institutional depository ensures the completeness and continuity of the scientific outputs of the institution itself and actively promotes the development of the institution, it has acquired support from more and more institutions and has become the mainstream tendency in the development of OA depositories.

1.3 Current Development of OA Depositories in China

OA depositories started relatively late in China and include mainly the following ones: China Science and Technology Theses Online (http://www.paper.edu.cn/), China Preprints Service System (http://prep.istic.ac.cn/eprint/index/jsp), Qiji Papers Library (http://www.qiji.cn/), OA Repository of the Hong Kong University of Science and Technology (http://repository.ust.hk/dspace/), Online Chinese Research Theses Database of the Chinese University of Hong Kong (http://www.usc.cuhk.edu.hk/wkgb.asp), arXiv.org Science Online China (http://xxx.itp.ac.cn), Preprints Theses Database of National Science and Technology Library (http://preprint.nstl.gov.cn/newprint/index.jsp), Preprints Theses Database of Mathematics Research Institute of Beijing University (http://www.math.pku.edu.cn:8000/inst/preprint/index.php), Preprints Theses Database of Mathematics Science Study Center of Zhejiang University (http://www.cms.sju.edu.cn/index.asp?ColumnName=pdfbook), and Preprints Theses Database of the Mathematics Department of East China Normal University (http://euler.math.ecnu.edu.cn/preprint/).

In general, the numbers of OA repositories in China are still small and the development of the OA repositories of different subjects is uneven, with science, especially mathematics, developing quickly.

2. Applied System Software Used in OA Repositories

The main technical problem involved in OA repositories is the applied system software. According to statistics from DOAR, there are 54 pieces of applied system software that have definite names of the 798 OA repositories, of which 228 use indefinite applied system software. It is seen that there are many pieces of applied system software used in OA repositories and they develop very quickly. Since the principles and purposes of the design of those pieces of applied system software differ one from another, the OA Repositories can choose appropriate applied system software according to the ranges of the contents of their materials and the characteristics of their management. In the following part, I will introduce the two most widely used pieces of applied system software worldwide, DSpace and Eprints.

2.1 DSpace

The DSpace system is an open source software which was developed jointly by MIT and the HP Company, the purpose of which is to realize the accessing, labeling, issuing, permanent storage and open access of the scientific research results of academic institutes. It is one of the most widely used types of applied system software in OA repositories. According to the statistics from the DOAR, of the 798 OA repositories, 141 use DSpace system software, while the ROAR statistics show that the number of OA repositories that use DSpace system software is 175. Any institute, or even any private individual, can download the DSpace software for free and establish their own OA repositories. The download address is http://sourceforge.net/projects/dspace.

The characteristics of the DSpace software are as follows: 1) Dspace software supports various digital forms, including texts, pictures, videos and sounds; 2) users can modify the software according to their own needs; 3) Dspace software supports institutional repositories; 4) it permits the submitter of the paper to manage the accessibility of the contents; 5) in the process of paper submission, DSpace software can use DC metadata to submit the contents and store the results in a related database where items can be looked up through an index server; 6) combined with OCLC and OAICAT, the DSpace software can fully support OAIV2 Contract adopting Handle used in CNRI to establish sole label frame. The DSpace software provides the possibility for realizing the exchange of metadata among different databases, and even the mutual accessibility of resources among different OA repositories.

2.2 EPrints

EPrints is the creation software used for OA repositories developed by Southampton University. It's purpose is to help academic institutions store their research results and increase accessibility to them, so as to extend the influence and prestige of the institutions. The first edition of Eprints was issued at the end of 2000, and there are altogether twenty three editions now. Eprints is the most widely used OA repository applied system software. The statistics from DOAR show that 175 OA repositories use DSpace system software is, while the statistics from Eprints Free Software shows that there are 213 OA repositories using EPrints software. Although the tacit structure of EPrints is the institutional repository, it can also be used to create subject-based repositories. EPrints can be downloaded for free from http://www.eprints.org/software/download/.

The characteristics of EPrints are as follows: 1) EPrints can support and be compatible with various metadata standards; 2) it uses modules provided by the software to update and increase new tools and functions; 3) it supports the storage of various text forms, and even a single text can be stored in various forms; 4) completeness of data in OA repositories is checked automatically; 5) the papers that are submitted can be saved in the form of texts, condensed texts, or can be mapped automatically from existing websites through a designated URL; 6) all submitted papers are first stored in a buffer and the papers in the buffer can be accepted, refused or sent back to the authors for revision.

3. Key Problems of Developing Open Access Repositories and Related Solutions

3.1 Quality

One of the important premises for academic publishing is the high quality of the publications, and, therefore, the quality of documents is the key problem concerning whether open access repositories, and even open access publishing, can undergo a better development. A series of evaluation index systems and quality control mechanisms exists in traditional academic publishing. Recently, concerning most open access journals, a way of appraisal through discussion among people in the same field has been adopted to improve the quality of publications. However, concerning open access repositories, the author is only required to submit the paper in accordance with certain academic norms in Word or PDF format. Generally speaking, the content is not examined. At present, people in academic and publishing circles are worried about the following problem: whether open access publishing without quality control mechanisms will degenerate the quality of academic publications and result in a large quantity of junk papers. Relatively speaking, the quality of post-print documents in open access repositories is better, so the key problem is to guarantee the quality of preprint documents in open access repositories.

In recent years, some open access repositories have been aware of the importance of quality. For instance, in order to improve the quality of papers in its repository, arXiv introduced an examination and verification mechanism that requires inactive researchers to get authorization from active researchers in the same field when they submit pre-prints. Meanwhile, it is trying out an e-system of expert examination of drafts in e-preprint archives in physics and simulating a traditional draft examination process to assess the quality of the submitted paper.

3.2 Operating Costs

Compared with traditional academic publishing, the costs of publication and transmission of open access are much less, but open access repositories still incur expenses for long-term preservation and maintenance of the information in repositories. This is true of especially, open access repositories providing free storage and free visit service to users that neither charge users any ordering or visiting fees nor charge authors any publication fees. As a result, a key problem for open access repositories is to guarantee long-term, stable and reliable operating costs during the process of development.

Under current conditions, open access repositories have been mostly established by organizations such as specialized academic associations, research centers, government organs, colleges and their libraries, based on their needs for research. Therefore, the operating costs of open access repositories are mainly borne by these organizations at present. Meanwhile, operating costs are subsidized by some social funds and advertising earnings, and, thus, the problem of operating costs of open access repositories is well-solved. Further, it is believed that other ways of making profit can be found to enrich the operating funds of open access repositories along with development.

3.3 Data Sharing

At present, most open access repositories require the submitted paper in Word or PDF format without specific and standardized norms or unification. In the meantime, articles submitted to open access repositories are not further organized, indexed or filed. As a result, it is a key problem to perform trans-depository searches and mutual operations among different open access depositories and, therefore, data sharing of document information is in the process of development.

The emergence of OAI Protocol (OAI-PMH) makes it possible to solve the problem of data sharing among open access repositories. OAI Protocol is a mutual operation plan proposed by the OAI (Open Archive Initiative) in terms of preprints. It achieves mutual operations among different databases in the mode of metadata harvest and forms a mutual operation framework irrelevant to application and, therefore, provides efficient tools for mutual operations and searches among different open access repositories. In this way, data sharing is realized. Presently, many open access repositories have adopted the OAI Protocol. Further, much of the software of open access repositories applications follows OAI Protocol, so the open access repositories established using such software as Eprints also follow OAI Protocol. In this way, data sharing among open access repositories is to some extent realized.

3.4 Copyright

In the above section, it is learned that documents in open access repositories include preprint documents and post-print documents. Correspondingly, copyrights of open access repositories shall be discussed in terms of preprints and post-prints. As for preprints, open access repositories preserve the author's copyright. Authors have the freedom to store their works in any open access repository without violating current copyright law and causing disputes concerning copyrights. However, as for post-prints in open access repositories, disputes concerning copyrights arise. For the sake of business monopoly, publishers always ask authors to totally transfer relevant copyrights to the publishers themselves when they agree to publish the works. In this way, the authors lose their copyrights and cannot freely store articles that have been published in traditional carriers.

As open access publishing is widely recognized, due to pressure, some publishers have allowed authors to store post-prints in open access repositories. But, there are still many publishers who forbid authors to do so. Some open access repositories adopt a compromise to solve this problem, that is, the way of corrigenda. In this way, authors are not required to directly submit the original texts of the published articles, but to submit illustrated versions different from the preprints. Through corrigenda, the researchers can actually obtain the final versions of the articles indirectly and, therefore, the problem of copyright in open access repositories is solved.

4. Conclusion

The emergence of open access repositories as one of the important forms of realizing open access publishing makes up the deficiency in academic publications. It is a new mode of academic publishing within the Internet environment, so it deserves the attention from academic and publishing circles. In the long run, the further development of open access repositories will head in two directions: one is to establish an open access repositories union, and the other is to strengthen the cooperation between open access repositories and publishers.

REFERENCES

Dickson, David. "Open Access Archiving: An Idea Whose Time Has Come?" 2005 <http://www.scidev.net/Editorials/index.cfm?fuseaction=readEditorials&itemid=150&language=1>.

Jin, Shukuang. "New Model of Information Exchange in Digital Age: Open Access." *Information Research* (2006): 3.

Jiang, Ruiqi. "The Development of Overseas Open Access Repositories." *Information and Documentation Services* (2005): 11.

Li, Guangjian, Yongwen Huang and Li Zhang. "IR: Present Situation, System Structure and Development Tendency." *Journal of the China Society for Scientific and Technical Information* (2006): 2.

Li, Ruoxi and Ying Huang. "International Academic Publishing Open Style Visit: Practice and Front Questions Research Progress." *Acta Editologica* (2006): 8.

Li, Wu. "Two Main Vehicles of Open Access Publishing." *Journal of Academic Libraries* (2005): 4.

Lin, Menghua. "Open Access Repositories Based on OA." *Information and Documentation Work* (2005): 6.

Suber, Peter. "Open Access Overview: Focusing on Open Access to Peer-Reviewed Research Articles and Their Preprint." 2006 <http://www.earlham.edu/~peters/fos/overview.htm>.

Xu, Liujing. "OA Repositories in Practice." *Digital Library Forum* (2005): 8.

Multimedia Electronic Magazines: Revolution of Magazines in terms of Content and Format in the Age of New Media

Jiang Chengsong & Li Ziwei

1. The General Situation of Electronic Magazines

The study of electronic magazines began in the 1970's. In China, the first electronic magazine—ShenZhouXueRen (《神州学人》)—emerged in 1995. The traditional definition of the electronic magazine is: a serial that has the common characters of the traditional serials, and can be gained through electronic media in the form of digital being.

The electronic magazine is often recognized as the electronic version of the magazine, while its content is often the same as that of its paper form. It's often only a supplement to the original paper magazine, and sent by e-mail through the Internet, or by other means of communication.

It's often simply expressed in the form of texts and pictures that are organized by the hyperlinks and issued by the original paper magazine publisher. However, over the past two years, the multimedia electronic magazine, which integrates audio, video and text, has been brought out. It is issued with the advanced P2P technology. It includes FLASH's, video clips, background music, 3D and so on. Its content is livelier. It provides varieties of reading modes, such as online or offline reading, opening IE directly, or through independent executable files or the reading software. It fully plays the multimedia and interactive advantages of digital information, and its content is no longer a simple reproduction of the paper-form, printed magazine.

This kind of magazine can be called a new generation electronic magazine (it also can be called a digital magazine, web magazine, multimedia magazine, and so on. In this paper, we call it a multimedia electronic magazine)—a true multimedia magazine. Its publishers can be the traditional magazine publishers, professional multimedia electronic magazine publishing organizations, even ordinary Internet users. This new magazine has research value, because it has great innovation in the aspects of form and the methods of operation.

This essay focuses on the multi-media platform for its gathering the functions of producing, publishing, subscription and sending through the study course of multi-media magazines. We are able to have a view of the panorama of the multi-media electronic magazines from this study. At present, only several comparatively big web platforms, such as XPLUS, ZCOM, POCO, received alternatively more than thousands of U.S. dollars of venture capital from (ACER, Commercial Bureau, Lenovo); the Carlyle Group and IDG provide the services of magazine downloads and subscriptions.

This essay talks about the new electronic magazines through the example of XPLUS, which is an interactive web platform of multimedia electronic magazines developed by Beijing New Digital and Communications (XinShuTong) Company. It sends and subscribes multi-media, electronic magazines through the Web. It is the first domestic, interactive platform of multimedia, electronic magazines provided with the venture capital from ACER, Commercial Bureau and Lenovo. It has millions of members. Obviously, it is a typical case for analysis.

2. Characteristics of the Multimedia Electronic Magazine—taking Magazines on the XPLUS for Examples

Firstly, we can carry out a general analysis on the magazines of XPLUS. The categories, names and publishers supplied by XPLUS can be seen on www.xplus.com.cn. There we will find some characteristics of the magazines on XPLUS as follows:

1. The rich categories and clear pertinence. The magazines on XPLUS gather 16 categories, such as fashion, life, music, finance and economics, views, male and female. The content is mostly aiming at the young, not the elderly or the infants. That's because the multi-media, electronic magazines are transmitted through networks, computers and other digital terminals. Obviously, the elderly and children are not the primary users of these media.

2. The diversification of publishers. The traditional magazine publishers provide electronic copies on the basis of paper copies, such as XinWei (《昕薇》), China Fortune, Football players. Further, a few special producers and content providers of electronic magazine, like COLDTEA and MUZINE, work like content packagers. There are also personally-produced magazines that have low standards and qualifications. They do it just for fun.

3. Dynamic and youthful magazine titles. Many electronic magazines adopted fancy names such as Beautiful Me, Trend Popular, Young, E-SHOW Fans, etc.

Through the comparison between multimedia, electronic magazines and traditional, printed magazines, we can find some other characteristics of the multimedia electronic magazines.

2.1 Multimedia promotes interactivity of e-media.

In these multimedia e-magazines, readers can watch colorful and varying pictures, listen to music and enjoy videos. After turning to a certain page of the magazines, readers can still have his own choice of what to read, he can choose the music he likes and the videos he wants to watch. The readers can access the contents of the magazines by using the table of contents page like traditional magazines; in addition, they can still choose the information they want in a specific page.

Magazines like Man WO! (《男人志 WO!》), provided by XPLUS, even contain some kind of scenario in which the readers can interact with the people in the magazine and their choices in the interaction process will determine what will be contained in the scenario's next step. During this process, magazines are no longer passively read by the readers, rather, they are full of interaction, like games. Through this process, the features of the e-media is dug out.

The e-magazines make changes not only on the contents carrier or the way contents are displayed, but also about the contents bias.

As for contents, early XPLUS e-magazines mostly deal with music and fashion. Now foreign language study, economics, science and technology and so forth are under coverage by the magazines. But fashion magazines are still the most popular. Those beautiful garments, makeup and celebrities, interactively displayed using the flash technology, draw the eyeballs of the young aged network users.

All media have their biases. Harold Adams Innis thinks most communication media has some kind of bias, which can described in terms of time and space. A communication medium either tends to last in time or transmits very easily in space. The colorful, dynamic e-magazine can really give spatial, visual and audio shocks to readers, but when it comes to the dimension of time, will the depth of the information be affected? In other words, while the e-magazine's ability to manifest dynamic, entertaining visual contents is without doubt, is it suitable for the e-magazine to carry serious in-depth contents? This issue needs to be considered continuously when editors run their e-magazines.

2.2 Automatic send, quick circulation and zero cost.

There is a Chinese saying, "Good wine's fame can also be prohibited by a long, narrow street." Circulation is always an essential part of running a magazine. Circulation costs of traditional magazines compromise a great proportion of the total cost. This is especially the case when it comes to magazines that have a specific kind of readers and a small circulation. Sometimes managers have to sacrifice circulation to cut costs. For example the magazines may only be able to be attained through the mail, which means readers cannot get them from retail stores. On the other hand, for the multimedia e-magazine, client-side software automatically downloads the magazines from the press or the press platform, which only needs a few minutes to transmit a magazine. This new circulation method cuts people, resources and money needed for the traditional way to circulate a magazine, which also makes possible the multimedia e-magazine's most attractive merit of being "free".

Aside from these merits that traditional magazines do not have, multimedia magazines also consider users' reading habits. They have covers, back covers and tables of contents. The sound of turning to a new page is also simulated. Out of consideration for reading habits, some multimedia magazines even provide ways to drag the mouse to make the magazines go to the next page in addition to a traditional "next page" button.

2.3 Cooperate with other Internet services.

E-magazines can be read in two ways: online reading, download, and then read it. No matter which one we choose, the only thing we should do is to connect it with a hyperlink, through which we can easily combine the e-magazine with network services. For example, "Love Movie," which is multimedia e-magazine that is mainly about movies, can provide the service of downloading movie posters as screen wallpaper. And the e-magazine "MUZINE" can provide people with the ability to watch and listen to music online. Further, we should consider e-magazines as one sort of service and combine that with other Internet services like e-commerce. South Network's multimedia e-magazine WuZhi (《物志》) claims itself as a new e-magazine that integrates original works, blogs, forums, messages and online broadcasts. After registration, readers can not only make comments and exchange thoughts, but also enjoy the services of online shopping and sending multimedia messages. Like XPLUS, the Poco e-magazine platform provides services like downloading magazines in addition to instant communication, document sharing, multimedia broadcasting and searching. Just as the CEO of Poco said, the e-magazine is just a small part of the services they provide; they place high importance on Poco's community values. The readers of the community have high loyalty and purchasing ability, so it is certain that Poco can find new business opportunities among its readers. We can say the e-magazine is not only the combination of network and magazine, it is also the combination of different network media types. In the future, its terminal reading equipment will not be confined to the computer screen, but will be able to be transplanted to PDA, Mobile and TV screen too.

2.4 Ease of feedback and collection of readers' data.

XPLUS has an integrated feedback program in the magazine, when readers take any actions, the program will send statistical data to the magazine provider, such as the number of downloads amounts of a magazine, time spent by readers, readers' appetites, the number of clicks. Take the XPLUS, for example; its reader questionnaire can provide eight percent to ten percent of feedback. According to the feedback, the magazine publishers can set up their development strategy and adjustments based on this real time data. The most important aspect is that they can set the rates for ads. Those data can also attract ad customers. It is very difficult to quantify the data of the traditional magazine. The effectiveness of the reader questionnaire of the traditional magazine is below 0.1 percent. The concrete experiences that the readers will have can be gained by finishing the complemented reader questionnaire; after answering the questions, readers only need to click the button. All of this makes the collection of data very easy, and the collaboration of readers and editors close.

2.5 Clear target, attracting more advertisers.

iResearch's market survey pointed out that more than half of e-magazine clients are between the ages of eighteen to twenty four, the other twenty eight percent of readers are twenty five to thirty, and the age of thirty one to thirty five take the other eight percent. Clear and centralized readers make it easy for the e-magazine to attract advertisers. Meanwhile, e-magazines can find precise statistics on the number of clicks an advertisement receives, which is helpful for exploring their efficiency, making advertisement strategies and developing special advertisement patterns. Besides this, e-magazines can subdivide contents better than traditional magazines can, which means the contents of an e-magazine can be better combined with its advertisements.

2.6 Multi-agent, diversified profit model.

Profits are crucial to the survival of XPLUS and the magazines based on it. XPLUS gains its profits by allowing content providers to publicize their magazines on the platform, helping them to edit their contents and advertising their commodities. The multimedia e-magazines built on it, on the other hand, earn their profits mostly from advertisements and some Internet, value-added service. All these will be discussed below.

Overall, the differences between the multimedia electronic magazine, the paper-form, printed magazine and the traditional electronic magazine can be summarized in the following table:

Table 1. (Continues on following page)

Contrast items	Paper-form printed magazine	Traditional electronic magazine	Multimedia electronic magazine
Vector	Paper	Electronic net and internet	Internet
Form	Cooperation set paper	HTML files or e-magazine	A file packaged by a special program
Content	Text and pictures	Text and pictures, organized in the form of hyperlink	Flash, Video clips, Background music, 3D and so on

Table 1. (Continued)

Contrast items	Paper-form printed magazine	Traditional electronic magazine	Multimedia electronic magazine
Issue method	Entities issue net: distribution channels retailers distributors	Sent Subscription list through email	Automatically sent to the Subscribers' computer
Feedback form	Mail questionnaires	E-mail reply	Background program records the reader's reading behavior; readers sent back the questionnaires after completing them
Added service	Present	No	E-mail service, online Community, short message; mobile
Profit model	Advertisement and partly issue profit	Payment for download	Advertisement-internet value-added service

Admittedly multimedia e-magazines have their shortcomings:

1. In order to read a multimedia e-magazine on XPLUS, a reader specifically designed for this platform, which is usually not compatible with other platforms such as ZCOM, is needed.

2. The content together with the feedback program is encapsulated into the e-magazine, which makes it use significant amounts of storage, which in turn makes the magazines not suitable for long-term collection. Besides, the magazines cannot be printed like common electronic documents, so they cannot be saved like normal magazines. Also, some magazines suffer problems from slow transmission speed.

3. Although the e-magazine is designed to make it look like a traditional magazine, most people can still feel the difference from a paper-based magazine due to the screen.

4. The contents of the magazine and the advertisements are merged together seamlessly. Even some of the magazines on the XPLUS are produced purely for the purpose of advertising. Readers are likely to get confused about which parts are advertisements and which parts are the actual magazine contents.

The father of modern communication, W. Shramm, proposed a formula for people's decisions on selecting media. It suggests that whether a medium will be chosen or not is decided by the comparison of the profits it can produce and the costs people need to pay. Multimedia e-magazines already have substantial contents. Also they are provided without any charge and easy to read and subscribe to. Their merits far outweigh their shortcomings. No wonder they have become more and more popular.

3. Business Model and Development Trends of XPLUS

The growing emergence of multimedia electronic magazines has greatly changed the value chain of magazines. In China, only formal publishing institutions with sales figures can publish paper magazines. The enlarged editions cannot be published by just any institutions. In the publishing of paper magazines, there are the Copyright Laws of The People's Republic of China, regulations of magazine management, contemporary regulations of magazine management and other laws and regulations as well as production regulations. As far as multimedia electronic magazines are concerned, although some laws and regulations can offer limitations, they are aimed at the whole Internet and content management. Compared to traditional paper magazines, the regulations are less strict. There is fundamentally a threshold on entering the market. In addition, because there is no need for paper and printing expenses, the cost of online magazines is low, and also has few risks.

As a result, someone who wishes to produce a magazine can make his or her dreams come true. As online magazine software, XPLUS provides a tool for readers to produce magazines of their own. Such software is not only convenient, but also easy to operate, through which readers may produce and issue a pleasing electronic magazine.

What's more, some studios have begun to produce their own magazines in groups and some traditional media also started the business of producing multimedia magazines. *Net Jockey*, which is regarded as online musical magazine produced by China International Radio (CIR) and Yihe radio, Xiwei, and *Southern People Weekly* Magazine have selected XPLUS as their distribution platform, providing another channel to expand their brand effect.

As a result, if some businesses intend to publish their magazines (either for the public or as internal magazines), they can publish multimedia magazines. For example, *Dream Flight Communication*, which was produced by Dream Flight Information Technology Company in Guangzhou, can show its productions on multi-media magazines. Even these businesses can only offer materials, and entrust the production to XPLUS and other technology providers.

"For free" is the most attractive feature among on the Internet, as well as the key factor for why multimedia, electronic magazines can be popular. However, providing free online service such as online magazines needs profits to support development. How can multimedia electronic magazines on XPLUS and other platforms make a profit?

Nowadays, in the performance of online magazines, Feixing, whose website produced Wo, and other online magazine producers have leveraged the content of magazines to earn advertising fees. Such magazines are suited to the youth market, and, therefore, they are apt to be popular with advertisers. In the meantime, they can count data such as click rates, so as to analyze advertising effects, map out advertising strategies and promote models for advertising profits (such as payment according to advertising click rates). XPLUS is determined to regard the totally impartial data of circulation and reading as the only basis to decide the advertising content and value, in order to create a new commercial model. In addition, because the contents of multimedia magazines are subdivided into more categories than traditional magazines, some multimedia magazines can integrate more content with more advertisements. Making use of the value-added services of the Internet, content providers can earn more profit. However, XPLUS and other magazine distribution platforms charge content providers who need to distribute magazines on such platforms.

As a result, regarding those producers of multi-media, online magazines, what they need to do is optimize content continuously and attach importance to brand value, so as to attract advisers. All of these are the same as traditional magazine publishers. Among such platforms, XPLUS should make efforts to be an abundant and convenient "magazine supermarket" by gathering more attractive content, increasing consumers and optimizing distribution.

It is obvious that these characteristics can be exchanged. Distribution platforms of magazines can be the producers of the magazine while the producers of the magazine can not only issue magazines on their own platform, but also expand distribution channels by means of other magazine issuing platforms.

The differences of the marketing chain between multimedia, electronic magazines and traditional, paper, and printed magazines are as follows:

Fig. 1. Traditional paper-printed magazine

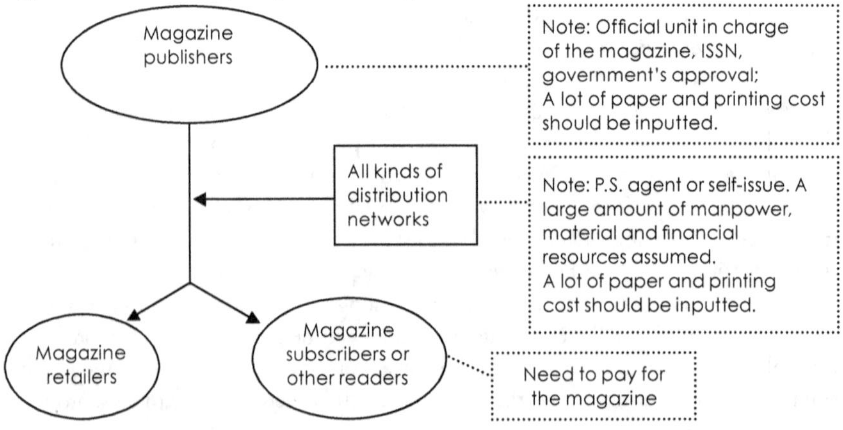

Fig. 2. Multimedia electronic magazine

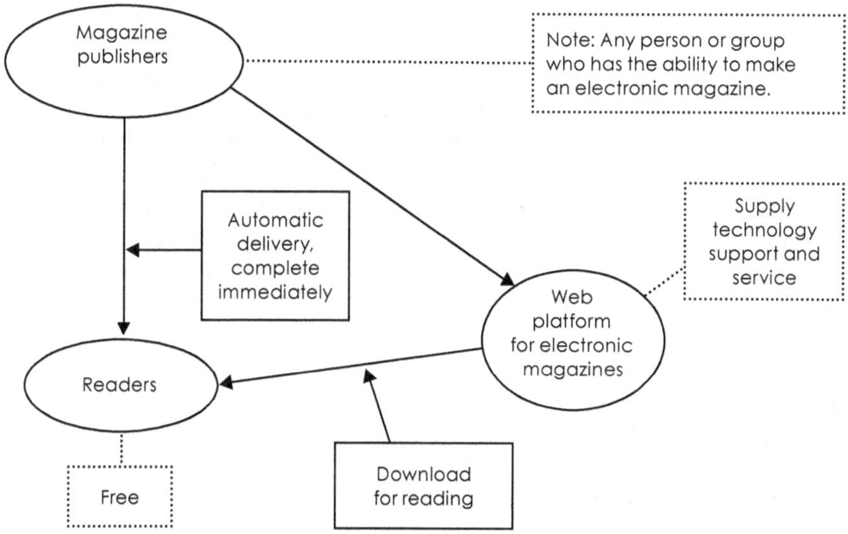

The multimedia magazine is not only the extension of the traditional magazine. As stated above, it will be integrated with Internet services and become "the media of mutual marketing," which should be the fantastic future of the multimedia magazine. XPLUS is just the beginning of the integration. Being a platform for transmission, XPLUS is not only a solid channel, but a mutual magazine forum, where readers can discuss and share ideas with publishers of the magazine, as well as ask questions about the software. With large numbers of registrations plus hot forums, XPLUS can provide other network services.

4. Conclusion

However, there exists no supervision for the magazines because they have fewer restrictions on access. Many electro-magazines include erotic content, which is popular among teenagers. Therefore, they need to be regulated. Obviously, traditional regulation methods will be not suitable here.

According to a report from iReasearch, in China, the number of users of digital magazines is around 20 million, and will reach eighty two million in 2010. The market scale of the digital magazine was 20 million Yuan in China in 2005, while it will become 1.25 billion Yuan by 2010. It is believed that the electro-magazine is becoming more and more popular, and also its appearance and profit mode are becoming better and better.

At present, we do personal research into XPLUS for future applications, whose patterns and modes are changing. XPLUS may be a flash in the network or something that could produce a new industry. The core value of our research consists of focusing on how to integrate types of media, rebuild the traditional value chain and find a creative profit mode in times when media is expanding greatly.

Though the multimedia magazine has grown fast, it's just the beginning compared to the traditional magazine's 340-year history (in 1665, in the sense of the modern, the first magazine, *The Scholar*, was produced in Paris). At the same time, people cannot change their reading habits in a short time; the structure of magazines won't change thoroughly. But it represents one trend, one possibility and one option in society. We will watch the process despite whether it evolves or not.

REFERENCES

Innis, H. A. *The Bias of Communication*. Beijing: China Renmin University Press, 2003.

Li, Yulin and Liu Cangde. "Electronic Journals and College Library." *Sci-Tec Information Development & Economy* (2006): 38.

Multimedia magazine, "How Can You Make Money?" *Multimedia Magazine*. 18 Oct. 2006. <http://column.chinabyte.com/335/2350835.shtml>.

Schramm, W. and E. Porter. *Men Women Messages and Media: Understanding Human Communication*. Beijing: Xinhua Publishing Press, 1984.

Sohu.com IT Channel, China Digital Magazine Research Report. 23 Oct. 2006 <http://it.sohu.com/20060402/n242594301.shtml>.

Sohu.com IT Channel, China Digital Magazine Research Report. 23 Oct. 2006 <http://it.sohu.com/20060402/n242594458.shtml>.

A Study of Advertising and Marketing of Digital Magazines in China

Wang Bo

1. Introduction to the Digital Magazine

"Digital magazine" refers to the combination of video, audio, picture and word, emphasizing on interactivity and multimedia, in the third generation of electronic magazines spread through the P2P platform.

The digital magazine has flourished since 2006. Because of its rich model of expression, segmental targeted audience, and accurate transmission mode, the digital magazine has pioneered a new information transmission channel. Additionally, without limits on the copies produced, no expenses for paper and printing, and the low cost of publishing, the advantages of the digital magazine are extremely obvious. A statistic from Penn Well Corporation showed that compared with traditional magazines, the costs of paper and transport of digital magazines save 50%, which means each magazine saves 1.1 to 1.5 dollars. As for magazines with international editions, the proportion is 75%.

The profit-making mode of the digital magazine is an important issue which has been widely discussed. The available profit-making modes are as follows: the first is to charge readers; the second is to gain revenue from advertising; the third is to expand value-added services. Nowadays, nearly all digital magazines are free of charge in order to gather a large number of readers. It is predicted that by 2010, circulation revenue will only account for 12% of the total revenue. Although it seems practical to develop value-added services, it is only at the experimental stage and has a long way to go before realizing profits. Therefore, advertising revenue becomes the only profit-making mode of the digital magazine.

2. The Present Situation and the Prospect of Digital Magazine Advertising in China

First of all, let's look at the present situation and the prospect of online advertising in China, which is the environment that digital magazine advertising relies on. An overview of the advertising revenue of China's media in 2005 shows that the advertising revenue of television is 32.4 billion Yuan, of newspapers is 27.2 billion Yuan, of magazines is 1.8 billion Yuan, of broadcast is 3.4 billion, and online advertising gets 3.1 billion. (Figure 1)

Fig. 1. 2005 China Media Advertising Revenue

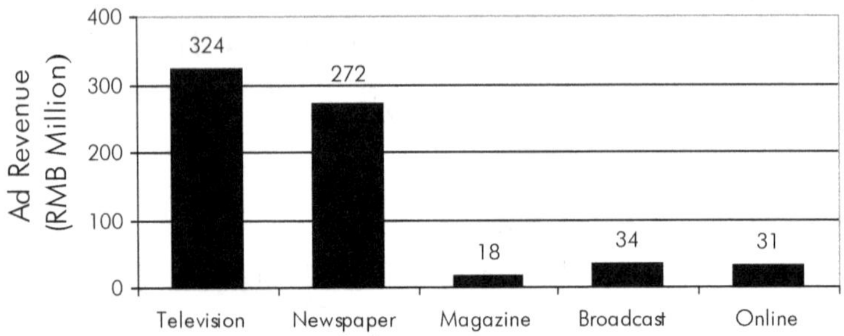

China's online advertising revenue reached 3.1 billion Yuan, ranking fourth among all media channels. For the first time its income exceeded magazine income. Advertiser Ogilvy's latest statistics show that the online advertising market of China increased by 77.1% compared with 2004. It is predicted that China's online advertising market will reach 4.6 billion Yuan in 2006 and hit 15.7 billion Yuan by 2010. Media professionals quoted in local media say that the traditional print media will no longer dominate the market with challenges from new media channels such as the Internet.

Within the healthy development of online advertising, digital magazine advertising has also increased rapidly. According to the China Digital Magazine Research Report in 2005 (abridged version) by iResearch, the advertising revenue of digital magazines in 2005 was 20 million Yuan. iResearch predicted that by 2006, digital magazine advertising revenue will have a rapid growth to 90 million Yuan in China. By 2010, China would have its digital magazine advertising revenue expanded to 1.1 billion Yuan. (Figure 2)

Fig. 2. 2005-2010 Total Advertising Revenues of China Digital Magazine

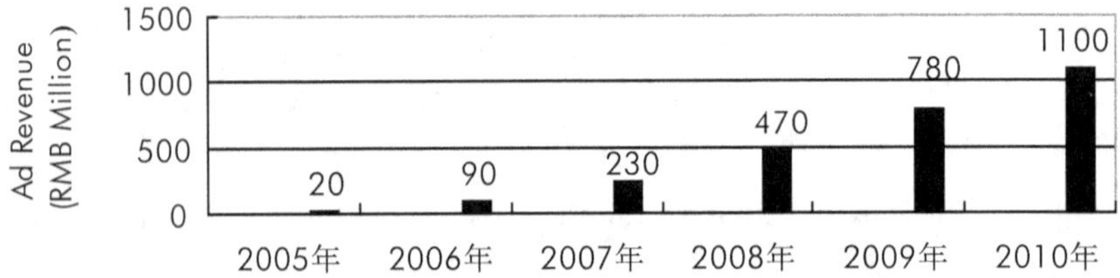

3. Marketing Mode and Character of Digital Magazine Advertising

With the rich media technology, the digital magazine has brought advertising marketing to a new era. Around 1995 was the birth of the first GIF banner. Two years later, an American company broke through the traditional online advertisement format, putting the game into banner ads. It was a revolution of online advertising both in content and form, and regarded as the birth of rich media advertisement. With the form of websites, pictures, hyperlinks, etc., rich media advertisement transmits to audiences accepting of the experience a distinctly different and visual shock. A survey showed that the click rate of the rich media advertisement is increased by 600% compared with the traditional advertisement.

The definition of rich media advertisement is controversial. Cheng Gang, director of the Advertising Department of Beijing University explained: "In China, rich media advertisement describes a broad range of interactive digital media that exhibits dynamic motion by taking advantage of enhanced sensory features such as video, audio and animation. In foreign countries, it points to an advertisement form which is different from traditional advertisement with the characteristics of interactive, attractive, rich information, and complies with the regulations of IAB (Interactive Advertising Bureau); the connotation is wider."

3.1 The Advertising Marketing Mode of the Digital Magazine

The advertising marketing mode of the digital magazine is as follows:

Fig. 3. Advertising Marketing Mode of the Digital Magazine

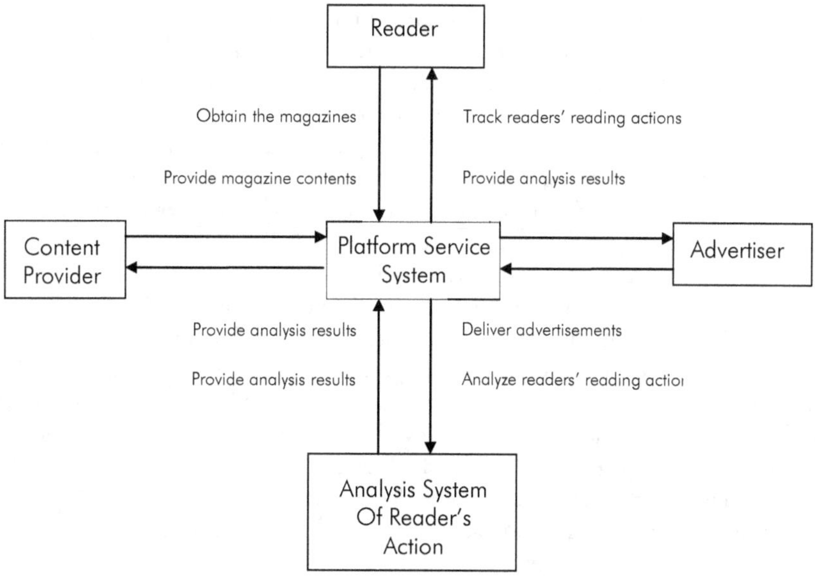

First, content providers provide magazine contents to platform service systems of digital magazines; second, when readers download magazines from the platform, the system tracks their information and reading actions, such as their locations, which magazine they download, and the time they spend on each page, etc. The selected datum will be sent to an analysis system of the reader's actions; third, the analysis system of the reader's actions analyzes the datum and concludes the interests and hobbies of readers. The results will be provided to content providers and advertisers, respectively. According to the results, content providers can improve the contents, and advertisers can recognize the composition and characteristics of readers, which is helpful to delivering advertisements. Finally, advertisers deliver advertisements to magazines through the platform service systems.

3.2 Characteristics of Digital Magazine Advertising

Advertising in the digital magazine has become interactive with the following features:

(1) Rich content and interactive form.

First, because of the participation of the rich media, the content of advertisements is abundant. It is characterized by integrating flash cartoons, video clips, background music, and even 3D special effects, offering richer content, and using advanced P2P technology for publication. Such elements attract readers to click on the advertisement, improve contact between readers and advertisers, and create satisfied reading experiences.

Second, it is interactive. Readers can not only appreciate the advertisement, but also be involved with it, watching it just like they are playing a game. Further, they can visit the advertisers' get the websites latest news about new products, join activities, send e-mail and communicate with the advertisers online. For example, Xplus is planning to introduce a value-added service—VOIP. It provides a button on the advertisement page: if readers push the button, they can talk to the advertiser immediately online. Through this page, readers can enjoy a series of services like viewing the product's pictures, comparing the functions, and even purchasing products.

(2) Tracking reader's reading actions online.

With the support of this technology, the digital magazine can track reader's reading actions, and feedback the advertising effect. In general, if a reader wants to read a digital magazine, he will download and install client terminal software first. Then, as soon as he downloads a magazine and reads it, the service platform can track the information about which magazine he downloads, when he reads it, how long he reads and stays on every page, etc. On the basis of such information, the system can analyze and conclude the characteristics of the reader, like living habits and consuming ability. The results can be transmitted to advertisers, and kept in the platform, preparing for the next advertisement delivery.

(3) Realizing accurate delivery.

After the marketing stage of dimension and segmentation, media advertising has approached the era of accurate delivery. It is said that the digital magazine takes on the advertisement mode of accurate delivery, accomplishing a task which is impossible for traditional media. Even reading the same digital magazine, readers could view different advertisements. That is because when a reader opens client terminal software, the platform will find his reading action report immediately and carry the advertisement he is most likely to be interested in to the magazine. This unique characteristic of the digital magazine has attracted many prominent manufacturers to deliver advertisements, such as Dell, DHC, eBay and so on.

4. The Problems of Digital Magazine Advertising

Although the prospect of digital magazine advertising is brilliant, there are still some problems.

4.1 The Aspect of Circulation

Circulation refers to the number of downloads of the digital magazine, including both downloads via the client-terminal, and direct downloads via web browsers. When advertisers deliver advertisements to the publication, circulation is always considered one of most important factors.

Recently, in digital magazines, the circulation of the bestsellers is about 0.3 million per month, which is a long distance from the click ratio and page view of the websites, such as Sina, Sohu, and Yahoo. Generally, famous websites have over 100 million registered readers worldwide, over 400 million daily page viewers, and over 60 million active readers for a variety of fee-based services. In order to achieve advertising quotient and share the market size of online advertising with these famous websites, it is an urgent matter to improve the click rate and circulation of the digital magazine. Xu Ning, assistant manager of VIKA, once said in a speech entitled "How to Do Digital Magazine Advertising Brand Marketing." "First, we should gather the number, then the segment." The advantages of digital magazine advertisement, such as tracking readers' actions and delivering them accurately are only significant in terms of a certain number of circulations. If the circulation is small and limited, everything would be meaningless.

4.2 The Aspect of Content

The content of digital magazines mainly comes from two sources: one is co-operated with established paper media magazines, and the purpose of the digital platform is to spread the digitized content of magazines via the Internet. Take Xplus and ZCOM for examples. Xplus signed a contract with the paper media magazines *like Economic Observer, CEO & CIO, ELLE, Vogue, Life Style,* and *The First. In Xplus,* 30% of the magazines are digitized content of paper media magazines. ZCOM signed a contract with *New Finance, Global People, Civilization, Digital Times, New-Youth, Golf Tattler,* and *Public Computer* in 2006. So far, more than 60 paper media magazines have published their digital magazines through the ZCOM platform. The other source is original creation. It also can be divided into two ways: one is provided by professional studios and producers, the other is by netizens.

The two sources have disadvantages, respectively. First, the function of most digital magazines cooperating with paper media magazines is to change the paper media into online media instead of involving it in content creation. It is not good for the long-term development of digital magazines if they rely totally on the contents of traditional paper magazines. The worse situation would be that the digital magazine becomes a simple e-version of the traditional magazine. Secondly, the original source is in an introductory stage; some original magazines are manufactured in a rough and slipshod way. So far, few of them have achieved a huge circulation.

Some professors ahev pointed out: "The digital magazine can be read, but does not need to be read." The problem is that the content of the digital magazine is weaker than its form. Cartoons, music, and games give readers visual and auditory shock;, however, it can only attract them for a short time; the barren content would make the digital magazine lose all its readers eventually. Moreover, the transmission and sharing of online technology, to a degree, make the form of the digital magazine easy to imitate. So the content is its core competence.

The principle that content is king applies to digital magazines as well as to traditional magazines. It is the content that attracts audiences and fosters their loyalty to the magazine. Therefore, the digital magazine should create its own unique content.

5. Conclusion

As Yu Gan, CEO of Xplus, has pointed out: "It often requires a process for every new advertisement and transmission form to be recognized and accepted. We should try our best to develop at this stage; it is impossible to achieve success in a short time." Although the prospect of digital magazine advertising is brilliant, it has a long way to go in order to achieve better development in the digital environment.

REFERENCES

"Accurate Delivery of Xplus Attracts Advertisers." 18 Sep. 2006 <www.sina.com.cn>.

"China Online Advertising Report 2005." Vers. Simple. 18 Sep. 2006 <http://www.iresearch.com.cn>.

"China Digital Magazine Report 2005." *China Digital Magazine*. 21 Sep. 2006 <http://www.iresearch.com/html/digital_magazine/detail_free_id28028.html9>.

"China's Online Advertising Becomes 4th Biggest Advertising Channel." 17 Sep. 2006 <http://english.iresearch.com.cn/html/online_advertising/detail_news_id_6668.html>.

"Digital Revolution of the Magazine Transferred By Electronic Technology." *China Book Business Report.* Trans. Zhang Zhuying. 2004.

"The Digital Magazine Flourished: the Form Is Better than Content." 18 Sep. 2006 <http://www.cnetnews.com.cn/news/net/story/0,3800050307,39450682,00.htm>.

"Digital Magazines Gives Birth to the New Form of Advertisement Delivery." 17 Sep. 2006 <www.iresearch.com.cn>.

Li, Na. "The Outlet of the Digital Magazine." *CEO & CIO.* 2006.

Fan, Lili. "Make Readers Like Your Advertisements: Xplus's New Profit-Making Mode." 18 Sep. 2006 <www.xplus.com.cn>.

"Rich Media Advertising Development Expects Diversification." *IT Times.* 16 Feb. 2006.

"Xplus Makes a Display of Its Ability, Win the Asian Top 100 of Red Herring." 19 Sep. 2006 <www.xplus.com.cn>.

Yu, Gan. "Visiting Silver Times: Digital Magazine Faces Integration." 2006. 17 Sep. 2006 <www.sina.com.cn>.

Zhang, Danyi. "The Form of the Digital Magazine Is Better Than Its Content." *Weekly Computer Newspaper* 2006.

Zhang, Danyang and Li Liling. "The Digital Magazine in Web 2.0." *News Practice* 2006: 31-32.

Zhao, Ruihua. "Narrow Advertisement: The Attempt of Advertisement Accurate Delivery." *Journalist* 2006: 75.

Self-Publishing on the Internet

He Ziyue

1. The Definition and Characteristics of Self-Publishing

The Definition of Self-publishing

There are many different physical formats for sharing information: paper manuscripts, pictures, information, audiotape, videotape, and others. The activity of publishing can generally be described as the act of putting these various media, which are written, selected, edited, and processed, into print or electronic format, and then distributing them to users through certain kinds of carriers. From this point of view, the understanding of publishing can be divided into three basic processes: editing, printing, and distribution. But as science and technology have rapidly developed, and the Internet has become more accessible to the average person, a new form of publishing, called Internet publishing, has sprouted.

The fifth regulation in The Temporary Provision on Internet Publication Supervision defines Internet publishing as the act of distributing information over the Internet. It refers to the activity of Internet information providers putting their own originals or others' writings which are selected and edited online or sent to terminals on the Internet for the public to browse, read, use and even download. In this definition, "print" and "circulation" have been replaced by "online circulation," and editing is done by individuals. In Internet publishing, the material does not need to be physically distributed to users, as opposite of the traditional publishing methods. Only with a computer and a phone line or a wireless connection can we access any online materials.

We usually call "individual publishing" "self-publishing" to distinguish it from governmental, official or organizational publishing, even though "Internet publishing" covers more than just self-publishing. In other words, self-publishing refers to the publishing activities of editing, printing, and distribution that are all executed mostly by an individual. Currently, self-publishing is predominately accomplished through the Internet.

If we look to early manuscripts from ancient times, it is clear that self-publishing existed long ago. Ancient preachers started to publish their ideas largely through self-publishing in the Spring-Autumn and Warring States Periods (770-221 B.C.) in China. After printing was invented during the periods of the Sui and Tang dynasties, ancient China gradually came to develop three types of publishing: *official*, *individual, and workshop.* Among the three forms, self-publishing played a key role in individual printing and workshop printing. With the birth of the modern press, the individual acts of editing, printing, and distribution have become more complex, and also more segmented. In other words, the individual steps of writing, editing, publishing, and distributing material are often performed by different people or entities. Under these conditions, the traditional individual self-publisher cannot compete with those using more formal, organized, mechanized means. Consequently, traditional individual self-publishing gradually declined.

The Characteristics of Internet self-publishing

Since the emergence of the Internet, the act of publishing has developed new characteristics. Writing, editing, publishing and even distributing are more easily executed and integrated with each other. The situation of the Internet is just like the Age of Spring-Autumn and Warring States Periods. Thanks to the new technology, self-publishing, which was common two thousand years ago, has recently been reborn. Compared to traditional publishing, self-publishing has the following obvious different characteristics:

1. Individuality and variation of publishing models. Unlike papers, which generally have certain patterns and static contents, the content of self-publishing is more flexible and varied. The Internet can even automatically supply its users with materials and services tailored to fit their personal preferences. For instance, some websites can provide contents that are personalized to each individual user, based on personal information or preferences filled out by the user upon his or her registration with the site.

2. Simplicity, speed, affordability, and ease of use. The traditional publishing process is as follows: author's writing, rewriting, proofreading, typesetting, printing, binding, transportation, bookstore, readers. But the steps of Internet publishing are: the creation of a distribution platform on the Internet, author's writing, uploading, reader (there is no time and place limitation), interaction between authors and readers. Self-publishing cuts out many of the middle steps of traditional publishing media. It is low-cost and fast, and has no time constraints like traditional publishing.

3. Interaction. One great advantage of self-publishing over traditional publishing is its ease of receiving feedback from users of the materials. In self-publishing, the author as well as the reader inspire and communicate with each other. To a certain degree, the author, the compiler, and the reader work together as a whole to create the final product.

4. The key difference between traditional publishing and self-publishing is that the format of paper print media tends to have significant barriers to access. For instance, in the editorial process, a piece must undergo selection, review, and final approval. Most people have no chance of ever publishing their own writing in their lifetime because traditional publishing has such a high threshold of accessibility. But the Internet grants individual people publishing authority and simplifies the publishing process. Self-publishing on the Internet skips the editorial processes; authors can have their writings published as long as they possess the basics of computer skills.

5. The defining feature of self-publishing is individualization. Traditional media are often organized by the government, institutions, and social organizations, while self-publishing mainly relies on personal implementation, on independent publishing. For instance, the average blog is owned and written by one individual author. Although there is a disparity between the power held by media-producing institutions and the power held by self-publishing individuals, the emergence of blogs has given individuals the ability to compete with institutions.

2. The Models of Self-Publishing

The existence of self-publishing on the Internet has developed with the following basic conditions. First, the Internet provides self-publishing with strong technical support and a free publishing environment. From the beginning, the whole idea is to develop a "decentralized, open, shared, and interactive" Internet, namely, one that has no absolute center, reflecting the way that the infrastructure of the World Wide Web enables users to express their views freely and easily. Second, the spread of the Internet over the world is exploding. The number of Internet users across the globe has been skyrocketing over the past few years. The Internet has proven to be surprisingly useful as a new kind of marketing tool. Furthermore, the application of various self-publishing technologies laid the foundation for the rapid development of these publishing activities (such as blog and wiki technology). Therefore, shortly after the birth of the Internet self-publishing activities flourished.

Fora and BBS which are commonly seen across the Internet can all be included in the scope of self-publishing. This essay is not going to analyze every available method of self publishing, but rather will focus on more common methods which have become very widely used. The following are the major models of self-publishing:

Personal Websites.

Currently, there are a large number of individual web pages on the Internet which were created by individuals in order to express that individual's opinions, and to disseminate personal information. Therefore, it is clear that these web pages represent a model of self-publishing. Personal websites have the ability to deliver the author's writings to the whole world, but in practice, they usually are unable to compete for more than a few readers in the vast media sea. They often do not transcend the level of interpersonal communication, and consequently it is possible for such a site to become an isolated island of information. Information on the Internet is plentiful and widespread, and while the quantity of information steadily rises, the average personal website gets lost in the ocean of information.

Blogs

The blog is a newer, easier-to-use version of the personal website. While it is easy for personal websites to become isolated islands of information with few readers, blogging websites supply bloggers ("blogger" refers to the author and editor of a blog) with network platforms and easily operated templates. Instead of having to write the entire code for a webpage, a person using a blogging website can simply type his or her text into the template, press a few buttons, and then the text is instantly published. In this way, a large number of blogs can be pooled under one blog website, thus forming a mass disseminative momentum, overcoming personal websites' shortcomings of weak disseminative ability.

The significance of blogs goes beyond simply promoting interpersonal communication. Some scholars have seen blogs as a form of mass media, one which gives common people the right to speak. In 1998, an article entitled "A White House Trainee involved with the President of the United States" shocked the whole world. It was first published by a writer named Matt Drudge on his own blog. This attracted the attention of CNN, and finally led to the worldwide exposure of President Clinton's scandal. This incident shows the amazing power of blogs.

Listservs

Listservs are similar to blogs in terms of the technology they use. In fact, some listservs can be used as a mode of blogging. But by their very nature, blogs operate pull technology, in other words, the author must try to draw readers to his or her blog in order to get his or her information read. Listservs, on the other hand, use push technology, meaning that the author sends the material directly into the inboxes of her readers; readers do not have to search for the information.

At present, there are some aggregations of listservs on the Internet. The Hill Network (http://www.cn99.com) in China is one such platform. The Hill Network was founded in November 1999, and was used to issue journals and newsletters via listserv. So far, its listserv has accumulated 38,000 publications.

Wikis

The first wiki was wikiwikiweb, which was an online help manual for software. The inventor of wiki technology thought that if people all over the world wrote what they knew on wikiwikiweb, then all software problems could be solved when all the knowledge was put together. Later, this way of organizing knowledge was noticed by a person named Jimmy Wales, who quickly combined the wiki with the encyclopedia. So, another popular method of Internet-based self-publishing was born, one named Wikipedia.

Wikipedia operates very differently from blogs. It combines a high degree of editing with low barriers to authorship, because anyone can log on to wiki websites and contribute information on any subject that he or she chooses. In the same way, Wikipedia stimulates the sharing of knowledge--tens of thousands of people contribute to it voluntarily every day. Because of its simple organizing mechanism and tremendous disseminating effect, Wikipedia has expanded and developed rapidly. Just five years, there have appeared more than 50 different versions of Wikipedia in various languages. The number of entries in Chinese and English is constantly increasing. There are over 200,000 entries in Chinese now. Wikipedia is a big victory for self-publishers. While many people blame blogs for their often mundane subject matter and language, one must be amazed at the strict editorial eye and the mutual respect displayed by users of the wiki technology. The Wikipedia created and maintained by average citizens has become the world's fastest-growing and most frequently used encyclopedia.

Publishing On Demand (POD)

Publishing on demand is a new way of publishing, which provides a limited amount of book printing and sales service based on the needs of readers in a short period of time. Because its editing, printing, publishing, and distribution are based on the needs of readers, so it is also a kind of self-publishing. Publishing on demand can be win-win for publishing companies and for self-publishing authors. It allows publishing companies to avoid the inconvenience of potential overstocks and shortages, and to make the books at their lowest possible cost. For self-publishers, the advantage of publishing on demand is that it can satisfy their desire for publishing books on paper media with quality comparable to that of widely produced, mainstream books. Publishing on demand, which commonly relies on the operation of Internet-based marketing, can communicate with readers and help writers sell their books on the Internet. It is worth noting that self-publishing is a major part of publishing on demand.

In addition, the online Internet studio (it has different names) is another model of self-publishing. For example, the famous Little Studio provides a long term multimedia-making and website-compiling service. Strictly speaking, these self-publishing activities on the Internet tend to be specialized and the Little Studio is just one kind of self-editing activity.

3. The Prospects and Strategies of Self-Publishing

3.1 The Relationship between Self-Publishing and the Publishing Industry.

Early self-publishing was a means of personal communication and study. But as more advanced self-publishing technologies, like blogs, were developed and became popular, self-publishing became more widespread and developed its own identity. At present, self-publishing has become a powerful model of communication that cannot be overlooked, and it deserves the full attention of the publishing industry. The author believes self-publishing plays the following roles:

Self-publishing can be seen as a step in the "the content industry." The term "content industry" refers to the group of entities which provide consumers with various information products through a variety of digital terminals. The process relies on the content products database and uses software and hardware freely. China has basically formed a content industry, which includes six players in the process—content providers (the publisher and so on), technical services providers, operators, distributors, buyers and terminal traders. At present, from the operation of self-publishing, we can see that self-publishing has been playing the role of content provider involuntarily. For example, as just mentioned, it is obvious that the self-publishing model "listserv" has an important place in providing information. Another example is the multimedia magazine. *Trend* is one such Internet magazine published on http://www.poco.com. Compared with print media, the content of multimedia is more plentiful and varied and most of the content comes from content providers.

Self-publishing can serve as a supplement to traditional publishing. It is obvious that self-publishing has fewer requirements than traditional publishing, as it is more accessible for everyone to publish their writings. In the publishing on demand mode, which combines the average individual's self-publishing and authorized traditional publishing, self-publishing becomes a possibility. Another is the wiki mode, the time and energy consumed in traditional publishing activity was changed by its magic mechanism.

Some self-publishers can become formidable competitors for mainstream media. Self-publishing media, such as blogs, have potentially challenged the mainstream media hegemony. The American blogger Matt Drudge first showed the world the potential strength of blogs in the year 1998. For half a year after he published "The Scandal of Clinton and Lewinsky," he led public opinion while the mainstream media followed him. But we must point out that only a few blogs can develop into mass media, and most of them will remain on the level of interpersonal communication. Therefore, the competitive capacity of blogs among future media is not strong, although they have a symbiotic relationship with mainstream media.

3.2 The Strategies of Self-publishing

Self-publishing has very few rules. Blogs, wikis and listservs are all nearly without barriers to access; that is to say, they avoid four major steps in the traditional publishing process--no editing, no printing technology, no or at very low cost, no form, and no system. Because of this, many people worry about potential problems, such as whether or not the self-publishers will be responsible, and whether they will deviate from existing policies, laws and regulations. Facing these doubts, the author points out that the following areas require attention and consideration:

The establishment of a sound mechanism for self-publishing.

Here, the term "publishing mechanism" refers to a quality control mechanism in self-publishing which shields the system from bad apples. In wiki technology, for example, the system encourages knowledge sharing, open editing of contents and mutual respect. Registered users have a clear purpose of sharing their knowledge, this purpose acts like a filter to weed out potential spoilers.

Second, competition can play a positive role in self-publishing. Because users want to publish their best work so as to gain attention, if they violate the rules or attack other people, they may lose readership and their reputation.

Third, self-publishing is an individual activity, and most users see it as their own space and cherish it very much. For example, the self-respect and self-discipline of bloggers has been a central topic of discussion in the blogosphere. As experience tells us, by relying on the power of goodwill and of software technology, it is possible to establish a governing mechanism in the world of self-publishing and to make that mechanism unnoticeable. This way, not only is it possible to maintain the close relationship between self-publishers and the average person, while making self-publishers remain conscious of the need to comply with the rules to some degree.

The promotion of self-discipline

It should be pointed out that there are some unexpected instances in self-publishing activities sometimes. After an unexpected event occurred, the site "Blog China" noticed the importance of advocating self-discipline and drafted an official proposal called the "Bloggers' Code of Ethics." This was the first time Chinese bloggers have been made aware of the importance of self-discipline; not just blogs, but other forms of self publishing as well should be self-disciplining. This has to do with more than just personal reputation; it also relates to the ability of the author's work to survive and to the destiny of self-publishing itself. Therefore, the author believes, a specialized association should be developed to formulate rules of self-discipline, in order to encourage Internet users to fulfill their responsibilities towards society as the role of self-publishing gains new levels of importance.

The enhancement of the interaction between self-publishing and Internet publishing

At present, large scale blog activity has already started on websites, such as Sina, Netease, etc. It is evident that self-publishing has been developing rapidly, affecting Internet publishing and eventually impacting traditional publishing. So, the author suggests that the mainstream media, publishers, and the government should pay more attention to self-publishing.

First, the traditional media should take bloggers under their wing to guide them and help them organize, so that self-publishing and traditional media can work in a complementary fashion. On one hand, the speed of the delivery of the news and information on traditional media networks can be greatly improved; furthermore, it can enhance the close relationship between media producers and media consumers.

Second, self-publishing activity should be paid enough attention in the "chain of content industry." Self-publishing has become a special way of creating content on the Internet. When traditional media is put online, the result is simply the electronic version of the paper product, but self-published material on the Internet is irreplaceable. Moreover, the very best self-published content can also be published again in traditional media. The same content can be published multiple times, unearthing the potential of multiple formats of media. Furthermore, there are many self-publishers who also engage in more traditional studio publishing activities, using both means to complement each other. Traditional publishing enterprises have the potential to use the self-publishing model to disseminate information in multiple means.

REFERENCES

Fang, Dongxing, ed. "The Competition, Symbiosis, Problems and Tactics between Blog and Traditional Media: The Meaning of Brief Study of Blog Interpersonal Communication." *Modern Communication.* 2004. 80-66.

"Publishing." *Encyclopedia of Editor in Practice.* Beijing: China Book Press, 1994. 150.

Yu, Min. *Publishing.* Beijing: China Book Press, 2003. 311.

Zhao, Zizhong. *A Study on Content Industry: The Core of Digital Media.* Beijing: China Media University Press, 2005. 15.

Blog Publishing and Its Copyright Protection

Li Yan

The history of blogs can be traced back to the report of "the Clinton Event" of 1998, which, together with reports on "9.11" made blogs a main means of communicating in the network. In 2002, blogs were introduced to China, and attracted people's attention after Wang Jipeng's "Internet counter-yellow event," and the sexual diaries of Mu Zimei. In the past two years, blogs have become a hot topic both in the net world and society. According to the 2005-2006 China Internet Industry Investigation Report issued by the Chinese Internet Association Exchange and Development Center in December 2005, the number of blogs globally in 2005 broke 100,000,000; in China they have reached 16,000,000, and will grow to 60,000,000 in 2006. At the same time, blog publishing gradually aroused people's interest both as a more advanced e-publishing method with huge commercial value, and as a publishing mode which would have a profound influence on the traditional publishing industry. Therefore it seems necessary to consider the issues of its connotation, its extension, its characteristics and its copyright protection.

1. The Connotation and Extension of Blog Publishing

Blog is the abbreviation of "Weblog," which means a network diary, and refers to a kind of individual cyberspace where an individual issues his or herdiaries and readers can attach commentary to them. When translated into "blogger" in China, it may also refer to the person who issues the individual information. Blog publishing should be understood as a new way of e-publishing, which means a blogger utilizes his blog to issue information. The contents, namely the issued information, may be original or reprinted, and its forms may be in text, pictures, videos and so on.

The common characteristics of blog publishing and traditional publishing are that they both include the stage of editing, of duplicating and of distributing. But these are performed differently online. The editing process of blog publishing refers to bloggers collecting source materials to create or reprint the works of others. Compare this with traditional publishing: the difference lies in the fact that the editing of blog publishing can be completed by one blogger himself; he is the author and the editor. Duplication in blog publishing refers to a blogger uploading his work to the blog website server, then the general netizens access it and it duplicates the work in their computers to read, thus the work is distributed. Unlike traditional publishing, blog publishing does not need ink and paper, and does not need transportation and storage. Revising the publication is as easy as picking up an oyster with three fingers. Moreover, in traditional publishing, we actually sell the visible information carriers—printed paper, recorded tapes or burnt discs. But in blog publishing, websites provide fee-free contents and by enhancing the click rate they attract investments from advertising agents.

The extension of blog publishing involves the following two aspects:

1.1 Relationships among Electronic Publishing, Net Publishing and Blog Publishing.

Fig. 1: The relationship among e-publishing, net publishing and blog publishing.

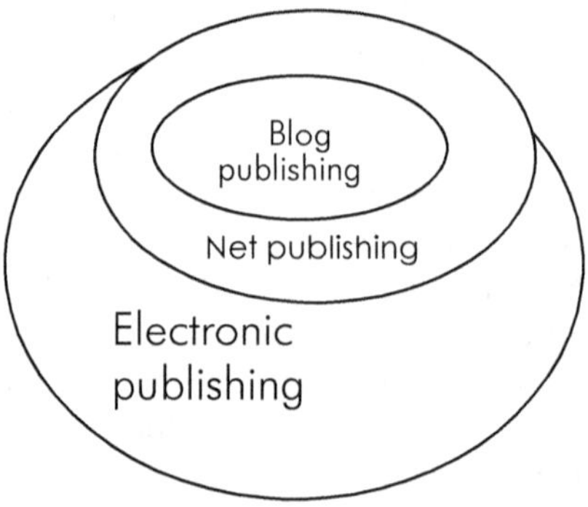

Net publishing is one type of electronic publishing, and "refers to an online communication behavior conducted by Internet information providers, who collect and edit works of their own or of others, and publish them on the net or transmit them to the terminals of the subscribers through the Internet, for the public to glance, read, use or download." Both net publishing and electronic publishing are realized through computers. But the carriers of electronic publishing are richer, like compact discs, floppy disks or the Internet; therefore, electronic publishing can include net publishing. Blog publishing, which is a kind of net distribution, belongs to net publishing. It is noteworthy that blog publishing is different from those thoroughly studied ways of net publishing like the e-book. The goal of blog publishing is not to make profits, but to satisfy the blogger's psychological need to unburden himself; therefore, normally the readers are allowed to duplicate information on the premise that there is no encroachment upon copyright; with e-books and other net publications that have to make money, duplication is not allowed in principle, and must put into consideration many questions including how readers pay for their reading, how to count precisely the number of sales and how to limit and protect the readers' rights to duplicate and collect.

1.2 Types of Blog Publishing

First is pure blog publishing. This requires that a blogger finish all the work like planning and creating it online. It suits a more individual network writer who produces and markets it all by himself. The second is publishing by reprinting. That is to collect and edit good work already online whose publishing value has been proved by the reprints and comments it attracts. This second way demands the location and publication the good manuscripts by earlier network writers. The last is a pattern that unifies traditional publishing and blogging. It is when, before publishing a book, one blogs certain chapters of the work in series, then analyses the feedback and data like the number of readers, commentary and responses it receives, thus providing a good basis for judgment on the prospects of the publication. This type of publishing, however, will more benefit serialized books. As a brand new publishing module with new ideas and new ways, it will cause a revolution in the publishing industry, and will bring to the publishing industry infinite prospects and opportunities for development.

2. Characteristics of Blog Publishing

2.1 Compared with traditional publishing

Besides the virtualization of the publications, blog publishing also has these characteristics: no threshold for publishing, a short publishing cycle, low publishing costs and effective interactions.

2.1.1 No threshold for publishing

A traditional publishing organization must be set up legally, and accept management surveillance, while blog publishing only needs registration with a free blogsite, and mastering basic computer operations. Blog publishing easily supplies the possibility of realizing the common dream of publishing or being a writer.

2.1.2 Short publishing cycle

Traditional publications must go though the author-publisher-distributor-reader flow. But blog publishing can be renewed whenever necessary, can be realized by just some clicks on a mouse after the work is done, and can be done as the occasion arises.

2.1.3 Low publishing costs

Traditional publication demands manpower and physical resources, such as the author, the editor and the publishing house to produce a book; it needs materials and requires transportation and storage to reach the readers. But the costs of blog publishing are extremely low because it can be done without these physical requirements.

2.1.4 Effective interactions

In traditional publishing, readers can only give feedback to the author directly or indirectly after the publication has gone through an entire publishing cycle. But in blog publishing, readers may make comments while reading, enjoying instant exchange of ideas with the author and with each other.

2.2 Compare blog publishing with other online publishing represented by e-books

Most present online publications came from the digitization of copyrighted works; thus, they have experienced the long cycle of traditional publishing; blog publishing is still faster and cheaper. Additionally, blog publishing is original, fee-free, personal and more direct.

2.2.1 Original

Although blogs can be reprinted, most of them are original. Whether they record the writer's thought processes path and divulge the innermost feelings, or exchanges information and explore academic questions, all bear the intense mark of being individual. But e-books and other online publications came from the digitization of copyrighted work, and are similar to reprinting.

2.2.2 Fee-free

In blog publishing, anyone can access the blogger's individual cyberspace to share his work for free. To a great extent, the fee-free aspects determine the popularity and high click rates of blogs, and this demonstrates the latent, huge commercial value of a blog. Readers of e-books and other online publications generally need to obtain the right to read through a purchase; only after putting in their user name and password can they register and read.

2.2.3 Personal

Firstly, being a kind of network diary, the contents of a blog publication are mostly individual experiences. But those of e-books and other online publications are normally academic. Secondly, the subject of blog publishing is the blogger. But producers of e-books and other online publications are "Internet information service providers authorized by the news publishing administrative department and the telecommunication management structure and engaged in the Internet publishing service."

2.2.4 More direct interaction

E-books and other online publications came from the digitization of copyrighted work, so they, too, must go through an entire publishing cycle, thus giving blog publishing the advantage that the author and the readers can exchange their ideas much more directly and easily.

3. Blog Publishing Involving Copyright Protection Issues

In March 2006, a female blogger, Qin Tao, sued the Sohu.com Corporation in the Beijing Haidian District Court, claiming that this web site had encroached upon her blog copyright. This is the first domestic lawsuit about blog infringements. From then on, people started to pay attention to the copyrights of blog publishing. Blog copyright related issues can be classified into three types. The first is disputes over blog copyrights. These are normally started by websites or traditional media illegally reprinting blogs without getting the bloggers' approval, or by encroaching upon the blogger's right of authorship. These take Qin Tao suing Sohu.com as their representative. The second is the more and more heated traditional publishing of blog works, i.e. blog works are edited and published in a traditional way. The website Blog China once promoted two blog books: Xie Yun's *My Ten-Year Occupation* and Li Lusha's *Going Out of my Working Unit*. Thereafter, the first click-rate ranking blog of the Sina.com — Xu Jinglei's blog anthology *Old Xu's Blog* and a Shanghai undergraduate, Qiao Qiao's *The Biography of Qiao Qiao's Engagement* were published one after another. The third is the gradual emergence of studies on blog copyrights. In May 2006, "the First International Cooperative Copyright Promotion Conference of China," conducted in Changsha, aroused people's great interest.

These events helped to bring the newly sprouting blog copyright protection issues to the publics attention. While blog publishing fulfils the social functions of disseminating and accumulating information with low, or even no, cost, it also raises questions about the protection of technology and demonstrates the laxness of related laws. To protect blog copyrights we have to establish a sound protective framework. No matter how mature a technology is, there will always be some loopholes, and moreover, technology is always changing, but laws tend to be static. Therefore, to protect blog copyrights we must take existing laws as the basic foundation and adopt them to technical and other protective measurements.

3.1 Copyright Law of the People's Republic of China, Correlative Laws and Blog Copyright Protection

It cannot be denied that both blog publishing and traditional publishing are the crystallization of human wisdom, though they have huge differences in shape. In the network environment, the duplication and transmission of digital work are simple, so it's very difficult for bloggers to control the dissemination of their own work. "Each stipulation of copyright in article 10 of the Copyright Law can be applied to all digitized works' copyrights. Disseminating the work through the network to the public belongs to the proper use of work stipulated by Copyright Law. The copyright owners enjoy the right to use the work or permit other people to use the work, and obtain rewards from the permissions." Therefore, the author's right of publishing, right of authorship, right of alteration, right to keep the integrity of the work, right of use, right to obtain rewards and other traditional copyrights should and can be applied to the domain of blog publishing.

In addition, the stipulations of the legitimate reprint, the authorized reprint, as well as payment for a published piece according to the Copyright Law and the correlation law are also suitable in blog publishing. Article 32 of the Copyright Law revised in 2001 stipulates explicitly that "after a work is published, other newspapers or magazines may reprint it or print it as an abstract or as reference materials, except where the copyright owner has declared that reprinting or excerpting is not allowed; however, compensation shall be paid to the copyright owner according to the regulations." Afterwards, in 2002, "the Supreme People's Court hearing related to the computer network on the copyright law applicable to disputes over the interpretation of a number of issues" extended this paying reprint permission system to the Internet and websites.

Finally, blog copyrights should be managed by collective copyright managing organizations according to Article 8 of the Copyright Law. Bloggers often do not have enough time and energy to negotiate and charge individual users or commercial websites one by one for rights infringements, and are unable to effectively supervise the service conditions of their copyrighted work. Therefore, providing permission for use of a blog work, and managing usage fees and other items uniformly through the collective organizations of copyrights can realize the above stipulations of related legitimated reprints, the authorized reprint, as well as the payment for published pieces.

3.2 "Protection Rule on Rights of Information Network Dissemination" (the Rule) and Blog Copyright Protection

The Rule that was adopted on July 1, 2006 made an explicit explanation of the formerly fuzzy concepts in the domain of information network dissemination. The Rule had a great impact on blog publishing.

The right of information network dissemination in the Rule has a vital significance in blog copyright protection. In blog publishing, since the creation is in real-time, carried online, and the work is issued in the network once it is completed, the rights of publishing and of information network dissemination of bloggers are simultaneously exercised, and it can be understood as the blogger tacitly approves that his work be disseminated through the network when completed, i.e. the blogger has intent expression to tacitly exercise his right of publishing through the network. Some websites intentionally confuse the two, and argue that the "right of information network dissemination is similar to the right of publishing," and is silently exercised, so they needn't get the blogger's agreement to reprint his work. But the two are essentially different. Right of publishing is "the decision whether a work will be revealed to the public or not." This right only involves the work which has already been completed, not yet published. Once a work is revealed to the public, the right of publishing is fulfilled and the author's right of publishing does not exist anymore. "Right of information network dissemination " refers to "the right to provide blog works to the public through wired or wireless ways to enable the public to obtain the work at the time and place designated by the blogger." "Right of information network dissemination" can be exercised with no limitations in the protecting period. The blogger can decide freely later exercisings of rights. Therefore, other websites and third parties must utilize the blog work under the blogger's agreement. Otherwise, they encroach upon the blogger's right of information network dissemination and must suffer the corresponding legal consequences.

Besides, the Rule stipulations that are about the rights and the obligations of the network service provider regulate the respective responsibility of blog websites and bloggers when blog copyright disputes arise. A blog website is a network platform, but the content is uploaded by bloggers. When a blogger encroaches upon other people's copyrights, like plagiarizing other people work, illegally reprinting other people's work and other behaviors, the blog website needn't undertake the responsibility, but if the copyright owner submits a warning, the blog website must remove the illegal content, otherwise they must suffer joint liability.

REFERENCES

Copyright Law of the People's Republic of China. 2001.

"General Administration of Press and Publishing." *Temporary Provisions on Administration of Internet Publishing.* 2004.

Hu, Dechi. "The Online Publishing and the Digital Copyright Protect." *Seeking.* (2003): 158-160.

Hu, Feilong, and Ping Zhou. "Blog and Blog Publishing." *Publishing Research* (2003): 56-58.

Interpretation of Certain Questions on Suiting Law about the Computer Network Copyright Disputation Case. Supreme People's Court. 2000.

Protection Rule on Right of Information Network Dissemination. 2006.

Zhang, Ye. "Appearance of the Question of Blog Copyright." *China Intellectual Property Rights Newspaper.* 2 June 2006: 11.

Research On the Application of OAI—PMH and Its Static Repository

Lu Xiaohua & Tong Wen

1. OAI-PMH and Its Working Principle

1.1 The Background of OAI-PMH

In the era of information explosion, everyone searching and exchanging information desires to obtain the access of the special specific contents they need. Metadata refers to describing, managing and utilizing the digital information resource in the network environment, which provides a mechanism of accurate description of data content, semantics and service. However, the diversity of digital information resources has brought a corresponding diversity of metadata formats, the access environment and so on.. This inevitably restricts the sharing, collection, exchange and utilization of the information resources, and brings inconvenience. Thus, a protocol of interoperability among metadata is required. OAI-PMH (Open Archives Initiative for Protocol Metadata Harvesting) is such a protocol which meets the requirement. It provides the organizations releasing net information of a interoperable framework which has nothing to do with the application.

OAI was first established at the Santa Fe conference in 1999, OAI-PMH version 1.0 was released in 2001, and version 2.0 which was released in 2002 is the OAI-PMH we are discussing.

1.2 The Working Principle of OAI-PMH

OAI-PMH has provided a interoperable framework based on metadata harvesting openly, which is conducted by the organizations releasing net information. The framework includes the data providers and service providers.

The data providers release the metadata, and the service providers send "Request" to the data providers, and with the "Response" metadata provider further value-added services.

OAI (Open Archives Initiative) originated from the electronic publishing industry, with the purpose of facilitating the exchange of academic researches for researchers from different areas under the net environment and avoid shortcomings of long publishing cycle and high cost in paper periodicals. With the development, the goal of studying OAI extends to all data formats, including all academic digital resources; OAI provides a new model of academic discussion and exchanges, which is beneficial for copyright protection as well as information sharing. Digital academic exchange is easier and more extensive, with a compatibility of all kinds of multi-media formats and data formats to increase the types of digital data access. In addition, compared with traditional interoperable protocols such as Z 39.50 and NCSTR. OAI-PMH is superior in operation of simpleness, opening and flexibility. As a result, an increasing number of trade staff from publishing, library information, computer and other fields pay close attention to the OAI-PMH.

Fig. 1: The Schematic Drawing of OAI-PMH Model

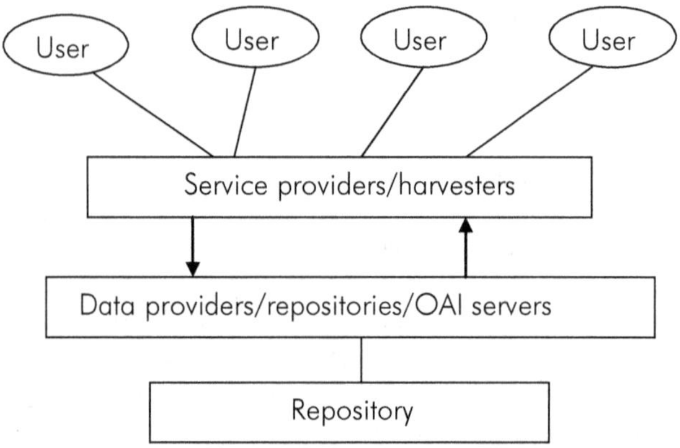

2. Application of OAI-PMH

So far, there are many getway websites, organizations and agencies using OAI-PMH when working with searching and sharing information. The number of the application projects of OAI-PMH overseas is not small, such as NSDL (National Science Digital Library), whose aim is to build the biggest and the most diversified national science digital library and provide varied digital resources for users of all levels. OAI-PMH plays the most important role in NSDL project. Metadata is its core component , which stores all kinds of metadata. First, search metadata from the information repository of the data providers with OAI-PMH. Then, integrate them with those obtained in other ways. The processed metadata are sent to metadata repository with OAI-PMH. Finally, the service providers in NSDL harvested all kinds of metadata through OAI-PMH to serve users. Apart from this project, there are the OINI of German, the CIMI of Australia and so on . . . There are many domestic application projects as well, for example, "system of knowledge repository" and "the knowledge network management system" are based on OAI-PMH to release and share digital resources. Currently, this system has been used in the database such as Chinese excellent doctoral/master's paper full-text knowledge database, Ancient document of Chinese medicine knowledge database and Chinese folk music digital library project and so on.

In publishing industry, the server system and types of database which publishers use are obviously different. Along with the development of network information exchange among heterogeneous database also has posed a challenge to publishers. Consequently, OAI-PMH attracts publishers. The cross-sharing of metadata information was based on OAI-PMH, with which publishers provided readers with access to publication metadata. Users could search any needed content conveniently, and solve the link restrictions. In addition, publishers use OAI-PMH to realize exchange and interaction of metadata, which guarantees users the accuracy and authority of information and protects the rights and interests of authors and publishers themselves.

Although publishers using servers based on OAI-PMH is still at an embryonic stage, there are examples of good applications, for instance: publisher Inderscience.

Inderscience is a publisher of international journals in the fields of science, engineering and technology, management, law and business administration, energy, environment and sustainable development and so on. Inderscience cooperated with a project team of EEVL (The Internet Guide to Engineering, Mathematics and Computing), and integrate the metadata of their publications to external services, especially the cross-referencing services. Here, OAI-PMH provided a free access, which helped the searchers to harvest, index and search metadata about the products through the searching engine, organizations, websites or any server based on internet. Users were enabled to share the latest abstract of the articles from Inderscience, which enhanced the loyalty and celebrity to some extent.

OAI-PMH is a good choice for publishers with advanced technique and abundant fund like Inderscience, and yet is inappropriate for small publishers with backward technique, less content resources and renewal speed.(especially the publishers who published only one or two journals) The solution is to introduce static repository and static repository gateway.

3. Static Repository and its Application

3.1 Static Repository and Static Repository Gateway

Although OAI–PMH is simple and easy, there are many limits in use. It is suitable to large-scale organizations and institutions, such as Internet-based digital library and some large/medium-sized publishers. But for small publishers who don't have enough fund and technology, it is necessary to introduce a Static repository and Static repository Gateway. Static repository allow small publishers to participate in information sharing based on OAI-PMH instead of full repository of digital information they are incapable to support.

A static repository is actually an XML file, which includes all metadata, identifiers and datestamps, and is mainly used for metadata harvesting are less than 5,000 records. Certainly, the metadata in static repository is only relatively static, and it can still handle changes to the collections. A static repository Gateway provides a portal for one or more static repositories. A static repository can be accessed online through a permanent Internet address. This file is an OAI-PMH data provider when registered in a static repository gateway (see Figure 2).

Fig. 2: The relations among Static repository, Static repository Gateway and OAI-PMH harvester

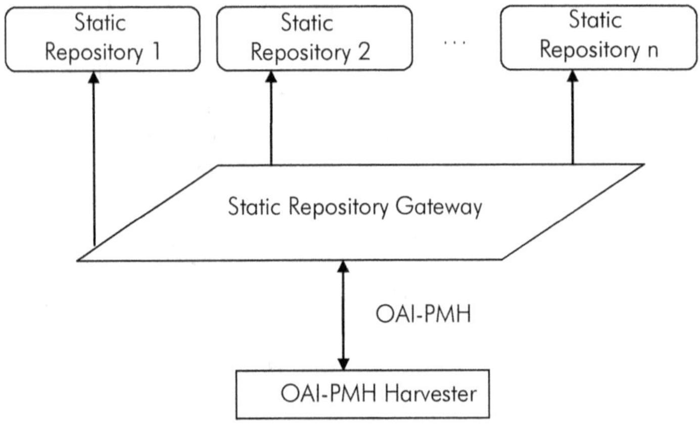

3.2 The Application of Static Repository

In some countries, researches on the application of static repositories are already in operation, such as the research done by Open Language Archives Community (OLAC) and the one of Los Alamos National Laboratory (LANL). As to the publishing field, the Static Repository Gateway and Toolkit (STARGATE) project is on the road. [6]STARGATE project is a low introductory research project of static repository which is developed for the sharing of publishers' metadata on the basis of the progress of OAI approach. The project is built on the technical architecture developed by the PALS I project carried out at Heriot Watt University in 2003. Specifically, it implements a series of static repositories of publisher metadata to demonstrate the interoperability of the OAI-PMH based static repositories. Static repositories had been implemented successfully within OLAC as a means of widening participation in OAI-based systems and services. Meanwhile, the triumphant application of static repositories in the HaIRST project had been regarded as another success since the one made by the FAIR Programme of Joint Information Systems Committee (JISC).

STARGATE project started on October 1st 2005 and came to its end on June 21th, 2006. The project was funded by JISC and was undertaken by the Centre for Digital Library Research at the University of Strathclyde for an investigation of the applicability of it. Four small publishers of e-journals named Journal of Digital Information, Information Research, Library and Information Research and Information Scotland had participated in the research work of the project.

STARGATE project had demonstrated the interoperability of the exposed metadata through harvesting and cross-searching via a static repository gateway, and conducted a critical evaluation of the static repository approach with publishers and service providers. John Robertson, STARGATE project officer, said the OAI approach had the benefit of associating the publisher with the metadata. "We want to promote the use of the OAI protocol primarily because it is easy to find papers online from an institutional repository but you don't find a link to the publishers", said John Robertson.

The project had lowered the technical barriers to the implementation of OAI-PMH, and enabled small publishers of electronic resources to participate more readily in OAI-PMH based disclosure and delivery services. STARGATE had created four static repositories on the basis of metadata provided by publishers, three of which contained their own journal's metadata and was registered and exposed through the gateway. In the process of the project, the low-cost function of static repositories had been showed up. Being a study case, STARGATE provided guidance for others to master this technique. To be specific, it can be concluded as follows. Firstly, the project provided guidance on the elementary and other related techniques of OAI-PMH based static repositories. Secondly, the techniques that the project took to set up static repositories according to existed digital information and what it declared for the standardization of metadata are referential. And it also touched on the set up of static repositories by using data and VB module. Finally, it indicated the conditions needed for the implementation of static repositories and the benefit that it would bring to publishers.

4. Conclusion

We are advancing to the Information Times characterized by the blast of digital information. In this era, the trend of transmitting and sharing of the digital information and services can not be reversed. The coexistence of different organizations, technology platforms and methods for searching and sharing information calls for a consistent criterion. Being an open standard for the exposure and harvest of metadata, OAI-PMH facilitates the communication between data and service providers. With the participation of publishers, searchers are able to quote articles with standardized format more exactly and obtain series of articles related to a certain topic of journal more easily. The application of OAI-PMH in the publishing field is of great potential. In the digital publishing field, OAI-PMH and static repositories would catch more and more attention with its extensive implementation. Therefore, it would provide technical support for the scalability and sustainable development of the whole digital era.

REFERENCES

Arms, William Y., Diane Hillmann, Carl Lagoze, Dean Krafft, Richard Marisa, John Saylor, Carol Terrizzi, and Van de Sompel. "A Spectrum of Interoperability: The Site for Science Prototype for the NSDL." *D_Lib Magazine*. 8 (1), 2002.

Caldwell, Tracey. "Stargate opens up OAI access to all." *Information World Review*. 15 Mar. 2006. <http://www.iwr.co.uk/information-world-review/news/2151986/stargate-opens-oai-access>

Dong, Hui and Ding Botao. "Study on OAI—PMH." *Book and Intelligence Knowledge*. 2004. (6)

Inderscience Publishers Ltd. <http://www.inderscience.com/mapper.php?id=11>

Li, Yongwen. *Research and Implement of OAI-based Integrated Information Retrieve System*: [Degree Paper]. Sichuan: School of Library of Sichuan University, 2004.

Liu, Xiaoming. *A Framework for Building Federated Digital Libraries Based on Metadata Harvesting*. Department of Computer Science, Old Dominion University, 2001.

STARGATE. <http://cdlr.strath.ac.uk/stargate/outputs.htm>

Analysis of the Marketing Model of POD Publishing

Liu Yongjian & Zou Rui

1. Introduction

In recent years, printing on demand (POD) has been an important component of the publishing industry to which it has brought far-reaching impacts. POD is a publishing methodology in which a copy is not created until an order is received. Compared with the conventional method of book publishing, POD is easier, faster, and generally more reliable and affordable.

Through the advanced technologies of digital printing and network distribution, POD can satisfy people's special needs for books by customizing the publishing process. Even an out-of-print book could be offered to readers through the network and digital printing technology within minutes. Unfortunately, POD has been a critical problem in the publishing industry for many years, mainly due to its controversial marketing model.

2. Marketing Model

With the POD publishing model, books are sent directly to retailers and individual readers and in principle are rarely passed on to wholesale distributors or made available in the mainstream markets such as bookstores. Therefore, the printing quantity of a book is solely determined by the actual demand. For instance, some POD book publishers such as iUniverse, Publish America, and Xlibris were quick in exploiting the advantages of POD and were able to add thousands of new books to their marketing lists and inventory. However, this was achieved at the costs of neglected, poor quality of book content, binding, and cover design, which is the very reason that their books ended up being rejected by readers, bookstores, and book reviewers. Consequently, POD is considered as a practice of low-efficiency publishing. This, to a large extent, could be attributed to its form of self-publishing. The market is dominated by the requirements of consumers since it is still a buyers' market.

Although POD saves marketing and distributing costs, it also diminishes profits for distributors and wholesalers, which means that distributors and wholesalers, who are familiar with the market and distribution channels, are ecluded from the business chain. Without effective marketing support, it becomes very difficult for

POD publishers to gain accurate and timely information about the needs of the market, which inevitably makes them slower in responding to market changes.

3. Integrated Marketing Communication of POD

The conflict between POD's marketing and operating modes forces publishers to attach importance to the details during the marketing process. Lauterborn's (1990) theory of 4C's emphasizes that marketing strategies should be planned from the consumers' perspective. This theory can be used for analyzing the awkward situation of present POD publishers for self-publishing. The so-called four C's are: Customer solution, Customer cost, Convenience, and Communication. Obviously, the POD market, to which publishers have devoted a lot of passion, could only be developed rapidly through stirring up customers' enthusiasm, seeking their approval of POD, and developing a good interactive relation between customers and POD publishers.

3.1 Customers' Needs and Wants

Meeting consumers' wants and needs is not about emphasizing institutional features and merits. Times have changed and the product characteristics must now match what the consumer specifically wants to buy. Undoubtedly, publishing on demand means that customers' demands take the highest priority. The press should focus on their choice of publication themes and publish books that will be popular among readers and have lasting value. Appreciation of readers is one of the most important preconditions of POD. One needs to admit that POD has limitations in publishing some kinds of books, such as novels, poetry, and anthologies, because these books do not have stable demand and could easily be pirated. Another reason is that these books rarely receive advance payments from wholesalers, which is not acceptable to the revenue model of POD. The press will face high risks because delayed payments affect capital turnover, which makes it very difficult for them to attract investments. However, POD is quite suitable for publishing reference books, academic books, and books that traditional publishers are reluctant to reprint due to the high costs of low quantity printing and stock maintenance.

In addition to the quality of book content, POD presses should pay adequate attention to book binding, cover design, and packaging. The press could make use of new technology instead of the traditional, high cost technology of offset lithography to publish unique books. Medium or small-scale presses could compete with big ones by utilizing new technology. Moreover, POD books and traditional books seem rather comparable in quality. The quality of a paperback or deluxe edition POD book is almost the same as the traditional offset print version.

3.2 Acceptable Cost to Consumers

Price setting needs to take the consumers' expectations and psychology into consideration. The product price may be the only part of the consumer's cost structure.

Cost is more encompassing, including things like opportunity cost. The objective of setting prices based on consumers' perception of costs is also to serve the consumers' needs better and shorten the selling process. Actually, the price anticipated by customers is often lower than that by the publisher.

Too high a retail price is the critical problem of POD publishers in their bookselling process, and is also its disadvantage, undoubtedly. This is because, for POD, the unit cost of each copy of a book is fixed, which leaves little room for profit increase, while the unit cost of each copy of a book printed with offset lithography will decrease as the print quantity goes up. For example, the cost of a 196-page 6×9 deluxe edition with four-color printing is CHN ¥10.00, but it could be reduced to ¥8.00 if it is printed 500 copies at one time, and even lower than ¥5 if the print quantity exceeds 1000. So, most books are not fit for POD publishing, especially under the condition of a large market demand. The price margin of POD is narrow and hard to decrease. At this moment, POD publishers can utilize their advantages at their own expense: they need not pay too much attention to cost reduction, for the low quantities of selling caused by weak market demands and low marketing costs caused by the narrow target audience. Usually, the customer's anticipated price of POD books is higher than that of conventional books. With the development of printing technology, the cost of POD books will be gradually lowered. Finally, both sellers and buyers will benefit a lot from POD publishing.

3.3 Convenience

Across the board, consumers are demanding convenience in every aspect of their lives. Higher education is slowly responding to this demand with such services as online registration, distance learning, and Web-based components to coursework. Consider all possible definitions of "convenience" as it relates to the consumer's wants and needs. Convenience may include aspects of the physical or virtual location, ease of access, transaction service, and time and hours of availability.

POD publishing itself has greatly simplified the marketing process. Customers only need to make a call to the POD publisher who holds the copyright to get one of their favorite books. However, the variety of POD books is relatively less than that of traditional books. With its high cost and low profit as additional factors, it is no surprise that reprinting published books remains the main business of POD publishing nowadays. Few POD presses bring new books to market. Meanwhile, any POD publishers wanting to enlarge or enter a new market have to depend on traditional publishing and its marketing channels to sell the books. In any case, POD publishing is more complicated, because of the following two disadvantages:

1. Returning books is not allowed. This makes bookstores reluctant to sell POD books or sign a sales contract. Allowing goods to be returned

is the key to book distribution, and the existence of stocks diminishes the significance of POD publishing. That's the conflict.

2. The discount rate is too low. Traditional publishers can quickly bring their books to the market by offering a discount rate as high as 45%, but POD publishers can hardly afford to do so. With less discounts possible for bookstores, POD publishers have greater difficulty in getting bookstores to agree to sell their books or push their books into the distribution system, which in turn hinders the selling of their books online.

Development of POD was restricted by the above two disadvantages for a long time, which increases the difficulty of evaluating the popularity or market share rate of POD books in the book review and publication fields.

3.4 Communication with Customers

Today's media-savvy consumers can spot a sales promotion from thousands of miles away. Technology and access to the Internet have enabled the dissemination of information specific to each person's needs. Many media work together to present a unified message with a feedback mechanism to make the communication bidirectional. Essential are an understanding of non-traditional media, such as word of mouth over the Internet, and an appreciation of how it can influence where you stand in the consumer's mind. Now, more than ever, effective and personalized communication is crucial to marketing success.

Since the costs of production organization and royalties are reduced, POD publishers should invest more in marketing and advertising. Common sales promotion tactics include book reviews, book signing, and author interviews. However, in an era of integrated marketing communication, sales promotion should focus on the readers' rational or emotional desire. For example, the marketing of academic books should be directed to the rational desire of consumers, and emphasize the book's authority and science, while marketing of pop readings should appeal to the customer's emotional desire and transform his/her emotional attachment into a sales transaction.

The press should not limit its marketing scope to known audiences and overlook the necessity of developing new consumer bases. On the contrary, publishers should make full use of the present advantages to advertise themselves to known customers, so that potential customers can be attracted to make sales transactions. Moreover, positive comments by known customers are the best advertisement for books, and such comments could spread quickly in different social groups and reach potential customers as quickly as possible. This spreading mechanism makes it a promotion tacticsuperior to any other marketing strategies. Customers of POD tend to be socially and spatially concentrated, which works to even greater advantage for the publisher's promotion campaign.

4. Conclusion

At present, some technological disadvantages still exist for POD publishers, but POD can nevertheless play an important role that conventional publishing can hardly replace. The success of POD publishing relies not on printing technology, but rather on the efforts made by publishers to attract readers, specifically theme planning, editing, and marketing.

References

"Book Publishing Through POD." *Wikipedia.* 1 Jun. 2006. <http://en.wikipedia.org/wiki/Publishing_on_demand>.

Hang, M., and J. Liu. "Knowledge Marketing: New Market Mode in the Era of Kowledge Economy." *Policy-Making Reference.* (1999): 5.

Lauterborn, R. "New Marketing Litany: 4P's Passes; C-words Take Over." *Advertising Age.* (1990).

"Marketing Mix." *Wikipedia.* 8 Jun. 2006 <http://en.wikipedia.org/wiki/Marketing_mix>.

McCarthy, J. E.. *Basic Marketing: A Managerial Approach.* Homewood: Irwin Publishing, 1960.

Moskowitz, H. R., and J. Beckley. "The It!™ Knowledge Warehouse: Large-Scale Concept-Response Databases Using Conjoint Analysis, Segmentation, and Databasing for Development and Marketing." *The Week Of Workshops, Advertising Research Foundation.* (2002).

Pickett, R. "Self Publishing tools: Print on Demand (POD) publishing." 19 Jan. 2006. <http://www.associatedcontent.com/article/18320/self_publishing_tools_print_on_ demand.html>.

Application of Mobile Payment Based on SIM Cards in Electronic Commerce of the Book Industry

Zhao Dan

1. Development and Existing Problems of Network Payment

With the continuing development of electronic payment on networks in China in recent years, the electronic payment system, which is an important part of electronic commerce of the book industry, has developed greatly. The following table shows that the trend of purchase payments on the network in the last five years has turned to electronic payment, and it annually increases in percentage.

Table 1: Statistics of types of payments for network purchases in China from 2002 to 2006. (Multiple choices for the year 2006.)

	Network payment (credit card or debit card) (%)	Cash on delivery (by cash) (%)	Bank remittance (%)	Post remittance (%)	Mobile payment (%)	Others (%)
2002.1	28.1	42.8	4.9	24.0	-	0.2
2002.7	30.7	33.1	6.0	30.0	-	0.2
2003.1	31.1	33.3	6.9	28.4	-	0.3
2003.7	33.2	29.6	10.2	26.8	-	0.2
2004.1	36.0	27.9	13.2	22.7	-	0.2
2004.7	37.9	24.4	18.1	18.9	-	0.7
2005.1	41.5	24.7	16.7	16.7	-	0.4
2005.7	48.4	23.3	16.6	10.9	0.3	0.4
2006.1	61.5	36.1	25.8	18.2	3.5	0.9
2006.7	73.8	28.1	15.2	12.4	2.4	2.0

Meanwhile, there are some problems with network payment, although it has already become a major choice.

First, Trojans and many baleful viruses, which are wide spread on the network, greatly undermine the security of network payment. In the investigation of "the biggest problem of network transactions currently deemed by users" made by the China Internet Network Information Center (CNNIC), we can see that users worried about the security for network transactions in the following years:

Table 2: Worry about security of network transaction in the past five years. (multiple choices for year 2006).

	2002.1	2002.7	2003.1	2003.7	2004.1	2004.7	2005.1	2005.7	2006.1	2006.7
Security (%)	31.0	22.1	23.4	25.1	28.1	28.9	34.3	26.9	-	61.5

Secondly, although the generalization of the Internet is rapid in China, some users feel it is inconvenient to pay for purchases on the network. In the same investigation as above, made by CNNIC, we can see the users' evaluations of "easy to use" network payments:

Table 3: The percentage of "inconvenient to pay" deemed by users for network transaction in the past five years (multiple choices for year 2006).

	2002.1	2002.7	2003.1	2003.7	2004.1	2004.7	2005.1	2005.7	2006.1	2006.7
Inconvenient to pay (%)	11.8	13.0	10.8	9.9	7.4	6.8	5.1	6.3	-	21.7

A new kind of electronic payment, i.e. mobile payment, can effectively solve the problems of "security" and "inconvenient to pay" for network transactions. In the following, I shall introduce this type of payment, and, based on this, bring forward a new type of mobile payment, i.e. mobile payment based on SIM cards.

2. Mobile Payment and SIM Card Mobile Payment

2.1. Mobile Payment

Mobile payment is through the binding of a cell phone number and bankcard account or bank account of a user, providing cell phone users with individual financial services anytime and anywhere, based on Short Message Service (SMS for short), Voice, WAP, etc. Some developed countries already provide the service of mobile payment for users. Presently, some initial attempts at mobile payment have occurred in China, e.g., for the users of "Go Tone" in Zhejiang Province.

2.2. Merits and Demerits of Mobile Payment

Compared with conventional payments (e.g. cash on delivery, bank remittance, post remittance), the merits of mobile payment are obvious. Even compared with the current major payment means, e.g. network payment, mobile payment has its advantages:

First, mobile payment is simpler and easier to use. Consumers buy the things they want on websites, and when payment is required, they only need to interface with several service providers such as China Mobile or China Unicom. In contrast, with network payment, there are numerous issuers in China. Some payment can only be made with some kinds of bankcards, while other kinds of bankcards are not accepted, which cannot be solved in a foreseeable time. For most bankcards with the function of network payment, a complicated authentication process is needed before the issuing of the card. All these reasons make the users who are new to the network feel at a loss.

Secondly, compared with payment made with computers, mobile payment has strong mobility, and is convenient and fast, which can be widely used in virtual and real purchases.

Finally, and also significantly, mobile payment is more secure than payment made with computers. Financial crimes on the network occur frequently, which challenges the security of network payment. On the network, hazardous viruses steal the accounts, passwords, and verification codes from users, which not only has a high potential of doing damage to users, but also threatens the electronic banks heavily and brings about a trust crisis for them. Compared with computers, the cell phone has smaller memory, fewer usable resources, and simpler functions; however, these give the cell phone a strong immunity against viruses, and make it hard for network criminals to do damage to users who pay through mobile payment.

Of course, mobile payment has its shortcomings. Currently in China, many mobile payments are made through SMS, yet SMS is delayed from time to time. Although the delay of most SMS is very short, when the conditions of the mobile network become worse, a delay of several minutes or even longer is possible.

Despite these shortcomings, the number of cell phone users is huge, and the major domestic service providers and banks have a positive attitude toward value added services including mobile payment. Now, the technology for mobile payment is almost mature, and the 3rd Generation communication network (3G for short) is also forthcoming. All these will greatly extend the value added services based on cell phones, and as a supplement for network payment, mobile payment is sure to develop greatly.

2.3. SIM Card Mobile Payment

Generally, current mobile payment is based on the cell phone itself, and has nothing to do with the SIM card. However, with the increasingly strong functions of SIM cards, it is possible to realize mobile payment on a SIM card, which is done by putting the function module and interface of mobile payment on the SIM card, not on the cell phone. (It is similar for a UIM card of the CDMA system, yet this article takes the SIM card as an example.) This is realized by designing the functions of menu setup and selection, input and output, display, and short message sending, on the SIM card, according to the specs of GSM11.14 (which defines the toolkit for SIM cards) or OTA. Its functions are similar with those of web pages made with simple HTML language.

Besides the merits of mobile payment mentioned above, SIM card mobile payment has its special merits:

First, for some simple mobile payments made through general short messages, a better human-machine interface can be achieved if the payment is on a SIM card: flexible menu selection, input prompt, error prompt, etc.

Second, complicated mobile payments (such as those having a complicated human-machine interface), are hard to realize on low-end cell phones; however, if this complicated payment is made on a SIM card, then low-end cell phones can also use this payment function. Thus, the function of the low-end cell phone is extended.

Additionally, SIM cards are issued by only a few service providers, while cell phones are produced by many producers, with many types of cell phones even for a single cell phone producer. Thus, SIM card mobile payments can achieve the unification of a human-machine interface, which decreases operation difficulty during the payment.

Finally, the functions of SIM card mobile payment are easier to be made diverse and individual. Presently, the major service providers in China offer various package services for different types of users, and the design of detailed functions of SIM card mobile payment can also consider different types of users.

The SIM card mobile payment outlined here is not aiming to substitute for the mobile payment based on cell phones. Mobile payment based on SIM cards, because of its special merits, especially its suitability for low-end cell phones, should become a supplement to the mobile payment based on a cell phone that has not existed long in the market, and promote the development of mobile electronic commerce (including electronic commerce of the book industry).

3. Technical Realization of SIM Card Mobile Payment

3.1. Realization of Mobile Payment on the SIM Card Side

To realize mobile payment on the SIM card side, application software for SIM cards must be designed, and the application software completes the mobile payment. From the top layer, the application software should provide users with an interface of mobile payment, with the functions of menu selection, user input, sending messages to the server, processing and showing messages from the server, data encipherment and decipherment, etc.

For example, for mobile payments for electronic commerce of the book industry, the following user interface is provided by simple application software:

"Bookstore A"

"Purchase books"—select a bookstore—>"Bookstore B"——>input book name or code——>done

"Bookstore C"

The above application software can be realized by Java, OTA, etc., however, because the Virtual Machine of Java is involved with intellecutal property rights and its code is relatively large, Java is not used widely in the SIM card market in China. The dominant software is the OTA technologies developed by China Mobile and China Unicom.

On SIM cards, the layers of software are as following:

Figure 1: Layers of software on SIM cards

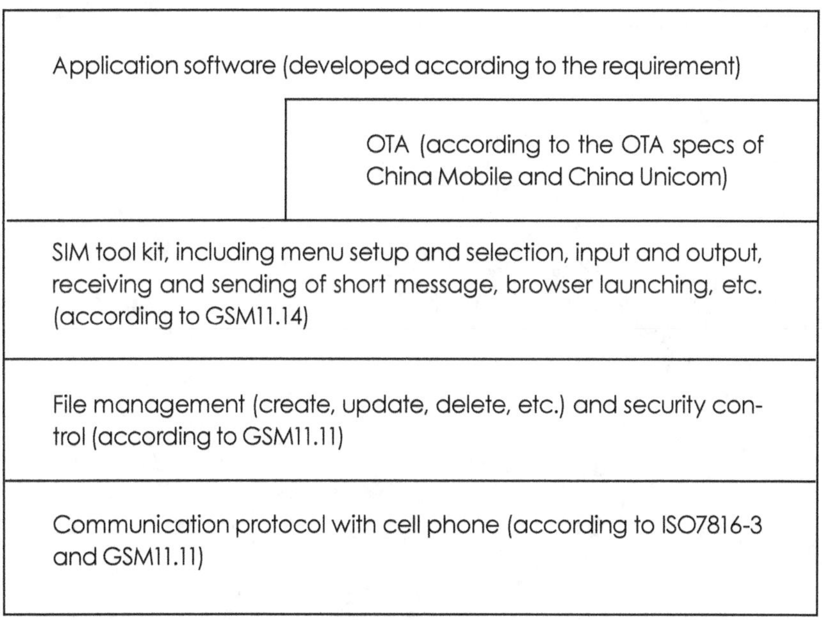

In the above figure, the lower three layers have the basic functions of an operating system, and, thus, are often called the COS (Chip Operating System).

OTA is built on the COS, and is composed of five parts: the interpreter, the part that packs and unpacks Mobile-Originated short messages (MO messages) and

Mobile-Terminated short messages (MT messages), remote file management, the part that guarantees security of data, and many tool-functions.

When developing application software with OTA, the application software will be developed according to OTA specs and the requirements for the software, and when finished, the software is in the form of a bytecode (something similar to Java). The bytecode can be put in a SIM card directly, or can be downloaded from a mobile network by a MT message, i.e., Over the Air (OTA for short). The interpreter is responsible for interpreting and executing the bytecode, and if interaction with the server is needed in the execution, then the part packing and unpacking MO messages and MT messages is called to interact with the server.

The part that guarantees security is responsible for the confidentiality, authenticity, and integrity of data or message.

3.2. Network Topology of SIM Card Mobile Payment

The interaction between the application software on the card side and the server at the network side is through Short Message Service. The topology of the whole system is as following:

Figure 2: Topology of the OTA system

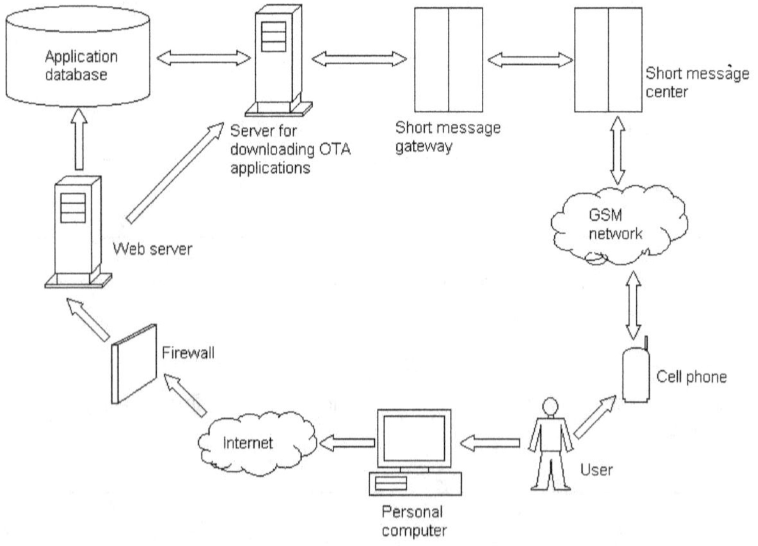

Except the server for downloading OTA applications (the OTA server for short), there is nothing special about other structures on the network side. The OTA server can be designed according to OTA specs and to the detailed requirements of mobile payment.

A user can also tailor the application software on his SIM card through the Internet, which is connected to the OTA server, as shown in the above figure.

4. Conclusion

Now, the development of electronic commerce of the book industry is rapid, yet the security of payment is always a concern for users. USB keys can improve the security of network payments; however, whether it will be accepted on a large scale by the users of electronic commerce of the book industry is unknown, because of the cost.

So, with a huge number of users, fast and secure mobile payment is no doubt an important supplement of network payment. The new mobile payment, i.e., SIM card mobile payment, which is based on OTA technology, better serves the requirements of micro-payment, and better serves the users with low-end cell phones, and, thus, is obviously a good choice for electronic commerce of the book industry. I hope this paper can promote research on payment through electronic commerce and the development of electronic commerce of the book industry in China.

REFERENCES

"ETSI Digital Cellular Telecommunications System" (Phase 2). *Specification of the Subscriber Identity Module - Mobile Equipment (SIM - ME) interface* (GSM 11.11 version 6.2.0 Release 1999).

"ETSI Digital cellular telecommunications system" (Phase 2+). *Specification of the SIM Application Toolkit for the Subscriber Identity Module - Mobile Equipment (SIM-ME) interface* (GSM 11.14 version 7.5.0 Release 1998).

Huang, Kaiqing. *Introduction to Technology of Modern Publication*. Shanxi: Economy Press, 2004.

"Implementation Specification of Downloading Monternet SMS Service Menus on STK SIM Over The Air" (Phase 2). *China Mobile.*

Zhou, Rongting. *Network Publication*. China Science Press, 2004.

Terminal Consumption Analysis of the Online Publishing Industry Chain

Wu Mei

Publishing insiders divide the history of online publishing into three periods: 2000 to 2003 is the period of perception and initiation; 2004 to 2005 is the period of exploration; since 2006 is the period of development. With the gradual development of online publishing, its industrial chain is forming step by step. It has broken the traditional operation of "author—publishing house—wholesaler—retail dealer—reader," and changed to flexible operations, such as "author—individual website—reader," "author—publishing house—website—reader," and "author—online bookstore—reader." All forms are in progress on a global scale.

But, the fine ecological conditions of an industry not only is the rational sequence of the division of labor, but also depends more on absorbing terminal expense needs. In other words, sustainable development can be realized only in circumstances of needs that have to be changed into benefits.

Online publishing has developed for about ten years in our country. The problem of insufficient effective demands in the terminal expense is always in online publishing. Although the book quantity has increased quickly in recent years, and the consuming group that enjoys online publishing services with online reading, online loading, and special RDR has increased year by year, the rise can still not satisfy the needs of the whole industrial chain's virtuous circle. The fee that consumers pay for online publishing services is so little that it can't balance the cost charged early in the links of the online publishing industrial chain, not to mention gain a profit from it. Therefore, this article has made a preliminary analysis of the terminal consumer pattern of the Chinese online publishing industrial chain and the demand. Then it discusses the bottlenecking in the Chinese online publishing industry.

1. The Terminal Consumer Pattern of the Online Publishing Industrial Chain

We can divide the terminal expense pattern of the online publishing industrial chain into three kinds according to the paying pattern: read for free, pay for reading, and reading with ads.

1.1 Read For Free

In this expense pattern, obtaining publications is free of charge. Now, news forums, some email publishing, and most of Web publishing belong to this pattern. This publishing pattern also needs funds, but the funds needed can be acquired without commercial operations. For example, news forums are usually funded and assisted by government departments, nongovernmental organizations or publishers.

Although this terminal expense pattern of the online publishing industrial chain—read for free—may have many consumers and great influence, noncommercial operation limits the development of its scale. Because online publishing is in no need of paper, and without such interlinks as printing, binding, drying out, and transporting, without middlemen who withdraw profits, the cost of online publication is lower than that of traditional paper books. Containing the same content, the price of e-books is usually equal to one-third of paper books or lower. However, online publishing and distribution also cost labor and money. There are the costs of the online publishing software, which is not cheap, and of copy money and copyright royalties. Taking account of all these costs, the cost of online publication does not drop greatly. The terminal expense pattern of read for free operates only in the limited drive that is necessary and with support provided by relevant departments. It leads to the phenomenon in online Chinese information—"much general information, little practical information: much second-hand information, little original information."

1.2 Pay for Reading

At present, a few email publications, online magazines and online journals are maintained by subscription. Online publishers usually provide contents or catalogues of several past books for consumers to read for free before subscription. Then consumers will decide whether they will subscribe or not. The price of subscribing to online publications is usually much lower than that of buying printed matter. In the traditional publishing industry, it's not easy to balance expenditures with income; however, for the online publisher, the chance of gaining profit increases because of the relatively lower costs and the economy of scale of online subscribers.

Certainly, the main body of terminal consumption with pay in the online publishing industry still is online database services. For instance, full text inquiry services in databases are provided by WanFang Data Co.ltd, which can be used after payment. Licensed consumers can browse and seek all contents of the database and are charged 0.10 Yuan to 3 Yuan for the information they acquire. This service depends on the scale and quality of its information services. Therefore, online publishers must take account of the brand and the scale of its information services. At present, information services that require payment mainly provide literature in the sciences and commercial information.

1.3 Reading with Advertisements

Reading with advertisements is not exclusive of the two terminal consumer patterns mentioned above. It's pay for reading for publishers and read for free for consumers, and is the most attractive terminal consumer pattern in the online publishing industrial chain.

Read with advertisement refers to when online publishers provide some pages as advertising pages in the first pages or reading pages of publications, and charge the advertisers who use these pages to advertise.

The advantage of online advertisement is obvious: it spreads quickly and broadly, is easily accepted and is relatively cheap. A recent investigation indicates that advertising on web pages is more beneficial to propagating the brand image than advertising on TV, and a lot of firms have gradually scrambled toward the Internet to advertise. However, facing the excessively crowded Net today, online advertisements usually make consumers lose their patience. And ostentatious advertisements or too many advertisements also easily cause readers to feel ill and result in losing their interest. Therefore, how to adapt online advertisements to readers to keep consumers in the long run is an important problem the pattern of reading with advertisements has to resolve; that is one of the terminal consumer patterns in the online publishing industrial chain.

2. The Terminal Consumer Demands of the Online Publishing Industrial Chain

2.1 Terminal Consumer Demands of Individuals

With the gradual popularization and development of the Internet, the number of netizens in our country has increased quickly and their reading demands make them a very big potential market for the terminal consumer demands of the online publishing industrial chain.

However, it is necessary for demand to become the driving power of the healthy development of the online publishing industrial chain that they must change into profit. But, now, the concept of "Net is free" is in vogue. Most online readers are used to acquiring online resources for free, and anticipate it. The result is that the visitor count will be big if provided with free e-books, and most visitors will be at a loss when confronted with charges. The loss outweighs the gain. The profits from consumers are less than the decreased profits of advertisements.

However, some websites try bravely to carry out paying for reading, such as the famous online literature website, QiDian Chinese literature (http://www.cmfu.com), which began in June 2002, and concentrates on the development of original literature.

These kinds of websites provide a platform for many articles which are difficult to published formally. The pay pattern of websites let many idealistic writers receive income in the process of writing and impulses and boosts the whole process of writing. The realization of the terminal consumption makes terminal demands change into visible terminal profits successfully and promotes the virtuous circle and development of the whole online publishing industrial chain. It makes online publishing a publishing form that is equal to traditional publishing.

2.2 Terminal Consumer Demands of Libraries

Online fantasy novel websites, as the forerunners of the revolutionary online publishing pattern, have developed the brand new pattern "Net—Net." The rapidly growing quantity and demands of netizens must induce many more publishing houses to enter into online publishing. Then, the supply of online e-books will be increased. However, mature consumers of online publishing in China do not lie in individual readers, but depend on libraries, which are the terminal consumers in the great demand for book databases.

It is well known that libraries of colleges, universities, middle and primary schools and public libraries are gathering book resources and readers, which own comparatively advanced network environments and computer applications. At the same time, there are many factors that are beneficial to the terminal consumption in this market.

With the intervention of the network, the place of traditional libraries is changing. The traditional consultancy centre position is replaced by the network, step by step. Libraries are no longer measured by the books they own, but by all the kinds of information they can provide for readers.

The concept of "quantity of copies" of the traditional publishing industry chain also applies to e-books; the terminal consumer demand of libraries will become an enormous driving force of the online publishing chain.

3. Bottlenecks of the Terminal Consumption in the Online Publishing Industrial Chain

Today, publishing insiders pay close attention to and place their hopes broadly on online publishing. However, many bottlenecks such as electronic payments, reading habits and reading equipment make the terminal consumption weak, which objectively restricts the sustainable development of the online publishing industrial chain.

3.1 Electronic Payments

The realization of the terminal consumption in the chain depends on the support of an electronic commerce system.

Generally speaking, the terminal consumption still mainly uses the type of payment that integrates electronic payment with cash. The promotion of paying for reading is necessarily held back.

3.2 Reading Habits

For now, the number of people buying books on the Internet is much fewer than that of people buying books at bookstores. Though it is not the defect of online publishing itself, it is the biggest adverse condition of online publishing. It's not easy to change readers' reading habits and modes of thinking from reading paper books to browsing screens.

There is still a problem of application and popularization even with a digital library.

Nowadays, there are many college and university libraries that have bought all kinds of digital information resources. But the application levers of teachers and students are different. Some teachers and students even may not have tried making use of a digital library to search for required knowledge and have not attempted the new reading mode.

3.3 Reading Equipment

Though e-books can be browsed and read on a PC directly, small, portable handheld readers, have much more obvious advantages to satisfy the terminal consumer demand. However, most online publications today are still electronic editions of paper books and primeval electronic readers mainly imitate the paper book habit that results in the advantage of "traditional reading habit" being much more apparent.

However, with the advance of time, the function of handheld readers will be improved more and more, which will lead to the rise of sales and the steady decline of prices. It's an inevitable trend of the electronic products developed in the information age. What's more, the development of mobile telephone net play technology means we can use a mobile telephone as handheld reader to browse or download online novels, which may be the solution to the bottleneck of the terminal consumer reader equipment in online publishing.

We are expecting that the mode of read with pay or advertisements will be widely popularized and bottlenecks of the terminal consumption in online publishing will be solved. With the full satisfaction of the terminal consumer demand, we will gain wonderful future of online publishing's great development.

References

Chen, Fang. "Market? Copyright? Industry chain? The Three Key Problems in Online Publishes." *China Publishing.* (2004).

Liu, Jingjing and Qiong Wu. "Digital Publishing." *Computer World.* (2005).

Zhang, Jianting and Ye Zou. "Two Online Publishing Patterns." *Publishing Research.* (2005).

Zhou, Rongting. "The Charging Pattern of Online Publishing." *Publishing Research.* (2000).

Investigation on the Networking of China's Copyright Trade

Wang Xiaoyan & Yang Xianghui

With the rapid development of the Internet, the integration of the Internet and the traditional book industry has become an inevitable trend. Networking in copyright trade could facilitate copyright negotiations and accelerate the speed of trading. The network of international publishing has been growing very quickly, and copyright trade has also been at the level of online transactions. Therefore, China's copyright trade through the Internet will also be further developed. To achieve this aspiration, we conducted a thorough investigation and analysis on the networking status of the copyright trade in our country from four aspects: management, information, transaction and agents.

1. Investigation of the Networking Status of China's Copyright Trade

1.1 Networking Status of China's Copyright Trade Management

The network management of the copyright trade refers to the way in which the central and provincial government quickly and widely disseminated through the Internet the copyright trade-related policies, laws, regulations and notice to the units and individuals at all levels and in all fields related, and timely feedback through the Internet in order to further improve the efficiency and effectiveness of the management. China's copyright trade administrations are the National Copyright Administration of the People's Republic of China, the Copyright Protection Center of China and the Regional Copyright Bureau. Meanwhile, the China Copyright Association is the only representative community; the regional copyright associations are social service agencies; the regional copyright protection organizations are society groups. But all of these associations and social organizations don't have their own website.

As seen in Table 1, The National Copyright Administration of the People's Republic of China paid more attention to network management. In September 2000, it launched its official website. Its main job is the administrative management of copyright. There are exhaustive copyright statistics and information feedback on the website, but it doesn't have an English version.

Table 1: The networking status of China's National Copyright Trade Administration

Name	Website	English Version	Information Feedback	Copyright Statistics
National Copyright Administration of the People's Republic of China	http://www.ncac.gov.cn	No	Yes	Yes
Copyright Protection Center of China	http://www.ccopyright.com.cn	No	Yes	No
	http://www.ibexnet.org/copyright	Yes	Yes	No
China Copyright Association	No	No	No	No

The China Copyright Protection Center has set up its own trading website, named China's Copyright Trading Information Network. It also set up its own research-based website. The former provides information about the copyright trade and copyright advisory service. The latter is mainly on copyright research and some basic copyright trade service. The China Copyright Association is an academic social community. It is still in the initial stages of networking. So far it does not have its own website.

Of the 42 municipal Copyright Bureaus, the networking status of the Beijing copyright bureau is the best. It not only has an English website, but the copyright information feedback services are also very good; they do not however have the statistics service. The Copyright Bureaus in Sichuan province and the Chongqing Municipal Bureau have their own websites with information feedback and works registration statistics for every year. But they don't have an English website, which is not convenient for foreign enterprises to understand and exchange information. About 59.52% of the following forty two copyright bureaus do not have their own websites. 33.33% of the copyright bureaus have only a joint Chinese website with the municipal Press and Publication Bureau. They have done a good job on the administration and services of the copyright trade, but are lacking statistics.

Table 2: The networking status of China's Regional Copyright Bureau (Continues)

Name	Website	English Version	Information Feedback	Copyright Statistics
Beijing Municipal Bureau of Copyright	http://www.bjcab.gov.cn	Yes	Yes	No
Tianjin Municipal Bureau of Copyright	No	No	No	No
Hebei Bureau of Copyright	No	No	No	No
Shanxi Bureau of Copyright	No	No	No	No
Neimonggu Bureau of Copyright	http://www.nmgnews.com.cn	No	Yes	No
Liaoning Bureau of Copyright	No	No	No	No
Jilin Bureau of Copyright	http://xwcbj.jl.gov.cn	No	Yes	No
Heilongjiang Bureau of Copyright	No	No	No	No
Shanghai Municipal Bureau of Copyright	http://cbj.sh.gov.cn	No	Yes	No
Jiangsu Bureau of Copyright	http://www.jsxwcbj.gov.cn	No	Yes	No
Zhejiang Bureau of Copyright	http://www.zjxwcb.gov.cn	No	Yes	No
Anhui Bureau of Copyright	No	No	No	No
Fujian Bureau of Copyright	http://www.fjxwcbj.gov.cn	No	Yes	No

Table 2: The networking status of China's Regional Copyright Bureau (Continues)

Name	Website	English Version	Information Feedback	Copyright Statistics
Jiangxi Bureau of Copyright	http://www.jxcbj.gov.cn	No	Yes	No
Shandong Bureau of Copyright	http://www.sdxwcb.gov.cn	No	Yes	No
Henna Bureau of Copyright	No	No	No	No
Hubei Bureau of Copyright	http://www.hbnp.gov.cn	No	Yes	No
Hunan Bureau of Copyright	No	No	No	No
Guangdong Bureau of Copyright	http://www.xwcbj.gd.gov.cn	No	Yes	No
Guangxi Bureau of Copyright	http://www.gxpress.gov.cn	No	Yes	No
Hainan Bureau of Copyright	No	No	No	No
Sichuan Bureau of Copyright	http://www.sccopyright.org	No	Yes	No
Guizhou Bureau of Copyright	No	No	No	No
Yunnan Bureau of Copyright	No	No	No	No
Chongqing Bureau of Copyright	http://www.cqppb.gov.cn	No	Yes	Yes
Tibet Bureau of Copyright	No	No	No	No
Shanxi Bureau of Copyright	No	No	No	No
Gansu Bureau of Copyright	No	No	No	No
Ningxia Bureau of Copyright	No	No	No	No

Table 2: The networking status of China's Regional Copyright Bureau (Continued)

Name	Website	English Version	Information Feedback	Copyright Statistics
Qinghai Bureau of Copyright	No	No	No	No
Xinjiang Bureau of Copyright	No	No	No	No
Copyright Bureau in Shenyang City	No	No	No	No
Copyright Bureau in Dalian City	No	No	No	No
Copyright Bureau in Changchun City	No	No	No	No
Copyright Bureau in Nanjin City	No	No	No	No
Copyright Bureau in Qingdao City	http://xwcbj.qingdao.gov.cn	No	Yes	No
Copyright Bureau in Wuhan City	No	No	No	No
Copyright Bureau in Guangzhou City	http://www.xwgd.gov.cn	No	Yes	No
Copyright Bureau in Shenzhen City	No	No	No	No
Copyright Bureau in Changsha City	No	No	No	No
Copyright Bureau in Xi'an City	No	No	No	No
Copyright Bureau in Chengdu City	http://www.cdbpp.chengdu.gov.cn	No	Yes	No

1.2 The Networking Status of China's Copyright Trade Information

The network of copyright trade information refers to the use of the Internet to provide access to copyright and trade information and to exchange information. The copyright trade information here is information in all aspects, including the author, works, copyright transactions, copyright information about sales and what is being sought, copyright owner, etc.

The networking of copyright trade information is the main part and the most realistic value in copyright trade networking. Some daily updated information is comprehensive, including "the introduction of foreign copyrights," " the copyrights of Hong Kong, Macao and Taiwan regions," "the mainland original manuscript" and " mainland copyright exports," for instance, Beijing copyright agent Ltd. Some are only providing annually updated information about the local copyright exports without the import information, such as the Chongqing Municipality and Sichuan Copyright Bureau. In short, the information provided by these websites is diversified in degree, but also has unique features. This shows the relative maturity of the networking of China's copyright trade information.

1.3 The Networking Status of China's Copyright Trade Transaction

Copyright trade transactions conducted through the Internet is network trading. There are many procedures during international copyright trade. Through the Internet, publishers can communicate with foreign publishers, and quickly resolve related issues.

In foreign countries, "International Copyright Online" (www.copyright.com) is a very good platform for network transactions. Domestically, the main organizations of copyright trading are the Copyright Protection Center of China, various publishing houses, copyright agent limited and some private companies. There are two kinds of copyright transaction network platforms: one is an integrated network platform, and the other is a network platform built by the publishers themselves.

The former are mainly "Chinese Copyright Online" (www.copyrightonline.com), "Beijing International Copyright Trade Online" (www.copyright-china.com), "China Copyright Information Online" (www.ccopyright.com.cn, held 'by China Copyright Protection Center), and "Chongqing Copyright Trade Online (www.cqca.com.cn). "Chinese Copyright Online" was started on September 1, 2006 by China Publication Online (BOOKICP), which is a prelude to the networking of China's copyright trade. In addition, so far, "Chongqing Copyright Trade Online" is the first integrated copyright trade network platform in the western region. The latter are mainly East China Normal University Press (www.hdsdbook.com.cn), QiLu Press (www.qlss.com.cn), and China Communications Press (www.ccpress.com.cn). These network platforms cover the domestic and international copyright trades, contract review, copyright registration, display of works, copyright protection, legal services and so on. All domestic and foreign publishers and copyright holders are free to release information and to negotiate through e-mail.

These operating network platforms have achieved some success. The Hunan Copyright Agency is a good example. In addition, Tianjin Education Publishing

House's *Find Guilbaud*, Liaoning Education Publishing House's *Dinosaurs to Dodos: An Encyclopedia of Extinct Animals*, and The People's Literature Publishing House's *Oxford English Literature History*, are all found and traded though the Internet. As far as the private companies go, they have relatively little involvement in copyright transactions for their unreasonable status. But there are exceptions. For example, Beijing Caiwei Culture Consultation, Ltd., the Beijing Bridge Book Publishing Company, and Danqing Books, Ltd., have also successfully carried out the copyright transactions though the Internet.

1.4 The Networking Status of China's Copyright Trade Agents

The agency is one of the hallmarks of a mature market. Approved by the State Department, the National Copyright Administration has set up twenty four copyright agents since 1988. These agents set up a powerful impetus to China's copyright trade.

Table 3: The networking status of China's copyright agents (Continues)

Name	Website	English Version	Information Updating	Copyright Information Providing	Copyright Transaction Platform
China Copyright Agent Ltd.	No	No	No	No	No
Beijing Copyright Agent Ltd.	http://copyright-china.com	Yes	Yes	Yes	Yes
Tianjin Copyright Agent Ltd.	No	No	No	No	No
Shanghai Copyright Agent Ltd.	http://cbj.sh.gov.cn/copyright	No	Yes	Yes	No
Guangxi Wanda Copyright Agent Ltd.	No	No	No	No	No
Liaoning Copyright Agent Ltd.	No	No	No	No	No
Heilongjiang Copyright Agent Ltd.	No	No	No	No	No

Table 3: The networking status of China's copyright agents (Continued)

Name	Website	English Version	Information Updating	Copyright Information Providing	Copyright Transaction Platform
Hebei Copyright Agent Ltd.	No	No	No	No	No
Henan Copyright Agent Ltd.	No	No	No	No	No
Anhui Copyright Agent Ltd.	No	No	No	No	No
Hubei Copyright Agent Ltd.	No	No	No	No	No
Hunan Copyright Agent Ltd.	No	No	No	No	No
Shandong Copyright Agent Ltd.	No	No	No	No	No
Jilin Fangda Copyright Agent Ltd.	No	No	No	No	No
Jiuzhou Multimedia Copyright Agent Ltd.	No	No	No	No	No
Chinese TV Program Agent Ltd.	No	No	No	No	No
Shanxi Copyright Agent Ltd.	No	No	No	No	No
Sichuan Copyright Agent Ltd.	No	No	No	No	No
Guangdong Copyright Agent Ltd.	http://www.gdcopyright.org.cn	No	No	No	No
Copyright Agent Department of China Book Trade Ltd.	No	No	No	No	No

At present, China's intermediary organizations of copyright trade development are not yet mature, and only a few organizations run well. Looking at the ninteen copyright agents in Table 3, only Beijing and Shanghai have their own websites, on which they offer a large amount of copyright trade information, including such features as overseas copyrights, Hong Kong, Macao and Taiwan copyrights, mainland creative works and copyright exports. Meanwhile, Acting Beijing Copyright Limited Liability Company offers an English version platform. Nearly nintey percent acting copyright companies do not boast their own websites and copyright information, and ninety one percent are without trading platforms. This situation is not conducive to China's copyright trade development in the network age.

2. Analysis on the Networking Status of China's Copyright Trade

Compared with developed countries in publishing, China developed the networking of copyright trade only recently. Although China has made great progress in many respects, there is still a big gap. As seen from the above survey, key issues existing in the process of the networking of China's copyright trade development are as follows:

2.1 Networking Construction on Information of Copyright Management Bodies Generally Lag Behind

China's copyright management mostly focuses on administration. Foreign publishers or copyright agents know Chinese copyright policies by visiting the official websites, such as copyright bureau and the like, which have a mission to link inside and outside information about copyright supervision. So, they should find their websites on the base of an international standard. A survey shows that 59.52 percent of copyright bureaus have no websites, and most others do not have English versions or columns meeting foreign requirements. There is more administrative supervision than there is service given, which makes copyright communication inconvenient.

2.2 Network Information on Copyright Trade is Scattered, Networking Development Unbalanced

First, there is not a recognized authoritative network platform in the domestic area for copyright information release. Second, network providers are mostly centralized in Beijing and Shanghai. The regional imbalance is not conducive to fully exploring and utilizing excellent copyright resources, or to helping China's copyright trade prosper. In addition, there are some shortfalls, including slow updates, incomplete information and so on.

2.3 Online Trade of Copyright Still in Initial Stage

At the present time, using the network to transact is just the beginning. There are few units doing business online. Most of them make the network a new propaganda tool, without any attention to building a database for copyright trade. There are both objective reasons and subjective factors. People have been accustomed to negotiating face to face for a long time. However, with the expansion of copyright turnovers and the extension of geographic zones, the advantage of online trade becomes more obvious. Online copyright trade will be an important tool.

2.4 Copyright Intermediaries Are Incompetent in Trading

Copyright agents play an important role in the copyright trade overseas, which has developed quite well. At the same time, the number of China's copyright agents is small because of administrative approval. What's more, many copyright agents did not run or run well. Few of them ran well in exchange information or trading online. This situation and some mechanisms influence the process of networking of the copyright trade badly.

3. Some Suggestions for the Networking of the Copyright Trade Development of China

3.1 Copyright Administrative Department Support to Perfect the Copyright Trading Platform

There are some problems with copyright information platforms, like information decentralization, renewal deferment, poor content and function. To improve Chinese copyright information platforms, the model of international advanced platforms could be referred to; all levels of copyright managements and associations should cooperate fully, and supply a network platform that publicizes the latest and relative convergence and credible information. From an information platform, visitors can see the general situations of bargaining companies or individuals, contacts, bibliographies, book covers, content abstracts, quotations, book reviews of best sellers, classic works, etc. At the same time, it may explore how to realize online trade, such as online copyright admission and cession, and so on. In addition, the information platform should offer some information about present international copyrights, net-copyright publication, copyright forums and international book merchants.

3.2 Participants in Copyright Trade Should Strengthen Their Awareness of the Network, Reform Their Own Wesbite Contents

"International Copyright Online," set up by a group of experts with profound net management experience and publishing knowledge in 1999, is reflecting the development trend of net-oriented, international copyright trading. It is has a new operation idea and running method, and it is truly a net copyright trading platform within copyright information exchange, copyright trading and management. Nearly one hundred domestic presses and agents have registered, but the others don't pay enough attention to networking. What's more, even those who have registered are limited to publicity, not engaged in e-commerce, and some bibliographies are not even displayed.

21CN is the age of the network economy. Participants in copyright trade should enhance their network awareness and reform the website contents, developing the existing online book information into a copyright communication center, taking a show of sample books and partial contents, and offering detailed information to their intended presses, agents and book explorers, such as information about a certain book being sold its special language copyright, who owns its copyright and how to contact the owner, and so on. The information should material and useful.

3.3 Establish and Improve an Available Bibliography Database, which Enables It to Offer Basic Information for Net Copyright Trade

An availability bibliography database is the basic information of the publishing and distribution industry, for which the application and development of the network supplies more universal and convenient conditions. As far as promoting the networking of China's copyright trade, an availability bibliography database is the groundwork of a works and copyright information database, as well as an important function and proportion for the copyright information platform. It can comparatively concentrate information, such as new books, best sellers, constant books, classic works domestically, and the author, will act for or permit, and the entire copyright information of books or works. In this way, it will make searching and using information convenient for the domestic consumer, and enable China's latest books or works and important books to be publicized and popularized in a timely manner by the network in favor of copyright exports. Now, China publishing groups are embarking on the construction. The database will promote the networking of copyright trade in the foreseeable future.

Transformation and Innovation in the International Book Trade Based on New Technology

Yao Yongchun

Owing to the rapid development of digital technology and networks, digital publishing has developed very quickly in recent years. It is open, global, low-cost and highly efficient. By means of information technology and Internet platforms, this new book publishing model can provide knowledge and information service to a no-region-boundary "virtual world marketplace" twenty four hours a day. It has maximally satisfied the need of the book trade between different countries and time zones for proceeding without time-space limitations. Consequently, there are some transformations and innovations appearing in the international book trade.

1. Influences on the International Book Trade by New Technology

The new pattern of book publication and consumption, such as electronic publishing, open access publishing, print-on-demand, reading online, e-commerce, etc., is changing the traditional relationship of the international book trade increasingly. It has brought not only challenges but opportunities to the international book trade market.

1.1 Improving the Efficiency of the International Book Trade, Optimizing the Global Allocation of Publishing Resources

A high-speed information transmitting channel has been opened up on a global scale based on new technology. Through the Internet, book publishers and book import and export agents can create direct links to readers and writers. They can not only get business information but communicate simultaneously in real time. That is to say, the demand–supply information can be exchanged more effectively than before. So, the uncertainty in the international book trade will be decreased, and the blindness in market development will be rectified, time lags and mistakes in decisions will be reduced, and the quality and efficiency of the trade will be improved.

On the other hand, the plenitude of book trade information will weaken the monopoly that came into being because of inadequate information exchange or information asymmetry in the world book market. However, it gives more opportunities to book publishers and agents to choose book products and trade partners all over the world, which is helpful for them to allocate resources rationally and dynamically on a global scale.

1.2 Excavating the Potential of the World Book Market, Expanding the Scale of the International Book Market

With the content digitization and corresponding expansion of publishing online and the electronic book market, the international book trade will expand as well. It is reported that the revenue of Chinese publishing online amounted to 3,500,000,000 Yuan in 2004, and the output of network academic documents nearly reached 500 million Yuan in 2005.[1] In the USA, the categories and the sale of electronic book increased by 20% and 23%, respectively, in 2005 as compared with last year.[2] For Reed Elsevier, online information accounts for about 70% of the total revenue from the USA and the whole world; in contrast, paper publications only account for about 30%.[3] The gradually growing digital publications break the physical limitations of traditional books, periodicals and newspapers. They are transferred with intangible digital data and transmitted at high speed online, so it is easier for them to spread and to be purchased all over the world. As a result, the capacities of the international book trade are expanding.

The scale of the world book market will also expand because of the increasing business opportunities brought by e-business. Because of the Internet, almost all publishers and book import and export agents can collect information on readers who visit their websites and build up their own databases. It is easier to carry out one-to-one sales promotion to every reader according to his preference, to arouse readers' potential desires for purchases and to change it into real consumption, ultimately. Moreover, the application of e-business makes it feasible to order, deliver books and pay money through the Internet, which gets rid of the obstacles in the traditional international book trade due to the space and time limitations. Under the new circumstances, enterprises can overcome the regional inferior position and do electronic business without any time-space restrictions. So, the market potential can be excavated sufficiently. Besides, the charm of digital reading and the convenience and high speed that readers experienced in buying books online will attract more readers. Thereby, the multinational individual book trade may thrive.

1.3 Decreasing the Costs of the International Book Trade, Accelerating the Flow of the International Book Trade

Based on new technology, most of the trade information, even the product itself, can be transferred in digital rather than in paper form. Therefore, the distance and time consumed in the international book trade will be shortened, and the procedure and process will be simplified. The cost of purchasing and marketing will decrease and the flow of trade will accelerate.

First, the purchasing costs will decrease. In the traditional international book trade, both trading parts promote their products and look for their customers by giving out book catalogues, and sending out book samples, personal selling, taking part in book fairs, and so on. The cost is high, but the efficiency is low. In addition, the processing activities such as negotiation, ordering and delivery, selling and paying, are usually carried out in different places, and the procedure of drawing and transferring business documents is so complex that it easily leads to delays and errors. However, relying on new technology, the trade operating system will realize informatization. All processing activities, like business information sales, negotiation, order and delivery, selling and paying, can be carried out online. So, the process will cut time, the transaction will accelerate, and the cost will be reduced.

Second, the stocking cost will decrease. The cycle of one deal in the traditional international book trade is so long that it usually takes several months to stock goods. The stocking cost is comparatively high. But under the circumstances of new technology, the international book trade will be undertaken step by step without paper documents. As a result, the trading period will be shortened and the stock will decrease. Especially, with the popularization of POD and publishing online, with the realization of publishing by order and producing and supplying in real time, the notion of zero stock and zero goods return is hopeful to become a reality.

Third, promotion costs will be reduced. According to a calculation by an American company, the promotion cost is 50,000 U. S. dollars per month when printing a goods catalog, while it is 100 U. S. dollars when showing goods on the Internet. Therefore, it can not only expand the coverage area of advertisement and strengthen the advertisement's effect, but also reduce the promotion costs. In fact, the majority of publishers and book import and export agents have already delivered their goods catalogues on the Internet. Besides, the duty-free condition of present e-commerce will also bring about a positive effect on book trade globalization. The trade flow will accelerate and the trading volume will increase.

2. The Trend of International Book Trade Based on New Technology

As a new publishing model, digital publishing and e-business will endow the international book trade with some new characteristics.

2.1 The Diversification of Trade Participants

Digital technology exposes the value of publishing content to the utmost degree, which lowers the entrance threshold of the publishing industry. While the traditional publishers are busy adjusting to the new role of content supplier, some content congregators have begun to invade their "descendent territory". For example, Google's book searching plan, Microsoft's searching in real time plan and Amazon's upgrading search are being carried out. These search engines not only build up an international information platform for publications and readers all over the world, but bring convenience to readers who can buy books from different countries. Meanwhile, small and medium publishers, even the authors themselves, have the chance to participate in book exportation directly because of the digitalization of books. Therefore, search engine companies, online bookstores, small and medium publishers, authors, etc. may become important entities in the international book trade, except for the traditional book import and export agents, multinational publishing houses and big publishers.

With the number of trade participants increasing, its impact on traditional international book trade agents must be acknowledged. Based on the prior technological conditions, the degree of specialization of the international book trade is high. For example, special knowledge and skills are necessary to apply for an import and export license, to conduct the affairs of customs, and to negotiate with foreign partners. The complex trade flow and procedure endows traditional agents with competitive advantages. However, with the development of online publishing and digital publishing, and with the maturity of related technologies such as online paying, it is probable that publishers can carry on international book trade on their own. They don't need agents anymore. Nowadays, some special publishing houses in the United States and Europe have been producing and selling books online, and many presses have also set up specific departments to promote online publishing and e-paper integration. Therefore, the function of traditional book import and export agents will be weakened, and their role will diminish. They are facing the fate of being abandoned by presses.

2.2 The Complexity of the International Book Market Structure

Digital technology creates conditions for producing and selling content, products and services in small amounts and individually. More and more types of peculiar book markets and individual operations will appear in networks, the no-region -boundary "virtual global market." Besides the traditional special and mass markets, a new small size market that is related closely with individual, custom publishing will take form gradually, which not only will bring new market chances to the international book trade, but also result in the complexity of the international book market.

On the other hand, the new forms of books such as databases, multimedia, electronic books, publish on demand, print on page, mobile phone novels, etc., will enrich the product structure of the international book trade tremendously, which will change the proportion of tangible and intangible trade overall. Intangible trade will be more important than before. In some peculiar marketplaces, for instance, information services and reference book markets, digital publications will probably become the main business type. Besides, online services will also become an important trade field. Services related to product importing and exporting will increase rapidly. For example, updating the content of digital publications for free and providing long distance learning will become increasingly popular.

Moreover, the international book trade imbalance pattern may worsen. With the generalization of new technology, especially the EDI technique, the technical obstacles to the flow of information gradually become clear. Hence, the information comparative advantage in the international book trade is becoming more and more important. In 2001, the United States and most countries of the European Union declared that companies that haven't adopted EDI to handle procedures as of 2001 would not be elected as trade partners and their deals would be postponed. But, as we know, for most developing countries it will take a long time to construct their information infrastructural facilities. Under such circumstances, the tendency will be more obvious that the developed countries dominate the international book market.

2.3 The Cut of the Trade Process

There are about twenty links, from business negotiation to contract fulfillment, in the traditional international book trade. But under network business and the Electronic Commerce environment, because the information can be transferred digitally, many steps, such as document printing and mailing, goods shipping and receiving, etc., are probably left out. As a result, the trade technological process will be greatly shortened. With the process reduction, it is easier for book import and export enterprises to manage to monitor the whole operation in real time and to improve the efficiency of management. So, to be sure, a new trade process management pattern will come into being.

In addition, the challenge led by the application of new technology to the traditional international book trade regulations should not be ignored. Most activities of the traditional international book trade are governed by domestic law instead of international law, so there inevitably exits many restrictions from different countries. These restrictions work against the development of the transnational digital publication trade, which has faced the global market from the very beginning. Therefore, some new regulations on trade safety, taxing, finance settlement, etc. have to be made and the macro management of foreign book trade in every country has to be perfected in order to create a fitting platform for the international book trade in the digital era.

3. Innovation in the International Book Trade Based on New Technology

While the new technology endows the international book trade with new characteristics, it also brings about some innovations on the operating mechanisms and managing patterns of the international book trade. Three aspects among these are worth close attention: the role of traditional book import and export agents, marketing ideology and model, and human resources development.

3.1 The Role Transformation of the Traditional Book Import and Export Agent

As an important circulating channel, the traditional book import and export agent always plays an essential intermediary role in international book trade logistics, business stream and information stream. But as stated before, it is facing the danger of being abandoned in the process of the international book trade. Therefore, the book import and export enterprise should change its intermediary role into a service enterprise step by step.

First, it can provide effective consultant services to publishers and readers in different countries. Publishers and readers can do their research about demand and supply information on the network conveniently and quickly, but it's still difficult for them to obtain valuable information rapidly. The reasons are obvious. The information on the Internet is numerous and jumbled and it's hard to discern which is true or false. Publishers and readers are not familiar with the international book market. But to some extent, it isn't difficult for book import and export enterprises. Because of the traditional division of work, they know the domestic and foreign book markets very well. They can take advantage of their dominant position in trade information resources to develop consultant services actively and provide valuable trade information to publishers and readers.

Secondly, it can provide publishers with more well-rounded specialization services. Besides traditional services, such as agencies, applying to the customs, goods check-ups, storing and transportation, buying insurance, filling out all kinds of documents, settlements of exchange, etc., book import and export enterprises ought to provide publishers with more detailed information on products, prices and channels, integrated after-sale services, and promotion services on the Internet and exhibitions at home and abroad. For example, Amazon makes a feedback platform for publishers. Through the feedback system, all the publishers know clearly their online selling information.

Thirdly, it could provide a trust-based value. Mutual trust ensures international book selling proceeds without obstacles. However, the establishment of mutual trust comes from long-term relationships. For those publishers and readers who lack experience in the book trading business, it would become a threshold. So, the book export and import enterprises could apply their established business reputations to matching jobs for the niche markets and make selling and buying possible.

3.2 The Transformation of the International Book Trading Concept

Digital publishing and network technology has brought forth a new way of international book trading—online sales. Online sales have greatly promoted the buyers role in the international book market with its characteristic of two-way exchange of information, which makes it possible for interactivity between the buyer and the seller at any time, in any place. Buyers have taken part in the book trading process and the market has turned from a seller-dominant market into a buyer-dominant "soft market."

The book trading concept has also brought forth methods of buying and selling. Offering diverse extension services, such as free services, fee-based services, per-view-based services, and even a customized service for a niche market or a specified reader, would become a trend. Establishing localized websites and customized online shops, working cooperatively with search engines, offering a user-friendly interface and diversified linkages would become the content of the services provided by the international book trading companies.

3.3 The New Aspect of the HR Development of International Book Trading Companies

In order to adapt to the development of digital publishing and e-commerce, to integrate it in the operation of management, international book trading companies must prepare a group of experts in these areas. These staff must have knowledge and experience in the operation of the traditional market and skills of online operations as well, which would become a has-to-be-tackled challenge for all international book trading companies.

REFERENCES

Andrews, Peluzzi. "The Challenge on Publishing Online by the tendency of Net Publishing and Paper Publishing." 31 Aug. 2005. <http://www.chinapublish.com.cn>.

Li, Bing. "Lecture in the 'Beijing International Forum on Publishing Industry 2006." 28 Aug. 2006. <http://www.chinapublish.com.cn>.

"The Retrospect of OA Publishing in 2004". 31 Aug. 2005. <http://openaccess.bokee.com/1435190.html>.

Wang, Xinmin. "The Prospect of Network Marketing from Electronic Commerce." *Publish Economy*: 6. 31 Jan. 2008.

Yu, Yongzhan. "New Technology and the Future of Publishing Industry." 28 Aug. 2005. <http://www.chinapublish.com.cn>.

Zhao, Zizhong. *On Content Industry: the Core of New Medium.* Beijing: Communication University of China Press, 2005.

Comparison and Drawing of Copyright Collective Management in China and Abroad in an Internet Environment

Hu Bo

After the promulgation and enforcement of "Administration Regulation in Copyright Collective Management" on March 1, 2005, the premier, Wen Jia Bao, mentioned intellectual property rights three times in a government working report given at the 10th NPC convention on March 5, 2005. It's obvious that, along with the development of the Internet and a digitized society, our government is paying more attention to ways to strengthen the protection of intellectual property rights. Meanwhile, the propagation of digital information over the Internet has made information resources widely utilized and shared. Numerous cyber citizens can review numerous bits of information from all over the world without stepping outside their door. The Internet and modern life have become vitally interrelated. The information spreading over the Internet plays a more and more important role in promoting human progress and development. To explore a balanced existing copyright system, fast-paced digital technology and information society, during the past few years, pertinent individual enterprises, governments and international organizations have been actively researching input and control technologies in order to build the foundation of digital copyright collective management. For instance, Japan has already built an information center for digital transmission and authorization, while the United Kingdom and France are attempting to combine electronic authorization and data exchange. Countries all over the world are trying to implement the idea of collective management of digital works by establishing a digital system of copyright collective management through the application of the Internet and digital techniques. Despite a lot of so-called "digital copyright management systems," many procedures have yet to be completed by human assistants. Only a few of them offer support twenty four hours online for inquiring about user prices and acquiring digital authorization and/or digital content. But over all, having had a few highly effective trials, especially in the developed countries, some collective management organizations have shown outstanding achievements in digitalization. Their advanced experience provides a valuable reference in this field.

1. Comparison of Copyright Collective Management between China and Foreign Countries in the Internet Environment

1.1 Collective Copyright Management is Already Becoming the International Trend in the Network Environment

The collective management of copyrights came to Europe in late eighteenth century. At present, some developed countries, such as the United States, the United Kingdom, Germany and Japan, have founded organizations of copyright collective management for various fields of works.

Satellite Instruction, passed by the EU Council in 1993, regulates that cable retransmission rights can only be exercised by a collective administration. Member states should ensure that all rights owners and related rights holders can only authorize or reject the cable operator's cable retransmission rights via collective management associations. The copyright management associations are defined as "any organization that makes copyrights or related rights management its unique purpose or major objective." If a copyright holder does not transfer his/her rights to the association of copyright collective management, his/her rights are considered to be transferred to a collective management organization in the same field. By having more collective administrative organizations to manage the same kind of works, the rights holder can freely choose one of them as its mandatory rights administrator. Along with the development of digital technology, the usage of works increases everyday, and the traditional collective administrative organization is faces two problems: categorizing the works and the authorized users so as to collect the copyright licensing fee and distributing it to the authors in a satisfactory way. It's not easy to manage every single copyright in an information society. In the green paper, "Copyrights and Related Rights in the Information Society," the Commission of the European Communities consolidates the self-managed rights and points out that the information society does not assent to abandon the collective administration conducted by the organization of collective management.

1.2 The Austere Reality Faced by Our Country's Copyright Collective Management

In its long past, our country has lacked legal regulation and practice in collective management. For a long period of time, because of planning and half-planning economic systems, copyrights were not acknowledged and protected as private property. When a copyright is approved as private and ought to be protected and rewarded, we have to make our way through practice to the goal of consummating the protection and ascertain a way of gaining rewards. Starting from the 1980s, various copyright agencies and copyright usage transmission organizations were formed by the government. They're similar to, but not exactly the same as organizations of collective management. Not until 1992 was the first genuine organization of collective management set up, named the Chinese Music Copyright Association, whose duties were to manage the members' rights of selling, performances and broadcasts. By the beginning of 2005, the "Regulation and Administration of Copyright Collective Management" was promulgated and put into effect by the State Council. It indicated that our copyright collective management is standardized, even though it started up much later than western countries.

2. Comparison between Domestic and Foreign Collective Copyright Management Organizations

2.1 Worldwide Copyright Management Organizations

There are several international copyright organizations or worldwide collective copyright management organizations formed by international copyright treaties, such as the International Federation of the Phonographic Industry (IFPI), the International Confederation of Societies of Authors and Composers (CISAC) and the International Federation of Reproduction Rights Organizations (IFRRO). According to the collective management based on international copyright treaties, for licensing works among the international members, copyright management organizations in each member state have established an inter-agency coordination system so as to locally protect the rights of foreign collective management organizations who sign copyright protection agreements. This mode has been adopted by national music management organizations in over 170 countries. The works of creators from any of the member states are protected according to the agreement. However, for the best practice, this kind of inter-protection needs to be legislated and transferred.

2.2 Official or Semi-official Collective Copyright Management Organizations

The publishing industry forms the collective copyright management organization, according to civil government supported copyright laws. Most countries adopt this organizational model. Collective management organizations of this kind are given monopoly authority by federal officials or non-official administrations to influence the monitoring of information nationally, avoid duplicate organizations and coordinate with the international collective management organizations. Under the principal of "same rights, sole management organization in a country," which was defined by WIPO in copyrights and neighboring rights, the Chinese collective management organization has been practically classified into music production and non-music production. Music production has been protected by the China Music Copyright Association, and non-music production has been protected by the China Copyright Centre.

2.3 Civilian Collective Copyright Management Organizations

European and American countries have established collective copyright management systems for about 200 years. In these countries, copyright is considered the same kind of property as a flexible asset or tangible asset. Thus, collective copyright management was treated as a commercial activity in law. Collective copyright management organizations have been established according to the Company Law or Competition Law, and restricted by the Anti-Monopoly Law. Continental countries have been more cautious toward collective copyright management and generally have adopted special legislation that can be categorized into two models: one is individual legislation, such as Germany's "Collective Copyright Management Law"; the other is implied legislation, which is adopted as one or more chapters in a copyright law. On Dec 22, 2004, China issued the "Collective Copyright Management Regulation," which stipulates that Chinese citizens, corporations and other organizations that are entitled to the right of copyrights by law can set up a collective copyright management organization.

3. Chinese and Foreign Solutions for Collective Management of Copyrights in the Network Environment

3.1 Foreign Solutions for Collective Management in the Information Network Environment

In the green paper, "Copyrights and Related Rights in the Information Society," the Commission of the European Communities says, "The information society does not assent to abandon the collective administration conducted by organizations of collective management. On the contrary, based on the benefits of the rights holders and users, it's necessary to establish a new organization for creating a multimedia-based system to empower a traditional organization to ensure rights licensing is easy, adequate, highly efficient and cost-effective. As a result, the Commission of the European Communities has worked out the multimedia-based VERDI project, including the member states of Germany, Italy, France and Finland. It carries out substantial analysis on European copyright conditions of a wide range of works, from sound effects, image, video and audio works, to literary works, computer software, databases and video games, in order to set up a European-wide copyright management database and an internet based licensing system.

In 1996, France set up a collective management organization, SESAM, to manage all of France's authors' associations. After SESAM collects the works intended to be used, using conditions such as volume of copies, sale price and location, from the rights user, its copyright license acquiring program issues an online and offline right of performance and license of copying, confirms the intended use of the works and its copyright tax.

In 1998, the "Author and Related Collective Management Association in Multimedia Clearing Center (CMV)" was set up in Munich, Germany. Instead of issuing copyright licenses, it provides copyright and related information about music, literature, art and visual arts online 24 hours, every day and responds to the user in two weeks after transferring the user's request to a related organization of collective management and collecting the management fee.

3.2 Progress in Legislation of Copyright Collective Management Related to the Information Network in China

It's an irresistible trend to protect the technology by copyright law as digitization and the Internet become more popular. Our country has also chosen the copyright law as the protection model: In 2001, the "Copyright Law" amendment and "Regulations for the Protection of Computer Software" officially established the protection for managing electronic information of technology and rights.

Our country has made remarkable progress in constructing the system of copyright collective management. The eigth amendment of the Copyright Law is regulation about copyright collective management. It defines the characteristics, legal status, fundamental authority and supervision of the collective management system. Furthermore, the "Copyright Collective Management Regulation on Administration," promulgated on December 28, 2004 by the State Council, clearly defines copyright collective management, specifying its setup procedure, organization structure, content of the activities, supervision and legal liability. What is worth paying more attention to is that the twenty fourth item in this regulation specifies the legal liability of the organization of copyright collective management, saying they should "build a rights information inquiry system to serve rights holders and rights users" and that "replies to rights holders and rights users about inquiries into rights information will be managed by the organization of copyright collective management." It also specifies the legal obligation for not building the rights inquiry system. The thirty second item specifies that the organization of copyright collective management ought to 1) record the situation of the usage of works licensing, licensing fee collection and distribution, the managerial fee and usage. Such information shall be accessible for the rights holders and users; 2) provide the rights holders easy access to inquire about or copy the financial report, work report and other business materials. The forty seventh item specifies that "the collective management organization of copyrights being responsible for distributing the copyright fee, ought to build a rights usage inquire system for the interests of rights holders and rights owners." This regulation has established the very necessary foundation of law for the digitization of our country's copyright collective management.

4. Comparison of the Copyright Collective Managing Pattern in the the Network Environment

4.1 Compelling Pattern

In the network environment, it's very easy for the user to gain works over the Internet, which makes authors a vulnerable group. It's reasonable to force the published works managed by the national united copyright collective management into a compelling pattern, though it violates the private right autonomy rule. The collective copyright management defined by two treaties of WIPO is voluntary instead of compelling. It not only shows due respect to private rights, but also upholds the principle of automatic copyright protection. In general, compelling the collective copyright management system declares in the form of law that some rights must be exercised by the collective copyright administrative organization, the rights holder has to accept this, or, otherwise, lose those rights. The compelling pattern entices the collective copyright organization to represent all rights holders and empowers the organization's role. In 1995, France introduced a compelling collective management based on exclusive rights and voluntary licensing and stipulated that rights holders have to claim their rights through the collective copyright management organization. The EU Council stipulated in the Satellite Instruction, issued in 1993, that cable broadcasting rights can only be exercised by collective copyright administration. Northern Europe and Russia implemented an extensible membership-based collective copyright management system. That being said, the collective copyright management organization is entitled to exercise the rights holder's rights if the rights holder doesn't clearly declare his/her opposition.. At present, the Chinese copyright protection centre collects and distributes the contribution fee in a similar way.

An interactive representative agreement is set up between the collective copyright management organizations in European countries. According to this agreement, a collective copyright management organization in any European country is entitled to manage the rights of rights-holders and rights-users within the country. When any conflict happens, the organization represents the foreign rights holder or rights user to defend his/her rights.

4.2 Voluntary Pattern

Out of respect for private interests of copyrights, in the spirit of copyright protection and autonomy, the copyright holder can decide the way to protect his/her copyright at will when the collective copyright management organization in our country is optional. The eighth item in the Copyright Law says, "The copyright owner and related copyright holder can authorize the collective copyright management organization to exercise the copyright and related rights." When the rights holder doesn't authorize the collective copyright management organization to manage his/her works in the collective way, by default the rights holder has to manage the rights on his/her own.

4.3 Compromising Pattern

In the network environment, the copyright protected by the Copyright Law is vulnerable. It's trivial, inefficient and nearly impossible to have every rights owner sign an authorization agreement with the collective copyright management organization. Therefore, the Copyright Law specifies clearly that by default, the rights owner is assumed to agree on delegating the collective copyright management organization to protect his/her works when he/she doesn't clearly indicate an objection to having the collective copyright management organization manage his/her rights. It saves lots of trivial paperwork. On Nov 22nd, 2000, the Supreme Court released the "Explanation on Applicable Law for Cases Related to Computer Network Copyrights," and explained that "for those works published on paper or spreading on the Internet, the website who copies and compiles these works is not violating the copyright if it pays the required licensing fee and lists the reference, unless the rights holder or its deleted network provider claims no copies and compilation." It implies that the rights holder should designate a collective copyright management organization to manage his/her rights protected by the Copyright Law.

In the meantime, the compelling collective copyright management policy is not adequate in our country, while the traditional version is still in progress, not to mention the version for network information resources. As is outlined in the explanation of the law, it is legal to propagate works whose rights are not declared.

5. Improve our Country's Copyright Collective Management System in the Network Environment

5.1 Consummate Copyright Collective Management Related Legislations

From the above comparison, it can be concluded that our copyright system is responding quickly to the challenge from the innovation of digital technology. Compared with the developed countries, our collective copyright management system is by no means less proficient than theirs in many aspects. However, in proportion with the domestic demands of digital copyright collective management, the system is inadequate and needs to be consummated in legislation.

First, the regulations for technical protection measures need to be refined. One ought to admit that technical protection measures were added to the revised Copyright Law, to some extent, targeting the execution of regulations from WCT and WPPT, instead of the needs of digital collective copyright management. Since it involves many-sided benefits for the rights holder, rights user, procedures and production industry, from the practical need as a developing country, our country adopted a prudent choice in legislation to prohibit the behavior of eluding copyright enforcement. It is comparatively sagacious. But, from the perspective of the trend of digital copyright protection, especially the demands on digital collective copyright management, there are existing disadvantages in the current regulations because it is quite difficult to investigate the responsibility of a single rights evader since the behavior is dispersed and concealed. Moreover, the equipment assisting the evasion of technical protection measures puts the rights of the rights holder in a very uncertain state, and this is the biggest threat to digital collective management. Therefore, under certain circumstances, it is necessary to prohibit the production and supply of such equipment.

Secondly, regulations about rights administration information need to be refined. Although the current Copyright Law describes "deleting or changing the rights administration information without permission from the rights owner or related rights holders" as infringing upon a copyright; it doesn't precisely define the content of "rights administration information." It's too simple and basic to make smooth the execution of the law. It's suggested to clearly define "rights administration information" in related legislation, referencing relevant international treaties and the conventions of every country. Furthermore, due to the copyright protection automatic acquisition principle, rights administration information is the premise of copyright protection. But inadequate and disordered information of rights administration results in great difficulties in copyright protection and management under the network environment. So, it's suggested that we stipulate in related legislation: 1) All copyright-protected works managed under collective copyright management should use the rights administration information in general. 2) They should formalize the rights administration information in a unified, standard form. 3) They should include the following information in the right administration information: conditions to use the work, the way to use it and the copyright declaration, etc.

Last, enforce the collective copyright management organization must inform making rights information accessible to the public as its duty. Indeed, due to the importance of the rights information in collective copyright management, the Collective Copyright Management Regulation stipulates the duty of the collective copyright management organization to provide the rights information to the public. However, it doesn't declare the way of providing the information and information updates. In order to adapt to the demands of digital collective copyright management and avoid wasting the public or the users time searching for related information, it's suggested that the following item be added to the "Collective Copyright Management Regulation": The collective copyright management organization should provide online or other remote electronic access to the information for the public. The information for the public should be updated on time when it's changed.

5.2 Construct a Platform for Our Country's Digital Copyright Collective Management System

To respond to the new problems in copyright creation, protection and utilization in the digital age, on March 1· 2005, the Collective Copyright Management Regulation was promulgated and its twenty fourth article stipulated that "the collective copyright management organization ought to set up a rights information inquiring system for the rights holders and rights users. The rights information inquiring system should include the name of the works, the name of the rights holder and authorized management duration of the copyright category and works managed by the organization." But, so far only the China Copyright Protection Center (http://www.ccopyright.com.cn) provides some information about those authors without a contact, forwarded by the China Copyright Licensing Fee Collecting and Distributing Center. No influential digital copyright trading system has been built and it does not match the expanding copyright industry in our country. So, what content should be included in a perfect digital collective copyright management platform?

First of all, it's a copyright information inquiry platform. The platform provides a copyright information inquires service to allow members to inquire about the copyright information via the Internet. The rights information in general includes the following: author name (person or company), name of the work, kind of work, rights duration, outline of the work, authorization conditions, licensing fee, publisher and contact. Any rights user can easily search via the Internet for rights information about the works on demand. Through this platform, the works users validate whether the desired work is managed by the collective copyright management organization, and if so, he/she can further find out the licensing fee for using it, and then confirm if he/she is authorized to use it by the organization.

Then, it's an online copyright trading platform. This platform includes digital signature, licensing fees, authorization means, digital works downloads, electronic payment, third-party authentication and so on. Via the Internet, 1) the copyright user can obtain a legal license for the desired work; 2) the rights holder can collect the licensing fee for his/her work on time; 3) the collective copyright management organization can manage the works of its membership from all over the world. It's valuable to reference a relatively mature online business model to build a twenty four hours online copyright trading platform. The Japan online authorization system (http://www.elicense.co.jp) and U.S. BMI digital authorization center (http://www.bmi.com) are typical platforms of such kind.

In order to keep the network development sound and keep the information accessible, it's necessary to enforce communication and cooperation between the collective copyright management organizations and the network service provider. It's also beneficial to the network service provider. In order to attract more visits to the websites and gain more ads, the service provider always must try all means to enrich their websites with abundant information or multimedia. Too many works are used in the websites to require that the service providers gain licenses from and pay the copyright holders one by one. It's cost-ineffective and impractical. It could dampen the enthusiasm of the network service provider and eventually reduce network efficiency and damage the benefits to the network user. On the principle that cooperation is better than counterwork and prevention is better than penalty, the network service provider could work together with the collective copyright management organization. The network service provider could legally use thousands of the works managed by the collective management organization without signing an agreement with each individual rights holder, as long as it signs an agreement with the collective management organization. On the other hand, the collective copyright management organization could prevent copyright infringement by providing copyright protection information periodically to the network service provider so that the provider could search and inquire if any broadcasting information infringes on any copyrights.

REFERENCES

Cao, Shihua. " Digital Intellectual Property Rights Collective Management in Digital Times." *Electronic Information Property Rights* (2006): 2.

Cao, Shihua. "Interaction Between Technology Innovation and Collective Copyright Management System in Digital Age." *Law Review* (2006): 1.

Huang, Xianrong. "Study On Network Information Resources Copyright Collective Management System." *Knowledge Of Library and Information* (2005): 2.

Li, Hongwu. "Monopolization and Limited Monopolization: Collective Copyright Management Expanding in Information Network Times." *Knowledgy Of Library and Information* (2005): 4.

Li, Yan and Xia Kali. "Network Time Calling For Copyright Collective Management System." *Publishing and Printing* (2005): 1.

Zhang, Guizhen. "Basic Analysis In Copyright Collective Management of Network Works." *University Liabrary And Information Tribune* (2002): 9.

Zhang, Lin. "Copyright Collective Management System Self-examination and Restructure in Digital Time." *Gui Hai Collections* (2005):6.

An Exploration of Product Development Tactics of College Textbooks in China

Liu Yindi

In recent years, the higher education enterprise in China has obtained a historical advance; this advance has inevitably led to the development of the college textbook publishing industry. Foreseeing the college textbook market's broad prospects, many publishing houses began to work on college textbook publishing. But in light of present circumstances, many publishing houses have very big zones or error in their college textbook product development, such as repeated publications, "textbook localization," and so on. The low level of the product development pattern has seriously fettered the development of the college textbook publishing industry. So I will discuss specifically the product development strategy of the college textbook including topic selecting, commissioning, book examining and processing, and book revising.

1. The strategy of selecting a topic for a college textbook

College textbook publishers should grasp the following two main points of the topic selection process.

First, the publishing house must carry on a full investigation and study on the book market. At present, the universities adjust their curriculum frequently and cold subjects can become hot subjects in a short time, therefore "to publish a book, investigate and study the market first" makes more and more significant sense in the college textbook publishing domain. Moreover, in the college textbook publishing domain, college presses have enormous superiority in conducting investigations and studies of the book market. College presses should utilize their superiority to understand positively the present situation of school teaching and the direction of educational reform, and participate actively in research, thus, allowing them to promptly understand the requests for textbooks and the demands in the teaching process, and then collect first-hand information to help the presses work out a plan for a selected topic.

Second, the publishing houses must publish textbooks that reflect their own identity. Therefore, for college textbook presses whose market is the college teachers and students, confirming their identity should be very urgent. At present, in the college textbook publishing domain, the phenomenon of duplication is extremely serious and, at the same time, massive, similar textbooks are published. Certain textbooks involved in certain popular disciplines collide, and textbooks for some specialties even have several dozens of editions promoted in two or three years. The repetition and identification of selected topics causes blind competition among the college textbook presses; therefore, the college textbook publishing houses must take as their key point the tactic of establishing a clear identity. Moreover, as soon as they form their own identity, they have to maintain it diligently and strengthen it unceasingly, and extend the scope of selected topics on the basis of that identity's being maintained. Presses should not give up too easily the original characteristic of developing new kinds of textbooks which they may not have the ability to deal with, even though some disciplines become feverishly popular.

2. The strategy of commissioning

After a publishing house formulates a plan for the selected topic, it must organize authors to complete the manuscript according to a plan. The college textbook publishing house must pay attention to the following aspects in the commissioning process.

First, college textbook presses must depend thoroughly on college publication resources thoroughly. For example, He Shengsui, president of Fudan College, believes that with the aid of Fudan College's celebrities and publication resources, Fudan College Press has advantageous superiority in the college textbook and scholarly publishing area. Thus, we can see that there is vital significance for college textbook publishers to utilize college publication resources fully. Certainly, when we use these outstanding resources in the publishing process, we also have to know that we absolutely cannot abuse them. For it is very common that many college teachers take college textbook publication as a platform and tool that can help them pull advance their academic status and assess their scholarly work. They take part in college textbook writing in abundance no matter what their own academic level is or what significance their own specialty and discipline has. This creates many problems in college textbook publishing; for example, more and more college textbooks are recommended by their professors to their students that have been written and contributed to by themselves. This might inevitably result in the decrease of quality of college textbooks and the increase of returns.

Next, the editors must pay great attention to communication with the authors. Every outstanding publication organization must contain a high level and stable author pool to guarantee the high quality of publications; no outstanding editor would neglect the author pool in order to guarantee an outstanding and remarkable publication style.

As editors in the college textbook publishing area, they have to communicate with the related authors after the authors are selected. First, the editors need to make the authors understand who are intended readers of the textbook. In the college textbook compilation process, a very prominent question is whether the textbook has a very clear reader in view. Too theoretical training textbooks or too superficial teaching materials for graduate students would hamper their sales. Therefore, the first step in commissioning a book is to deliver related information to the authors. Second, the editors must communicate regarding aspects of the college's own strong suits and characteristics of the discipline, and its prospects for development. There are so many different disciplines in so many universities, a publishing house couldn't publish all the necessary textbooks; therefore, the editors should analyze with the authors the characteristics and main features of similar book markets. Finally, the editors also have to communicate with the authors in sentiment, because the majority of authors in the college textbook publishing area are professors and scholars who have a quite high academic level and attach importance to the interaction of emotions.

3. The strategy of examination and processing

The examination is the core link in textbook publishing work, because a first-class selected topic does not necessarily mean first-class publication. The authors of college textbooks are renowned scholars who generally enjoy great prestige; therefore, the editors are apt to be awed, when they don't want or dare to modify the drafts, then it is easy to create "real problems" in college textbooks. The editors' laziness and eagerness for instant success and immediate profits make up the other side of the coin. They just take it for granted that these textbooks that are compiled by famous experts and scholars will be of very high quality so they don't read the manuscript carefully. Moreover, a large number of editors in college presses compile dozens of kinds of textbooks a year at present, and this makes it hard to guarantee quality.

In the college textbook editing process, there are several points the editors need to know:

First, the editors must strictly control quality. This is a basic requirement in book publishing and it is even more significant when we speak of college textbooka. On the one hand, college textbooks, which are taken as fundamental to transmitting the society's culture and education, shoulder the responsibility and the mission to "proselytize, instruct and dispel doubts." If the mistakes in college textbooks are not corrected in time, they might be very bad influences an entire academic circles over a very long period. On the other hand, they target consumers of college textbooks are college teachers and students who have a very high scientific and cultural level; therefore, they are more sensitive to the textbook's quality. If they find a certain textbook's quality is not high, not only could this textbook's sale be affected, but also the entire publishing house's prestige and image would be harmed. There are many academic related scandals that have occurred recently; many people denounced the professors' degeneration in these incidents, but at the same time they also reflect the shortcomings of the editing function in college textbook publishing.

Second, college textbook publishers must acquire brand consciousness and value the binding and layout of college textbooks. A commodity needs packaging. No matter how good the commodity is, unsuitable packaging will make it unlikely to be sold well. College textbooks are still a kind of commodity; they also need good binding and design to establish and maintain the identity of the textbook and enhance the college textbook's sale. In fact, speaking of the binding and design of college textbooks, a series binding and design style always plays a vital role in promoting the brand influence of the textbook and expands the sales volume. Textbooks that sell very well in the college textbook publishing domain are generally serialized at present. For example, Beijing College Press's serial textbook named *Face the 21st Century Curriculum Textbook* adopted the same or similar title page and papers, Shanghai Communication College Press's serial textbook named *21st Century Higher Vocational Education General Textbook* adopted the similar mounting and design, and South China College of Technology Press's *The 21st Century Computer Science and Technology Serial Textbook* also adopted the same tactic. These textbooks have continuous and serialized characteristics in the binding and design so they make a profound impression on the consumers, and, of course, obtained a large sales volume.

4. The strategy of revision

One of the most prominent problems is that textbooks are universally aging. So-called "textbook aging" refers to the phenomenon that textbooks are relatively lagging, namely textbooks have not been able to reflect promptly the newest academic developments, achievements, knowledge and concerns. Therefore, it is very important for publishers to revise college textbooks on the basis of the original edition. In the revision process, we must pay attention to the following several points:

First, the publishers must renew the editions promptly according to the discipline's development. But we must know that the textbook's aging does not always relate to time. Some textbooks published for only one or two months might still stand in the row of the aged books; while some textbooks, though published twenty years ago, are still in use and worshiped as classics in the discipline, like some textbooks in science. The foundational contents are relatively stable in these disciplines, the formula and the basic theory are irrevocable, and so they don't need frequent revisions. The current problem of college textbook aging is manifested when the methods, data or correlated cases are obsolete. Moreover, a book's life cycle is very short in some disciplines that reflect the development of science and technology; therefore, the publishers must renew the edition promptly.

In recent years, a lot of domestic college textbook publishing houses paid more attention to renewing textbooks; they regard revision as a significant link in college textbook construction. But at present, many publishing houses in China are suspected of following blindly and deceiving readers in college textbook revisions. Some so-called new textbook editions, which were published recently, mostly plagiarized the old textbook directly or indirectly. The publishers published and sold the textbooks that are crowned with a new title on the slightly modified first-edition textbook's content. This does not only deceive readers but also destroys the press's prestige.

Next, college textbook publishers could carry on the strategy of developing "integrated textbooks," which are very common in western countries. Most higher education curriculums are included in higher education have been computerized in the United States and the majority of contents in textbooks might achieve human-machine interaction and self-study. Textbook integration does not only need a complete set of books, in the time of networks, it also demands that publishers to do two jobs. One is to provide new services, including the emerging electronic publications, the network forum, the network resources storehouse, the network classroom, the network community and so on. For example, Fudan College Press developed *the 21 Century College English Audiovisual and Speaking Course of Study* in 2005 and the complete set of the *21st Century College English* online study platform, a new kind of service. The other is that publishers have to provide new activities, including conducting training, developing teaching discussion, training teachers, promoting textbooks, etc. For example Foreign Language Teaching and Research Press occupied the college English textbook market very quickly through their excellent services in the development process.

Certainly, the development of "textbook integration" also demands that the press have abundant strength resources to underwrite its projects. When interviewed by the *China Press and Publishing Journal*, Zhang Zengshun, editor-in-chief of the Higher Education Press, told the journalist that the Higher Education Press invested 15,000,000 RMB to the college English educational reform project. For many small publishing houses, this huge investment might cause them to shrink back at first sight. Moreover, the present integrated textbooks only involve English and computer teaching; therefore, there is an imminent and bright prospect for the development of integrated textbooks in the college textbook publication domain in China.

Finally, the publishers must lower the price of re-published textbooks. A college edition textbook's renewal frequency is speeding up in China at present, which is important progress. But the problem is that publishing houses utilize the chance of textbook revision to raise the textbooks' price. The debate on rising textbook prices draws more and more attention. The U.S. Public Interest Research Groups published a second report on how the price of textbooks had pushed the struggle over American textbooks' prices to a new climax. The PIRG urges publishing houses to produce inexpensive textbooks, as many as possible, so as to avoid sacrificing educational value.

In fact, the problem of textbooks' high prices doesn't only exist in the United States; it is also very common in China. Most college textbooks are reprinted ones in China, as we know; the cost of reprinting is lower than original editing, so the price should be at least no higher than the original. But at present the price of a newer edition is much higher than the previous one in the college textbook publishing domain. It is very unreasonable to raise the price of college textbooks, and lowering the price of reprinted college textbooks should be the strategy that the enterprise must consider in the long run. Some large-scale publication groups have already realized the negative effects brought by the high price of college textbooks in the United States. Within several years, Pearson has established a complicate textbook system from a simple one. They developed several different levels of the textbooks when they revise them, and the cheapest ones, namely the so-called electronic books, are at half the price of the textbooks sold on the market. Readers might purchase some chapters alone on-line, and then share a book with their friends by\ purchasing the password. The method Pearson employed is a kind of strategy — lowering the price of a textbook through integration. It has been proved that publishers in China should study the strategy which Pearson adopted because it is not only an effective method which could reduce the price of the college textbook, but it also would give an impetus to the development of the college textbook publishing industry in China in the long run.

From the analysis above, we know that the university textbook publishing domain is a domain has dynamic prospects, but the problems existing in product development hamper the promotion of university textbook publishing. I hope my suggestions involving the university textbook product development flow, including selecting a topic, commissioning books, examining and processing books, and revising books can enlighten publishers and give impetus to the development of the university textbook publishing industry.

REFERENCES

College English Educational Reform Project. <http://dean.xjtu.edu.cn/Content/2004/4296132822.html> 9 Apr. 2006.

Cong, Xiaohong. 'On the Topics Selection and Compilation of College Textbook." *College Publishing.* 2003: 30-33.

Li, Li. "Pearson Education: Assistant in Study." *China Book Business Report.* 2004: 13.

Li, Ye. "The Principles of Marketing." Guangzhou: Guangdong Higher Education Press, 2003.

Sun, Chenglin. "College Press and Higher Education Textbook Publication." *Theory and Practice of Higher Education in Building Material.* 2000: 119-120.

Tang, Shenping. "Shallow Discussion On the Development of Textbook Integration in Net Age." *China Publishing Journal.* 2003: 22-23.

Wang, Dong. "The Problems in the Revision of Higher Education Textbook." *China Book Business Report.* 2005: 8.

Wu, Ping. *The Theory of Edition.* Wuhan: Wuhan College Press, 2005.

You, Jianzhong. Foreign publishing news. *A Vast View on Publishing.* 2004: 32.

Zhao, Yingying. "Higher Education Textbook Is Facing Struggles." *Journal of the CPPCC.* 2004: (4).

The Negative Effects of Editorial Planning on Academic Researches

Zhao Jianguo & Chang Chunqiao

In the field of academic research, "It can be said that characteristics that distinguish modern editing from traditional editing lie in high planning consciousness and explicit planning behavior." "During editing, the autonomy of editors manifests itself in planning. In the past, editors were confined to the office and lacked autonomy, so they could only passively receive completed works, and spent most of the time reading and polishing those manuscripts. Now, editors concentrate on the planning of selecting topics. They get closer to authors, readers and the market. They collect information, select topics and invite authors to write manuscripts. All of these activities show the autonomy of editors." Planning weighs heavily both in modern editing and editorial theory. "No matter, judging from the practice of editing, the quality of editing or from the effectiveness of editing, planning always plays an important role." Planning is so important that it affects the concept of editing. Yang Huanzhang has said, "Editing means the act of creating a new work after planning, checking and revising manuscripts." Planning already becomes the beginning and essential factor of editing. Because of these significant changes, it is said, "a new epoch of editors is approaching in the field of Chinese publishing."

In China, editorial planning as the intensification of the independence of editors did not win much recognition in theory nor in practice until China's reform and opening-up, especially after the transition to a market economy.

In the early 1990's (before 1992), people created a brand new concept—the "planning of selected topics." The one who is responsible for an edition is to be called "planning editor"; at the same time, some publishing houses also set up planning editors' offices.

Planning appeared earlier in magazines and newspapers.

What is "editorial planning"? And what do planning editors do?

They are called "commissioning editors" in English publishing houses. Commission means "entrusting some person to do something." According to the explanation in the *Printing and Publication Dictionary* (2nd Edition) by P. H. Collin, 1997, commissioning editors are "the editors who are responsible for proposing a conception of books and inviting the authors to work it out."

In the U.S., a primary mission of commissioning editors is looking for appropriate authors and asking them to write books with the ideas of the editors and the sales staff; this is called the editorial planning of books. Editorial planning of academic periodicals includes establishing certain columns and inviting scholars to write manuscripts on hot academic topics. Sometimes editors ask someone to write controversial articles acting as targets; then editors write editors' notes and invite other authors to discuss it, about which it is quipped that the editor is the father and the author is the mother.

As we all know, academic books and academic periodicals are the main stage for showing academic research. Editorial planning has entrenched itself into an impregnable position. What effects does this have on academic research? We should affirm that the successful editorial planning of academic books brings positive effects. For example, the series of "World Classics Translated Into Chinese" issued by the Commercial Press had published 4,000 titles by 2004. They are still being published now. All kinds of published academic works could stand the test of time and gain a shower of praise. Some of them have been printed many times. The *Social Contract*, by Jean Jacques Rousseau had been printed seventeen times by April 2005, becoming a famous brand of the Commercial Press, and a model for publishing academic works in China. The positive effects of planning of books were summarized like this: "(1) It has significant effects on publishing of series of books. (2) Activities for reading or popularizing knowledge were planned by editors. (3) Best sellers on social problems were planned by editors too." Successfully planning academic periodicals had positive effects on academic fields and the society, such as, the discussion of the human spirit or academic specifications. However, those who are not academic researchers can hardly understand the negative effects of editorial planning on academic researches, and that is why I write this article.

Firstly, the editorial planning of books is mainly considered regarding the market, not academic books themselves. Successful planning always put academic value in the first place, just like the series of "World Classics Translated Into Chinese" issued by the Commercial Press, which is rare. Seeing the economic benefits the Commercial Press obtained, some other publishing houses copied their ideas. But they were not good gatekeepers, so there were poor academic effects and economic benefits. "As a working method, editorial planning means editors design working goals with their own initiatives according to the demands of market and the needs of readers. Editorial planning is a kind of editing of ideas. It means editors work it out and learn from the authors' ideas, which is a perfect combination of editors' ideas and authors' ideas." "To remain invincible in fierce competition, elaborate planning based on careful investigation and analyses of the market is necessary, which is both a whole design of editing and organization of editing." "With the features of planning, foresight, originality and initiative, editing becomes a kind of creative activity, which can keep a hold on the market and make every effort to publish fine books." As can be seen from the views set out above, editorial planning is associated with meeting market requirements. Academic works have no competitiveness so academic works would not be chosen by editors. Editors invite authors to write books with selected topics. On the other hand, academic works written by scholars are out of the market. Scholars have to pigeonhole the books or publish them at their own expense. Mostly, famous works can be planned and published successfully, but creative works can seldom be successfully planned for the simple reason that creative works can barely be mass-produced by planning.

Natural and social sciences cannot ignore the market or be totally controlled by it. Editorial planning of books with the market as the orientation is inimical to publishing creative works. As some scholars said, in recent years creative works are small in scale and original books are hardly to be seen. One of the reasons is that publishing houses place too much emphasis on the editors' planning. "Original academic works and literary and artistic works could not be created by the editors' planning." Here is a formal discourse on editorial planning of academic creative works.

Secondly, the editorial planning of academic periodicals considers the hot issues and local flavor, not academic research itself.

It is necessary that periodicals pay attention to academic hot issues, such as the column "Strategy of Sustainable Research" in the Journal of Beijing University, because they could be the sales hook or be reproduced frequently. Also, it is effective to edit columns with local flavor, such as "Culture Research of Shang Dynasty" in the Journal of An Yang, or "Culture Research of Wu Xi" in the Journal of Su Zhou. Academic researchers know that valuable and creative academic topics are not hot issues. Academic topics are limited by editing with local flavor. It is a happy coincidence when valuable academic topics happen to be the ones chosen by editors, but it seldom happens. Editorial planning of some academic periodicals highlighted certain academic topics, but accidentally obstructs some other significant academic topics. Editorial planning has caused an imbalance of academic works. Academic periodicals should act as stages both for exchanging ideas and presenting various academic topics.

Thirdly, those works written with the editors' ideas are not the most satisfactory works of the authors. Each author has his special accumulation of knowledge and writing style, which is hard accord with selected topics. So authors have to copy and apply editors' ideas without any change; as a Chinese saying goes, "cutting the feet to fit the shoes."

Fourthly, editors have a voice in choosing topics, but scholars are in a position of authority in that choice, though topics chosen by editors are not worse than topics chosen by scholars. Generally scholars always attend to the needs of the development of study, and editors satisfy the needs of society or the overall layout of periodicals. If editors negotiate with authors well, they will choose satisfactory topics for both of them. In fact, because of the authority of editors, scholars often bend to editors' ideas. Editorial planning is called "initializing control," which means editors control everything after selecting the topics. Editorial planning decides what to write about. Works written by scholars became processing assignments of editors.

The publication of books has its own rules; so do academic periodicals and scholarly research. However, they have a common purpose to promote the progress of academic researches. The core of progress and prosperity in academic research is academic innovation. Academic innovation exists in the research of scholars, not the research of editors, which may depress editors. But it is true. Academic research is controlled by editorial planning. Nevertheless, we cannot rely solely on a planned economy to speed up economic growth. We must primarily rely on a market economy. So it is with academic research, which is full of contingency and uncertainty. Academic research needs more freedom and more flexible conditions than economic activities do. Scholars should not follow the planning of editors; on the contrary, the editors' planning should serve the scholars' academic innovation. Editors should keep abreast of the latest research developments. In particular, those achievements characterized by primitive innovation should be the first choice of editors. Valuable topics do not exits in the office of editors, but they can be found during communication between editors and authors. To a certain degree, the situation where editorial planning directs academic research has to be changed.

How to properly handle relations between editorial planning and unsolicited manuscripts is the same question as editorial planning and observed rules of academic researches. It is generally believed that many unsolicited manuscripts have been rejected, and only a small portion of them can be published. Two authors, periodical editors, mentioned this in an article: "Editorial planning would be the mainstream of publishing, and there would be fewer unsolicited manuscripts." Basic research and creative research is hard to predict and to be accepted by people who are limited to existing ideas. Creative works contain two aspects, which are invention and great breakthrough in thoughts. With great enthusiasm and belief, scholars make achievements themselves or were supported by leaders of their vision. Their academic works were not planned by editors, such as with Einstein's theory of relativity. Those achievements of free research made monumental contributions to science.

Therefore, please leave space for unsolicited manuscripts. Please pay attention to unsolicited manuscripts while considering editorial planning.

Some of the unsolicited manuscripts are really competitive though they are quite different from planned ones. What a pity to reject all the unsolicited manuscripts! The freedom of the press is impaired if only planned works can be published. There is no freedom of academic research without freedom of the press. Leaving space for unsolicited manuscripts should become a working convention of publishing houses and academic periodicals, which is favorable to academic innovation.

REFERENCES

Chen, Cuiling. "Popularity of Editorial Planning." *Editors Bimonthly* (1997): 4.

He, Juling. "The Subject of Editing." *Journal of Shan Xi Normal University* (2003): 1.

Lin, Suifang. "Editorial Planning and the Effects." *Journal of He Nan University* (2003): 6.

Liu, Jianmin, and Yongchun Li. "Editorial Planning of Academic Periodicals." *Theoretical Investigation* (2002): 4.

Wang, Huasheng. "Planning: A New Idea of Editing." *Journal of the People's University of China* (1998):4.

Wang, Jianhui. "The Philosophical Connotation of Editorial Planning." *Editors Bimonthly* (1998): 1.

Zhou, Xiaoyan. "Planning of Editing." *Journal of the People's University of China* (1998): 6.

A Comparative Study of Magazine Advertising of China and Western Countries

Wu Yun

Magazines are important advertising media and advertisement is the economic mainstay in magazine management. Most advertisers believe that the magazine is an economic advertising medium that has a longer period of validity and less cost in comparison with TV and newspapers. So concerning the development of the magazine industry, it's significant for magazine publishers to get stable and high income from advertising.

Content is the core of magazines, and distribution and advertisement are the two wings of magazine management. These three parts form the lifeblood of the magazine. Magazine publishers in western countries have some wise ideas and strategies that might be useful for Chinese magazine publishers. In order to develop the Chinese magazine industry, Chinese magazine publishers should acquire the idea of "content is king," set up brands depending on quality the of magazines, attach more importance to magazine distribution and advertising, and build up their own competitive power.

1. Analysis of Magazine Advertising Management of Western Countries

According to data from the International Federation of the Magazine Press, in 2005, the advertising income of the magazine industry in the USA, Germany, Japan, France and the UK were, separately, 17.23 billion US Dollars, 4.25 billion US Dollars, 3.24 billion US Dollars, 3.16 billion US Dollars and 2.39 billion US Dollars. Magazine industries in developed countries can supply 10 percent of the annual total advertising income, and in some countries the percentage can even reach thirty. Magazine publishers in western countries always highly emphasize the importance of advertisement, and many magazines in western countries provide 1/3 or 1/2 of total pages for advertisement.

Magazine publishers in the developed countries determine their characteristics and orient themselves toward the most attractive points for readers and advertisement customers, according to the relation of magazine sales and advertising income. For example, the annual advertising revenue of some medical magazines in the USA has exceeded 10 million US dollars. These medical magazines have their own readers, such as medical professionals, and fully exploit advertisement resources depending on their readers. We can draw the following conclusion: advertisement also plays an important role in business and professional/trade magazines' management and Chinese publishers should learn actively from western publishers in this field.

A means usually used by many magazine publishers in western countries is to give subscribers high discounts or provide magazines to readers for free, while their main source of income exists in advertisement. For instance, many magazines in the USA provide a discount as high as about 20% of the magazine price in order to obtain subscribers. They don't get too much from distribution, but they earn more from advertisement. In the top twenty magazines in the USA, there are only two magazines, TV Guide and Reader's Digest, of which distribution income surpasses advertising income. Magazine publishers in western countries also innovate ceaselessly forms of advertisement. In order to develop their advertising business, many Japanese magazine publishers cooperate with managers of Internet and mobile phone companies.

Almost all the consumer magazines in western countries receive no subsidies or funds from the government, and must make their livings by themselves. Magazine publishers earn profits from distribution and advertisement. They usually maintain stable prices; if the cost in one field rises, they will try to depress the cost in other fields. In the gross incomes of magazines in western countries, advertising revenue of consumer magazines generally occupies 30% to 70%. So consumer magazines in developed countries provide many advertising layouts, classify various advertising types and arrange different levels of pricing. On the other hand, business and professional/trade magazines could can some subsidies for their intimate relations with all sorts of enterprises and guilds. So there is great difference among different kinds of magazines in quality of design and printing, some magazines are simple while some are luxurious.

The advertisement marketing of magazine publishers in western countries consists of selling, management, promotion of sales and manufacturing. Many magazine publishing companies in Germany attach importance to collecting customer information and making address classification cards; they choose various ways to promote advertisement sales based on these customer resources. The Fogel Publishing Group of Germany focuses on publishing IT magazines and automobile magazines, and its main measure to control costs and gain profits is to promote advertising.

In order to meet the competition in the advertising market head-on, magazine publishers in developed countries not only continuously innovate competing means, including putting magazine advertisements on TV, but also conduct an advertising agent system. Advertising companies are agencies between publishers (including other media) and advertisers, and they recommend different advertisements to magazine publishers. This can help magazine publishers reduce the costs of seconding used to seek advertisements and obtain a more stable advertising income.

All publishers will use media to promote a new magazine. Magazine publishers in developed countries put great emphasis on the promotion of new magazines. For example, the general interest magazine Focus, published in Germany, promotes itself by TV advertisements. Besides advertisement, magazine publishers in developed countries also pay attention to investigating markets and reading customers statistical cards in order to collect market information and adjust magazine content and publishing means on time.

2. Analysis of Magazine Advertising Management of China

In 2005, advertising income in China reached 141.6 billion (RMB) Yuan, of which 2.49 billion (RMB) Yuan is from magazine advertising. Although there is great disparity between China and developed countries in the market revenues of magazine advertising, Chinese magazine advertising income has grown very rapidly and the rate of increments has kept above 20% for some years. All these have indicated that Chinese magazine advertising can continue to grow.

There are two characteristics of Chinese magazine advertising management for the macro-angle. One is the small scale of the magazine advertising market, and the other is its unstable operation. The small scale of the Chinese magazine advertising market is manifested by sales. In China, magazines own a small advertising turnover of only 1% in comparison with newspapers, television and radio. And the market scale of Chinese magazine advertising is also a little low compared with magazine advertising in western countries.

The other characteristic of Chinese magazine advertising management is the unstable operation of the whole magazine advertising market. The scale of the magazine advertising market and its undulation are intimately related too the scale of the magazine consumer group and the different characteristics of the operators in different fields. As we all know, the scale of the advertising market is large if the scale of the consumer group is large, and if an advertiser puts more emphasis on long-term strategic investment, the investment for advertisement is more stable.

There are some Chinese magazines that have great circulation such as *Readers* (whose monthly circulation has exceeded 8 million copies) and *Bosom Friend* (its monthly circulation has exceeded 4 million copies). But these magazines are out of the top 10 magazines in advertising income in China. The top 10 magazines in the annual list of Chinese magazine advertising, such as *ELLE, COSMOPOLITAN* and *Shanghai Style,* usually do not do well in distribution. Why do advertisers give up magazines that have great circulation and invest in the magazines that don't have as great circulation? Obviously this condition is related to characteristics of the industries that advertisers belong to.

As a mass medium, magazines are connected intimately with advertisement. Advertisement depends on certain industries that support the media advertising market. Fundamentally, the expansion of the advertising market is decided by the investment scales of relevant industries, and the tendency of the investment in advertisement is a symbol of industry prosperity. Because different media have different characteristics, the advertising market of consumer magazines is obviously dependent on IT, cosmetics, clothing, telecommunication, and automobile industries, while business and professional/trade magazines are mainly dependent on the investment scale of particular industries. Some industries change rapidly, bringing in change to the operation of advertising. At present, the investment of eight industries, including IT, cosmetics, electronic, automobile, lifestyle, education and telecommunication has occupied above 60% of magazine advertising income in China. These industries are all in their in terms of booming in terms of advertising investing. Nowadays, Chinese enterprises are improving their brand values and renewing their products. In this situation, managers cannot ignore the significance of advertisement and must realize that the first thing they should do to expand their market is to improve investment in advertisement. In recent years, just the increasing advertising investment of these industries has supported the increase of advertising income of fashion and economic magazines. And it has been the main power in promoting the expansion of the Chinese magazine advertising market.

In addition, there is another reason for the large validation in the Chinese magazine advertising market. The main magazine advertising markets are located in a few cities such as Beijing, Shanghai, Guangzhou and Shenzhen. The advertising market in these cities will surely influence the operation of the whole magazine advertising market in China.

From the above analysis, we can conclude that there are some problems in the operation of Chinese magazine advertising such as small market scale and large variation, and these problems are concerned with the subdivision of the consumer group, the developing conditions of industries and regional culture and economy.

In the micro-angle, some Chinese magazine managers have attempted to increase advertising income. Many magazine advertisements are designed for specific markets. For example, 70% of the advertisements in *Cute* are for cosmetics. Conditions permitting, some magazines adjust their publishing cycles or add new content in order to increase the volume of ad pages. In comparison with other media, the main weakness of magazine advertising is the long publishing cycle. The adjustment of the publishing cycle and magazine content will increase magazine advertising income, but there is a big risk in doing so. If magazine publishers are short of market superiority and economic power, the publishers dare not to do so. But as far as the whole magazine industry is concerned, there are still many Chinese magazine managers with obsolete ideas of management, which hinder the development of the Chinese magazine industry.

Many magazine publishers in China haven't found their own effective ways to exploit the advertising market. Magazine publishers' ideas and means of operation are not the same in deciding whether to depend on themselves or professional advertising agents. The common means of magazine publishers in developed countries is signing contracts with advertising agents, who usually buy most of the advertising pages of magazines; only a small quantity of advertising pages are bought by advertisers straight from magazine publishers. It costs much more for magazine publishers to find for advertisements by themselves. Many magazine publishers in China anticipate that the advertising market has a bright future and are adding personnel engaged in advertisement. Their actions are effective in the near future, but not advisable long-term strategies. Chinese magazine publishers must investigate carefully develop out the advertising agent system in China, and still need support from departments of publishing administration and magazine publisher associations.

Chinese magazine publishers must improve their ideas and levels of manufacturing of magazine advertising. In China, the proportion of advertisements in newspapers is regulated, while there is a lack of relevant regulations for magazines. Most magazines put colorful advertisements on covers and interleafs, and there are black and white advertisements on a few inner pages of magazines. But magazine advertising has no diverse forms and no manifest difference from advertisement in newspapers At present, the design of magazine advertising is not novel in China, and there are still some problems in the manufacturing of magazine advertisements such as rough quality of printing.

3. Conclusion

There's great disparity in magazine advertising income between China and developed countries. But the incremental rate of magazine advertising income is rising fast, and the developing space of Chinese magazine advertising is great. Further, there is great disparity in advertising strategies and advertising forms between China and developed countries.

Fundamentally, the development condition of magazine advertising is decided by the situation of the national economy and relevant markets. Advertisement is a barometer of the national economy, and the stable development of the national economy is the basic impetus for increase in the advertising market. Advertising revenues of developed countries occupy 5% to 8% in state revenues. The growth of the Chinese advertising market has just started and Chinese advertising revenue only occupies about 1% on state revenue. The increment rate of the Chinese advertising market has exceeded the increment rate of the national economy and the proportion which advertising revenue occupies in state revenue will increase continuously. The reform of the Chinese press and publishing systems is being carried out. After China's entry into the WTO, retail and wholesale publishing businesses in China have been gradually opened to foreign capital, which will promote the advancement of the market economy of the publishing industry and drive the development of the magazine advertising market.

After China's entry into the WTO, some international media groups began to deal with magazine advertising in China and this will have immediate impacts on the Chinese magazine publishing industry. Chinese magazine managers should improve the condition of magazine management in the following aspects:

1. Magazine managers should enhance consciousness of advertising management and make advertising management more canonical, standard and integrated. The designers should design more attractive advertisements in order to improve their effect. Above all, magazine managers should not one-sidedly emphasize advertising income, but grasp the style and characteristics of magazines.

2. Magazine managers should improve the quality of magazines and innovate unceasingly in order to expand magazine circulation. Magazine quality, circulation and advertisement depend on one another. In order to increase advertising income and make magazines prosper, magazine publishers should attach great importance to distribution, and manage to improve the publication's quality of content and form.

Chinese magazine managers and advertising agents should quicken the innovation of advertising strategies. They can actively innovate advertisement forms that should transform visual from functional advertisements, possess more originality and integrate with some of the burgeoning media such as the Internet.

It is a reasonable choice for magazine managers to seek appropriate collaborators and benefit from each other for the sake of increasing advertising revenue. For instance, *Globe,* published by the Xinhua News Agency, is cooperating with *The Global Observer* ,published by the China International Publishing Group. The two magazines have different visual angles and content, and can make use of mutual advantages so as to enlarge influence in the advertising market, and win market predominance.

REFERENCES

Husni, Samir and Emily Main. "Life After Death in the Magazine Industry." *Publishing Research Quarterly.* Summer 2002: 3-11.

"International Federation of the Periodical Press (FIPP), and Zenith Optimedia." *World Magazine Trends 2005/2006* (2006).

Johnson, Sammye and Patricia Prijatel. *The Magazine from Cover to Cover: Inside a Dynamic Industry.* Trans. Wang Hai. (Beijing: China Renmin University Press, 2005).

Kim, Hank. "Free or Fee?" *Ad Age Global*, June 2002: 16-18.
Morrish, John. *Magazine Editing: How to Develop and Manage a Successful Publication*. (London: Rutledge, 2003).
Sun, Yanjun. *Periodicals in China*. (Beijing: China Social Sciences Press, 2003).
Wu, Yun. "Comparative Analysis of Chinese and Foreign Periodical Publications." *China Periodical Yearbook 2002/2003*. (Beijing: Encyclopedia of China Publishing House, 2003): 178-185.
Wu Yun. "Comparative Analysis of the Consumer Market of Chinese and Foreign Periodicals." *China Periodical Yearbook 2003/2004*. (Beijing: Encyclopedia of China Publishing House, 2004): 159-167.

The Viability of Copyright Protection Systems

Liu Chunnian

1. Brief Description of Copyright Protection

Copyright protection systems are composed of the 5W's; that is, why-where-who-what-which. Brief terms are shown in Table 1.

Table 1. Five Ws on copyright protection systems

Why	Why is there copyright protection?
Where	Where does copyright come from?
Who	Who owns the copyright to a work?
What	What can be copyrighted?
Which	Which material cannot be protected by copyright?

W1: Why is there copyright protection?

The economic philosophy behind the Copyright Clause is the encouragement of individual effort by financial benefit, which is the best way to advance the public welfare by promoting and disseminating knowledge. Copyright law is intended to serve as a regulatory scheme that balances the competing rights and interests of three different groups: creators, entrepreneurs, and the public. The primary objective of copyright is not the right of the author or publisher to gain a profit, but rather, to promote the progress of science and useful arts. Thus, copyright protection serves as a means by which a crucial societal purpose is achieved.

W2: Where does copyright come from?

Copyright law's authority is derived from the U.S. Constitution (Art. I, Sec. 8, cl. 8.), which empowers the American Congress "To promote the Progress of Science and Useful Arts. . . by securing for limited Times to Authors . . . the exclusive Right to their . . . Writings . . ." As a result, the American Congress passed the Copyright Act, a federal statute, to carry out the constitutional mandate and to implement the specifics of copyrights.

W3: Who owns the copyright to a work?

Obtaining a license from the author is necessary to exercise one of the rights exclusively reserved for the copyright holder under the statute. Generally, the copyright is owned by the person (or persons) who creates the work. For all practical purposes, the employer is considered the work's author. For example, artists often assign or transfer their rights to a publisher or recording company for the opportunity to get their music heard by the public.

W4: What can be copyrighted?

Copyright is a protection that covers published and unpublished literary, scientific and artistic works, whatever the forms of expression, provided such works are fixed in a tangible or material form. This means that if you can see it, hear it and/or touch it - it may be protected. If it is an essay, if it is a play, if it is a song, if it is a funky original dance move, if it is a photograph, HTML coding or a computer graphic that can be set on paper, recorded on tape or saved to a hard drive, it may be protected. Copyright laws grant the creator the exclusive right to reproduce, prepare derivative works, distribute, perform and display the work publicly. Exclusive means only the creator of such work, not anybody who has access to it and decides to grab it.

W5: Which material cannot be protected by copyright?

Ideas, procedures, principles, discoveries, and devices are all specifically excluded from copyright protection, as are articles having a utilitarian function. Also, works that are not "fixed in any tangible form" are prohibited from protection, since fixation is a requirement for copyright under the statute. Names, titles, and other short phrases are also excluded from copyright protection. This is because the degree of creativity is simply too minimal to meet the threshold requirement that at least a minimum amount of original expression must exist before copyright protection may be attached to a work.

2. Principles of Balance and Limitation on Copyright Protection Systems

2.1 Typical Bills of Copyright Protection Systems

There are no "international copyrights" that enable you to protect your work throughout the world. However, most countries are members of the Berne Convention and the Universal Copyright Convention (UCC), which allow you to protect your works in countries of which you are not a citizen or national. Still, we have other important treaties to watch for. Under these treaties, some works may be protected. Typical bills on copyright protection and their main characters are listed in Table 2.

Table 2. Typical bills of copyright protection

Typical bills	Main characters
US Copyright Act of 1976	Very useful to explain the objectives and limitations of this national act.
The Berne Convention	The world's oldest international copyright treaty, signed by 159 countries. All the member nations are required to provide the same copyright protection to all nationals in all the member nations. This treaty is much broader in scope and offers far more protection than the USC.
Digital Millenniums Copyright Act(DMCA)	The DMCA is a complex set of laws that make major changes in the US Copyright Act of 1976 to address the digitally networked environment, and aims to protect the author's copyright stronger than before.
The EDRI Directive	The European counterpart of the DMCA but has a more extended scope. It aims toward the harmonization of certain aspects of copyright and related rights in the information society.
Copyright law of PRC	Copyrights involve personal rights and property rights. Personal rights include the right to sign, the right of publication, the right of alteration, the right to keep integrity, and the right to withdraw works. Property rights include the right of use and the right to remuneration.

2.2 Principles of Balance on Copyright Protection Systems

One of the fundamental issues of copyright regulation is how to define the principle of balance between authorship and readership in the digital era. This issue, in particular, has been seriously raised as it breaks up the balance of the groups that belong to the Internet service providers. The copyright owners are looking for a certain level of responsibility and participation from service providers to police copyright violations. However, Internet service providers are responding to such requests by maintaining that the copyright owners "want service providers handcuffed to unrealistic policing efforts, while realistically concerned about protection of their works."

A new right within copyrights is called transmission. However, there has been a debate on whether a digital transmission is a distribution of a copy to the public. If every digital transmission were defined as an infringement of copyright law, many people are worried that public access to information would be seriously restricted. Copyright owners are willing to accept the proposal that every digital transmission is defined as an infringement of copyright law. They believe that, with the proposal, they will be able to control all performances of copyrighted works, not just the public performances and public displays that the existing law grants to copyright owners. On the other hand, schools and libraries argue that it is not appropriate to regard every transmission as regulated by copyright, and the proposal can seriously restrict the primary purpose of copyrights.

Some hot debates on the balance of copyright protection are listed as follows:

Does copyright protection infringe upon free speech?

Assent: Unbridled copyright power will threaten something equally important: the right to listen, read, and research without having to pay a toll any time a private citizen wants to gather information for his or her own use.

Opponent: Cyberspace is little more than a vast copying machine for pirated software, CDs,, and movies.

Can HTML coding and webpage layouts be copyrighted?

Assent: HTML coding and webpage layouts cannot be copyrighted!

Opponent: A webpage layout may be copyrighted if it is actually written and/or designed by the author and has been fixed in a tangible medium by being saved to a hard drive.

Does somebody own the "new" version right when he or she takes someone else's writings, text, html or graphic image and changes it around to suit his/her needs?

Assent: If somebody has changed someone else's writings, text, html or graphic image around to suit his or her needs, he or she owns the "new version."

Opponent: If somebody has done any of that with the original owner's permission, and according to owner's terms and conditions, then he or she owns the "new" version. If not, he or she may be committing copyright infringement and/or plagiarism.

Should hot-linking and spider harvesting be considered an infringement of copyright?

Assent: It is not the Internet service providers' responsibility to police latent copyright violations.

Opponent: Hot-linking or spider harvesting is not only a kind of, but may also be construed as copyright infringement in some cases.

Should locking or trapping other web sites or pages in one's frames be considered as infringement of copyright?

Assent: It is acceptable to lock or trap other web sites or pages in one's frames to ease navigation within a site.

Opponent: Showing someone else's web page through the use of frames is extremely rude and may be construed as copyright infringement in some cases.

Should Fonts and Dingbats be protected by a copyright?

Assent: Typography may not be protected by a copyright, and once created becomes public domain.

Opponent: Original fonts and dingbats are a means of expression that may be fixed to a tangible medium when created, and hence become protected by a copyright owned by the creator.

2.3 Limitations on Copyright Protection

Fair use

The legal definition of what constitutes fair use is ambiguous in U.S. copyright law, and only a court can determine with authority whether a particular use is fair use. It is unlikely, therefore, that we will be able to build certain systems that can reason about what uses are fair in the foreseeable future. Use of copyrighted works or portions thereof, for any other purpose is not deemed fair use. That includes copying text or scanning pictures from postcards, magazines, books or any other work.

Licenses implied in fact

Fair use allows limited use of another's work without approval, but other uses may be approved by implication. For example, when a message is posted to a public email list, both forwarding and archiving seem to be implicitly allowed. It is reasonable to assume that such liberties are okay if not explicitly forbidden. However, when forwarding, archiving or, say, using part of a message, be careful not to change the original meaning. No one implicitly authorizes another to attribute to them an embarrassing message they did not write.

Express licenses

To address some issues, one web author posts this amusing notice:

> Warning: I reserve the right to use any email you send to me. If you do not want your email to be used in such a manner, mark it confidential.

That seems reasonable; many email copyright problems could be avoided if list owners would broadcast, at least on initial subscription, a similar notice.

3. Effect of the Present Law on the Duration of Copyrights

3.1 Three Basic Questions about the Duration of Copyrights

When mentioning the duration of copyrights, three basic questions should not be ignored. See Table 3.

Table 3. Three basic questions on the duration of copyrights

Question	Answer
Question 1: When does Copyright Protection begin?	Copyright protection begins when any of the above described work is actually created and fixed in a tangible form.
Question 2: When does Copyright Protection expire?	Dates in a copyright statement do not refer to when that copyright will expire. Expiration of a copyright actually takes place later.
Question 3: How long does copyright protection last?	Not uniform. For example, America and China have different rules. See Table 4.

Table 4. Different terms of copyrights between America and China

Countries	Duration of Copyrights
America	In 1998, the U.S. Congress passed the Copyright Term Extension Act, amending the Copyright Act and extending the duration of copyright protection for works by an additional twenty years. Under the legislation, newly created works are generally afforded copyright protection for a period of seventy years after the life of the author. Works created for hire and owned by corporations are protected for ninety five Years. This trend of granting additional protection for works has steadily expanded from Congress' original term, in 1909, of 28 years from publication to its current grant of the life of the author plus 70 years, to exploit the work exclusively.
China	In China, the term of protection for the rights of publication, use and remuneration of a citizen's works is the entire author's life and fifty years after his death, with the deadline being December 31st of the fiftieth year after his death. The term of protection for the rights of publication, use and remuneration of the works created by a legal person or an entity without legal personality is fifty years; the deadline is December 31st of the fiftieth year after the works were first published. But no protection shall be granted to works unpublished within fifty years after completion. Afterward, the copyright of the work will revert to the public domain and become public wealth.

3.2 Circumvention of Copyright Protection Systems

It is perfectly understandable that copyright owners, anticipating that the eventual enactment of a new copyright law that will extend the duration of all copyrights then subsisting, should seek to continue protection for copyrighted works that would otherwise fall into the public domain within the next few years. However, other factors must be weighed.

The proposed legislation—which exceeds what is required by the WIPO treaties—extends beyond the subject matter of copyrights to prohibit the manufacture, import, offering to the public, provision or otherwise trafficking in any "technology, product, service, device, component, or part thereof" intended to circumvent technological protections of copyrighted works. A copyrighted work that is no longer in the market may not be accessible for reading or analysis even by a lawful owner of a copy, because the copyright owner no longer provides the services. Upon expiration of the copyright, the passage of a work into the public domain may be impeded by technological protections. A work may become permanently inaccessible if the medium or format in which it is fixed becomes obsolete and the copyright owner does not choose to invest in migration to a new format or medium. In any of these circumstances, circumvention of technological protections would be lawful and appropriate in order to preserve and/or make the work accessible to legitimate users. This would be impossible if the necessary technology is not available.

Research in computer science and related fields may involve products and technologies that fall under the prohibitions of this bill even though this research is not intended to circumvent technological protections of copyrighted works. In particular, the development of new technological protections requires the ability to test them with the strongest possible circumvention technologies.

3.3 Chinese Specific Points for Copyright Authorities

Chinese copyright authorities are looking for breakthroughs in key cases and intensify their administrative enforcement efforts.

1. To conduct examinations and checks after special campaigns on, for example, combating cyber infringement and piracy, to prevent the resurgence of already dismantled illegal organizations.

2. To crack down especially on illegal operations which profit by providing film, music and software downloads through the Internet and look for breakthroughs from here, with a view to settling a number of key cases, closing down a number of websites and punishing a number of offenders before the end of this year.

3. To carry out efforts to "straighten out and crack down on production lines of pirated optical discs," and actively coordinate with CD-duplicating

parties to streamline optical disc production companies. In this process, priorities need to be identified, enforcement needs to be rigorous, and penalties need to be made as harsh, heavy and quick as possible.

4. Actively coordinate with authorities such as the Committee on Education, Science, Culture and Health of the National People's Congress to review progress in the implementation of copyright law across the country.

4. Conclusion

The viability of copyright protection systems can be complicated and uncertain. One can also readily see that nearly all recent works are automatically protected by copyright and will remain under the law's protection for many more decades. Still, the application of these bills ultimately has the promise of solving only the copyright issues. The use of a particular work may raise other legal concerns beyond copyright. Those issues will be the subjects of future studies in connection with this project.

REFERENCES

Berne Union for the Protection of Literary and Artistic Property. <http://www.law.cornell.edu/treaties/>.

Bitlaw - A Resource for Technology Law. <http://www.bitlaw.com>.

Brownlee, Lisa M. "Recent Changes in the Duration of Copyright in the United States and European Union: Procedure and Policy." 6 *FORDHAM I. P., MEDIA & ENT. L.J.* 579 (1996).

Bryce, Shauna C. "Recent Development: Life Plus Seventy: The Extension of Copyright Terms in the European Union and Proposed Legislation in the United States." 37 *HARV. INT'L L.J.* 525 (1996).

China's Action Plan on IPR Protection 2006 <http://www.smg.cn/root/news/>.

Colby, Richard, Helen Sousa, Eddy Baker and Otto Harbach. "The Road to a Copyright Term of Life Plus Fifty Years." *COMM. & L.* (1984).

Gifford, Christina. "The Sonny Bono Copyright Term Extension Act." *30 U. MEM. L. REV.* 363 (2000).

"Digital Millennium Copyright Act." *Public Law 105-304* <http://thomas.loc.gov >.

Ginsburg, Jane C. "Copyright Legislation for the Digital Millennium." *23 COLUM.-VLA J.L. & ARTS* 137 (1997).

Epping, Jerome N. Jr. "Harmonizing the United States and European Community Copyright Terms: Needed Adjustment or Money for Nothing?" 65 *U. CIN. L. REV.* 183 (1996).

Hamilton, Marci A. "An Evaluation of the Copyright Extension Act of 1995: Copyright Duration Extension and the Dark Heart of Copyright, 14." *CARDOZO ARTS & ENT LJ* 655 (1996).

Hatch, Orrin G. "Toward a Principled Approach to Copyright Legislation at the Turn of the Millennium." 59 *U. PITT. L. REV.* 719 (1998).

Jaszi, Peter A. "Goodbye to All That—A Reluctant (and Perhaps Premature) Adieu to a Constitutionally-Grounded Discourse of Public Interest in Copyright Law, 29." *VAND. J. TRANSNAT'L L.* 595 (1996).

Lavigne, Joseph A. "For Limited Times? Making Rich Kids Richer Via the Copyright Term Extension Act of 1996." 73 *U. DET. MERCY L. REV.* 311 (1996).

Patry, William. "The Failure of the American Copyright System: Protecting the Idle Rich." 72 *NOTRE DAME L. REV.* 907 (1997).

"The Public's Right of Fair Use FAW."<http://fairuse.stanford.edu/>.

Reese, Anthony. "Reflections on the Intellectual Commons: Two Perspectives on Copyright Duration and Reversion." 47 *STAN. L. REV.* 707 (1995).

Reichman, J. H. "Evaluation of the Copyright Extension Act of 1995: The Duration of Copyright and the Limits of Cultural Policy." *14 CARDOZO ARTS & ENT LJ* 625 (1999).

Segal, Adam P. "Zombie Copyrights: Copyright Restoration under the New § 104a of the Copyright Act." *13 COMPUTERS & HIGH TECH: L.J.* 71(1997).

Ubertazzi, Luigi Carlo. "The "Butterfly" Case or EC Term of Protection Directive and Transitive Law, 31" *IIC: INTERNATIONAL REVIEW OF INDUSTRIAL PROPERTY AND COPYRIGHT LAW* 142 (2000).

"What is Copyright Protection?" <http://www.whatiscopyright.org>.

Overview of China's Copyright Permissions from 1996 to 2005

Cai Yun

At the 13th Beijing International Book Fair (BIBF) held from August 30 to September 2, 2006, China's copyright permissions achieved a surplus for the first time in twenty years. The copyright permission items broke through 12,000, creating a new record. The items of signed copyright export contracts achieved a historic breakthrough, reaching a total of 1,096, an increase of 98.2%. There were 891 import contracts, an increase of 6.7%. The ratio of copyright imports and exports is 1.23:1. The rapid development and this historic breakthrough of China's copyright permissions in recent years not only benefited from the increasing overall strength of our publishing industry, but also benefited from the past ten years of reform and development operations. So it will be useful to sum up experiences and promote even greater development of China's copyright permissions in the future by conducting an overview. Recalling the history of China's copyright permission over the past decade, China's copyright permission market has great potential.

1. The BIBF (Beijing International Book Fair) in the Past Decade

Since 1986, the BIBF has been successfully held for ten times. In accordance with "Bring the world's first-class books into China, introduce Chinese books into the world" as the theme, BIBF has played an important role in promoting international technological and cultural exchanges, expanding cooperation in publishing and copyright permissions and developing the book import and export trade. Now, it has become a large fair of copyright permissions, book trades, cooperating publishing and cultural exchanges, and is considered one of the most influential publication exhibitions in Asia and even the world.

After more than ten years, the BIBF's function has changed from purely book displays to pragmatic copyright permissions. The scale is bigger and bigger; the level is higher and higher as well. The number of booths grew from 200 in the very beginning to nearly 1,000 now. And the number of exhibits increased from 5,000 in the first session to more than 100,000. Despite the low turnover rate of BIBF in past decades, the average of all transactions accounted for 68.99% of China's total copyright transactions in the year (see Table 1). It has proved that it is the most important copyright permissions event in China's publishing industry.

Table 1: Statistics of BIBF in 1996-2005

Year	Session	Number of Copyrights Transactions	Turnover Rate	Account for China's Total Copyright Transactions in the Year
1996	6th	2500	2.69%	78.99%
1998	7th	4200	4.20%	69.34%
2000	8th	6879	6.88%	86.19%
2002	9th	8106	8.11%	63.16%
2003	10th	8129	8.13%	47.87%
2004	11th	8250	8.16%	62.94%
2005	12th	9236	7.70%	74.42%

2. Sketches of China's Copyright Permissions in the Past Decade

2.1 Ten Years Copyright Permission Volume

After more than 10 years of recovery since China's reform and opening up, China's copyright permissions entered into the golden period of development around 1996. According to the statistics of the National Copyright Administration, China's total copyright transactions were more than 90,000 titles from 1996 to 2005, of which 83,372 were newly introduced titles, and 8,523 titles were output (see Graph 1).

Graph 1: 1996-2005 China's Copyright Transactions Profile (unit: species)

Year	1996	1997	1998	1999	2000	2001	2002	2003	2004	2005
Import	2915	3224	5469	6459	7343	8250	11517	15555	11746	10894
Export	250	353	588	418	638	653	1317	1427	1362	1517
Import / Export	12:1	9:1	9:1	15:1	12:1	13:1	9:1	11:1	9:1	7:1

(Source: National Copyright Administration http://www.ncac.gov.cn. Search date Aug. 18, 2006)

As to the amount of imported copyrights, the growth has accelerated since 1996. And there was an increase of 69.6% in 1998 compared with 1997 before the steady increase in the next few years. It exceeded 10,000 titles in 2002 and finally achieved a maximum 12,516 titles in 2003 (See Graph 1). Since 2003, China's book market has suffered a decline in sales and huge growth in inventory. China's copyright permissions of 2004 were affected, going through the first negative growth for many years, and continued to fall in 2005. After a complete breakdown of the book economy bubble in 1997, China's copyright permissions began to see a sound and rational development.

To the amount of exports, the trade deficit is obvious. The ratio of imports and exports was about 11:1 (see Graph 1).

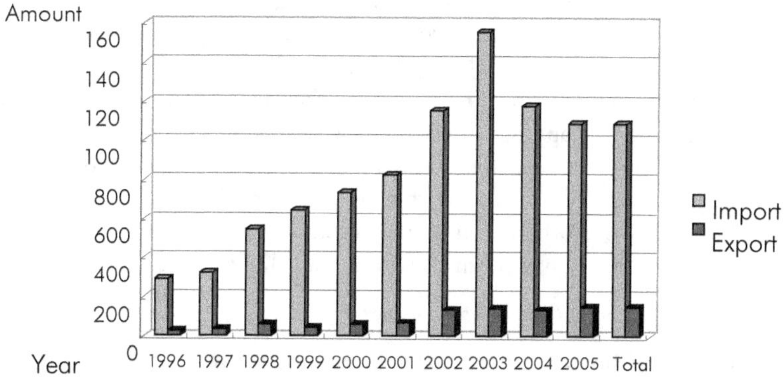

Table 2: 2003-2005 Copyright Exports Statistics (unit: species)

Regions \ Years	2000	2001	2002	2003	2004	2005
Taiwan	212	187	755	472	55	669
Hong Kong and Macao	38	80	352	178	372	169
Korea	33	7	103	89	114	304
Japan	6	12	18	15	22	15
Singapore	8	1	—	9	30	43
USA	2	6	9	5	14	16
United Kingdom	2	1	6	2	16	74
Germany	0	1	2	1	20	9
France	0	0	1	11	4	7
Russia	—	—	0	1	0	6
Canada	1	10	0	—	0	0
Total Export	6638	653	1317	1427	1362	1517

(Source: National Copyright Administration http://www.ncac.gov.cn. Search date Aug. 18, 2006)

2.2 The Geographical Market Structure of China's Copyright Permission and the Product Characteristics

The geographical market structure of China's copyright permissions

The source of copyright imports is mainly the United States, Britain, Japan and other developed countries. Take the year 2003 for example, when the largest number of copyright introductions occurred, China's total copyright import volume was 15,555 titles, and the top ten countries and regions were the United States, Britain, Taiwan, Japan, Germany, France, Hong Kong, the Republic of Korea, Russia and Canada.

The export region is mainly in East Asia and Southeast Asia. As Table 2 shows, mainland China's major copyright export is to Asian countries and regions that are closely linked with Chinese culture and history. Taiwan and Hong Kong are the largest trading partners. China's copyright exports are steadily improving compared to Japan, Singapore and other Asian countries and regions. Particularly, China's copyright exports to Korea have been rising dramatically in recent years.

Product characteristics of China's copyright permissions

The contents of imported books have become much more diverse. The focus and the higher demand force copyright imports are closely linked with social and economic development, which decides the direction of copyright introductions. The mainstream of introductions in the 1980s was literature and social science, IT books for the end of the 1990's and into 2000, and economic management books came into the lead most recently. In recent years the introduction of bestsellers has also been increasing, such as J.K.Rowling's Harry Potter published by the People's Literature Publishing House, Spencer Johnson's Who Moved My Cheese published by China CITIC Press, Elbert Hubbard's A Message to Garcia published by Enterprise Management Publishing House, Robert Kiyosaki's Rich Dad, Poor Dad published by Beijing World Publishing Company, and so on.

Then, seeing the subjects of copyright output, the subjects that reflect Chinese history and culture still play an important part in exports, such as ancient classics, scenery, monuments, ancient architecture, arts and crafts, literature, history, medicine, and so on. The output volume of technology and scholarly books has gone up significantly in recent years, owing to the government's encouragement and publishing houses' efforts in improving the quality of title selection and publication. The structure and quality of China's exported books have made gratifying progress. Take the example of an excellent copyright exchange in 2004 for example, the outstanding exported books including: *Gaoshiqi Classical Scientific Series, Uncle Yang Liwei Talks about Spaceflight, China Strategy, Computer Immunology, Introduction to Modern Environmental Science, Higher TCM Reference Books, Interesting Story of Chinese History, Princess Derling,* and *Business Wisdom: the Wealth Secret of Wenzhounese.*

3. The Status of Participant Publishers

3.1 The Development of Participant Publishers

For one thing, a number of publishers who participate in copyright importing take the opportunity of establishing and consolidating their brands. Their characteristics are as follows:

First, some publishers have made are long-term plan on copyright imports in order to upgrade products, improve efficiency and create brands. These imported books not only brought publishers, but also bring about great economic efficiency. The sales of the imported books of some publishers have already accounted for the majority of their total sales.

It can be clearly seen from Table 3, that, in 2003, the sum of the top 10 publishers' copyright import volumes accounted for 1/3 of the total copyright imports. The number of every publisher's imported books is decisive. The copyright import volume of Foreign Language Teaching and Research Press accounted for nearly 98% of its annual new publications. And more interesting, China CITIC Press's imported books were more than double the number of its new published books.

Table 3: 2003 Top Ten Presses on Copyright Import

Name of the Press	Import Volume (species)	The Proportion of New Published Books (%)	2003 Rank
China Light Industry Press	212	69.06	No.129
China Youth Press	218	59.89	No.87
Posts and Telecom Press	255	29.38	No.29
Science Press	293	15.01	No.4
Publishing House of Electronics Industry	393	32.01	No.15
China Ren Min University Press	421	54.60	No. 20
Foreign Language Teaching and Research Press	576	98.00	No.5
China Machine Press	621	39.25	No.16
Tsinghua University Press	845	67.38	No.7
China CITIC Press	996	237.71	No.104

Secondly, the introductions strive to achieve global, synchronized publication. For example, with books like *Harry Potter,* introduced by People's Literature Publishing House, *Guinness World Records,* introduced by Liaoning Education Press, the follow-up of *Left Behind,* introduced by China Workers Press, Chinese publishers have been trying to launch the Chinese version with other versions simultaneously.

Third, the operation of Chinese publishers in copyright permissions is more skillful. At the 2000 Frankfurt Book Fair, 21st Century Publishing House, associated with the Sesame Press and Taiwan Penguin Books Company, dealt with foreign publishers. They bought the parts that they needed. The three publishers shared the fee of translation and printing, saving a huge sum of money. The foreign publishers were also pleased because the Chinese versions were sold at one time. Several domestic publishers also tend to choose fixed foreign publishers for an intensive cooperation and monopolized exploitation.

Fourth, the scale of introductions expanded; the brand and characteristics are gradually notable. Characteristics have been formed in certain, such as computer books. The "big four" are the Publishing House of Electronics Industry, China Machine Press, Tsinghua University Press, and the Posts and Telecom Press. For art books, the "big four" are the Yilin Press, Shanghai Translation Publishing House, the Writers Publishing House, and the LiJiang Publishing House. And for foreign language learning books there are the Foreign Language Teaching and Research Press, Shanghai Foreign Language Education Press, the Foreign Languages Press and the Commercial Press.

Fifth, it's common for publishers to use the Internet and other advanced ways to upgrade traditional copyright permissions, to search for information, to look for works, and to negotiate royalties.

For another thing, publishers who can export copyrights mainly own distinctive books and integrated strength, such as the Foreign Languages Press, New World Press, Beijing Publishing House, China Machine Press, Foreign Language Teaching and Research Press, Jiangsu Children's Publishing House, Zhejiang Children's Publishing House, Liaoning Children's Publishing House, Weilai Press, and the Tianjin Science and Technology Publishing House. Their common features are: first, their books are suited to foreign markets; second, they have staff familiar with copyright permissions; third, they all attach importance to copyright permissions. The performance of these publishers is not only outstanding in copyright exports but also excellent in copyright imports.

After nearly a decade of efforts, publishers that had notable achievements in copyright permission began to emerge, such as the Encyclopedia of China Publishing House, Publishing House of Electronics Industry, the Foreign Languages Press, Posts and Telecom Press, Joint Publishing Company, China Light Industry Press, World Publishing Company, Science Press, China Ren Min University Press, Yilin Press,

Liaoning Education Press, Guangdong Education Publishing House, Shanghai Foreign Language Education Press, Chongqing Publishing House, and the Hainan Publishing House.

3.2 The Geographical Distribution Features of Participant Publishers in China's Copyright Permissions

China's copyright imports in geographical distribution are extremely uneven. It can be seen in Figure 1 that Beijing is number one in introduction volume with 38,632 titles, which accounted for 59% of the total import volume, putting it far ahead of other provinces and municipalities. In general, the copyright permissions are more active in the economic and cultural centers and developed coastal regions. The copyright introductions in underdeveloped regions such as Inner Mongolia, Guizhou, Qinghai, Tibet and other provinces lag far behind the former, and in some areas there is even no record of copyright introductions.

Figure 1: 2000–2005 Copyright Introductions of the Top-10 Provinces (unit: species)

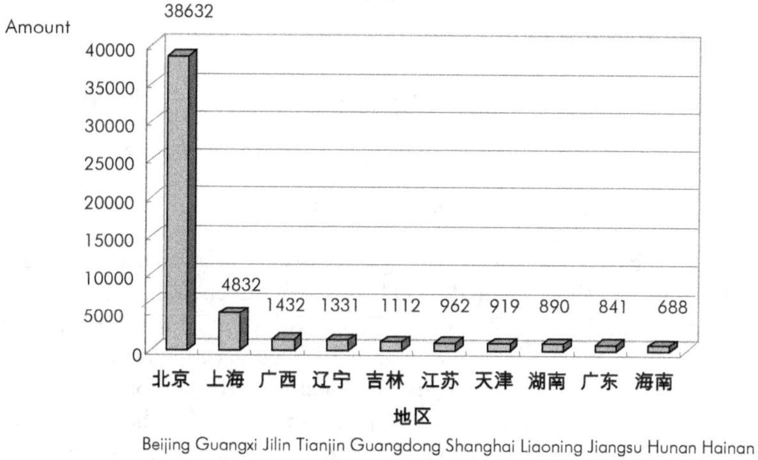

(Source: National Copyright Administration http://www.ncac.gov.cn. Search date Aug. 18, 2006)

In the output of copyright, Beijing's copyright exports are absolutely leading with 2,964 titles, three times that of Shanghai, which is the number two. The rest were scattered in Liaoning, Jiangsu, Hubei, Zhejiang, Henan and other provinces and municipalities (see Figure 1). Comparing Figure 1 with Figure 2, the top four provinces and municipalities of China's copyright imports and exports are the same: Beijing, Shanghai, Liaoning and Jiangsu. It shows that copyright importing and exporting in these four districts is very active and prospering. However, the latter ranked Hubei, Anhui and Henan provinces in Figure 2 are not included in Figure 1. The main reason is that, in addition to the attention paid to copyright exports, they also have relatively rich publication resources of copyright output.

Figure 2: 2000–2005 Copyright Output of the Top-Ten Provinces (unit: species)

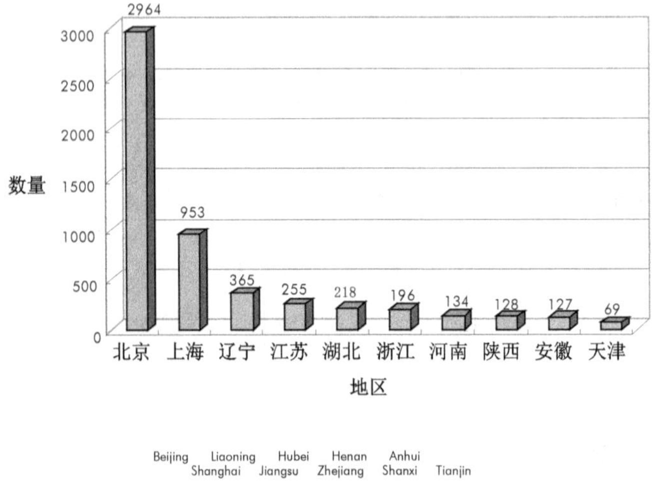

(Source: National Copyright Administration, http://www.ncac.gov.cn. Search date Aug. 18, 2006)

4. The Outlook

According to the WTO is opening agreement, China opened to foreign investors the retail and wholesale markets of books, newspapers and journals in 2003 and the end of 2004, respectively. In order to cope with competition from open markets after joining the WTO, the government has [encouraged Chinese publishers to go out of China and compete in the international market.] put forward the "go out" strategy on publications and conducted policies to encourage the export of cultural products. At present, the operation of the "go out" strategy has the support of government, trade organizations, and the publishing industry.

The reform of the publishing system in recent years has become the inner motivation of the "going out" strategy. And the experimental unit of publishers in the reform is becoming the main force in copyright permissions. In addition, the further enhancement of the overall strength of our publishing industry will provide the "going out" strategy a good foundation. There were 220,000 kinds of books published in 2005, an increase of 6.8% over last year, including 129,000 kinds of new books with an increase of 5.7%. Besides increasing varieties, more and more publishing groups and book publishers have paid more attention to brand building and the planning of masterpieces and international publications. Owing to the increasing of composite strength, China's economic and cultural influence in the international community has been further expanded. With the progress of China's book copyright permissions in quantity and quality, there will be huge potential in China's copyright permissions.

REFERENCES

"Analysis on China's Copyright Permission: <http://www.hebcph.com/>. 16 Aug. 2006.

"The Behavior of Copyright Permission is more Sensible and the Output Quality Has Been Markedly Improved." *Publishing Reference* (2005): 9.

Beijing International Book Fair: <http : //www.bibf.net/> 18 Aug 2006.

Cui, Hongwei. "The Orientation of China's Copyright Permission." *Press and Publishing Exchanges* (2005): 4.

China's National Copyright Administration: <http://www.ncac.gov.cn>.

Kai, Ya. "China's Copyright Permission." *Publishing Economy* (2005): 9.

"The Previous Statistics of Beijing International Book Fair." <http://www.china.org.cn/>. 16 Aug 2006.

Xia, Kali. *Analysis on China's Book Copyright Permission*. Wuhan: Wuhan University, 2004.

Xin, Guangwei. *Copyright Exchange and Chinese Publishing.* Chongqing: Chongqing Publishing House, 2003.

Contributors

Cai Yun
School of Information Management, Wuhan University, China

Chen Wuwei

Robert E. Evanson
Former President, McGraw-Hill Education, USA

Fang Qing & Tao Li
School of Information Management, Wuhan University, China

Gao Hong
Hengyang Normal College, China

He Yun
School of Information Management, Wuhan University, China

He Ziyue
School of Art & Law, Wuhan University of Technology, China

Henan Sun
Centre for Publishing Studies, University of Stirling, UK

Hu Bo
South China Normal University, China

Huang Kaiqing & Zhou Guobiao
School of Information Management, Wuhan University, China

Huang Xianrong
School of Information Management, Wuhan University, China

Shay Humphrey
M.S. in Publishing Program, Pace University, USA

Jiang Chengsong & Li Ziwei
Department of Information Management, Nanjing University, China

Jiang Ling
School of Information Management, Wuhan University, China

Li Jianwei
College of Journalism and Communication, Henan University, China

Li Xinxiang

Li Yan
Shanxi Normal University, China

Lian Xiaochuan
M.S. in Publishing Program, Pace University, USA

Liang Chunfang
School of Literature Humanities, Zhejiang Gongshang University, China

Lin Yuyin
College of Liberal Arts, Guangxi University for Nationalities, China

Liu Canjiao
School of Management, Xiangtan University, China

Liu Chunnian
Nanchang University, China

Liu Jinhong
School of Information Management, Wuhan University, China

Liu Yindi
School of Information Management, Wuhan University, China

Liu Yongjian & Zou Rui
Wuhan University of Technology, China

Lu Xiaohua & Tong Wen
School of Information Management, Wuhan University, China

Luo Zichu & Dai Yang
School of Information Management, Wuhan University, China

Niu Xiaohong
School of Information Management, Wuhan University, China

Sherman Raskin
Director, M.S. in Publishing Program, Pace University, USA

Ursula Rautenberg
Friedrich-Alexander-Universität, Germany

Sun Fan
School of Information Management, Hei Long Jiang University, China

Wang Bo
School of Information Management, Wuhan University, China

Wang Qiuju & Wang Hongmei
Hebei University, China

Wang Songmao
School of Journalism and Communication, Wuhan University, China

Wang Xiaoyan & Yang Xianghui
School of Information Management, Wuhan University, China

WU MEI
School of Information Management, Wuhan University, China

WU PING
School of Information Management, Wuhan University, China

WU YUN
School of Information Management, Wuhan University, China

XIAO LEI
School of Information Management, Wuhan University, China

XU LIFANG & XU QI
School of Information Management, Wuhan University, China

YAO LEI
School of Information Management, Wuhan University, China

YAO YONGCHUN
School of Information Management, Wuhan University, China

ZHANG MEIJUAN
School of Information Management, Wuhan University, China

ZHANG WENHONG
Beijing Institute of Graphic and Communication, China

ZHANG ZENGSHUN
Higher Education Press, China

ZHANG ZHIQIANG & XING PENG
Institute of Publishing Science, Nanjing University, China

ZHAO DAN
Zhejiang Gongshang University, China

ZHAO JIANGUO & CHANG CHUNQIAO
Journalism and Communication Institute, Henan University, China

ZHU JINGWEN & SUN JUE
School of Information Management, Wuhan University, China